Between Being and Time

Between Being and Time

From Ontology to Eschatology

Edited by Andrew T. J. Kaethler
and Sotiris Mitralexis

LEXINGTON BOOKS/FORTRESS ACADEMIC
Lanham • Boulder • New York • London

Published by Lexington Books/Fortress Academic

Lexington Books is an imprint of The Rowman & Littlefield Publishing Group, Inc.
4501 Forbes Boulevard, Suite 200, Lanham, Maryland 20706
www.rowman.com

6 Tinworth Street, London SE11 5AL, United Kingdom

Copyright © 2019 The Rowman & Littlefield Publishing Group, Inc.

Chapter 3: This chapter appeared in *Christian and Islamic Philosophies of Time*, edited by Sotiris Mitralexis and Marcin Podbielski, 87–120. Wilmington, DE: Vernon Press, 2018. Used with permission.

Chapter 10: Some quoted material in this chapter is taken from *Slavery and Freedom*, by Nikolai Berdyaev. Translated by R. M. French. San Rafael, CA: Semantron Press, 2009. Used with permission.

Chapter 11: A previous version of this chapter appeared in *Storia e mistero. Una chiave di acceso alla teologia di Joseph Ratzinger e Jean Daniélou*, edited by Giulio Maspero and Jonas Lynch, 399–411. Roma: Edizioni Santa Croce, 2016. Used with permission.

All rights reserved. No part of this book may be reproduced in any form or by any electronic or mechanical means, including information storage and retrieval systems, without written permission from the publisher, except by a reviewer who may quote passages in a review.

British Library Cataloguing in Publication Information Available

Library of Congress Cataloging-in-Publication Data

Names: Kaethler, Andrew T. J., editor.
Title: Between being and time : from ontology to eschatology / edited by Andrew T. J. Kaethler and Sotiris Mitralexis.
Description: Lanham : Lexington Books-Fortress Academic, 2019. | Includes bibliographical references and index.
Identifiers: LCCN 2018055992 (print) | LCCN 2019003094 (ebook) | ISBN 9781978701816 (Electronic) | ISBN 9781978701823 (cloth)
Subjects: LCSH: Ontology. | Time.
Classification: LCC BD331 (ebook) | LCC BD331 .B436 2019 (print) | DDC 111—dc23
LC record available at https://lccn.loc.gov/2018055992

To Fr. Matthew Baker (1977–2015)
And they that be wise shall shine
as the brightness of the firmament

Contents

Acknowledgments	ix
Introduction: Feast of the Transfiguration, 2018	xi

PART I. RETHINKING ONTOLOGY WITHIN HISTORY

1 Ontology versus Fideism: Christianity's Accountability to History and Society — 3
Haralambos Ventis

2 Ontology, History, and Relation (*Schesis*): Gregory of Nyssa's *Epektasis* — 23
Giulio Maspero

3 Syn-odical Ontology: Maximus the Confessor's Proposition for Ontology within History and in the Eschaton — 37
Dionysios Skliris

4 The Liturgy behind Liturgies: The Church's Metaphysical Form — 65
David W. Fagerberg

5 The Kantian "Two-Images" Problem, Its Lesson for Christian Eschatology, and the Path of Maximian Analogy — 83
Demetrios Harper

PART II. BEYOND BEING AND TIME: ESCHATOLOGICAL HERMENEUTICS

6 Zizioulas and Heidegger: "Eschatological Ontology" and Hermeneutics — 99
Matthew Baker

7 What Does "Rising from the Dead" Mean? A Hermeneutics
of Resurrection 125
Maxim Vasiljević

8 Ecstatic or Reciprocal Meaningfulness? Orthodox Eschatology
between Theology, Philosophy, and Psychoanalysis 143
Nikolaos Loudovikos

PART III. PERSONHOOD BETWEEN ONTOLOGY AND HISTORY

9 The Ontology of the Person—An Outline 163
Christos Yannaras

10 Berdyaev's Solution to History: Redeeming Persons
in Historical Love 173
Daniel S. Robinson

11 Joseph Ratzinger's *Imago Dei* Anthropology: The
Reconciliation of Ontology and Salvation History 189
Isabel C. Troconis Iribarren

12 Praying and Presence: Kierkegaard on Despair and
the Prolepsis of the Self 205
Chris Doude van Troostwijk

PART IV. POLITICS BETWEEN BEING AND TIME

13 Mapping the Theo-Political: Metaphysical Prolegomenon
for Political Theology 221
Jared Schumacher

14 The Eucharist Makes the Church Repent: Eucharistic
Ecclesiology and Political Theology 247
Daniel Wright

15 How Realistic Are Christian Politics? A Case for
Eschatological Realism 265
Logan M. Isaac

Bibliography 277

Index 293

About the Contributors 297

Acknowledgments

We are grateful for all the contributors and for those who attended the conference in Delphi, Greece, that first inspired the volume. Special thanks are due to Alexis Torrance who provided the edited version of Matthew Baker's piece (chapter 6) and for Katherine Baker who gave her kind permission to publish Baker's work. We would also like to thank Chris Doude Van Troosstwijk for his assistance in looking for a publisher. In regard to publishing, we are thankful for the folks at Lexington Books/Fortress Academic, in particular Michael Gibson who started the project with us and for Gayla Freeman and Neil Elliott who completed it. Lastly, we thank our families and friends for their loyalty and support. This volume ultimately grew out of the soil of friendship and is itself testimony to the relational ontology found here within.

Introduction

Feast of the Transfiguration, 2018

Andrew T. J. Kaethler with Sotiris Mitralexis

"Who will lay hold on the human heart to make it still," Augustine asked, "so that it can see how eternity, in which there is neither future nor past, stands still and dictates future and past times? Can my hand have the strength for this? (Gen. 31:29). Can the hand of my mouth by mere speech achieve so great a thing?"[1]

The questions surrounding the relationship between time and eternity, the one and the many, essentialism and anti-essentialism, or in short ontology and history, persist from the pre-Socratics to the present. Christian theology, itself imbedded in history, has had no small part in the dialogue both shaping and being shaped by the contemporary philosophical milieu. In *Introduction to Christianity*, a text that engages much with the question, Joseph Ratzinger lays out three major paradigm shifts that have transformed the ways in which we interpret reality.[2] These three paradigms or approaches to knowing mark different ways of conceiving of ontology and history and helpfully provide a lay of the land.

Skipping past pre-Socratic thought, Plato's notion of time as the moving image of eternity or the prime mover in Aristotle's thought, which is the *final cause* of change (teleology), represent what Ratzinger refers to as the metaphysical approach to perceiving reality. Eternal unchangingness provides, as it were, the platform from which the particular can move, change, and develop. The cosmos and its participants are conceived, as described in the poetic musing of John Millbank, as "particularized exemplifications of this All, possessed of a relatively stable substance, secured and defined by a specific participation in the All's universal essence."[3] According to the metaphysical approach, God is a pure thinking "thing," and the cosmos is, crassly speaking, a product of this thought. All being is what has been thought and is meaningful and true because of its relation to the *Logos*. Human thought is a rethinking of divine thought ("re-cognition"). My *logos*—my own reason—is in relation to God's *Logos*. Thus, thought is more real, solid, and unchanging than that which man creates within history, for whatever man creates is liable to corruption and eventual nonexistence. In contradistinction to the historical, truth is unchanging and eternal. Truth is found in metaphysics and its certainty is attested to by its unchanging nature, or in more Ratzingerian terms: according to the metaphysical approach being is truth, *verum est ens*.

The shift away from the metaphysical approach is marked by the thought of Giambattista Vico (1668–1744). Vico shifts away from *verum est ens* (being is truth) to *verum quia factum* (truth as fact). Following the logic of Aristotle, in which to know something one must know the cause, Vico maintains that the only things that we can know with certainty are those that concern man. As a result, history and mathematics replaced metaphysics as the primary science. Thereby, eventually history worked its way into other disciplines: philosophy (e.g., Hegel), theology (e.g., historical critical method and the rise of biblical studies as its own discipline), economics (e.g., Marx), and natural science (Darwin's theory of evolution). Through the historical lens everything is seen as a process. There is no "*is*" but rather what "*was*" and what "*may be*."

However, the certainty of *verum quia factum* could not be consistently maintained because of the inherent subjectivity involved in historical research. While the certainty of mathematics is objective, history involves interpretation. Thus, a new paradigm arose: the scientific/technological paradigm, or *techne*. This new paradigm of knowing is the result of mathematical thinking brought together with scientific empirical thinking, a shift away from fact in the past tense to the future tense of "makability": *verum quia faciendum* (truth as feasibility). Ratzinger writes, "The fact has set free the *faciendum*, the 'made' has set free the 'makable', the repeatable, the provable, and only exists for the sake of the latter. It comes to the primacy of the 'makable' over the 'made', for in fact what can man do with what has merely existed in the past?"[4] Put differently, our gaze shifted from the past to the future—progress.

Man, as a product of mere chance ("discovered" by history), now redeems himself by making himself and the world into what he wants. In essence he turns himself into God. While the ancients began their theoretical musings from God in order to understand the nature of man, moderns have inverted the order: man creates an understanding about God. To put it differently, God is recognized as the end result of *faciendum*, whereas for the ancients He stood at the beginning—a switch from receiving to making.

All three approaches seek to make sense of the world by looking in a specific direction. The metaphysical approach (*verum est ens*) gazes into the ether of Eternity; the historical approach (*verum quia factum*) looks to the past; the scientific/technological approach peers into the future. The break from the metaphysical is a far greater change than the move to the technological. *Techne*, we could say, is less a break than a shift, for the emphasis is still akin to the historical: the focus on process, on making and becoming. Both share in what Ratzinger calls the "know-make" relationship; we can only truly know what we have made or will make.

These *Lebenswelten* veil and unveil truth, create prejudices in the Gadamerian sense. Each approach parallels various theological and philosophical emphases:

1. Metaphysical (*verum est ens*): incarnational theology and essentialism.
2. Historical (*verum quia factum*): theology of the cross, historical critical scholarship, philosophy of spirit (*Geist*), and the emphasis on progress.
3. *Techne* (*verum quia faciendum*): an emphasis on eschatology, political theology, a rejection of "onto-theology," anti-essentialism, and transhumanism.

More could be added but this suffices to make the point. Most importantly it raises the ensuing question, in what paradigm is Christian belief most fully at home? Following the path forged by Ratzinger, belief does not wholly belong to any of the *Lebenswelten* (and we could add, any of the theological emphases). By its very nature faith concerns meaning and not primarily facticity, or verifiability. This is not to deny the metaphysical, historical, or 'technological' import but is a change in focus:

> Christian belief really is concerned with the *factum*; it lives in a specific way on the plane of history, and it is no accident that history and the historical approach grew up precisely in the atmosphere of Christian belief. And indubitably Christian belief has something to do with changing the world, with shaping the world with the protest against the lethargy of human institutions and of those who profit from them.[5]

Certainly Marxism did not arise out of a religious vacuum but grew out of a Christian-Jewish tradition that opposes the powers that oppress the weak. Ratzinger maintains that the present paradigm creates an opportunity for Christian theology to gain a "new understanding of the position of faith between fact and *faciendum*."[6] Yet, he makes clear that belief cannot rest completely on either plane of knowing. It cannot whole-heartedly accept the know-make relationship, for belief concerns a different relation, what Ratzinger calls the "stand-understand" relationship. Belief is trusting in something that one does not make and here taking a stand. "Essentially, it is entrusting oneself to that which has not been made by oneself and never could be made and which precisely in this way supports and makes possible all our making."[7] All meaning requires such a move; ultimately, created meaning is an oxymoron. "Meaning, that is, the ground on which our existence as a totality can stand and live, cannot be made but only received."[8]

What one steps beyond and stands firm on, what one receives, is not an impersonal "thing" but a person. We stand on the one who is Eternity, who is the Kingdom Himself, that is, Jesus Christ. That is, Christ simultaneously fulfills all tenses of reality: He *is* (Son) and *was* (Jesus of Nazareth) and *will be* (the Kingdom in person, *hē autobasileia*)—Alpha and Omega. This points to a common thread weaved throughout this volume: relationality. What stands *between* history and ontology is the *person* of Christ. With a properly understood Christology the tension between history and ontology is relationally retained, and thus we do not "end either in historical positivism or in an ahistorical gnosticism."[9]

BETWEEN BEING AND TIME

This edited volume came to fruition on the heels of a conference titled *Ontology and History: A Challenging and Auspicious Dialogue for Philosophy and Theology* that we—Andrew T. J. Kaethler and Sotiris Mitralexis—organized in May 2015, and which took place in Delphi, Greece. As a Catholic and Orthodox respectively the conference was ecumenically organized and likewise ecumenically represented by the participants. The present volume mirrors this to some extent, providing a wide array of diversity in approach.

The conference was, and thereby this volume is, dedicated to the memory of Fr. Matthew Baker (see chapter 6). A rising star in the Orthodox world, not to mention a scholar who shared my love of the theology of Joseph Ratzinger, Baker tragically was killed in a car accident on March 1, 2015, as he travelled home from celebrating evening prayer at Holy Trinity Greek Orthodox Church in Norwich, Connecticut. I am grateful to have corresponded with him through email leading up to the conference. In the emails, he wrote humbly, adroitly, and passionately about literature, theology (East and West), and philosophy—sadly I did not meet him in person. Yet, it is a blessing that we can connect with the profundity of his work here presented.

The first section of this volume, "Rethinking Ontology within History," presents five chapters that creatively seek to relook at the confluence of history and ontology. Haralambos Ventis examines the spurious dilemma that theologians have faced in order to preserve the meaningfulness of Christianity: ahistorical essentialism or an equally ahistorical insular fideism. Rejecting both options, Ventis sketches an alternative that embraces historical development and theology's responsibility to society (a community in the midst of flux), and yet is unmistakably ontological. Giulio Maspero explicates Gregory of Nyssa's relational ontology and draws the reader's attention to Gregory's conception of relation (*schesis*) and his notion of perpetual ascent (*epektasis*). Maspero argues that both notions, grounded in a Trinitarian ontology, make it possible to conceive of being and history as noncontradictory. Also exploring ontology as "on the way" (dromic ontology), Dionysios Skliris explores in great depth Maximus the Confessor's philosophical theology, where he claims to find a unique and bold valorization of history *via ontology*—in stark contrast to the widespread tendency in philosophy and theology to annihilate the importance of history *sub speciae ontologiae*. Like Maspero, Skliris highlights both movement and relationship—dromic ontology as an ontology of the *syn-od*—but through the Maximian triad of *logos*, *tropos* (mode), and *telos*. David Fagerberg, turning to Pavel Florensky, Alexander Schmemann, and Benedict XVI, comes to the question through liturgy. Too often liturgical theology splinters into historical and ritual specialization and overlooks *the* Liturgy behind the various liturgies. Fagerberg argues that we must understand the whole—a sort of metaphysics of liturgy—before we can understand the parts of the liturgy. Demetrios Harper discusses Immanuel Kant's philosophy of history. Kant has a forward-looking view of history in which by the overcoming of nature through rational self-legislation human persons will overcome irrationality and disharmony. History looks beyond itself to a future "transcendental utopia"; however, this utopia is a mere aspiration, a pointing toward something from which there is no reality—an ontological void. Harper provides an alternative perspective looking to Maximus the Confessor's eschatology with a particular focus on Maximus's use of *mimesis*. Unlike Kant, Maximus does not denigrate nature but sees the manifestation of the Creator in our spatio-temporal world. Christ fills Kant's ontological void; He makes present the end and purpose of history.

 The second section, "Beyond Being and Time: Eschatological Hermeneutics," examines how eschatology changes the way in which we "read" the world. Most notably, Martin Heidegger, Georges Florovsky, John Zizioulas, and Maximus the Confessor come to the fore as the authors grapple with the topic. Matthew Baker enucleates Heidegger's influence on Zizioulas's hermeneutics highlighting the categories of *ekstasis*, authenticity, and being-unto-death. Then Baker explores the implications of Heidegger's hermeneutics in Zizioulas's theological hermeneutics drawing attention to the eschatological emphasis which, unlike Heidegger, finds its locus in Christ and thus is a future that is already present. Maxim Vasiljević raises the question, Who is Christ not simply in a universal sense but in regard to one's own present reality? Engaging not only with the aforementioned authors, Vasiljević brings

Baker's work to bear on the subject who also finds the answer in a "hermeneutics of Resurrection." Nikolaos Loudovikos brings into conversation Origen, Ludwig Wittgenstein, and Sigmund Freud with the previous list of thinkers, and highlights hermeneutics as a way of being in which each person freely creates meaning. Yet, such meaning is not ecstatic—self-centered will to power—but reciprocal or dialogical. Ontology is understood in this light, what Loudovikos sees as an eschatological ontology. That is, ontology is understood as relational/dialogical unending movement or development. He critiques all attempts to engage with history and ontology that tend toward the ecstatic, tendencies he sees in Zizioulas, Christos Yannaras, and John Romanides (not to mention Western theology *in toto*).

The third section, "Personhood between Ontology and History," explores the theological anthropological question of what it means to be a person in time. All four chapters share in the claim that personhood is constituted by relation. Offering a summary and epitome of his ontology of personhood, Christos Yannaras argues that we cannot speak of personhood in terms of a phenomenal *what* but only as an active *how*. Existence concerns becoming and such becoming constitutes relations; God is Father, not some ontic necessary being but one who freely wills to exist, and love is the mode of His existence; this inaugurates, Yannaras argues, an ontology of freedom. Daniel S. Robinson explicates Nikolai Berdyaev's conception of history and its relation to a personal God. A witness to the violence of the Russian revolution, Berdyaev conceived of the problem of history as the problem of theodicy. Where is God's justice in the midst of human violence and viciousness? How can we reconcile the God of mercy with the unmerciful determination of history? In response, Berdyaev turns away from a conception of God as all-powerful to a co-suffering personal God. Only the voluntary passion of Christ can make sense of historical and theological reasoning. Isabel C. Troconis Iribarren shifts the third section in the direction of the West and explores Joseph Ratzinger's (Pope Emeritus Benedict XVI) *Imago Dei* anthropology. Ratzinger holds together the ontological and the historical by maintaining that the human person *is* one who finds herself by transcending herself in relation to others (ultimately *the* Other). In so doing, Troconis claims that Ratzinger holds together continuity and discontinuity. Chris Doude van Troostwijk explicates Søren Kierkegaard's conception of prayer and the human self, focusing on Kierkegaard's *Sickness unto Death*. Prayer is the dialectic counterpart to despair. Enrolled in his own brokenness marked by his inability to know his own self, man falls into despair—the historical realities of life reveal man's insufficiency. Yet, it is this experience that opens man to God's divine assistance (prayer) and thereby reveals man as he is: one whose self is found only in relation to the Eternal One.

Introduction xvii

The final section, "Politics between Being and Time," looks at the possibility of political theology. With the shift to the technological paradigm and the priority of making and feasibility and the corresponding eschatological emphasis political theology came into existence. The tension between future feasibility and a theology of incarnation has marked political theology from its conception. This is, in our eyes, an indispensable implication of inquiring into the convergence of ontology (eschatology?) and history, since the introduction of ontology into history—and vice versa—engenders the question of our *collective* task *within* history. When seen under a theological and, most pertinently, eschatological light, the question concerning history morphs into a question concerning our political coexistence (rather than, say, individual ethics). In other words, it is impossible to approach the march of ontology within history without also acknowledging the politically theological elephant in the sanctum. There is a *polis*, or at the very least the question concerning it, between the Incarnation and the Eschaton. Following a rough outline provided by Adrian Thatcher, Jared Schumacher develops a genealogy of the modern concept of ontology demonstrating the plethora of meanings that it has taken on. Schumacher argues that the modern anti-post-metaphysical usage of ontology rejects philosophical realism, and thus the discourse follows a rationalist or idealist track, both of which are problematic for theology. In response, Schumacher posits that in order for basic Christian doctrines to be retained and for Christianity to have a voice in the political realm, theology must recover its traditional metaphysical realism. Daniel Wright brings eucharistic ecclesiology to bear on the current discourse in political theology. Turning to William Cavanaugh and John Zizioulas, and rooting political theology in the eucharist, Wright argues that the Church's penitential action is prescriptive for political theology. In other words, eucharistic ecclesiology leads into political theology, the continuation of the eucharistic demand for repentance. Logan M. Isaac explores how John Howard Yoder and Reinhold Niebuhr employ Christian "realism" in regard to pacifism and justified uses of violence. Niebuhr uses realism to justify limited violence, but Isaac, turning to Yoder, finds fault with Niebuhr's realism. That is, it is not a biblical realism like Yoder's which is grounded eschatologically; Jesus's life was not just sacramental (ontological) but exemplary and thus political even in its seemingly extraordinary demands of pacifism.

The conversation does not end here. Theologians and philosophers will continue to dialogue about history and ontology. Nevertheless, with all the diverse perspectives represented in this volume, I think that each contributor can agree with Alexander Schmemann that "the Church is to be seen as the presence and communication of the kingdom that is to come. The unique—I repeat, unique—function of worship in the life of the Church and in theology is to convey a sense of this eschatological reality."[10]

NOTES

1. Augustine, *Confessions*, trans. Henry Chadwick (Oxford: Oxford University Press, 2008), 229.

2. I have used Joseph Ratzinger's work because he appropriately perceives that the most pressing theological question today concerns the relationship of ontology and history. His writings repeatedly engage with the question (e.g., Ratzinger's *Habilitationsschrift* on Bonaventure's theology of history and his monograph on eschatology). Lawrence Cunningham aptly notes that "Ratzinger's entire approach to the mystery of Christ attempts to hold in creative tension the truth of the Eternal Logos and the Logos made flesh." Lawrence S. Cunningham, "Reflections on *Introduction to Christianity*," in *Explorations in the Theology of Benedict XVI*, ed. John C. Cavadini (Notre Dame: University of Notre Dame Press, 2012), 150. See endnote 4 in chapter 11, "Joseph Ratzinger's *Imago Dei* Anthropology: The Reconciliation of Ontology and Salvation History."

3. John Milbank, *The All: A Philosophico-Political Polemic*, accessed July 6, 2018, https://tif.ssrc.org/2018/02/16/the-all-a-philosophico-political-polemic/.

4. Joseph Ratzinger, *Introduction to Christianity*, trans. J. R. Foster (San Francisco: Ignatius Press, 2004), 65.

5. Ibid., 67–68.

6. Ibid., 68.

7. Ibid., 70.

8. Ibid., 73.

9. Cunningham, "Reflections on *Introduction to Christianity*," 151.

10. Alexander Schmemann, "Liturgy and Eschatology," in *Liturgy and Tradition: Theological Reflections of Alexander Schmemann*, ed. Thomas Fisch (Crestwood, NY: St Vladimir's Seminary Press, 1990), 95–96.

Part I

RETHINKING ONTOLOGY WITHIN HISTORY

Chapter One

Ontology versus Fideism

Christianity's Accountability to History and Society

Haralambos Ventis

Since the dawn of its appearance, Christianity has been sold as an intellectually defensible faith. Be that as it may, the precise expression of this ongoing witness to outsiders has varied greatly throughout the ages, and its desired mode is still hotly debated today. At least part of the rivalry stems from the antinomic character of Christianity, which is both metaphysically laden and rooted in historical narratives, as well as liturgically structured as a synthesis of *lex orandi* and *lex credendi*. As a result of these distinct yet counterbalancing facets, theologians have long been faced with a spurious dilemma in their efforts to account meaningfully for the Christian faith: they have felt compelled either to uphold an ahistorical, essentialistic "natural theology," on one hand, or to restrict themselves to an equally ahistorical fideist perspective, irresponsibly insular from the world and averse to ontology and the materiality of life, on the other. In this chapter, following a review of these competing models comprising this fruitless quandary, I shall draw a rough sketch for an alternative tense but feasible manner of Christian testimony, one that is sincerely falsifiable and thus accountable to history and society, yet unmistakably ontological in outlook. My thesis presupposes the conviction that despite the fragile interplay between history and ontology undergirding the suggested project, Christians should not be thwarted from striving to vocalize an existentially meaningful and socially responsible witness of the Gospel to the world.

SOME PRELIMINARY REMARKS: PLATO VERSUS THUCYDIDES OR THE FLAGRANT INCOMPATIBILITY BETWEEN ONTOLOGY AND HISTORY

As anyone sufficiently trained in the history of Western metaphysics would readily admonish, any attempt to correlate philosophical ontology with history is bound to be doomed or, at the very least, appear to be suspect from the outset. For, while not necessarily synonymous with platonic dualism or inescapably marred by precritical (i.e., pre-Kantian) metaphysics, the very notion of metaphysical ontology evokes images of Parmenidean immutability and permanence. History, on the other hand, is the realm of Heraclitean flux and change, of constant transformation and arbitrary mess, best handled by a "nominalist" approach, even when allowing for distinguishable eras and trends. Worse yet, a religiously soaked ontology, even remotely or partially based on revelation, is fatally hindered from undergoing reconsideration and evolution, which are the lifeblood of any historically conscious system of ideas. No matter how intellectually polished, religions (particularly of the monotheistic sort) are adamantly resistant to change and are accustomed to pontificate rather than to engage in sincere dialogue with nonadherents—fallibility, proclaimed or actual, has never been the strong suit of religion. All this has naturally given a black eye to even sincere and well-meaning attempts at establishing links between religiously informed ontologies and social legislation, for obviously secular democracies are highly attendant to the need for change as they are to the emergence of new knowledge and the new needs of citizens, which demand fresh and often radical thought that goes beyond inherited dogmatisms and hardened preconceptions.

At the risk of blatant oversimplification, it could be argued that the advent of Modernity is correlative with the dwindling of ontological realism, whose touted demise inevitably compromised the standing of natural theology as well. Converging philosophical developments brought epistemology to prominence, a turn-about followed by an ascent of temporality as the premier arena of human thought and activity. Metaphysical speculation on the mysteries of an eternal heaven, whether Platonic, Aristotelian, or Christian, lost its appeal as post-Renaissance scientists began pondering the tangible wonders of our inhabited world in all its materiality and temporality. This landmark paradigm-shift occurred gradually, following William of Ockham's demolition of platonic-type Universals as mere *nomina*; Francis Bacon's glorification of empirical science in his *Novum Organum*; and the emergence of Empiricism proper (neatly summed-up in John Locke's dictum that "all things that exist are only particulars"). This process finally came to a head with Immanuel Kant's devastating critique of the Ontological Argument and the speculative ventures of all unrestrained, unaccountable metaphysics—a landmark point at the end of a cumulative development moving at the opposite end of Christian Wolff's ontological essentialism. In sum, the ascendancy of epistemology and temporality go hand in hand, although history is more like biology in its indeterminism and unpredictability as opposed to physics. In view of this strained relation between what is unashamedly static, essentialist, and *a priori*, and what is insubordinately transient, *a posteriori*, and focuses on particulars, it might seem that it has taken historiographers a surprisingly long time to uphold a nominalist approach to studying historical events. Eventually, of course, they did, albeit not without strong resistance.[1] Historian of note Paul Veyne, to cite but one case, belongs to those that championed the nominalist thesis in historiography, stipulating that historians ought to look chiefly at particulars, inasmuch as history is the study of the *change* of human practices, institutions, empires, and borders.[2]

POST-KANTIAN, POSTEMPIRICIST WAYS OF CHRISTIAN EVANGELIZATION: THEOLOGIANS GETTING THE MESSAGE IN TIMES OF ANTIMETAPHYSICAL ARIDITY

How did Christian theologians and theist philosophers of religion respond to this dwindling of traditional, precritical ontology, a predicament incurred not so much by the elevation of temporality per se but by the combined iconoclastic might of both logical positivists[3] and such influential postpositivists as Willard van Orman Quine and Ludwig Wittgenstein (all champions of the so-called "linguistic turn" in twentieth century philosophy)?[4] Interestingly, for reasons that will be broached shortly, Western theologians largely resorted to the convenient haven of fideism, while their Greek Orthodox counterparts went the opposite way of reinstating ontology at the heart of Christian dogmatics. Let us examine these two theological paradigms separately, beginning with fideism.

One of the major enforcers of philosophical immanentism (the restriction of all meaningful, valid knowledge to human experience only, at the expense of any hint of transcendence) has been the doctrine of *nonrepresentationalism*. This notion is an outgrowth of certain developments in British empiricism; it was initially precipitated by John Locke's absolutization of sense-data, which he posited as inescapable intermediaries between human perception and external objects—a decisive ploy further exacerbated by Hume's radical empiricism, which reduced causation to mere habit, as an unobserved entity. In its classical, consolidated version, however, nonrepresentationalism originates in the Kantian epistemological distinction between "phenomena" and "things-in-themselves." As instituted by Kant, this divide was meant to challenge the naive realist certainty that the spatio-temporal reality perceived by human subjects is an accurate representation of the world as such, apart from the human mode of its apperception. In its twentieth-century linguistic version, nonrepresentationalism conveys roughly the same skeptical epistemological reservation, an insistence namely that reality is decisively mediated throughout, except that it is now seen as filtered through language, not by means of our transcendental constitution. The bottom line with nonrepresentationalism is that it has decisively impaired (or so it seems) an entire cluster of pre-Kantian ideas related to Platonism and the tradition of the Cartesian *cogito*. These include realism, foundationalism,[5] natural theology, and all traditional ontological pursuits assuming the possibility of a direct cognitive access to the world and what is beyond it. Having dramatically undermined these exploits, nonrepresentationalism (transcendental or linguistic) conflates *what* is known with *how* it is (humanly) known, thereby inextricably annexing existents and ontology in general to our modes of conceptualization, in other words to the human cognitive horizon, whose impenetrable limits are nowadays seen as linguistic (cf. the early Wittgenstein's famous dictum, "the limits of my language mean the limits of my world," *Tractatus Logico-Philosophicus*, 5.6). In short, nonrepresentationalism is the staunch denial of the possibility of ever arriving at the bottom of "reality," much less of attaining an accurate and corresponding depiction thereof.

Because of its kinship with pre-Kantian forms of ontology, natural theology could not avoid falling into considerable disrepute either under the reign of nonrepresentationalism, having already been challenged on theological grounds by Reformed thinkers as an idolatrous hybrid of Jerusalem and Athens, hopelessly tainted by unbiblical philosophical ideas. Even prior to Kant, it had become obvious in Protestant circles that establishing necessary links between God and the external world was not only untenable but even blasphemous, and always at the price of neglecting the inner logic and beauty of the Christian faith itself. These cogent theological objections were now joined, as we just saw, by a sharp philosophical skepticism. Michael Sudduth sketches a handy summary of the negative consequences of the Humean/Kantian position for traditional natural theology:

> First, God is an unobservable entity and does not belong to the world of objects conditioned by the human mind. If causation is restricted to experience we could not be justified in reaching any conclusions about God being the cause of the existence of the cosmos or its order. Such a proof presupposes that causal chains can be extended beyond what is given to us by our immediate sense impressions. Secondly, Hume would grant that our past experiences of seeing human agents building houses provides some justification for our extrapolating a human agent as the cause of the house we currently observe. However, since we have never

seen universes being made by the deities we cannot properly form any justified beliefs about God being the cause of the universe and its order. Not surprisingly, Hume and Kant each rely on the restriction of causation to experience to dismantle the project of natural theology.[6]

In view of this immanentist intellectual milieu, realist or externalist theologians have found it increasingly difficult to engage in classical apologetics, say of the type instituted by William Paley, except at the cost of implausibility, irrelevance, and unforgivable quaintness. Interestingly, however, a sizable portion of theologians reared in the strongly antitheoretical insights of Martin Luther and other early Reformers (and such spiritual descendants as Kant, Søren Kierkegaard, and Karl Barth), have eagerly embraced this devastating critique of grand metaphysics and natural theology as a virtue, not a problem. Specifically, they see the indictment of ontotheology as an opportunity for the prophetic voice of the "God of Abraham, Isaac, and Jacob" (as opposed to the God of the philosophers) to be heard once again, in its unadulterated authenticity. In the words of one representative, Terrence W. Tilley, who sees the philosophical disease of Modernity as the valorization of pure theory and the degradation of practical, bodily, and emotional issues,

> some contemporary epistemologists have embarked on a practical path which must lead them to consider doxastic practices, the conditions under which they work, and the "noncognitive" ingredients necessary to knowing, including both personal attitudes and social conditions. . . . Ultimately it leads to a claim that the justification of religious belief is best understood not as demonstrating that an individual is entitled to hold some specific religious proposition, but as showing the wisdom of participating in a religious tradition, and, by implication, the wisdom of accepting the central and distinctive practices and convictions of that tradition.[7]

Tilley's statement captures well the legacy of a former generation of practical or internalist theologians, such as James William McClendon Jr. and James M. Smith, whose own intellectual lineage reaches back as early as Michel de Montaigne and Blaise Pascal. Tilley sees in the work of Montaigne and Pascal an interesting anticipation of current issues in the philosophy of religion, especially in the work of Montaigne, who was probably the first to draw explicitly the now established contrast between the *externalist* and the *internalist* or fideist models for witnessing to religious belief. As opposed to externalists, whose literary emblems are the characters of Cleanthes and Philo in Hume's Dialogues, internalists value inner coherence over rational demonstration or the usual evidences for the existence of God. Well-known internalists, aptly represented by Demea in Hume's Dialogues, are nowadays inclusive of those who generally belong to the contemporary stream of Reformed Epistemology, more poignantly represented by Alvin Plantinga, Nicholas Wolterstorff, and William Alston. A more extreme version of contemporary theologians averse to theistic ontology are the so-called radical "death of God" theologians (among whom are Mark Taylor, Charles Winquist, Robert Scharlemann, and Carl Raschke), whose more immediate inspiration comes from Nietzschean iconoclasm and Derridean deconstruction. Their far less radical counterparts, on the other hand, such as George Lindbeck and T. Z. Phillips, have written under the spell of a milder linguistic revolution that is Wittgensteinian as opposed to postmodern in its own non-representationalism, and based on a contextualist reading of the Austrian philosopher's so-called later period. Despite their differences in emphasis and inspiration, these scholars have all embraced fideism as their preferred model for doing theology, staunchly denying, with Barth, the notion of *analogia entis* along with the possibility and the obligation to arrive at God through arguments and demonstrations in favor of theism.

To get some flavor of this recent fideist predilection, let us take a closer look at the neo-Barthian approach represented by the so-called Yale School of postliberal theology and its most outstanding advocate, George Lindbeck. Lindbeck's model has afforded a luring alternative to those seeking a way out of the impasses created by the crisis of traditional apologetics.[8] In his now classic manifesto *The Nature of Doctrine*,[9] Lindbeck reinterprets Christian doctrines as grammatical rules *à la* Wittgenstein's concept of "language games." This new appraisal of doctrines sees them not as ontological statements referring to an external reality but as expressions and guidelines of the community's authentic ritual and liturgical praxis. Lindbeck's non-ontological interpretation of doctrines liberates theology from the arduous task of proving or establishing the truth of Christianity, switching as it does attention from the traditional, thorny question "Is faith *true*?" to the more accommodating "Is this or that belief *authentically* Christian?"

His purpose is to drive home to us that "[doctrines] are . . . second-order rather than first-order propositions and affirm nothing about extra-linguistic or extra-human reality."[10] For example, in our talk about God "the primary focus is not on God's being in itself, for that is not what the text is about, but on how life is to be lived and reality construed in the light of God's character as this is depicted in the stories of Israel and of Jesus."[11] This causes Lindbeck to conflict with the so-called "propositional model," which equates doctrinal formulations with (ontological) truth statements about God and the world. At the same time, Lindbeck is just as dismissive of "experiential-expressivism," a theological approach originating in the apologetic work of Friedrich Schleiermacher and more recently expounded by Bernard Lonergan and David Tracy. He sees the two models as corresponding to radically opposed approaches to religion and theology. The former, and oldest, approach has historically comprised the stronghold of traditional theologians who have used doctrinal propositions to objectively refer to transcendent realities all along. The latter model, by contrast (understandably championed by more liberal quarters), focuses on the believer's inner awareness, which is then linguistically externalized as the particular expression of a universally partaken transcendent reality. Despite being portrayed as opposites in his book, Lindbeck alerts us to a veiled but real fault shared equally by these approaches, meaning their incipient precritical foundationalism: he chides both for claiming to rest upon firm, albeit different, ontological pillars. These are comprised of objects, states of affairs, or transcendent facts for the propositionalists, and of emotions (the affective moods of believers) for experiential-expressivists; but for all their difference, both types of foundations are sold as yielding objective knowledge in the form of truth statements about the divine.

In contrast to those two, Lindbeck's "linguistic-cultural" countermodel is clearly antifoundationalist and internalist in character, redefining religion as a set of communal practices shaping one's life in its entirety, in conscious reaction to a widespread understanding of theology as a cerebral, theoretical endeavor reduced to self-contained, doctrinal propositions. "The latter," Lindbeck indicates,

> locates religious meaning outside the text or semiotic system either in the objective realities to which it refers or in the experiences it symbolizes, whereas for cultural-linguists the meaning is immanent. Meaning is constituted by the uses of a specific language rather than being distinguishable from it. Thus the proper way to determine what "God" signifies, for example, is by examining how the word operates within a religion and thereby shapes reality and experience rather than by first establishing its propositional or experiential meaning and reinterpreting or reformulating its uses accordingly. It is in this sense that theological description in the cultural-linguistic model is intrasemiotic or intratextual.[12]

Much the same holds for the internalism of D. Z. Phillips. Over the years, Phillips has established himself as an outspoken supporter of the beneficial theological appropriation of Wittgenstein's insights, one marked by strongly Kierkegaardian overtones. "Kierkegaard and Wittgenstein," Phillips states in wholehearted personal concurrence, "attacked philosophy's foundationalist pretensions. Philosophy does not provide its own yardstick by which our practices are to be assessed. Instead, it endeavours to give perspicious representations of these practices when we are tempted to become confused about them."[13] His main concern, more forcefully expounded in his elaborate critique of Alvin Plantinga's own foundationalism,[14] has been to show that the entanglement of theologians and philosophers in endless disputes over the reality of God and the truth of religious claims, mirroring in that respect the unnecessary philosophical exchange concerning realism and relativism, should rather be explained away as being due to grammatical confusions; in other words, as being spawned by misuses of language that, once removed, expose the pointlessness and vacuity of all positions involved. For in reality, Phillips holds, all sides have routinely, if mostly unconsciously, indulged in systematic linguistic abuse by drawing terms out of their appropriate context, thereby ending up talking past each other instead of making meaningful contributions to the dialogue. Thus, with the help of Wittgenstein's technique of linguistic analysis, metaphysical problems, including those of realism and nonrealism, may be harmlessly dismissed as pseudoproblems unworthy of serious attention and thought:

> The distinction between the real and the unreal is not given prior to the use of various language games. There is no Archimedean point outside all language games by which we assess the adequacy of language in relation to reality. Such a relation is a chimera. It is so easy to forget this when we discuss religion. . . . In saying [for example] that no-one would worship unless he first believed that God exists, the realist assumes that we are all realists with respect to religion, believers and atheists alike. This assumption hides the fact that, so far, no conceptual elucidation has been provided of what this prior belief in the existence of God amounts to. No intelligible account could be given of it. The realist will not allow any appeal to religious worship in elucidating the belief, since to do so, he claims, is to confuse religious belief with its truths. The religious life, he argues, is the fruit of the belief in God's existence which is its foundation. And so we have a search for a minimal, basic belief in the existence of God, one which involves no affective response. Such a search ends up with a marginal phenomenon far away from the realities of religion. The realist wants to insist, quite rightly, that God's existence, like the existence of tables and chairs, does not depend on what we say and think. But we must also realize that what saying this amounts to depends on what talk of existence means in these respective contexts. Wittgenstein's attack on realism applies to the belief that there is a chair in the next room, as it does to belief in God. Wittgenstein, however, is not advocating non-realist accounts of religious belief in face of the onslaughts of positivism. His philosophical insights cut through the dispute between realism and non-realism.[15]

It is worth mentioning that Phillips finds the terrain of theology particularly suited for elucidating Wittgenstein's thought and the contribution the latter can make to believers and nonbelievers alike, as soon as its crux is sufficiently grasped. This is because the torturing dilemma of realism versus nonrealism is more acutely manifested in contemporary efforts to either endow theology with a "scientific" grounding, or conversely (which in Phillips's and Wittgenstein's view amounts to the same thing) to discredit it as a primitive, pre-modem, "unscientific" discourse. "The trouble is that we discuss the inexplicable in a culture dominated, not by religion, but by science. We are thus tempted to treat the inexplicable as something which must have an explanation, but one which is unavailable to us." So, Phillips concludes, "Religion becomes a 'super-science' whose answers and explanations will be known after death. Religious mysteries are temporary mysteries. The hubris present in theodicies, with their available answers, now invades the heavens by insisting that we shall have answers there."[16] What Phillips is saying here is that the cardinal sin of many a philosopher of religion, and of no less a self-described "realist" theologian, has been the inclination (nurtured by an ill-conceived "scientific" attitude) to prove or verify what by nature resists all proof and verification, and which has repeatedly led to metaphysical nonsense, to intellectual dead ends. His answer to these and such alleged pseudo-problems, drawn as it is directly from Wittgenstein and skillfully unpacked in his critiques of John Searle, Terence Penelhum, Roger Trigg, Richard Swinburne, and Alvin Plantinga, is conceptual clarification and the realization that words, especially those employed in religious discourse, draw their meaning not in the abstract but from their concrete uses in particular forms of life, religion itself being seen as a par excellence form of life.

> Rightly or wrongly, Wittgenstein is accusing realism and non-realism of being idle talk; talk which takes us away from the directions in which we should be looking if we want to clarify the grammar of our beliefs concerning [such ordinary objects as] chairs. Similarly, the accusation against theological realism is that it is idle talk. If this accusation is a just one, realism has never been integral to faith. This does not mean that we must embrace non-realism. . . . Theological non-realism is as empty as theological realism. Both terms are battle-cries in a confused philosophical and theological debate.[17]

MEANWHILE IN EASTERN ORTHODOXY: SOME BELATED BUT PROMISING STIRRINGS

So much, then, for Western Christian fideism in a nutshell. Has there ever been a fideist counterpart in Eastern Orthodoxy? A tiny version of it could be claimed in the recent work of the Greek author Stavros Zoumboulakis, but is nowhere near the breadth and scope of fideism proper, as it is known in the West. Historical events have generally prevented Orthodox theologians from following up on and responding to challenges posed by Hume, Kant, the Enlightenment, and Modernity. A landmark turnabout in Greek Orthodox theology occurred with the emergence of the so-called "theological generation of the early '60s,"[18] an umbrella term referring to the collective effort of young Greek theologians to revitalize Christian witness and Church life in Greece, following a long period of stagnation caused by two factors: the institutional Church's introverted isolation from society, and the pernicious prevalence of a thick legalist pietism spread by lay Christian brotherhoods attempting to fill the gap. The team of revitalizers, whose more prominent and influential members include Metropolitan John Zizioulas of Pergamon, Christos Yannaras, and the Revs. John Romanides and Vassilios Gontikakis, among others, more or less converged on the pursuance of a twofold strategy: 1) a concerted return to the wealth of Orthodoxy's own patristic resources as a spiritual antidote to the alleged impasses of Western rationalism and scientism, and 2) a systematic attempt to counter the shallow, groundless piety of the then popular brotherhoods by reinstating ontology and personhood as prime theological categories in Orthodox theology. Their hoped-for goal was, and still remains, to fend off legalism by having morality flow from Christian ontology, and in particular from the ontology of the Trinitarian Persons, whose hypostatic otherness and diversity could (at least in principle) justify a broader, more open-minded and more compassionate anthropology and ethics.

Now, to the extent that these intellectuals deliberately rejected classical apologetics and turned their attention to the long-neglected patristic and liturgical dimensions of Christianity as a far more genuine witness to the Gospel from the inside rather than the standardized package of proofs and demonstrations supposedly documenting the existence of God, they may be said to have adopted an internalist (and confessionally tinged) reasoning that places them apart from the evidentialists. At the same time, however, they are at odds with internalists as well, insisting as they do that theological propositions are ontological in character (in the sense that they do make truth-claims) and that Christian theology *in toto* must be informed by a broader ontology based on a correct picture of God's being. Yannaras, in particular, began a promising and inspired but ultimately unfinished project titled *Critical Ontology*[19] with a view to subjecting Christian ontology to Popper's falsifiability principle—an admirable and badly needed aim, sadly easier stated than achieved. More will be said about it below.

In the meantime, given the immeasurable amount of water that has gone under the bridge since the dawn of this invigorating theological Renaissance in Greece, a reaction to it had long been overdue and was finally voiced in the unsettling prose of Stavros Zoumboulakis. A classicist with a keen eye for Jewish and Christian thought, Zoumboulakis sternly admonished Yannaras for prioritizing ontology over ethics, for glibly drawing a necessary link between morality per se and legalism—an arbitrary and irresponsible confusion akin to throwing out the baby along with the bath water.[20] For in this particular case, the denunciation of pious legalism and its deleterious effect on Christian spirituality came at the cost of also ridiculing the notions of philanthropy and especially human rights as non-Orthodox ideas uncritically and needlessly imported from the West. Zoumboulakis will have none of that. From his perspective, Christ did not found a system of metaphysics or an alternative ontology but a new mode of life based on the primacy of self-sacrificing love, obedience to the word of God, and concern for the least members of society. In view of this hermeneutic, the one-sided fixation with ontology monopolizing Greek theology from the 1960s onward blurs the lines between right and wrong and nurtures a diversion from history and society's ailments toward a nebulous metaphysics sometimes tinged with nationalistic cultural overtones. Such a thick layer of ontology may well block the humanity of marginalized people from sight, just as surely as legalist pietism has done all along, thus failing to promote the hard-earned dignity and freedoms afforded outcasts in secular Western societies from Modernity onward (which of course is not to say that human rights are better upheld by fideists or internalists, who are actually known to carry more grudges against Modernity out of a fidelity to the pristine core of the Gospel). Hence, ethics and the law as opposed to ontological engagements should constitute a first theology according to Zoumboulakis; accordingly, the best witness to the truth and philanthropy of the Christian Gospel is not metaphysical pursuits (apologetics and all)[21] but the love and concern displayed by Christians amongst themselves and especially toward outcasts: the foreigner, the needy, and the socially downtrodden (Zoumboulakis draws heavily here from the anti-ontological/ antimetaphysical heterology of Emmanuel Levinas).[22]

It seems to this writer that Zoumboulakis is largely, but by no means entirely, right on this issue, given the derision with which the culture of human rights and their furtherance has been treated by Yannaras and some followers, who love to dismiss it as reminiscent of a boy-scout mentality, supposedly feeding individualism and self-centeredness. Compassion and solidarity are prime theological arteries that must be extended to include unmitigated support to human and civil rights out of a genuine Christian commitment to hard-earned liberties and equality for everyone—they are not to be offhand dismissed or sacrificed to a "higher" metaphysics aloof to historical tribulations. Generally speaking, however, I concur with Yannaras and Zizoulas in their firm belief that Christian doctrines and theology must ultimately rest on solid ontological bedrock if they are to avoid collapsing to a caricature of the Gospel or being hijacked by the pious neo-Pharisees. Fideism may be partly correct, for after all no one can become truly acquainted with a religious tradition without delving firsthand into its inner logic and ritual. Certainly, religions are forms of life operating on a shared reasoning encompassing worship, creed, and personal conduct all at the same time; and it is this holistic experience, chiefly available from the inside, that accurately represents the gist of any given faith. Nevertheless, fideism suffers from serious faults too, and so can hardly suffice on its own for spiritual nourishment and a meaningful witness to those outside the faith.

Fideism is in fact uniquely prone to fundamentalism. That is because it insulates faith from any and all external criticism (and few things can reek of irresponsibility more than a self-righteous faith inimical to accountability), just as it blinds adherents from the ongoing challenges of history and the new, worthwhile demands of life as life evolves in new, unpredictable directions. At the end of the day, the internal logic of any faith may well turn out to be false and even deleterious for the sanity and safety of individuals and society at large. As the philosopher of religion Kai Nielsen rightly indicated, the participant's understanding of religious discourse does not give that discourse immunity against philosophical criticism, nor does it ensure the validity of logical coherence of religious language and its autonomous criteria of rationality—consequently, it is not a contradiction to speak of the possibility of an "ongoing but irrational form of life."[23]

For these and other reasons, Christianity is in dire need of a finely worked-out metaphysics and ontology, one endowed with strong intellectual and dialogical potential; because if anything, an intellectually advanced metaphysics constitutes a faith's sole chance at self-criticism, and can act as an impetus for it to engage in dialogue with something other than itself—something that a self-standing, self-perpetuating, introverted fideism can never provide, whether based on ethics, ritual, religious sentiment (as Friedrich Schleiermacher submitted) and/or communal linguistic practices, as Wittgensteinian theologians maintain. Hence, I salute Yannaras's endeavor to give Christianity a falsifiable critical ontology capable of making the faith accountable to history and the world.

Ideally and as promised, this would be an ontology liberated from preconceived axioms and *a prioris*; consequently, it would be earnestly receptive to the rough edges of historical indeterminism and perplexity, and thus subject to continued revision where its cosmological and anthropological insights are concerned (though not in terms of established Christology and Trinitarian doctrine). One of Yannaras's strong suits in that regard is the suggestion that truth is an intersubjective affair, always *participated into* with various degrees of success than actually *possessed* as an object. Unfortunately, however, for all of Yannaras's bloated ambitions and intentions, his project was done in the abstract and more with a view to demonstrating the intellectual astuteness of Hellenic Christianity than out of any sincere desire to make connections and bridges to real life; no concrete effort to subject the faith to crucial "crash tests" with social and historical reality is discernible in any of his project's propositions (the book is structured in the form of short, numbered sentences reminiscent of Wittgenstein's *Tractatus Logico-Philosophicus*). At the end of the day, Yannaras's programmatic ontology is tainted and hampered by its own latent *a priori*: that truth, though intersubjective, is ultimately confirmed by majorities, as in the conciliar resolutions of the Ecumenical Councils that settled Christian doctrines once and for all. No room is thereby allowed for the possibility that not infrequently, the truth is also salvaged and conveyed by an enlightened minority or by individual dissidents moving against the tide of popular platitudes and prejudices (as in the cases of St. Athanasius or St. Maximus the Confessor); nor is there a discernible willingness in this critical ontology to factor in unexpected possibilities and discoveries that should call for uneasy, even painful, reconsiderations of established beliefs and customs.

Still, the project of constructing a critical, falsifiable Christian ontology intersecting with history and time is worth pursuing and bringing to completion, for only then shall Christians truly become accountable to history, as the Rev. Georges Florovsky of blessed memory so wisely urged. At bottom, such an ontology would emulate Christ's bodily Incarnation, in the sense of following His risky trajectory from heavenly safety and immunities (i.e., from the bliss of eternity) down to the uncertainties and mess of history. To put it differently, the Christian truth must be constantly tested against the implacable complexities of human life and history, for it is after facing them squarely that it can correct itself, mature, and offer the world a realistic vison honestly liable to facts and life. This self-critical Christian ontology could greatly benefit from the rediscovery of Christian *eschatology*, a horizon that ensures that our Tradition is neither static nor complete but is still and always will be in the making, inasmuch as the vessel of the Church is still afloat on the ocean of time and has yet to reach the shores of the Eschata. Only upon arrival there, at our true homeland, where startling reversals of what was and is considered to be normal and acceptable await us, along the lines of Mt 20:16 ("so the last shall be first and the first last") and in the spirit of the radical social reversals incurred by Christ, shall we be entitled to speak confidently, from the benefit of hindsight. Until then, an eschatologically informed ontology will be open and alert to the new signs of the times and will regain its prophetic voice that was tragically lost as a result of institutional Christendom's absorption in false, conventional certainties and an idolatrous fascination with a glorious past.

CONCLUSION

Like counterfeit money, ideologies look real and cashable, but in fact often are not, their promises notwithstanding. They abhor history because history falsifies them, more often than not at the expense of both followers and unwitting victims sacrificed for the broader good. Ontology-laden ideologies, particularly of the religious sort, are the most dangerous ones, since they are sold as possessors of the unfalsifiable stamp of revelation or profess to convey a deeper than apparent, uncheckable knowledge of reality. Contrastingly, ideologies that claim to be (and demonstratively are) mindful of historical and other forms of contingency are healthier and more robust than their tightly sealed rivals.

Ontology, even on a minimal scale, is an unavoidable player in every nuanced attempt to make sense of human life and the world. Christianity, as a Trinitarian faith proclaiming the historical enfleshment of the Word, has its own resurrectional ontological commitments to offer and is unique among faiths in elevating love to the status of a prime ontology, by disclosing the very being of God as love (1 Jn 4:8). As a result, it cannot afford to shy away from ontology, either out of fear of ontology's unpopularity in our skeptical, postmodern milieu or because of a stubborn commitment to internal purity and integrity, as fideism shows. Christianity is intrinsically ontological throughout and only as such ought it to make a difference in the world, on condition, however, that its ontology be *porous* to history, as well as apophatic and falsifiable, that is, critical. This is an admittedly tall order. But Christianity is a tense faith, walking along the razor's edge from its inception as an uneasy intersection of eternity with history and of the being of God with the being of humankind in the Person of its founder.

NOTES

1. For example, Cody Franchetti authored a rather polemical paper "to discredit the idea that strict Nominalism alone be an apposite stance in conceiving history. Still, I believe," he further adds, "particulars to be the cornerstone for historical understanding; and yet, I am also convinced that historians who ignore universals and exclusively scrutinize particulars will find their work wanting of characteristics, which if overlooked, shall fatally compromise their historical apprehension. In other words, I wish to show that though particulars have a vital place in history . . . Nominalism is epistemologically deficient, especially in history, for universals are an inalienable aspect of human understanding, and thus are essential for a thorough conception of history and a comprehensive historical grasp: history's singularly extensive compass requires a broad vision that accepts both universals and particulars" ("Nominalism and History," *Open Journal of Philosophy* 3, no. 3 [2013], 401–412).

2. Paul Veyne, *Writing History: Essay on Epistemology*, trans. Mina Moore Rinvolucri (Manchester: Manchester University Press, 1984). Veyne pushes his nominalist thesis further in "Foucault Revolutionalizes History," in *Foucault and His Interlocutors*, ed. Arnold I. Davidson (Chicago: University of Chicago Press,

1997), 146–182. Murray Murphy advances a thesis similar to Veyne's in *Philosophical Foundations of Historical Knowledge* (Albany, NY: State University of New York Press, 1994), with an emphasis on scientific empiricism fashioned after Quine's own, as a way of countering the arbitrariness of historical subjectivism and generalizations. Veyne's radical nominalist historiography was strongly challenged by another historian of note, Marcel Gauchet in his important essay "Le nominalismehistorien. A propos de 'Foucault révolutionnel histoire' de Paul Veyne," *Social Science Information/Information sur les sciences sociales* 25, no. 2 (June 1, 1986), 401–419.

3. For more on Logical Positivism, see the now classic work by Victor Kraft, *The Vienna Circle: The Origin of Neo-Positivism, a Chapter in the History of Recent Philosophy* (New York: Greenwood Press, 1953).

4. Ludwig Wittgenstein and Willard Quine are among the premier champions of twentieth-century (postpositivist) linguistic nonrepresentationalism in English-speaking philosophy, bent on eliminating metaphysics and first-order, systematic philosophies structured in the traditional, pre-Kantian sense (an intention that I believe also applies to Wittgenstein's so-called later period, as outlined in his *Philosophical Investigations*; in this, I follow John Koethe, *The Continuity of Wittgenstein's Thought* (London: Cornell University Press, 1996), as well as the late professor Burton Dreben, whose seminar lectures on Wittgenstein and analytic philosophy I had had the good fortune to attend from 1994 to 1996 at Boston University.

Quine's thought, in particular, revolves around a cluster of highly popularized philosophical catchwords such as "indeterminacy of translation," "ontological relativity," "naturalized epistemology," "holism," and so on, all of which add up to his eliminative program to undercut the legitimacy of discourses involving extrahuman ontological categories. The resulting picture shows the concept of truth to be an "immanent" property, solely internal to linguistic contexts. For all the immense complexity of his life work, Quine was never too fearful of epigrammatic accounts of his program: "Truth is immanent and there is no higher. We must speak from within a theory." See Willard Van Orman Quine, *Theories and Things* (Cambridge, MA: Harvard University Press, 1981), 21–22. Now, should we also choose to be just as laconic in drawing a first sketch of his strategy and intentions, we could describe them in terms of a materialist and empiricist nominalism that not only relativizes reference to a high degree of indeterminacy (enough so as to decisively undermine the notion of independent, free-floating "meanings"), but even stretches the limits of language (as Wittgenstein did) to declare it coextensive with thought and the whole of reality. As opposed to the Vienna positivists, Quine disavowed the analytic/synthetic distinction in his famous essay "Two Dogmas of Empiricism," for the sake of embracing an all-encompassing Pragmatism, an enhanced and empiricized version of Carnap's reduction of reality to linguistic frameworks. See Willard Quine, "Two Dogmas of Empiricism," in *Problems in the Philosophy of Language*, ed. Thomas M. Olshensky (New York: Holt, Rinehart & Winston, 1969), 416–417. The question concerning the final defeat and demise of metaphysics, in the aftermath of the consecutive attacks launched against it by Immanuel Kant, Friedrich Nietzsche, Martin Heidegger, the Vienna Circle positivists, the aforementioned post-positivist nominalists like Wittgenstein, Quine, and

Richard Rorty, the French deconstructionists comprising the left-wing quarter of the "linguistic turn" in philosophy (most notably sporting Jacques Derrida), and other iconoclast theorists, is quite complicated and not half as straightforwardly answered as antimetaphysical champions believed or prophesied; for, if anything, in the years of recent past we have seen a resurgence and partial revival of metaphysics, if only initially as a descriptive account of reality, beginning with the work of P. F. Strawson, himself a scholar of Kantian proclivities, incidentally; see his *Skepticism and Naturalism: Some Varieties* (New York: Columbia University Press, 1985).

5. As J. Wentzel van Huyssteen explains, "Foundationalism holds that, in the process of justifying our knowledge-claims, the chain of justifying evidence cannot go on *ad infinitum* if we are ever to be in a position to claim that we have justified our knowledge. Thus, foundationalists specify what they take to be the ultimate foundations on which the evidential support-systems for various beliefs are constructed. The sort of features most frequently mentioned are self-evidence, incorrigibility, being evident to the senses, indubitability, and being self-authenticating and properly basic, that is, foundational.... To claim that knowledge rests on foundations is to claim that there is a privileged class of beliefs that are intrinsically credible and that are able, therefore, to serve as ultimate terminating points for chains of justification. These 'givens' could be anything from sense data to universals, essences, experience, and God's revelation. In this sense the 'doctrine of the given' can indeed be called the comrade-in-arms of all foundationalism." See J. Wentzel van Huyssteen, *Essays in Postfoundationalist Theology* (Grand Rapids, MI: William B. Eerdman's Publishing Co., 1997), 226. The Cartesian passage habitually cited as the inaugural statement of foundationalism is drawn from the four rules of Descartes' *Discourse on Method*: "The first rule was to accept nothing as true which I did not evidently know to be such, that is to say, scrupulously to avoid precipitance and prejudice, and in the judgments I passed to include nothing additional to what had presented itself to my mind so clearly and distinctly that I could have no occasion for doubting it. The second, to divide each of the difficulties I examined into as many parts as may be required for its adequate solution. The third, to arrange my thought in order, beginning with things the simplest and easiest to know, so that I may then ascend little by little, as it were step by step, to the knowledge of the more complex, and, in doing so, to assign an order of thought even to those objects which are not of themselves in any such order of precedence. And the last, in all cases to make enumerations so complete, and reviews so general, that I should be assured of omitting nothing" (*Descartes: Philosophical Writings*, ed. and trans. Norman Kemp Smith [New York: The Modem Library, 1958], 106–107). Now, at its most extreme form, the revolt on foundationalism feeds on the Nietzschean motto "There are no facts, only interpretations" (nowadays posited as: "There is no such thing as a transcendental signified"). In all its present and variant versions, antirepresentationalism relies on (and is in fact indistinguishable from) holism, a modern epistemological alternative to foundationalism with strongly contextualist overtones. Also known as "coherentism," holism may be designated as the epistemological attitude that in one way or another underdetermines the connection between theory and reality by denying a one-to-one correspondence between the two, granting only a wholesale correspondence at best. Holism should be basically

understood as a web, and may be best portrayed perhaps by Otto Neurath's famous metaphor of the "conceptual boat," whose point is to illustrate the sheer impossibility of establishing direct and unmediated links between our linguistic paradigms and extralinguistic reality. This is because we are visualized as being constantly adrift, a vessel amidst a boundless linguistic ocean and so forced to reconstruct the boat plank by plank while afloat, forever denied the chance to build it anew from the privileged point of an extralinguistic shore. Holism thus presupposes a special view of language as inescapable and overwhelming, as we shall see below. It is also best understood in its contrast to foundationalism, which as we have seen makes the determining factor of entities their own individual essences, as that which gives entities their identity. Being as they are realists and referentialists, foundationalists concentrate on the things themselves as indivisible entities, while holists focus on their relational situations. Theologian Nancey Murphy draws out a helpful comparison/contrast between the two epistemological models. Holist theories of knowledge, she says, "differ in several important respects from foundationalism. First, there are no indubitable (unrevisable) beliefs; nor are there any sharp distinctions among types of belief, only degrees of differences in how far a belief is from the experiential boundary. Second, for foundationalists, reasoning (construction) goes in only one direction—up from the foundation. For holists there is no preferred direction, and the kinds of connections among beliefs in the web are many. . . . In general, what 'holism' means is that each belief is supported by its ties to its neighboring beliefs, and ultimately, to the whole; the criterion of truth is coherence" (Nancey Murphy, introduction to *Theology without Foundations: Religious Practice and the Future of Theological Truth*, eds. Stanley Hauerwas, Nancey Murphy, and Mark Nation [Nashville, TN: Abingdon Press, 1994], 13). It is worth pointing out that holism by no means should be taken as antithetical to empiricism, since it allows for some degree of correspondence (Quine, one of the most influential contemporary holists, is an unmitigated empiricist, or better yet a postempiricist); but it is nonetheless true that holism weakens the link between theory and experience, depending on the degree of incommensurability that it places among paradigms (thus Rorty's holism is of the wholesale kind, and so miles apart from the empiricist and scientific contextualism of Quine). Holism, finally, as a constitutive aspect of contemporary nominalism, is central to Wittgenstein's later work on language (as it is to Quine's), and renders meaning relative to particular, historical, and contingent frameworks called "language-games"—that is, dialects shaped by the practices of different communities.

6. Michael Sudduth, *The Reformed Objection to Natural Theology* (London and New York: Routledge, 2009), 204.

7. Terrence W. Tilley, "In Favor of a 'Practical Theory of Religion': Montaigne and Pascal," in *Theology without Foundations: Religious Practice and the Future of Theological Truth*, eds. Stanley Hauerwas, Nancey Murphy, and Mark Nation (Nashville, TN: Abingdon Press, 1994), 49–74, 57.

8. Christian apologetics has seen a major revival since the end of the twentieth century (with various degrees of success) in the work of the so-called "evidentialists," those who maintain that religious belief must be justified (epistemically or ethically), if it is to be valid. Evidentialists include, among others, Richard Swinburne,

Laurence Bonjour, John Bishop, David Bentley Hart, and William lane Craig. See indicatively, William Lane Craig and J. P. Moreland, *Philosophical Foundations for a Christian Worldview* (Downers Grove, IL: InterVarsity Press). 2003; William Lane Craig, *Reasonable Faith: Christian Truth and Apologetics* (Wheaton, IL: Crossway, 1994); William Lane Craig, *On Guard: Defending Your Faith with Reason and Precision* (Colorado Springs, CO: David C. Cook, 2010); Richard Swinburne, *Is There a God?* (Oxford: Oxford University Press, 2010); Richard Swinburne, *The Coherence of Theism* (Oxford: Oxford University Press, 1993, 2nd edition); Richard Swinburne, *Faith and Reason* (Oxford: Oxford University Press, 1981, 2005); Laurence Bonjour, *The Structure of Empirical Knowledge* (Cambridge, MA: Harvard University Press, 1985); David Bentley Hart, *Atheist Delusions: The Christian Revolution and Its Fashionable Enemies* (Ann Arbor, MI: Sheridan Books, 2009). John Bishop raises the need for an ethical justification of faith; see his *Believing by Faith: An Essay in the Epistemology and Ethic of Religious Belief* (Oxford: Oxford University Press, 2007).

9. George Lindbeck, *The Nature of Doctrine: Religion and Theology in a Postliberal Age* (London: Westminster John Knox Press, 1984).

10. Lindbeck, 80.

11. Ibid., 121.

12. Lindbeck, *The Nature of Doctrine*, p. 114.

13. D. Z. Phillips, *Wittgenstein and Religion* (New York: St. Martin's Press, 1994), xviii. Contrary to some initial expectations, Phillips is highly critical of Lindbeck's internalism. admonishing it for "being still in the grip of the very confusion he hopes to eradicate." Cf. *Faith after Foundationalism* (London & New York: Routledge, 1988), 203. His critique of Lindbeck extends over four chapters (15–18) in this work. "What we have seen is that Lindbeck," says Phillips in a wrap-up comment, "while half-realizing that theological doctrines are not descriptions of an object given independently of them, cannot free himself from the tempting and prestigious grammar of that relation, a grammar drawn, in the main, from our talk of physical objects" (ibid., 205). By this Phillips simply means that Lindbeck drops two foundationalist theories only to embrace another, of his own making, instead of carrying out Wittgenstein's antitheoretical method of conceptual clarification to the end. "What is not realized," according to Phillips, "is that what we need is not another, better, theory to succeed foundationalism, but no theory at all. Instead of calling my remarks Faith After Foundationalism, they could equally well have been called Against Theory" (ibid. 195).

14. Phillips, *Faith after Foundationalism,* Part One, chapters 1–9, 3–127. While not being an evidentialist, Plantinga is nevertheless a foundationalist, insisting as he does that there exist "properly basic," as he calls them or warranted beliefs about God, that come naturally to us out of an inborn *sensus divinatis* and so are not in need of being externally proven. See Alvin Plantinga, *Warranted Christian Belief* (Oxford: Oxford University Press, 2000), and its prequels, *Warrant: The Current Debate* and *Warrant and Proper Function*, both published in 1993 also by Oxford University Press.

15. Phillips, *Wittgenstein and Religion*, p. xi.

16. Ibid., xvii.

17. Ibid., 35.

18. For an excellent detailed account of the origins, scope, and overall agenda of this important theological trend in Greek Orthodoxy, including earnest applause and criticisms to it, see the published proceedings of a conference held at Volos, Greece, in May 2005, titled "Turbulence in Post-War Theology: The Theology of the '60s,": Pantelis Kalaitzidis, Thanasis N. Papathanasiou, and Theofilos Abatzidis eds., Αναταράξεις στη μεταπολεμική θεολογία—Η "Θεολογία του '60" [*Turbulence in Post-War Theology: The Theology of the '60s*] (Athens: Indiktos Publications, 2009).

19. Christos Yannaras, Προτάσεις Κριτικής Οντολογίας (Athens: Ikaros Publications, 1985, 2010; in Greek).

20. Stavros Zoumboulakis, Το περιοδικό 'Σύνορο' και ο Χρήστος Γιανναράς. Η θεολογική πρόταση της αποηθικοποίησης του Χριστιανισμού ["The 'Synoro' Journal and Christos Yannaras: The Theological Proposal for a Demoralization of Christianity"], in Αναταράξεις στη μεταπολεμική θεολογία—Η "Θεολογία του '60" [*Turbulence in Post-War Theology: The Theology of the '60s*], eds. Pantelis Kalaitzidis, Thanasis N. Papathanasiou, and Theofilos Abatzidis (Athens: Indiktos Publications, 2009), 315–326.

21. In the history of Christian theology, the definition of Christianity as a practical, ethical, or moral ideal was first forcefully submitted by Albrecht Ritsch (1822–1889), who sought to revive the Kantian reconfiguration of the faith in terms of practical reason following the rigorous deconstruction of traditional metaphysics in *Critique of Pure Reason*.

22. Emmanuel Levinas, *Totality and Infinity: An Essay on Exteriority*, trans. Alphonso Lingis (London: Kluwer Academic publishers, 1991).

23. Kai Nielsen, *An Introduction to the Philosophy of Religion* (New York: St. Martin's Press, 1983); here cited from Walter H. Capps, *Religious Studies: The Making of a Discipline* (Minneapolis: Fortress Press, 1995), 257.

Chapter Two

Ontology, History, and Relation (*Schesis*)

Gregory of Nyssa's Epektasis

Giulio Maspero

Postmodernity seems to be presently at a crossroads, and two main possibilities lie ahead: either it develops into a *Hypermodernity* or it turns into an *Aftermodernity*. The outcome depends on the choice to go to extremes with the very premises of Modernity or to start a critical reconsideration of the premises themselves. History and being are the key elements in this choice because one of the main postulates of Modernity is the dialectic approach to their relationship.

With Modernity truth and being started to be seen as violent and to be understood as the source of a necessary dialectic. Postmodernity attempted to overcome this dialectical dimension through the negation of any difference. Paradoxically this brought about a bewildering flourishing of differences with the result that we now lack tools to manage the complexity.

The point is that differences are everywhere in reality and this is affirmed theologically. Difference is at the very root of reality because creation is founded on the vertical and fundamental difference between God and the world. This is horizontally reverberated in the differences between human beings at both a synchronic and a diachronic level—that is, in the social and the historical dimensions. But taking it one step further, modernity brought dialectics into God himself, so that every other difference is necessarily understood as dialectic too. This implies that both society and history break up into disconnected pieces. The more dialectics replace relationships, the more difficult it becomes to find something that can keep together both the inner and the outer world of the human person—that is, a common *logos*. The ecological, economic, and social crisis is just a result of this process, but when life is threatened, it is always good to go back to its sources. From the Christian perspective this means going back to Scripture and to those who received and thought through the gift of Scripture in the first steps of our journey.[1] The

Fathers of the Church are exactly what their name expresses: they transmitted Christian life and always "father" us—that is, they are a source that can help to deepen our understanding when we need it and lead our way when we get lost. In particular, Gregory of Nyssa's doctrine seems truly meaningful for the relationship of being and History,[2] so much so that he can be considered very postmodern, or better said, very *aftermodern*.[3]

RELATION

The key element that suggests this remark is Gregory's ontological conception of relation (*schesis*). His theology presents a radical reworking of this category which is applied *in divinis* (in God), in order to say that the personal multiplicity of the Father, of the Son, and of the Holy Spirit is within the affirmation of their absolute natural numerical identity. Classical metaphysics, in fact, had substance as the sole principle of distinction, but this could not be applied to the three divine Persons who are a single eternal substance. Thus, *schesis* was redefined, ceasing to be considered a mere accident, as was the case with Aristotle's *Categories*, so that a new ontological dimension arose that characterizes, in the case of the divine, the immanence of God's substance, that is, the inner dimension of God's nature.

The two different ontological frameworks, which characterize classical and Christian metaphysics, imply an extremely different conception of deification. In fact, in the case of Greek pagan thought there is just one graduated ontological order which joins God and the world, so that deification could consist in climbing the metaphysical ladder through the *logos*. This is conceived as an ontological mediator that leads from one level to the next, that is, as *necessary reason* that from cause to cause allows the wise to go back to the ultimate cause, which in the Platonic conception is identified with the sphere of ideas while in Aristotelian thought it is found in the unmoved mover—thought thinking itself. In both cases this process rising up from the world toward God requires an increasing abandonment of the material dimension, in the first case, or the potential dimension, in the second, to reach by intellect alone that which really is.[4]

This is reflected in a new vision of the created world in its relationship with the Creator. For example, the way of predicating in God and in the human person the virtues and spiritual faculties changes: in fact, the presence of a single ontological order leads to the necessity of highlighting the differences between the First Principle and the human person, and the distinction can be based only on ontological *deficit* and on the diversity introduced by the participatory structure. Whereas, in the Christian case the focus is on what ontologically unites the creature to the Creator—that is, relation, a principle of distinction that is unknown to classical metaphysics.

Philosophical deification essentially consists in moving up the ladder of being, travelling along the different ontological steps of thought that stand between the human person and God, like a Greek *meson*, a mediator of intermediate metaphysical density. In contrast, in the Christian context there is nothing between God and the world, and deification, which *in itself* is impossible because there is no access to the divine *from below*, becomes possible only by the gift of grace *from above*. God is so transcendent that He is able to lower Himself; not needing to statically defend His position, He makes Himself man, dynamically combining eternity and time in a relationship whose ontological strength is infinite since it is founded in the personal depth of God Himself.

The fundamental element from this ontological point of view is that between God and the world there is a true infinite gap.[5] The distinction between them is not based on the existence of different substances which occupy an intermediate position within the same ontology. But rather there are two different ontologies connected only by relations. Gregory, following in the footsteps of Athanasius and Basil, developed this doctrine to answer Eunomius, who spoke of the three Persons of the Holy Trinity as three different substances.[6] He did not use the names of the Persons but made an appeal to philosophical terminology. The Bishop of Nyssa explained:

> But I think the reason for this new invention of names is obvious to everybody: all men when they hear the titles 'father' and 'son' immediately recognize from the very names their intimate and natural relation to each other (φυσικὴν πρὸς ἄλληλα σχέσιν). Community of nature (τὸ γὰρ τῆς φύσεως συγγενὲς) is inevitably suggested by these titles.[7]

In this text the community of nature and the reciprocal relation are linked both in the divine dimension and in the created order. The very names of the divine Persons speak of such a relation that implies identity of nature between those who are linked by it.

Gregory here traces a parallelism between the two ontological levels. He is perfectly aware of the differences between them: in God *schesis* perfectly communicates the infinite and eternal divine nature, so that each Person is numerically the same substance, whereas at the human level it only communicates a participation into the human nature.

This can also be seen, for example, in his *Commentary on the Song of the Songs*. Elias Moutsoulas has highlighted that commenting on *Song of Songs* Gregory, unlike Origen, is mainly concerned about the ontological relationship between God and the human person.[8] The Cappadocian stresses at the same time the absolute difference between the divine nature and the world, on one hand, and the freedom of the loving relationship with the human beings, on the other:

> You are truly beautiful—not only beautiful, but the very essence (οὐσία) of the Beautiful, existing forever as such, being at every moment what you are, neither blooming when the appropriate time comes, nor putting off your bloom at the right time, but stretching (συμπαρατείνων) your springtime splendor out to match the everlastingness of your life—you whose name is love of humankind (φιλανθρωπία).[9]

In this text the language of poetry and ontology meet: the very name of God is Love, that is a relation that does not fade away but is stronger than the passing of time. History and eternity are knotted together by the verb συμπαρατείνω, that derives from τείνω just as ἐπέκτασις is its derivative. The latter comes from Phil 3:13, where Paul says: "Brothers, I do not reckon myself as having taken hold of it; I can only say that forgetting all that lies behind me, and straining forward to what lies in front (ἔμπροσθεν ἐπεκτεινόμενος), I am racing towards the finishing-point to win the prize of God's heavenly call in Christ Jesus."[10] Jean Daniélou defined *epektasis* as follows:

> For the Platonist . . . change can only be deterioration; for the spiritual and the divine are identical, and the divine is unchangeable. But once we establish the transcendence of the divine with respect to the created spirit, another sort of change becomes possible, the movement of perpetual ascent. This movement tends towards the Immovable, and under this aspect it is at the opposite pole to the meaningless motion of the material world: it is process of unification and concentration. But the ultimate unity and stability are never achieved; the soul is conceived as a spiritual universe in eternal expansion towards the infinite Darkness.[11]

The different meanings of the two forms derived from τείνω—συμπαρατείνω and ἐπέκτασις—are determined by the couple of prepositions which precede it: in the first one, *syn* ("with") and *para* ("by" or "alongside of") express the coextensive dimension that characterizes God's eternal ontology, in the latter, *epi* and *ek* express in the same time the simultaneous union (*epi*, Greek for "at" or "toward") and excess (*ek*, Greek for "out of") which mark the relationship between the creature and the Creator.[12] *Epektasis* and apophaticism—that is, the impossibility of expressing through human language the eternity and infinity of the divine being—in Gregory's theological architecture are the hallmarks of the new ontological framework characterized by the gap between the higher uncreated nature and the lower created nature.

In fact, only the Incarnation of the eternal Logos could have made known the higher ontology—that is, divine immanence—because only a free action of the Divinity could fill the infinite gap between the two natures. In this way, Christ is the *Logos* who becomes truly human without ceasing to be divine, in such a way that He is not *in between* the two ontologies, as the Arians thought, but that He perfectly belongs to both natures.

This means that only through Christ and His flesh can we come to know something about the Trinity whose splendor is excessive for our minds.[13] In Gregory's thought the apophatic dimension has a deep Christological dimension not always sufficiently stressed. For example, commenting on *Song of Songs* 1:16, the Cappadocian interprets the shadow by the bed of the Bride and the Bridegroom as a reference to the economy of Incarnation, because only through the "shadow" of the human nature of Christ the pure rays of divine glory could reach the creatures without destroying them.[14] This line of interpretation is typical in Gregory's theological grammar. For example, he reads the theophany of the Burning Bush as a prophecy of the Incarnation of the *Logos* in the Virgin's Womb.[15] The ontological gap implies that revelation always takes place through a veil.

This means that it is not possible to get to know God through a necessary connection of the divine substance and the created ones, but the infinite gap can only be filled by (free) relation. No name can express God's essence, but His relation (σχέσις) with the soul is a true name that makes known God as Love.[16] This is the experience of the Bride in the Song, who discovers within herself a path to get in touch with the Higher nature that ontologically *is* Love (ἀγάπη).[17] From this perspective, it is possible to see the theological meaning of the following definition:

> Love (φίλτρον) is the interior relation (ἡ ἐνδιάθετος σχέσις) to what is desired in the heart and is caused by pleasure or passion.[18]

So it is exactly the ontological reshaping of relation that makes possible to conceive *epektasis* as a dynamical relationship of history and being:

> [The soul] conformed to the properties of the divine nature, imitates the superior life (τὴν ὑπερέχουσαν ζωὴν), in such a way that nothing remains but the disposition of love (τῆς ἀγαπητικῆς διαθέσεως), which naturally tends toward the Good. In fact, love is this: the interior relation (ἐνδιάθετος σχέσις) toward that which is desired in the heart (τὸ καταθύμιον).[19]

For the soul to be similar to the divine nature, that is Love, it must have a *pure disposition* to love, that is, a pure immanent relation.

EPEKTASIS

This ontological understanding of relation seems to found the possibility of *epektasis*. One of Gregory's best descriptions of this infinite progress of the soul is his ontological interpretation of Moses's ascent:

> [Moses] shone with glory. Although exalted (ἐπαρθεὶς) by such magnificence, he still burns with desire: he is insatiable to still have more and still has thirst for that which constantly filled him to his pleasure; and, as if he had not yet enjoyed it, he asks for more: he beseeches God that He appear to him as He is in Himself and not merely in the measure in which he, Moses, can participate in Him.[20]

His desire grows in the measure that his relationship with God becomes stronger. It is fundamental that his participation is presented from the perspective of God's true being, and not from that of human potency. It seems that the new ontological dimension of relation changes the creature itself:

> It seems to me that Moses takes on these sentiments to create a disposition (διαθέσει) of soul that is enamoured of what is beautiful by nature.[21]

The terminology used by Gregory is that of disposition and of the relatives, which are those realities adverbially described as turned toward something else. Aristotle uses πρός τί πως ἔχειν as definition of relation.[22] Gregory defines human perfection in relational terms:

> Perhaps the perfection of human nature consists precisely in the disposition (τὸ οὕτως ἔχειν) to always want to have more and more good.[23]

So precisely the fact that deification is participation in God Himself through the personal relation with His infinite self implies that the desire of the finite creature is always full and always needs to be filled, because the very response of God makes the human person more capable of receiving Him:

> For this reason, the ardent lover of beauty (ὁ σφοδρὸς ἐραστὴς τοῦ κάλλους) welcomes within himself what sometimes appears to him to be only an image of what he desires, and he longs to be filled by the very figure of the archetype. This is the purpose of his audacious request, which goes beyond the limits of desire, that is, beyond the veils of beauty, no longer though mirrors and reflections, but face to face. The voice of God gives what is asked through the very refusal of it, showing in a few words an immeasurable abyss of thought. The generosity of God, in fact, agrees to satiate the desire of Moses, but does not promise to him rest or satiety.[24]

From this perspective, apophaticism is not a *no*, but on the contrary, is precisely the gift of the divine *yes* in the relation of mutual indwelling between finite creature and infinite Creator. Thus, to see God consists in never stopping to want to see Him, turning the gaze[25] always to Him (πρὸς αὐτόν) so that, paradoxically, Moses is filled with what he desires precisely because his desire is never fully satisfied (δι' ὧν ἀπλήρωτος ἡ ἐπιθυμία μένει).[26] According to Gregory, every ending is but a beginning, a new starting point of the ascent, in an ever-growing union, always perfect and always deeper; this is *epektasis*. Commenting on *Song* 2:6 Gregory has recourse to the image of the arrow that is shot toward the divine nature by the Archer—that is, Christ—but at the same time travels toward the infinite and has already achieved its goal resting in His hands.[27]

The desire becomes a constant disposition in the personal relation with God who dynamically unites the human person and God in an eternal movement. Apophaticism is thus the translation of divine transcendence and of its overflow which draws in participation. For this reason, just like desire, movement also changes meaning in the ontological grammar of Gregory of Nyssa:

> Therefore the reasoning shows that that which seems to be feared—I mean to say that our nature is mutable—is instead a wing for the flight towards the greatest things, since it would be a punishment for us to not be able to undertake a change for that which is better. Therefore let not he who sees in his nature the disposition to change become afflicted, but moving in every thing towards that which is better and transforming himself *from glory to glory*,[28] let him change thus, becoming every day constantly better, in daily growth, and perfecting himself always more, without ever being able to reach the limit of perfection. For in this consists true perfection: to never stop growing towards the best and to place no limits to perfection.[29]

Perfection is no longer static in the achievement of a goal,[30] because when the goal is a relationship with the One who is infinite and eternal then it is already reached within the dynamic of an always growing union. The human person is, thus, recognized as a pilgrim not simply provisionally but definitively, insofar as his eternal perfection and glory remain an eternal movement not only *toward* God, but *in* God. In this way the pilgrimage *in via* itself is recognized as a grace and a beginning of glory. Jean Daniélou has expressed this in a very effective form:

> This is essentially what Gregory is describing. Men always have the tendency to stabilize, to fix, the various stages of perfection which they have attained, and to see in the time-process a threat to their very transitory moments of happiness. They want to recover their past ecstasies, to go, like Marcel Proust, in

search of Time Past. For Gregory, on the contrary, the future is always better than the past. But to overcome this natural tendency of the soul, Gregory offers the support of faith, which is an adherence to a promise. Here we have the transition from poetry to prophecy, from the anthropology of the Platonists to that of the Bible. Paradise—and creation—is yet to come. We must no longer try to recall it, but to hope for its accomplishment. And thus forgetfulness, a sin to the Platonist, here becomes a virtue. We must leave the known to go towards the unknown, to go out, as Rainer Maria Rilke would say, into the Open.[31]

Both Andreas Spira[32] and Jean Daniélou[33] wrote on Gregory's conception of time stressing its ontological revolutionary meaning because the perfection becomes dynamic, while for Greek thought it had to be finite by necessity.[34]

UNION

If perfection is now recognized in dynamics, that means that a true revolution has changed ontology. It is a move away from the metaphysical thought that conceived of motion as potentiality, and Divinity, which has no potentiality because of its perfection, as static along with being. Again, with Jean Daniélou, we can see how deep the transformation was: "Now to overcome this difficulty Gregory had to destroy the equation: good = immutability, and evil = change. And consequently he had to show the possibility of a type of change which would not merely be a return to immobility—that is, to be a mere negation of change. Here then is the revolution in thought which Gregory accomplished."[35]

The eternal beatitude of the human person is thus conceived in a dynamic sense, creating a sort of continuity between grace, the ascension of the soul, mystical experience, and Heaven. Paul is an example of this, for he was initiated into Paradise and raptured to the third Heaven, as he reports it in 2 Cor 12: 1–4. For him, according to Gregory, the good reached did not become a term of desire (ὅρον τῆς ἐπιθυμίας),[36] but the beginning of a new upward surge:

> In this way he [Paul] taught us, I believe, that, regarding the blessed nature of the Good, a great part is constituted by what we sometimes find ourselves; but infinitely greater than what is grasped each time is that which remains still beyond that, and this experience is continually repeated for those who participate of the Good, insofar as one enjoys continual growth, which is actuated in the entire eternity of the ages through always greater realities.[37]

The reference to eternity has a clear ontological meaning, because in Gregory's thought the eschatological dimension corresponds to the definite condition of the human person according to God's will. Thus, the perfection of the human person is defined starting from the condition of the angels (τῇ ἀγγελικῇ καταστάσει).[38] The human person who remains faithful to God will reach the status of the angels whose wills are definitively turned to the Trinity in the perpetual progress of the *epektasis*. That is the perfection of the celestial creatures, whose impassibility (τῆς ἀγγελικῆς ἀπαθείας)[39] is once again a reinterpretation of the category of classical *apatheia*.[40] This no longer means the negation of the possibility of being moved, or therefore being emotionally moved, but rather the impossibility of being diverted from the definitive movement toward God through which the will and desire are definitively determined.

Moreover, this is carried out through mutual indwelling, as is seen in the sixth homily of *In Canticum*, where he comments on the meeting of the soul precisely with the Angels. In the text, *Song* 3:1–8, the route taken is traced from the soul to the encounter with the Groom and to the union which takes place thanks to this encounter, in the mutual indwelling, for which God is found in the soul and the soul is poured out in God (ὅ τε γὰρ θεὸς ἐν τῇ ψυχῇ γίνεται καὶ πάλιν εἰς τὸν θεὸν ἡ ψυχὴ μετοικίζεται).[41] It is this dynamic union, which is realized from power to power (ἐκ δυνάμεως εἰς δύναμιν, see Ps 83:8), leading into union with the One who is desired (ἐν αὐτῷ γενέσθαι τῷ ποθουμένῳ) embracing Him in oneself (ἐν ἑαυτῷ τὸν ποθούμενον δέξασθαι).[42]

Such a union takes place, however, in the darkness of the night, like the spousal union in the nuptial bed, because God is beyond all possibility of understanding. Therefore, the text of the *Song* shows a bride who does not manage to reach the Groom but after the encounter continually seeks Him. Thus, the union is apophatic precisely because it is relational.[43] In fact, paradoxically, specifically in encountering the ontological excess of God, which renders impossible intellectual comprehension of Him, the possibility of real union with Him comes about in the personal dimension of faith. Gregory shows, commenting on *Song of Songs*, that God is not in the mind of man, but abides in his heart. For this reason, he tells the bride:

> "*No sooner had I passed them by*, having departed from the whole created order and passed by everything in the creation that is intelligible and left behind every conceptual approach, than I found the Beloved by faith, and holding on by faith's grasp to the one I have found, I will not let go until he is within my *chamber*." Now the *chamber* is surely the heart, which at that moment became receptive of his divine indwelling—at the moment, that is, when it returned to that condition in which it was at the beginning when it was formed by the *mother* who gave it birth. We shall not go wrong to conceive the *mother* as the First Cause of our constitution.[44]

It is interesting to note how Gregory unites the exegetical perspective to the ontological perspective, reading the mother in whose house the bride accepts the Groom (see *Song* 3:4) as the first cause of all things, that is, God Himself, whose nature is absolutely transcendent.

Ontological language, Christological apophaticism, and *epektasis* are thus characteristic of deification according to Gregory of Nyssa who manages to hold simultaneously God's absolute transcendence and the reality of man's union with Him. This is also evident at the terminological level, because Gregory seems practically to be the only person to use, in order to indicate the final destiny of man, the expression "communion of the Divinity" (κοινωνία τῆς θεότητος), which Basil had used in an intratrinitarian sense to affirm the consubstantiality of the divine Persons.[45] Thus, in his *Homilies on the Beatitudes*, Gregory indicates the equivalence of such a communion with the divinity and the more common θεοποιεῖν:[46]

> Participation in the beatitudes is none other than communion with the divinity (θεότητος κοινωνία), to which the Lord raises us through what was said. It seems to me, therefore, that He, by the fact of having brought to its consequences the sign of beatitude, renders in a certain way god (θεοποιεῖν) whomever listens to and understands his discourse.[47]

Gregory, like his brother Basil of Caesarea, makes recourse to the expression κοινωνία τῆς θεότητος in a properly Trinitarian context, saying that both Eunomius and Sabellius made the doctrine Jewish precisely because they denied such a communion.[48] Nevertheless, in the final period of his discussion with the Neo-Arians, the bishop of Nyssa refines the language, introducing the distinction between communion and unity of nature:

> We, in fact, are introduced by the words of Scripture inspired by God to the mystery for which in the Father and in the Son we see not a communion (κοινωνίαν), but a unity of nature (ἑνότητα).[49]

The point is that κοινωνία τῆς θεότητος is declined in an economic and thus not immanent sense, in order to avoid a possible confusion between God and creature. At the same time this is evidence of how the power of deification is based, for Gregory, precisely on the economy itself, insofar as it is the reality of baptism and of the sacramental life that can elevate one to an authentic participation in the divinity.[50]

In this sense, Gregory's bold language is not based only on the powerful Trinitarian conception, but also, and at the same time, on the joining of this with the Christological dimension,[51] as is the case with the relation between economy and immanence, the interpretive key of Cappadocian theology. For this reason, the ideal axis that unites the divine infinity, apophaticism, and *epektasis* continues with the Sacraments and Christ Himself:

> He who has learned that Christ is the Head of the Church, consider first of all that every head is of the same nature (ὁμοφυής) and substance (ὁμοούσιος) with the body which is subject to it, and that there is a unique connaturality (συμφυΐα) of each part in relationship to the whole (πρὸς τὸ ὅλον), which thanks to a unique co-spiration (διὰ μιᾶς συμπνοίας) actuates the conformity of sensation (συμπάθειαν) of the parts together with the whole. Therefore, if something is external to the body, it is also totally external to the head. With this the reasoning teaches us that also each member must become that which the head is by nature, to be intimately united with the head (πρὸς τὴν κεφαλὴν οἰκείως ἔχῃ). And we are the members that complete the body of Christ.[52]

From this perspective the union of the human being with God is absolutely real and ontological. The new dynamical conception of eternity presents a continuity between history and heaven, so much so that it seems possible to speak of a true union of being and history. Gregory's line of reasoning can be sketched as follows:

1. In the Trinity relation is not an accident but perfectly communicates being.
2. Point one is reflected also in the created world where some relations communicate being, as in paternity and the transmission of human nature to offspring.
3. *Epektasis* is the maximum form of this communication because it brings true communion with the divinity.
4. In light of the aforementioned points, personal history and being are relationally and ontologically connected.

CONCLUSION

For this reason it remains absolutely impossible to *understand* God ("*avoir Dieu*") but the human person can truly *be* God ("*être Dieu*"), according to a magnificent expression given by von Balthasar, in the eternal movement of the *epektasis*.[53] Moreover, this possibility is ontologically based precisely on the radical distinction between God and the world, which, from the Trinitarian perspective, opens the possibility of an authentic relation between the Creator and the human person.

This makes it possible to conceive of both being and history as non-contradictory: *epektatis* is a clear manifestation of the new ontological conception developed by Gregory, because it connects being and history, as well as time and eternity, in a relational way. Movement is no more an effect only of potentiality but can be a manifestation of perfection, as perfection itself for the human person is an eternal movement toward and into the triune God.

If one assumes the perspective of relation, the apparent negativity of apophaticism reveals itself as an extraordinarily positive and disruptive statement in the *epektasis* because this communicates being and makes the partaking into the divine nature possible (see 2 Peter 1:4). The ontological approach has the advantage of emphasizing the radical novelty of Gregory of Nyssa's conception of history and of the relationship between time and being. This seems to be a true ontology of history that is no more the mere translation of a philosophy of history but is the result of the development by Gregory of an outright Trinitarian ontology.

NOTES

1. Joseph Ratzinger wrote that only through the first answer, in German *Antwort*, we can understand the Word, in German *Wort*: see Joseph Ratzinger, "Die Bedeutung der Väter für die gegenwärtige Theologie," *Theologische Quartalschrift* 148 (1968): 257–282, especially 275–276.

2. Jean Daniélou wrote: "Gregory was obsessed by the mystery of time, more than by any other problem. From his position at the meeting-point of Greek and Christian thought, he was conditioned to feel all the tragedy of time and its inexorable law; he knew the impatience that comes of waiting and the anxieties that attend the recurrence of things. But his response to this situation was not the platonic flight from time; it was the Christian affirmation of a true sense of time, giving it positive value as the stage and scene of a divine action." Jean Daniélou, *The Lord of History: Reflections on the Inner Meaning of History* (London-Chicago: H. Regnery, 1958), 153.

3. Cf. Morwenna Ludlow, *Gregory of Nyssa, Ancient and (Post)modern* (Oxford-New York: Oxford University Press, 2007).

4. See Giulio Maspero, "Patristic Trinitarian Ontology," in *Rethinking Trinitarian Theology: Disputed Questions and Contemporary Issues in Trinitarian Theology*, eds. Robert J. Wozniak and Giulio Maspero (London-New York: T&T Clark, 2012), 211–229.

5. A very interesting and balanced study on this subject is Xavier Batllo, *Ontologie scalaire et polémique trinitaire* (Münster: Aschendorff, 2013).

6. Gregory of Nyssa, *Contra Eunomium* I, 151,1–154,13: GNO I, 71,28–73,15 (GNO = *Gregorii Nysseni Opera*, Brill: Leuven).

7. Ibid., 159,1–160,1: GNO I, 75,1–5 (All translations are the author's except where otherwise noted).

8. Cf. Elias Moutsoulas, Γρηγόριος Νύσσης, Βίος, Συγγράμματα, Διδασκαλία (Athens: Eptalophos A.B.E.E., 1997), 97.

9. Gregory of Nyssa, *In Canticum canticorum*, GNO VI, 106,20–107,5: trans. Richard A. Norris, *Gregory of Nyssa: Homilies on the Song of Songs* (Atlanta: Society of Biblical Literature, 2012), 119.

10. Phil 3:13–14.

11. Jean Daniélou, *From Glory to Glory: Texts from Gregory of Nyssa's Mystical Writings* (Crestwood, NY: St Vladimir's Seminary Press, 1961), 56–57.

12. Cf. ibid., 59.

13. Cf. Giulio Maspero, "L'ontologia trinitaria nei Padri Cappadoci: prospettiva cristologica," in *Trinità in relazione: Percorsi di ontologia trinitaria dai Padri della Chiesa all'Idealismo tedesco*, ed. C. Moreschini (Panzano in Chianti [Fi]: Edizioni Feeria, 2015), 69–91.

14. Cf. Gregory of Nyssa, *In Canticum canticorum*, GNO VI, 107,9–108,4.

15. Cf. Gregory of Nyssa, *Oratio in diem natalem Christi*, GNO X/2, 246–247.

16. Cf. Gregory of Nyssa, *In Canticum canticorum*, GNO VI, 61, 13–17.

17. Gregory of Nyssa, *Dialogus de anima et resurrectione*, PG 46, 96C.

18. Gregory of Nyssa, *In Ecclesiasten*, GNO V, 417, 13–14.

19. Gregory of Nyssa, *Dialogus de anima et resurrectione*, PG 46, 93BC.

20. Gregory of Nyssa, *De vita Mosis* II, 230.1–6: GNO VII/1, 113–114.

21. Ibid., II, 231,1–2: GNO VII/1, 114.

22. Aristotle, *Categoriae*, 8a 31–32.

23. Gregory of Nyssa, *De vita Mosis* I, 10.4–6: GNO VII/1, 5.

24. Ibid., II, 231,5–232,8: GNO VII/1, 114,9–19.

25. Cf. ibid., II, 233,3–5: GNO VII/1, 114,21–23.

26. Ibid., II, 235,6: GNO VII/1, 115,13–14.

27. Cf. Gregory of Nyssa, *In Canticum canticorum*, GNO VI, 129,10–16.

28. 2 Cor 3.18. See Daniélou, *From Glory to Glory*, 69.

29. Gregory of Nyssa, *De Perfectione*, GNO VIII/1, 213,20–214,6.

30. See Jean Daniélou, "La Colombe et la ténèbre dans la mystique byzantine ancienne," *Eranos Jahrbuch* 23 (1954): 400–405.

31. Daniélou, *From Glory to Glory*, 61.

32. See Andreas Spira, "Le temps d'un homme selon Aristote et Grégoire de Nyssa," *Colloques internationaux du CNRS* (Paris 1984): 289.

33. Jean Daniélou, *L'être et le temps chez Grégoire de Nisse* (Leiden: Brill, 1970).

34. See Ekkehard Mühlenberg, *Die Unendlichkeit Gottes bei Gregor von Nyssa. Gregors Kritik am Gottesbegriff der klassischen Metaphysik* (Göttingen: Vandenhoeck und Ruprecht, 1966), 29–58, and Romano Guardini, *Das Ende der Neuzeit* (Basel: Hess Verlag, 1950), 13–15.

35. Daniélou, *From Glory to Glory*, 47–48.

36. Gregory of Nyssa, *In Canticum canticorum*, GNO VI, 245,22.

37. Ibid., GNO VI, 245,22–246,5.

38. See ibid., GNO VI, 134,10–11.

39. See ibid., GNO VI, 135,6. See also GNO VI, 254,1–4 where that dynamic impassibility, as a gift of the Logos which attracts from glory to glory, becomes a reason of kinship and brotherhood among humans and angels.

40. See Lucas Francisco Mateo-Seco, "Apátheia," in *The Brill Dictionary of Gregory of Nyssa,* eds. Lucas Francisco Mateo-Seco and Giulio Maspero (Leiden-Boston (MA): Brill, 2009), 51–54.

41. Gregory of Nyssa, *In Canticum canticorum*, GNO VI, 179,6–7.

42. Cf. ibid., GNO VI, 179,11–15.

43. Cf. Martin Laird, "Apophasis and Logophasis in Gregory of Nyssa's Commentarius in Canticum Canticorum," *Studia Patristica* 37 (2001): 126–132.

44. Gregory of Nyssa, *In Canticum canticorum*, GNO VI, 183,5–15: trans. Norris, 196–197.

45. Cf. Basil of Caesarea, *De Spiritu Sancto* 45: *Sources Chrétiennes* 17bis (Paris: Cerf, 1968), 406.

46. This is true in general, but Gregory tends to use *theopoiein* rarely: see Norman Russell, *The Doctrine of Deification in the Greek Patristic Tradition* (Oxford: Oxford University Press, 2004), 226.

47. Gregory of Nyssa, *Orationes viii de beatitudinibus* V, GNO VII/2, 124,13–18.

48. See Gregory of Nyssa, *Contra Eunomium*, III, 8, 23,3: GNO II, 247.

49. Gregory of Nyssa, *Refutatio confessionis Eunomii,* 40,10–13: GNO II, 328,16–19.

50. See Gregory of Nyssa, *In Canticum canticorum* GNO VI, 249,15. See also *Oratio catechetica magna* 37,119.

51. See Lucas Francisco Mateo-Seco, *Estudios sobre la cristología de San Gregorio de Nisa* (Pamplona: Eunsa, 1978), 257–258.

52. Gregory of Nyssa, *De perfectione*, GNO VIII/1, 197,19–198,4.

53. See Hans Urs von Balthasar, *Présence et pensée: essai sur la philosophie religieuse de Grégoire de Nysse* (Paris: Beauchesne, 1988), 81.

Chapter Three

Syn-odical Ontology

Maximus the Confessor's Proposition for Ontology within History and in the Eschaton

Dionysios Skliris

Ontology might be considered as the noblest philosophical endeavor. What could possibly be nobler for a great spirit, what could be more tempting for an ambitious thinker, what could be more particularly human, than thinking about being *qua* being? Can this noble endeavor tolerate the dust of time that is history, the frustrations of meaning, the absurdity, the inertia? In what follows we will examine Maximus the Confessor's (c. 580–662) concrete philosophical propositions that concern the relation between ontology and history, in which ontology is considered as having a historical character in an eschatological perspective.[1] We will condense the Maximian propositions to ten points, trying to develop them by showing their internal logical coherence.

1. INTRODUCTION: SOME CRUCIAL MOMENTS OF THE ONTOLOGICAL ENDEAVOR FROM ARISTOTLE TO HEIDEGGER AND A POSITIONING OF MAXIMUS IN THIS PHILOSOPHICAL QUEST

An initial issue that confronts us concerns the particularity of Maximus's position in the ontological quest. That is, before looking at Maximus's ontology of history, we should take a brief glance at some crucial moments in the history of ontology. To begin, it is necessary to turn to Aristotle who endeavored to study being *qua* being and thereby birthed the noblest discipline of philosophy—that is, "after the Physics" (μετὰ τὰ Φυσικά), or metaphysics. One could say that from Aristotle onward ontology is meta-physical in character. That is, we examine being *qua* being, in its purity, in order to then be able to explain the multitude of concrete beings. The movement of thought in metaphysical ontology is something like the following:

1. We ascertain the existence of empirical beings.
2. Then, taking them as our points of departure, we are elevated to being *qua* being.
3. It is only after having "solved" or at least "contemplated" this noblest problem of being *qua* being that we come back to the multitude of physical beings in order to examine how they are posed inside the amplest question of being *qua* being and how they are thus explained.

Nevertheless, Neoplatonism asked whether the "Being" which explains beings has in fact to be *above* being if it is to really explain them.[2] In other words, the question is whether a being that explains beings can share their character of being-ness or whether it has to transcend being if it is meant to account for them. This problem was connected to the Neoplatonic demand—which could also be seen as a Hellenic demand in general—to exalt simplicity as the character *par excellence* of divinity. The result is a theology in which God is absolutely simple, the One, even if this is to mean that He is above personhood, above consciousness, or even above ontology. In other words, if a "divine" One is to really explain the Many, then as One it has to be above the Being that will explain beings. Being and ontology are considered as including a fundamentally dual or schizoid character, since contemplating the One involves breaking it into subject and object.[3] In this view, for example in Plotinus, a radical metaphysical explanation of the existent will have to be elevated beyond being in a supreme simplicity which will explain being and ontology by "being situated" above them. This simplest One might be considered as Good in an eminent way, but not as Being, since the latter emanates from the One and is explained by it. Christian thought has rather brought "down to earth" this elevated Neoplatonic way of thinking—not only through the Theology of the Incarnation, where God becomes history, but also through a Trinitarian Theology, in which the Incarnation is intrinsically linked, at least in the economical revelation, to the Trinity. The Christian Trinitarian God is simple in His essence, but He is also a Trinity of Persons who hypostatize their essence in being personally willing and operating (ὑφιστῶντες, θέλοντες, ἐνεργοῦντες). There is a certain Christian revalorization of ontology after its positioning in the "second" realm, that of the Intellect, by Neoplatonists. What is more, this revalorized ontology enters history and *becomes* history, something which may arguably be seen as a distinctive contribution of Christianity. The connection of ontology and history, which constitutes the subject of our volume, is, in many ways, a particularly Christian achievement. It is a consequence of Incarnation—that is, the faith on the one hand that God as Trinity has ontology, and, on the other hand, that One of the Trinity enters history and offers ontology also to the latter. Or, what is more, that One of the Trinity *becomes* history and thus offers history, from the inside, the possibility to *be* in the ontological sense of being—the possibility to *become ontology.*

The Christian connection between ontology and history has had a different evolution in the East and in the West. In modernity, it was posed in a new way by Immanuel Kant, who reformulated the demands of René Descartes's rationalistic subjectivism. In addition, British empiricism took this connection in the direction of an interpretation of ontology as phenomenology: the object perceived is but a phenomenon once removed from that which is the Thing in Itself. The posterior German idealism with Fichte, Schelling, and Hegel put aside the unknowable Thing in Itself and restricted it to the phenomenon alone. Thus, ontology became associated with a certain type of phenomenology.

Hegel stepped beyond Fichte and Schelling by placing the phenomenon within history, as the Spirit which is developed inside the life of the subject will be considered as the same with the one which is developed inside history. In some sense, the Hegelian view constitutes an extreme consequence of the Christian association between ontology and history.[4] Yet, due to its extreme radicalization, the Hegelian view could also be considered as post-Christian. In Hegel it is the whole Trinity that enters history and not just the Son. In other words, nothing is left in ontology which is not *already* history. The Christian Trinitarian God enters history, and by doing so He transfers His Trinitarian ontological structure to it—that is, history itself becomes a Trinity of position, negation, and negation of negation or *Aufhebung*, echoing the three hypostases of the Father, the Son (as incarnation and sacrifice), and the Spirit (as communion and unity).

In Hegel, the two categories of history and ontology find their most radical identification since Trinitarian ontology becomes Trinitarian history, that is, dialectical history. Marx follows this (post-)Christian identification of ontology with history, but he reverses it. For him it is matter that proceeds through history from an (abstract) position to negation and through it to a negation of negation. The Christian theme of sacrifice (sacrifice of the Son) is turned into revolution, and the theme of unity and communion (the work of the Holy Spirit) is transformed into the goal of a future classless society.[5] The conflict between idealism and materialism—the Hegelian idealistic subject and Marxist materialism—and the two types of totalitarianism that grew out of each system of thought, instigated a new movement in philosophy, a movement aiming to undermine this dualism. The ontological question needed to be reformulated so that it would not be necessary to absolutize either spirit or matter and thereby lead to a sort of idealistic or materialistic domination.

We principally owe to Martin Heidegger such a reformulation of the ontological question—that is, the question of what is the significance of Being beyond special beings and beyond a subsumption of it either to spirit or to matter. Heidegger posed the question by distinguishing the ontological from the ontic—what concerns Being *qua* Being from what concerns any given concrete being. This contrast between the ontological and the ontic leads to a denunciation of the metaphysical tradition or to what he has termed "ontotheology." Heidegger denunciates a European philosophical tradition where God is considered as one "privileged" being which explains other beings by forming a unique series with them as if He were the first in a sequence, either temporal (in a very crude version), or causal, teleological or metaphysical (in more elaborate versions). Such an integration of God in a unique sequence with other beings could be considered as a "debasement" of God or Being. It is very interesting that it was an "atheist" philosopher (or rather a nontheist one) who revolted against the trivialization of God committed by Christian thinkers.

The acuteness of Heidegger's denunciation inspired a reformulation of the ontological question, a new way of approaching ontology that avoided naïve types of metaphysics. In regard to the question of the relation between ontology and history, this issue seems open. On the one hand, Heidegger seems to strip history of the immense carriage of meanings that were attributed to it, for example, by Hegel or Marx. What is more, Heidegger seems to conflate Being and Nothingness, and thus ontology and nihilism. On the other hand, it is in the horizon of time and the *Dasein* that beings emerge from Being, thus leading to an existential urgency to assume one's historical responsibility. A certain emphasis on history is thus present in a different manner.

The keenness of Heidegger's denunciation of the previous metaphysical tradition led theologians of the twentieth and twenty-first centuries to search for a mode of theology and ontology beyond metaphysics.[6] Theologians after Heidegger tend to reexamine their proper traditions in the light of the ontological question: this development took place in the transitory period of Modernism, on the borderline age after the collapse of modern ideals in the two world wars and before an eventual shift of paradigms that is still expected.

Contextually speaking, Maximus is an appropriate figure to bring into the conversation. Like us Maximus lived in a borderline period, at the end of Late Antiquity, when the Greco-Roman economy had collapsed after the Persian and Arab invasions. Maximus thematized history after having experienced the frustration of its meanings and after having traversed a great part of the Mediterranean as a nomad and a refugee.[7] Maximus's experience of the instability of history and its inscrutable meaning is comparable to the modern experience— a general loss of orientation—following the two world wars, the period of time in which the ontological question was raised in a new and more existential form. Maximus tried to contemplate historical trauma of his age through the categories offered by the fusion of Neoplatonism and Aristotelianism while trying at the same time to formulate the particularity of faith in Christ who has become history and yet also saves history by His resurrection. Maximus thus engaged with the problems of Aristotelian and Neoplatonist metaphysics, and in so doing historicizes it, even integrating it in a dialectical structure. Maximus opens metaphysics to the Resurrection and teleology to eschatology. In what follows I shall examine the particular points of Maximus' ontological proposition in the light of contemporary problems posed by the question of the association between ontology and history.

2. IS GOD THE TRUE BEING? OR IS HE BEYOND BEING?

The post-Heideggerian demand on theologians is to avoid considering God as one more being among many, even if He is to be considered the first one in a series that can be temporal, causal, teleological, or metaphysical. In regard to this demand, there are many different modes of theologizing. Such modes could be considered as original since the keenness of the Heideggerian criterion has led to a radicalization of theology. But they are not altogether new since the great mystics in the East, and also in the West, have always grasped God's radical otherness in relation to the world. One such mode of theologizing consists in attributing being to the world and considering God as beyond being, that is as "supra-essential," or even as beyond ontology in general. This way could perhaps somehow schematically be termed "apophatic,"[8] even though apophaticism is mostly a question of gnosiology and less of ontology *per se*. One different way of theologizing is to attribute being to God and deprive it of the world. The latter would thus be considered as lacking being per se, having a sort of "iconic" being, or a being according to participation or grace. If we are to put the post-Heideggerian question to Maximus, we would remark that his answer, which is in no way "ontotheological," has some fascinating surprises that are exceptionally appropriate for the present age.

Maximus begins by exalting God's absolute transcendence and alterity. This transcendence is connected to a radical simplicity.[9] Insistence on simplicity could lead to the conclusion that there is nothing opposite (ἐναντίον[10] or ἀντικείμενον[11]) to God. However, Maximus goes in a different direction and claims that what is "around God" (περὶ Θεόν) is His opposite.[12] This means that if Being has an opposite (ἐναντίον), namely "non-Being," then Being is not God-in-Himself but is "around God" (περὶ Θεόν). The same is valid not only for Being which has nonbeing as its opposite, but also for goodness as opposed to evil, truth as opposed to falsehood, immortality as opposed to mortality, beauty as opposed to ugliness, et cetera. God "in Himself" is beyond any characterization that could have an opposite (ἀντικείμενον). "Realities" such as Being, and in consequence Truth, Goodness, or Immortality and Unchangeability, et cetera, are "around God," whereas God as absolutely transcendent is beyond them.

In order to understand this, we have to examine his thought in relation to the modes of thinking that were dominant in his own age—as well as in the preceding centuries—such as Aristotelianism, Neoplatonism, and various forms of Gnosticism. Maximus's position constitutes an explicit opposition to the relevant position of Aristotle that substance (οὐσία) has no opposite. According to Aristotle, there are various qualities in each "first substance" (or "hypostasis," as it would later be termed), which are susceptible of opposite qualities. For example, a man, let us call him Peter, can be white or black, tall or short, et cetera, the latter being *qualities*. At the same time, he has a first substance, his "Peter-hood," as well as a second substance, his humanity, which make him be what he is. His "substance" or "essence" (οὐσία), namely his humanity which constitutes him as Peter, is not susceptible of an opposite. Maximus does acknowledge the philosophical advantages of such a position for distinguishing, for example, between substance and qualities, or between substance and accidents. At the same time, he is deeply aware that this Aristotelian position is linked with the belief in the eternity of the (created) substance and thus with the eternity of the world. But Maximus rejects the eternity of the world since as a Christian he believes in the creation of the world *ex nihilo* (*creation ex nihilo* preserves the freedom of both God and humans). For this reason, Maximus insists that substance has an opposite, namely nonbeing, due to the createdness of the world (*CChar* 3.28). Consequently, whatever is created, including created substances and essences, is "inside" an ontological "domain." Within this domain there is a wrestling between being and nonbeing. Such a wrestling does not take place in God, who does not have any opposite. Maximus's argument is deeply anti-Gnostic and anti-Manicheist—that is, antidualist. Maximus wants to absolutely assure that there is nothing "besides" God ("μηδὲν ἔχειν ἀντικείμενον συνθεωρούμενον," *AI* 37, 1296C). Consequently, God is not an essence, but supra-essential (ὑπερούσιος, *AT* 5, 1048D–49A), and in a similar way God is considered as "hypergood" (ὑπεράγαθος) and "hypertrue" (ὑπεραλήθης).[13] In an extreme apophaticism characteristic of the Areopagitic and Maximian tradition God is conceived as "hyper-god" (ὑπέρ-θεος).[14] God is beyond even simplicity itself (*TP9* 128A). He is also beyond the future, which is significant for eschatology—God *in Himself* is beyond eschatology.[15] Whenever we speak of an essence—or of a *logos* of essence—in God that is possibly contrasted to His existence or to His personal mode of existence, this is done in an abusive way, against as it were proper linguistic precision; Maximus sometimes describes this as a "supra-essential essence" in order to indirectly address this reality. At the same time, it is not only the term "essence" (οὐσία) that presents this particular problem, but also the term "being" (ὄν, εἶναι), since essence and being have nonbeing as an opposite (ἀντικείμενον). In this way, Maximus formulates a *hyperontology*, which brings him into sharp contrast with Aristotelianism, Gnosticism, and Manichaeism, and closer to a modernist denunciation of ontotheology. Yet, the Maximian project should not be viewed as a version of Neoplatonism. In the latter, what is at stake is the relation between the One and the many, the latter emanating from the One. By contrast, in Maximus, who is following a Biblical theology, the fundamental goal is to convincingly reject any ontological "reality" "besides" God. Of course, after the creation of the world there is in a certain sense an "ob-ject" *vis-à-vis* God, but this ob-ject is contingent—that is, not ontologically necessary—and is a product of the will and energy of God who is also present inside it through His *logoi* and energies (the latter could be termed as "pan-en-theism" in contrast to "pan-theism"). The world that is created *ex nihilo* is not therefore a real opposite (ἀντικείμενον) to God, even though it might be regarded as having an otherness due to the free action of creation and, what is more, due to the free offering of freedom and personhood by God to some of His creatures, like men and angels. In any case, Maximus and Neoplatonists share the demand for an apophatic hyperontology, but the philosophical landscape in the two cases is quite different. Neoplatonists focus on the production of the many by the One. Maximus focuses on the need that there be no opposite (ἀντικείμενον) to God; any otherness to God is created freely and contingently. One last but crucial point that needs to be made is that personal otherness inside God is not considered by Maximus as forming an "opposite" (contrast). The Son and the Spirit are persons in relation but not in opposition to the Father. Held by Maximus and the Eastern tradition, this relational emphasis differs from Western conceptions, where personal relations were sometimes conceived as *oppositiones relationis*, reaching up to the Hegelian dialectic.

The aforementioned differences do not exhaust the differences between Maximus and the Neoplatonists, and there remain some blind spots, which need to be examined and further explicated. So far we have seen that according to Maximus God in Himself does not have an opposite. On the other hand, in its historical mode of existence the created world, which does have an opposite—that is, nonbeing—is in a state of continuous friction between being and nonbeing, due to which it cannot be qualified as being properly speaking. This raises the following question: Is there any sense in which Maximus has an ontology, and where should one search for it? Notwithstanding what has been explicated so far, the answer is a positive one. Maximus has an ontology, and it is to be found in Christ.

3. THE LOCUS OF ONTOLOGY IS CHRISTOLOGY

Jacques Lacan has defined love as "giving something you don't have to someone who doesn't want it."[16] We could say something similar, yet different, about Being in Maximus's thought: Being is what is offered by God, while He himself transcends it, to a world which does not have it but strives for it. Of course the latter constitutes the difference between Maximus and Lacan. This gift of Being is Christ.[17] Christ unites in His hypostasis God who transcends Being and the created being which is not yet being. Maximus wrote that God can be qualified more as nonbeing than as being due to His transcending "being" ("Θεὸς . . . τὸ μὴ εἶναι μᾶλλον, διὰ τὸ ὑπερεῖναι ὡς οἰκειότερον ἐπ' αὐτοῦ λεγόμενον, προσιέμενος," *Myst* 110–11). God is thus so transcendent that He even transcends the categories of Being and nonbeing.[18] On the other hand, created being is so immersed in nonbeing that it too cannot be qualified as being. Being thus arises from the meeting of the two, namely of God-above-being and of created being which is not-yet-being. Consequently, the "locus" of ontology is Christology.

In any case, one has to admit that different positions of Maximus in different points of his work make his thought difficult to grasp. We shall nevertheless try to examine some of these points. Firstly, Maximus seems to distinguish between, on the one hand, God in Himself who does not have an opposite, and, on the other hand, realities "around God" (περὶ τὸν Θεόν), where one can detect Being, Truth, and Goodness as originating from God. The expression 'περὶ τὸν Θεόν' should be linked to its Cappadocian understanding—for example, in Basil of Caesarea (in an anti-Arian and anti-Eunomian direction)—and less to the theology of uncreated divine energies as formulated seven centuries later by saint Gregory Palamas. The latter was in his own turn influenced by Maximus but elaborated on this topic in order to correspond to contemporary theological needs (such as the need to qualify grace and the Thaborian Light as uncreated—that is, not created).[19]

What is characteristic of Maximus is that he has a personal/hypostatic approach that concerns the interaction between theology and economy. Before all ages the Son is begotten by the Father and the Spirit proceeds from Him. But in the Economy too there are some distinct hypostatic roles: The Father-Intellect (Πατὴρ Νοῦς) has the initial good will (εὐδοκεῖ) of creation, the Son-Logos (Υἱὸς Λόγος) as the Incarnated Word is the author par excellence of creation (αὐτουργῶν), and the Spirit (Πνεῦμα) cooperates in bringing it to eschatological completion (συνεργεῖ / τελοιοῖ).[20] The order of economy is not absolutely identified with the order of theology *ad intra*, but it is not independent or irrelevant to it. In a similar sense, the *logoi* of beings through which the world is created and eschatologically perfected constitute the good will of the Father-Nous (εὐδοκία) but are ontologically situated mostly inside the Son-Logos who is the Author par excellence of Creation[21] (αὐτουργῶν) and who is the only One Who is incarnated;[22] whereas, the Spirit cooperates (συνεργεῖ) in their eschatological accomplishment (τελοιοῖ). What we want to say is that the *logoi* are not just a "reality" "between" God and the world, which just "is there" in an impersonal way. The *logoi* too should be seen as having a personal structure, namely being the good will of the Father (εὐδοκία), being situated in the Son the Logos as their "accomplisher" par excellence (αὐτουργῶν), and being brought to eschatological completion by the Spirit (συμπληροῖ).[23] The fact that the *logoi* are "situated" in the Son is related to the Son being the Logos, while the Father is compared by Maximus to the *Nous*-Intellect Who has the good will exactly by being the *Nous*, the *Spirit* being the cooperator of the Logos.[24] Maximian ontology is structured in a personal way. The ontology "around God" is not just "something" between God and the world that is just "there." Being is originated by the "good will" (εὐδοκία) of the Father-"Intellect"; the ontological "locus" of being is *par excellence* the Son; whereas, the Spirit is the cooperator (συνεργῶν) and the completer (συμπληρῶν).

A thinker (either late medieval or modern) posterior to the debate between Thomas Aquinas and Duns Scotus (or, in general, to the relative debates between intellectualism and voluntarism or realism and nominalism in the West) might want to pose some philosophical questions to Maximus. For example, are the *logoi* of beings contingent or necessary? Hans Urs von Balthasar, has indeed posed this question.[25] We should note here that the question of the contingency of the *logoi* is not posed by Maximus himself. Maximus's own view is that the *logoi* are wills and intentions of God[26] which are situated in the Logos. In a similar sense we could say that the "Being" of God is a "supra-essential Being," because God in Himself transcends Being. At the same time, Being is initiated by God, and this initiation of Being in God has a hypostatical/personal structure as a "good will" of the Father, an "authorship" of the Son and a "cooperation" of the Spirit (εὐδοκία—αὐτουργία—συνεργία / συμπλήρωσις).

4. THE "LOCUS" OF CHRISTOLOGICAL ONTOLOGY IS HISTORY

If the "locus" of ontology is Christ the Logos, this means that the "locus" of ontology is also history. Christ is the Person Who is begotten from the Father "before all ages." He is the Author par excellence (αὐτουργῶν) of the *logoi*-wills of God. Consequently, He is the Author par excellence (αὐτουργῶν) of creation and the Incarnation (through the "good will" of the Father and the "completion" of the Spirit). Maximus's position concerning this point is very subtle. On the one hand, there is no *necessary* production of the world by God as in Neoplatonism. The creation of the world could be considered as contingent. On the other hand, the *logoi*-wills of God are uncreated. What is more, these *logoi*-wills are personal, because they are "situated" in the Logos who is the "Author" of their "logic" character in a similar sense to His being the "Author" of creation and the One to be incarnated. This hypostatic/personal glance at Maximus's ontology could arguably lead to an interpretative conclusion that in a similar way Son the Logos is the "Author" (αὐτουργός) of ontology with the "good will" of the Father and the cooperation of the Spirit. It could be pointed out that the world is contingent, as created *ex nihilo*, and that its existence is unnecessary. Nevertheless, the *logoi* are uncreated and in a similar sense Being too is uncreated and "around God." Therefore, in the post-Heideggerian question, whether Being is "on the side" of God or "on the side" of the world, and if we are allowed to put this question a bit too schematically, a (perhaps equally) schematic answer would be that Being is "on the side" of God. But Being is something more. It is personally structured and "situated" in Son the Logos. In other words, Being is not "just out there" as a heavenly "around God." Ontology is the affirmation of Being by God the Father in His Son with the cooperation or completion of the Spirit. Ontology is personal in its very character.

Yet, Son the Logos is the One who *becomes* history. This means that history becomes the locus par excellence of ontology. If we find in Hegel the most radical association of ontology with history, we could say that Maximus does not fall short of Hegel in such a connection. On the other hand, Maximian thought presents antidotes to some of the Hegelian shortcomings. For example, Maximus avoids a sort of historical pantheism by insisting on the contingency of world in itself.[27] Even though there is a certain dialectic in Maximus, this dialectic is absolutely free and does not necessarily include evil as part of the internal evolution of the Spirit.[28] For Maximus, evil is contingent, even if it can enter *a posteriori* in the divine "Economy"[29] mostly through the *results* of sin and not sin in itself. History is thus a place of free dialogue between God and man. We do not find in Maximus an ontologization of history or a turning of history into totalitarian historicism.[30] The connection between history and ontology takes place in the Person of Son the Logos who is the hypostatic "author" of ontology and who makes ontology become history, by becoming history Himself.

5. HISTORY AS "ICONIC" ONTOLOGY, THE *ESCHATON* AS THE TRUTH OF HISTORY

The world does not possess being in itself since it is indissolubly intermingled with nonbeing. It is the incarnated Christ who is the author of ontology and who is turning it into an ontology-in-the-becoming inside history. But this means that Maximus's view of history is dynamic and in a sense dialectical (hence the comparison to Hegel). It is a "historical" view of history and by this we mean that it is a view of history that leaves space for surprises, frustrations of meaning, suspense, unexpected interventions of grace. History is not just a static field for domination by structures that come from outside history and that are contemplated *sub specie aeternitatis*. The dynamic character of history is expressed by Maximus mainly by the distinction between shadow, icon, and truth (Heb 10:1). The Old Testament, in which the Logos is not incarnated yet, is a "shadow," where one can "hear" the "voice" of God without seeing Him.

The New Testament, where the Logos is incarnated and becomes flesh, is an "image," as we can now "see" the Incarnated Logos. But the truth lies in the resurrection of Christ Who introduces the eschatological mode of existence.[31] The truth of ontology and history is situated after the Second Coming in the *eschaton*, when the Christological mode of existence will be manifested and realized in all its ontological consequences. For this reason, inside history we only have ontology (i.e., proper ontological Being) as an "icon"; whereas, ontology proper—Being as such—is situated in the eschatological Christology.[32] This is also manifested through the triple schema "being"—"well-being"—"eternal-(well)-being" (εἶναι—εὖ εἶναι—ἀεὶ εὖ εἶναι).[33] "Being" refers to creation, "well-being" to history, and "eternal-(well)-being" to eschatology. The meaning of this triple schema is that true being is the eternal eschatological being in view of which being was created. Nevertheless, the passage to eschatology is mediated by history as an endeavor of well-being, meaning an effort to actualize the potentialities of natural creation (being) in view of the eschatological future (eternal well-being).

6. A DROMIC ONTOLOGY

The distinction between shadow, image, and truth at the end of history poses a view of history as a way, a "dromos," where being is not settled and achieved at the beginning but demands a certain itinerary until the end when it will become true.[34] The connection between ontology and history in Maximus means that ontology is *dromic*, that being is "on the way" ("καθ'ὁδόν"). In the next sections, we shall try to examine the different dimensions of this dromic ontology through some particularly Maximian triple schemas or double contrasts.

7. DIMENSIONS OF THE DROMOS: ΛΟΓΟΣ—ΤΡΟΠΟΣ—ΤΕΛΟΣ, ΕΊΚΩΝ—ΌΜΟΙΩΣΙΣ, ΑΥΤΕΞΟΥΣΙΟΝ—ἘΛΕΥΘΕΡΟΝ

The *dromos* has a beginning: it is God's *logoi*-wills for beings, which are "situated" in God the Logos.[35] It has a middle: the historical realization of *logoi* by concrete historical *tropoi* (modes). It has an end: the goal for which the world was created and which is the assumption of the world by Christ and its hypostatic union with divinity. The three "concepts" of *logos*, *tropos*, and *telos* are dialectical, as they are not defined ontically—that is, independently from one another.[36] On the contrary, they are, in a way, "breaking" the one into the other. For example, according to Maximus *logos* means a will of God for one being which is not identified with the created and fluid nature of this being, but is a "signpost" for the future. The fact that the *logoi* of beings are "situated" inside Son the Logos could also mean that the *logoi* are wills of God which disclose how God the Father wills a being or attribute to be incorporated in the incarnated Christ. For example, the *logos* of body and materiality that man shares with all other bodily and material beings is their reception in Christ thanks to the Incarnation. The same is true about the soul that man shares with animate beings. More concretely, the *logos* of the irascible part of the soul is the love of God,[37] the *logos* of desire is divine *eros* (*QThal* 55.313), whereas the *logos* of intellection, which man shares with angels, is the intellectual prayer (νοερὰ προσευχή, *CChar* 1.79) of Christ to His Father, et cetera. In this sense, the "concept" of *logos* breaks into that of the *telos*, since the *logos* does not have an independent existence but exists merely as a sign to the end. But it also "breaks" in the notion of *tropos* because it does not have an existential value, unless it receives a concrete historical realization by the *tropos*. The end is the hypostatical union between the created and the uncreated in Christ, the "mystery" for which the whole universe is willed before the ages in order to be recapitulated in Christ, according to Pauline theology.[38]

This end is not merely the last episode in a linear evolution of history. The *telos* is present already in the beginning inside the *logos* which is a signpost to it.[39] Besides, the *telos* is identified to a certain mode of existence that is the filial existence by which created being enters by grace and in the Spirit the filial relationship between the Son and the Father. The end is thus referring to eschatology—that is, to the eschatological mode of existence—but it is also present inside history, not only through the *logos* but also through the Resurrection that inaugurates the *eschaton*. The mode is conceived in the same way as a historical modification that is in dialogue with the divine *logos* in view of the *telos*. If the end is the divine filial mode of existing eschatologically as sons by grace,[40] then the historical modes are different modes through which each personal hypostasis is negotiating the call of the adoption. Inside history, modes might be tragic. For example, among the modes of sonship, one may find that of the "prodigal son," or of a son who is trying to deny his sonship or his call, like Jonah. But, in the end, the *logoi* are integrated in the Logos, and in the same way the many *tropoi* of the different hypostases will be incorporated in the mode of existence of the Son, without denying the freedom and contingency of history.[41] The fact that there are many modes inside history means that in the *eschaton* as well there will be different modes not of good and evil, but of a disposition (διά-θεσις)[42] toward the good omnipresence of God, as well as different modes of participation or nonparticipation in this presence (*QD* 19.5–21), which in the Maximian idiom are termed modes of "eternally-well-being" or "eternally-ill-being." *Logos*, *tropos*, and *telos* start in history, but are confirmed only in the *eschaton*. In the latter, the many *logoi*—that is, the different *logoi* of the existence of beings—are integrated inside Son the Logos Who reveals the logical meaning of all creatures; whereas, the multiple modes of the negotiation of this call to sonship will be incorporated in the unique mode of existence of the Son as modes of sonship by grace, bearing at the same time the contingent human disposition toward that call. Through this triple schema we could also understand better the characteristic Maximian contrasts between image and likeness or freedom and liberation (αὐτεξούσιον—ἐλεύθερον). The biblical theme of the creation of man according to the image and the resemblance of God takes an interesting Maximian twist: the image is a *logos* at the beginning of the way (dromos); whereas, the resemblance is a mode inside the *dromos* of history toward its eschatological end.[43] In the same way, the αὐτεξούσιον is the *logos* of human nature and this means that man can participate consciously in his movement inside the historical *dromos*, as well as that he has this possibility as a divine gift from the very beginning.[44] The ἐλεύθερον is, on the contrary, a liberation of man by the grace of God who comes to find and assume him inside the historical *dromos*.

8. THE FIVE DIMENSIONS OF BEING INSIDE A DROMIC ONTOLOGY: ΔΥΝΑΜΙΣ—ἝΞΙΣ—ἘΝΕΡΓΕΙΑ—ἈΡΓΙΑ—ΣΤΑΣΙΣ

The fact that ontology is dromic means that being is not given in its starting point, but traverses a certain trajectory until its eschatological accomplishment. Maximus receives from Aristotle a certain metaphysics of motion, where being is moved from potentiality (δύναμις) to actuality (ἐνέργεια) in order to be realized as well as to realize its ontology. Nevertheless, Maximus transforms this metaphysics in the direction of a historical and eschatological character. The field of this trajectory from potentiality to actuality is not natural teleology, a sort of physical time measuring the movement provoked by it, nor is biological maturation its goal. On the contrary, teleology opens up to eschatology in the sense that any finality of nature is realized historically in an itinerary toward its eschatological truth. Nature with its logical finalities is saved and confirmed, but it is realized and assumed by history. In other words, it is history that constitutes the horizon or even the goal of nature and not the opposite.

Dynamis means something else as well, namely the fact that in the beginning nature is not given as accomplished. It is absolutely fluid and fashionable. A being in its starting point has, on the one hand, a created nature which is in a state of potentiality and is fashionable, being able to develop historically.[45] On the other hand, it is a *logos* of God, for this nature is a signpost for how this nature is called to be in the future. If there is a certain anti-essentialism in Maximus, it is not an anti-essentialism of a voluntarist type, where man is called to counter an already given nature. Rather, it is an anti-essentialism in the sense that such a given nature never in fact existed. What does exist in the beginning is, on the one hand, an absolutely fluid nature, and, on the other, the dialogue with God's *logos* who directs us toward the future through propositions,[46] man's modal responses, and God's counter-responses through His grace.

Aristotelian teleology insisted mainly on the passage from potentiality to actuality (δύναμις—ἐνέργεια). Maximus completes this schema by ἕξις and στάσις, which are terms borrowed from Aristotelianism and Greek philosophy in general but conceived in a very particular way by Maximus.[47] *Stasis* is the eschatological end, where the *dromos* of history comes to a halt because it has arrived at its destination, which is the hypostatical unity of the created and the uncreated in Christ. *Stasis* is thus beyond *energeia*. In modifying Aristotle, Maximus conceives that the goal of being is not its actualization, but its accomplishment inside a goal (*QThal* 60.49–62) which presents a natural gap in relation to the actualization of nature inside history. *Hexis* is a relative station inside history. *Hexis*, or *habitus* in its Latin translation, means that history is not a continuous flux, an unattainable sequence of ungraspable moments like a Heraclitean river, a Cratylean flux, or a Post-Modern sequence of alterities. *Hexis* is a sort of mediation between *dynamis* and *energeia*.[48] Maximus includes the element of *dynamis*, that is of fluidity, but he also wants to introduce the element of *hexis* determined by the person as a stance inside history.[49] If *dynamis* is the changeability (τροπή) in the departure of history, *hexis* is a personal historical mode, which stabilizes this flux in order to express a personal disposition or stance like a crystallization of the historical dynamic (akin to Arthur Schopenhauer's view of art as a representation that crystallizes the will's vain hunting). *Hexis* is a mode of disposition of a person toward what is happening in history. It could thus be considered as a mediation between *dynamis* and *energeia* in the sense that in order to arrive at the actualization of nature (for nature to become something), it needs to pass from a personal modal and historical disposition. If *dynamis* and *energeia* mostly concern nature respectively in the departure of its trajectory and in its actualization, *hexis* is a personal dimension of being. At the same time, *hexis* can be considered as an anticipation of the eschatological stasis, in the sense that it is a relative stasis that dawns inside history before the final stasis in the *eschaton*.

The position of energy in Maximus's ontology means it is the person that actualizes nature and thus has a responsibility for its accomplishment. At the beginning of the *dromos* nature is a *dynamis*, but through the intervention of the person it is not only enhypostasized but also actualized—that is, accomplished.[50] The person is thus in dialogue with the divine *logos* of nature and proceeds to a historical negotiation of this logical call. Maximus sometimes uses a couple of terms "*logos* of nature"—"*tropos* of energy," which together with the Cappadocian couple "*logos* of nature"—"*tropos* of existence" means that the person makes nature not only to *sub-sist* (ὑπό-στασις) but also to *ek-sist* (ἔκ-στασις) and to be actualized. It is exactly this combination of *hypostasis*, *ekstasis*, and accomplishment/actualization that one could term a "dromic ontology." But the *energeia* is distinguished from the stasis, and this difference is very important. Inside history a first actualization of nature "takes place" through the hypostatical mode of existence, but this happens in view of the eschatological stasis. The distinction between *energeia* and *stasis* means that as Christians we are not content with a simple actualization of nature, but our goal is beyond that; it is in the eschatological enhypostatization of nature in the person of Christ and its consequent divinization. This eschatological mode of enhypostatization is inaugurated by the historical Resurrection but will be manifested in all its ontological fullness in the *eschaton* when it will be shown that human nature in its catholicity is received and actualized by the hypostasis of the Logos, which includes in itself the different hypostases of humanity. Every historical actualization of nature happens in view of the eschatological stasis.

The distinction between *energeia* and *stasis* is also formulated through the term *argia* (rest). This means that the actualization of nature by the *energeia* is no guarantee that this particular actualization will survive in the *eschaton* as it is. After the actualization there is a put to rest by death. This death is not simply a mystery that shows the otherness of mortal creation from the Immortal God. After the Crucifixion of Christ death is also something we could assume deliberately (ἑκούσιον πάθος), not of course in an absolute sense like Christ Who is absolutely free, but by the grace of martyrdom. By this voluntary death we put to rest the historical actualization of nature. The *stasis* of the *eschaton* is a new actualization after the bodily resurrection. Nevertheless, it is not a *creatio ex nihilo* but a *creatio ex vetere*.

This means that the historical *energeia* might survive even though we should remain apophatic about that and not wish to impose our conceptions on God's freedom. What we mean is that Maximus has formulated his eschatological hope by the term "διάθεσις" (disposition), which means that each person in the *eschaton* will retain a formation of her hypostatic receptivity according to her historical mode (*TP1* 21D–8A). The historical *energeia* is not something that will be discarded in death. We have a very serious responsibility for our historical *energeia* since nature, according to Maximus, is waiting for us as persons to actualize, even if we hope that in the end it will be actualized by Christ and thus saved by Him. The relation between *energeia, argia,* and *stasis* is expressed through the biblical image of the sixth, the seventh, and the eighth day.[51] The sixth day corresponds to the *energeia*—actualization of being inside history as a preparation (Παρασκευή in its etymological sense). The seventh day corresponds to the repose of Sabbath,[52] where the world is crucified and buried with Christ, since, as insists Maximus, "all the phenomena need crucifixion, . . . and all the intelligibles need burial."[53] The eighth day is the stasis in the *ana-stasis*, where being is resurrected in another form ("ἐν ἑτέρᾳ μορφῇ," Mark 16:12).

The fact that Maximus integrates rest (ἀργία) in his dromic ontology shows that he wants to break away from the closed Greek ontology. The goal of being is not only to be fulfilled like in the Aristotelian trajectory from potentiality to actuality but also to be crucified so that it may be resurrected through crucifixion. The characteristic example that helps us understand this dialectic is Christ's prayer at Gethsemane.[54] The prayer, as exposed by Maximus, contains three ontological moments:

1. Christ as a man expresses and affirms His natural will to live. In this way Christ actualizes the will for life (the importance of which was

conceived by Maximus much before Schopenhauer and Nietzsche) in a kind of sixth day.
2. This will for life does not take the form of an egoistic survival at all costs. On the contrary, the will for life is put to "rest" through the crucifixion of its natural self-sufficiency and is referred to the divine will of the Father.
3. It is only though this *argia* that the human will of Christ (as well as our own human will) for life will be eschatologically fulfilled as a communion of life through the Crucifixion and the Resurrection.

There is thus a certain dialectic between *energeia*, *argia*, and *stasis* that is expressed poetically as a dialectic between the sixth, the seventh, and the eighth day. The seventh day means that often God's will does not consist of a one-sided celebration of nature, but also includes its frustration of its limitation, at least in its lapsarian claim for self-sufficiency, so that it may be accomplished in an eschatological stasis that comes after the *argia* of the seventh day.

A similar triple schema is that of the historical time (χρόνος), the eon (αἰών), and the eschatological ever-moving stasis (ἀεικίνητος στάσις).[55] The time of the sixth day is when beings are actualized. In the eon, we have a sort of crystallization of the finalities, which are activated through history, in a seventh day of rest. In the eighth day beings are resurrected in another mode of temporality—that is, in a stasis where being and nature are inside God the Logos, but there is also another mode of motion since God cannot be exhausted in this stasis; from this arises another mode of temporality. We could understand this Maximian vision of the stasis, or rather the ever-moving stasis, through the expression that Christ is the "Locus of the Living" (Χώρα τῶν Ζώντων). The nature that is assumed and resurrected by Christ is not an individual nature, but the catholic nature of all of us.

"Christ is Risen" means that we are all risen, something that can already be seen in the experience of the saints but will completely be manifested in the *eschaton*. By having entered the human nature of Christ as many filial modes inside the One Filiality, we continue to move in the *eschaton* but in another way that consists of a coexistence of *stasis* and motion. *Stasis*, because the hypostatic union is a sort of Christian "unmoved prime mover," to put it in an Aristotelian manner.[56] That is, the hypostatic union is an eschatological end that moves history from its end according to an eschatological teleology. Maximus receives but also transforms Aristotelianism, because in the end the ideal is not only the *stasis*, but also a sort of eternal movement which shows that the transcendent God cannot be exhausted. Though God has offered the possibility of union with Him, he continues to set off a movement toward Him. As we have observed, God is in Himself beyond Being. Nevertheless, in the *stasis* of eschatological Christology, God offers Being. Eschatological

Christology is in the end an ontology, but it is an ontology of a Being that is simultaneously in rest and in movement. One could say that created nature, after having received Being by grace, is both at rest and in movement. It is in rest because it received being; it is in movement because it moves toward a God that is in Himself beyond Being. In this sense, even eschatological ontology is somehow a dromic ontology but with the important difference that it is a *dromos* where we have already reached the terminus, but continue nevertheless to move "from glory to glory" (2 Cor 3:18)[57] as the whole of humanity is united in an eschatological ecclesial mode.

9. THE HISTORICAL RESPONSIBILITY OF ONTOLOGY

The fact that Maximus uses all these terms and concepts in order to formulate his ontology might be exhausting for his reader, or it might be difficult for an "exegete" to grasp his thought in a definite way. This is exactly what dromic ontology is all about; it is an ontology "on the way," where "concepts" cannot contain it, cannot fossilize it in static schemas. Hence the polysemy, the tension, and the poetic openness that is so characteristic of Maximus. By focusing on this dromic ontology, we have tried to show the rhythm and the intensity of the Maximian vision rather than give final ontological answers. Another dimension of this complexity and of the tensions of Maximian thought is what we would call the "responsibility" of ontology. Maximus could be viewed as a responsible thinker who tries to do justice to different dimensions and moments of the human experience. For example, with *dynamis* he is trying to express the fluidity of nature in its departure as well as the intensity in the dialogue with the divine *logos* for it. With *hexis* he endeavors to designate how the person who is hypostasizing nature takes a stance in this dialogue in a relative historical stability before the *stasis* par excellence at the *eschaton*. With *energeia* his effort is to indicate the responsibility of human persons for the actualization of nature which is waiting to be accomplished by each one of us. With *argia* he stresses that this accomplishment might be a frustration of nature in its lapsarian demand for self-sufficiency. Consequently, the truth might be saved inside history not by the success of this world but by the defeated, by the "stones that are rejected" (1 Pet 2:7) in the buildings of history. With *stasis*, he attempts to express the eschatological end of the hypostatic union between the created and the uncreated in Christ Who, as the final cause of creation, does not constitute merely a final episode, but is present already in the beginning of history.

In order to understand this ontology of responsibility and the consequent responsibility of ontology—that is, the responsibility of Maximus as a thinker when he is ontologizing—one should think what would happen if one of the five dimensions of this ontology (δύναμις—ἕξις—ἐνέργεια—ἀργία—στάσις) was missing. An ontology without *dynamis* would be an ontology where nature would be accomplished and given in the beginning and where consequently the person could do nothing in regard to it other than adopt an escapist attitude toward its necessity. In other words, it would entail a deterministic ontology, which would provoke the tendency of an imaginary flight out of it and into a voluntarist personal freedom. If, on the other hand, we had an ontology of *energeia*, without having at the same time an ontology of *dynamis*, then the result would be an ontology without tension between protology and eschatology, where historicity and all its adventure would be lost inside a *tropos* of the energy, which would be repeated again and again in a sort of automatic unhistorical ethos. In this case, the *energeia* would be one-dimensional and it could not become the same *dynamis* for another *energeia*. Consequently, whoever is not coordinated with such an *energeia* would be excluded as a sort of pariah condemned in an ontological anathema. In other words, an ontology of *energeia* without *dynamis* would be an ontology of tradition at the detriment of radical originality. An ontology without *hexis* would be a sort of Cratylean or Post-Modern (e.g., Deleuzian) (non-)ontology of a perpetual historical flux, which would entail an unloving (ἀνέραστος) stance—one cannot fall in love with a flux or relate to a river. An ontology without (historical) *energeia* would be a mutilated ontology where nature would remain unactualized. Thus, nature could only receive passively as a sort of platonic *chora* (neither being nor nonbeing). As a result, the forms would come to dominate it from the outside—that is, either from a platonic past or from the future of eschatological stasis in a sort of inverted Platonism. An ontology without historical *energeia* would mean that history would be but a passive field where decisions outside history would come to be imposed upon it, or where static structures either from the protological past or from the eschatological future would come to dominate it. It would be an ontology where a sort of fearful structuralism would try to kill or at least repress the vigor and the unpredictability inherent in historicity. Inversely, an ontology without *argia* would be a moralist ontology that would celebrate moral achievements in a one-sided way. It would be an ontology of the winners, of petty-bourgeois families, where there would be no room for the defeated, for the foolishness for Christ, or even for monasticism in general, for what Giorgio Agamben terms "inoperativity" (*inoperosità*). It would be an ontological *Kaiadas* for all the stones that have been rejected but will become the cornerstone (1 Pet 2:7). An ontology without *argia* would be an ontology without the macarisms of the Sermon on the Mount, an ontology that would disregard the fact that God "has chosen the non-beings in order to abolish the beings"

(1 Cor 1:28), an ontology without the Cross (and possibly without Judgment). Finally, an ontology without *stasis*—that is, without ever-moving *stasis*—would be an eternal world of Platonic souls, an ontology of immortality maybe, but not of historical incarnation and eschatological resurrection. It would be an ontology without Christ, or, if we are to admit the equation of Christology with ontology, an ontology without ontology.

It is exactly the great responsibility that Maximus shows as a thinker that makes him formulate an elaborate, balanced, and multidimensional ontological vision in order to do justice to all the tensions that exist in the Christian spiritual life.

10. DROMIC ONTOLOGY AS AN ONTOLOGY OF THE SYN-OD

When developing Maximus's ontology, we have not exposed the significance of the Judeo-Christian conception of the "Fall." The reason is that we did not want to give a misleading impression that there are two ontologies, one before and one after the Fall. We believe that Maximian ontology is uniform because according to Maximus the Fall happened "simultaneously to the coming into being" ("ἅμα τῷ γενέσθαι," *AI* 42, 1321B). There is no ideal prelapsarian state that existed within time. What is crucial is that most of the schemas of Maximian ontology such as *logos—tropos—telos*, being—well-being—eternal well-being, image—resemblance, αὐτεξούσιον—ἐλεύθερον, sixth—seventh—eighth day, *dynamis—hexis—energeia—argia—stasis*, et cetera, are absolutely valid even after the Fall. Nevertheless, according to Maximus the Fall is a historical event. If we are to evaluate the Fall inside a dromic ontology, we would say, borrowing an expression of John Zizioulas's, that the Fall is a fall not from a perfect past where the perfection of man would have already been accomplished, but *a Fall from the future*, that is, from what man might have achieved had he not fallen. In such a view, we can understand the meaning of Adam's Fall only *a posteriori* by examining what was the case in Christ. In his dromic ontology Maximus also uses the triple schema "according to nature"—"contrary to nature"—"beyond nature" where the "according to nature" (κατὰ φύσιν) is the point of departure of a *dromos* which will eventually either fall into the "contrary to nature" (παρὰ φύσιν) or be assumed by the supernatural (ὑπὲρ φύσιν). To take one example that is already given, if the will for life is according to nature this point of departure cannot stay as it is; it will either fall into the egoism of survival at all costs, which is "contrary to nature," or it will be assumed by the supernatural sharing of life through the Crucifixion and the Resurrection.

What is then the difference between a lapsarian and a nonlapsarian mode of the *dromos*? One could put it in a very simple way that the Fall means having to make this *dromos* for one's own; whereas, the nonlapsarian mode would be to make this ontological *dromos* of history all together. For this reason Maximus posits that there are three components to the Fall—that is, egoism, pleasure, and *gnome*. *Gnome* means an initial disposition (διά-θεσις) that is at the outset connected to createdness and not to the Fall and which after the Fall turned into a conflict (διά-στασις)[58] inside nature and is tantamount to a tragic fragmentation of it. The *gnome* means that in a fallen world the *dromos* takes place separately for each person. Exactly what the Church is trying to do is to cure this fragmentation by calling us to an ascetic coordination of our gnomic wills,[59] so that the ontological trajectory of history take place by all of us together.[60] In the *eschaton* the gnomic will is conceded (*AI* 7, 1076BC), and it is therefore manifested that we are all members of a unique humanity that is received and resurrected by Christ as the "Locus of the Living" (Χώρα τῶν Ζώντων).[61] The *gnome* ceases then to be a conflict (διάστασις) and survives after having been conceded as a sort of "post-gnomic" will that is termed διάθεσις (disposition). The latter does not entail fragmentation like the historical *gnome* but does entail the possibility of a distinction between the "saved" and the "damned," in the sense that each person has a particular disposition (διάθεσις)[62] toward the omnipresence of God in Christ and in the Spirit. In the *eschaton* we expect the manifestation of what was inaugurated by the resurrection of the catholic human nature by Christ and which we now anticipate in the Eucharist. The Maximian vision is that movement is continued in the *eschaton* as an ever-moving repose. Therefore, we hope that there will be some sort of movement in the *eschaton* that will be different, some other mode of temporality, an entirely different mode than the diastematic time of history. There will be in the *eschaton*, we could hope, a different sort of *dromotic* ontology, in which we have reached the end but we will nevertheless continue to move. It will thus be a *dromos* made by all of us together, that is a *syn-od*.

Thus, if the ontology of history is an ontology of the way (ὁδός), the ontology of the *eschaton*, is an ontology of the *syn-od* (σύν-οδος). The latter means that we are all on the way together, inside the catholic human nature assumed by Christ as the "Locus of the Living" (Χώρα τῶν Ζώντων)—that is, as many sons by grace in the Spirit inside the hypostasis of the One Son Who is referring us to the Father. This etymological meaning of the *syn-od* could be seen as a Maximian version of the Heideggerian *Mit-sein*, that is, not only being together, but *moving* together both in the historical *dromos* and in the eschatological ever-moving *stasis*. It is this eschatological ontology of the *syn-od* that we anticipate in the syn-odicity of the Church inside history, not only in the Eucharist as an *Ex-od* and an Entrance (εἴσ-οδος), but also in the synods by which local Churches gather in order to manifest the synodical character of the *Ec-clesia*. Today, in an age where the synodical consciousness of the Orthodox Church is actively revived through the summoning of a Panorthodox Synod, our hope is that this dromic character of Christian ontology will be manifested anew. It is thus timely to formulate again our faith as to what we expect of the Church and its ontology. That is, we believe in the Ec-clesia as a *syn-od*, a being-together on the same way.

NOTES

1. A first version of this chapter appeared in Sotiris Mitralexis and Marcin Podbielski eds., *Christian and Islamic Philosophies of Time* (Wilmington, DE: Vernon Press, 2018) with the kind permission of which it is reprinted here.

2. See, for example, Dominic J. O'Meara, *Plotinus. An Introduction to the Enneads* (Oxford: Clarendon Press, 1993); John Bussanich, "Plotinus's Metaphysics of the One," in *The Cambridge Companion to Plotinus*, ed. Lloyd P. Gerson (Cambridge; New York: Cambridge University Press, 1996).

3. Maximus the Confessor is also feeling the need to respond to this line of argumentation. In *Capitum de Theologia et Œconomia Centuria* (henceforth *CGn*) 1.82, 1116B–17A, he tries to explain in what sense we should understand divine intellection in order to avoid a loss of divine simplicity.

4. See, for example, Charles Taylor, *Hegel* (Cambridge; New York: Cambridge University Press, 1975).

5. For the relation between Marxism and Christian Trinitarian Theology see Slavoj Žižek, *The Fragile Absolute; or, Why Is the Christian Legacy Worth Fighting For?*, Wo Es war (London; New York: Verso, 2000); Slavoj Žižek, *On Belief*, Thinking in Action (London; New York: Routledge, 2001); Slavoj Žižek, *The Puppet and the Dwarf: The Perverse Core of Christianity*, Short Circuits (Cambridge, MA: MIT Press, 2003).

6. See, for example, John Panteleimon Manoussakis, *God after Metaphysics: A Theological Aesthetic*, Indiana Series in the Philosophy of Religion (Bloomington: Indiana University Press, 2007).

7. For a possible influence of the events of Maximus's life in his thinking see Jean-Miguel Garrigues, *Maxime le Confesseur. La charité, avenir divin de l'homme*, Théologie historique 38 (Paris: Beauchesne, 1976), 35–82. For criticism on this line of interpretation see Marc Doucet, "Vues récentes sur les métamorphoses de la pensée de saint Maxime le Confesseur," *Science et Esprit* 31, no. 3 (1979).

8. For a very interesting attempt to link the apophaticism of the Fathers to post-Heideggerian thought see Christos Yannaras, *De l'absence et de l'inconnaissance de Dieu, d'après les écrits aréopagitiques et Martin Heidegger*, trans. Jacques Touraille, Théologie sans frontières 21 (Paris: Cerf, 1971); Christos Yannaras, *Philosophie sans rupture*, trans. André Borrély, Perspective orthodoxe 7 (Genève: Labor et fides,

1981); Christos Yannaras, *Person and Eros*, trans. Norman Russell (Brookline, MA: Holy Cross Orthodox Press, 2007).

9. Maximus is treating the question of divine simplicity and transcendence mostly in the following passages: *CGn* 1.48, 1100C–1101A; 1.82–83, 1116–17; 2.3, 1125D, 2.74, 1157D–60A; 2.81–82, 1164A; *TP9* 128A; *Myst* 437–85 (PG 91,680A–81C); *AI* 10, 1112D–13B, 1153B, 1180D–81A, 1196AB, 1205C; *AI* 15, 1216A–B, 1220AB; *AI* 16, 1221C–24A; *AI* 21, 1249C. Since Constas's critical edition names Migne's *Patrologia Graeca* column for each respective passage, while many scholars still depend on PG's *Ambigua*, we will use Constas's critically edited text while simply citing *AI* and *AT* with PG 91 columns for the readers' convenience, as PG columns can be easily traced back to Constas's pages, while the opposite is naturally not the case.

10. For the notion of ἐναντίον see *CChar* 3.28; *TP17* 212C–D.

11. *AI* 37, 1296B–C.

12. For the notion of περὶ (τὸν) Θεόν in Maximus see the passages: *CChar* 4.7; *CGn* 2.73, 1157BC; *AI* 15, 1220C ("Περὶ Θεὸν γάρ, ἀλλ' οὐ Θεός, ἡ ἀπειρία, ὅτι καὶ ταύτης ἀσυγκρίτως ὑπέρκειται"); *AI* 34, 1288B.

13. See *AI* 37, 1296C, where it is stated that God is beyond truth ("ὑπὲρ ἀλήθειαν").

14. For the meaning of apophaticism in Maximus, see the passages: *QThal* 55.41–47; *Myst* 103–26; *AI* 10, 1144A, 1165BC; *AI* 15, 1216B; *AI* 16, 1221CD; *AI* 17, 1229C; *AI* 20, 1240CD; *AI* 34, 1288B–89A; *AI* 71, 1409C.

15. See *AI* 37, 1296BC.

16. Jacques Lacan, "Problèmes cruciaux pour la psychanalyse. Séminaire [XII,] 1964–1965," ed. Michel Roussan (Paris: Editions de l'Association Freudienne Internationnal, 2000), seminar of March 17, 1965.

17. The Christocentric character of Maximian ontology is stressed in John Zizioulas, "Person and Nature in the Theology of St Maximus the Confessor, in *Knowing the Purpose of Creation through the Resurrection: Proceedings of the Symposium on St Maximus the Confessor, Belgrade, October 18–21, 2012*, ed. Maksim Vasiljević [Bishop Maxim] (Alhambra, CA: Sebastian Press & Faculty of Orthodox Theology, University of Belgrade, 2013), 85–113.

18. See *AI* 10, 1180D–81A: "Πᾶν γὰρ ὅπερ καθ' ὁτιοῦν τὸν τοῦ 'πῶς' ἐπιδέχεται λόγον, κἂν εἰ ἔστιν, ἀλλ' οὐκ ἦν. Ὅθεν τὸ θεῖον 'εἶναι' λέγοντες, οὐ τὸ πῶς εἶναι λέγομεν· καὶ διὰ τοῦτο καὶ τὸ 'ἔστι' καὶ τὸ 'ἦν' ἁπλῶς καὶ ἀορίστως καὶ ἀπολελυμένως ἐπ' αὐτοῦ λέγομεν. Ἀνεπίδεκτον γὰρ παντὸς λόγου καὶ νοήματος τὸ θεῖόν ἐστι, καθ' ὃ οὔτε κατηγοροῦντες αὐτοῦ τὸ 'εἶναι' λέγομεν αὐτὸ εἶναι. Ἐξ αὐτοῦ γὰρ τὸ εἶναι, ἀλλ' οὐκ αὐτὸ τὸ 'εἶναι.' Ὑπὲρ γάρ ἐστι καὶ αὐτοῦ τοῦ εἶναι, τοῦ τε πῶς καὶ ἁπλῶς λεγομένου τε καὶ νοουμένου. Εἰ δὲ 'πῶς,' ἀλλ' οὐχ ἁπλῶς, ἔχει τὰ ὄντα τὸ εἶναι, ὥσπερ ὑπὸ τὸ 'ποῦ' εἶναι διὰ τὴν θέσιν καὶ τὸ πέρας τῶν ἐπ' αὐτοῖς κατὰ φύσιν λόγων, καὶ ὑπὸ τὸ 'ποτέ' πάντως εἶναι διὰ τὴν ἀρχὴν ἐπιδέξεται."

19. For the relation between the Cappadocian/Maximian expression "περὶ τὸν Θεόν" and the Palamite theology of uncreated divine energies see Vasilios Karayiannis, *Maxime le Confesseur. Essence et énergies de Dieu*, Théologie historique 93 (Paris: Beauchesne, 1993).

20. For the notions of εὐδοκία, αὐτουργία, and συνεργία / τελείωσις / συμπλήρωσις as characterizing the three distinct divine Hypostases see the passages: *PN* 87–96;

AT 2, 1037C; *AT* 5, 1049D; *AI* 7, 1081C, 1128–29; *AI* 40, 1304C; *AI* 61, 1385D–88A; *QThal* 2.22–30, 19, 40.12–18, 60; *TP6* 68D; *TP20* 237D–40B.

21. See *AI* 7, 1081C; *AI* 10, 1128–29; *AI* 40, 1304C ("Θεός . . . ἐν τρισὶ τοῖς μεγίστοις ἵσταται, αἰτίῳ καὶ δημιουργῷ καὶ τελειοποιῷ· τῷ Πατρὶ, λέγω, καὶ τῷ Υἱῷ καὶ τῷ ἁγίῳ Πνεύματι"). In the latter, Maximus is following Gregory of Nazianzus. Nevertheless, in other passages, Maximus rather stresses the commonality of the divine energy of creation in which all the Three Hypostases participate. See for example, *QThal* 28.70–83. It seems then that there is a certain tension in Maximus's thought. The energy of creation is common but at the same time the αὐτουργῶν is the *Logos*. The creation of the world by the *Logos* seems to be linked to the fact that He is the only one Who was incarnated: *QThal* 60.117–120: "Ἔδει γὰρ ὡς ἀληθῶς τὸν κατὰ φύσιν τῆς τῶν ὄντων οὐσίας δημιουργὸν καὶ τῆς κατὰ χάριν αὐτουργὸν γενέσθαι τῶν γεγονότων θεώσεως, ἵνα ὁ τοῦ εὖ εἶναι δοτὴρ φανῇ καὶ τοῦ ἀεὶ εὖ εἶναι χαριστικός."

22. See *QThal* 60.94–105 (*PG* 90,624B–C): "Τοῦτο τὸ μυστήριον προεγνώσθη πρὸ πάντων τῶν αἰώνων μόνῳ τῷ Πατρὶ καὶ τῷ Υἱῷ καὶ τῷ ἁγίῳ Πνεύματι, τῷ μὲν κατ' εὐδοκίαν, τῷ δὲ κατ' αὐτουργίαν, τῷ δὲ κατὰ συνεργίαν· μία γὰρ ἡ Πατρὸς καὶ Υἱοῦ καὶ ἁγίου Πνεύματος γνῶσις, ὅτι καὶ μία οὐσία καὶ δύναμις. Οὐ γὰρ ἠγνόει τοῦ Υἱοῦ τὴν σάρκωσιν ὁ Πατὴρ ἢ τὸ Πνεῦμα τὸ ἅγιον, ὅτι ἐν ὅλῳ τῷ Υἱῷ τὸ μυστήριον αὐτουργοῦντι τῆς ἡμῶν σωτηρίας διὰ σαρκώσεως ὅλος κατ' οὐσίαν ὁ Πατήρ, οὐ σαρκούμενος ἀλλ' εὐδοκῶν τοῦ Υἱοῦ τὴν σάρκωσιν, καὶ ὅλον ἐν ὅλῳ τῷ Υἱῷ τὸ Πνεῦμα τὸ ἅγιον κατ' οὐσίαν ὑπῆρχεν, οὐ σαρκούμενον ἀλλὰ συνεργοῦν τῷ Υἱῷ τὴν δι' ἡμᾶς ἀπόρρητον σάρκωσιν." See also *QThal* 60.117–130 and *AI* 61, 1385D: "Σκηνὴ τοιγαροῦν τοῦ μαρτυρίου ἡ μυστηριώδης ἐστὶν οἰκονομία τῆς τοῦ Θεοῦ Λόγου σαρκώσεως, ἣν ὁ Θεὸς καὶ Πατὴρ εὐδοκήσας 'παρέδειξε,' καὶ τὸ Πνεῦμα τὸ ἅγιον διὰ τοῦ σοφοῦ Βεσελεὴλ προτυπούμενον συνεργῆσαν 'ἐτελείωσε,' καὶ ὁ νοητὸς Μωϋσῆς ὁ τοῦ Θεοῦ καὶ Πατρὸς μονογενὴς Υἱὸς αὐτούργησε, τὴν ἀνθρωπίνην φύσιν ἐν ἑαυτῷ 'πηξάμενος' ἑνώσει τῇ καθ' ὑπόστασιν."

23. *QThal* 2.23–6: "Ὁ Πατήρ μου ἕως ἄρτι ἐργάζεται, κἀγὼ ἐργάζομαι, ὁ μὲν εὐδοκῶν, ὁ δὲ αὐτουργῶν, καὶ τοῦ ἁγίου Πνεύματος οὐσιωδῶς τήν τε τοῦ Πατρός ἐπὶ πᾶσιν εὐδοκίαν καὶ τὴν αὐτουργίαν τοῦ Υἱοῦ συμπληροῦντος."

24. See *AI* 61, 1385D–88A: "Πλὴν ὅτι καὶ τῆς ὅλης κτίσεως, νοητῆς τε καὶ αἰσθητῆς, ἐστὶν εἰκὼν ἡ σκηνή, ἣν ὁ Θεὸς καὶ Πατὴρ, οἷα Νοῦς, ἐνενόησε, καὶ ὁ Υἱὸς, οἷα Λόγος, ἐδημιούργησε, καὶ τὸ Πνεῦμα τὸ Ἅγιον ἐτελείωσε."

25. Hans Urs von Balthasar, *Cosmic Liturgy: The Universe according to Maximus the Confessor*, trans. Brian E. Daley, A Communio Book (San Francisco: Ignatius Press, 2003), 163–64.

26. *QThal* 13.8; *AI* 7, 1085A.

27. For the contingency of creation in Maximus see the passages: *TP25* 272C; *Myst* 103–26. See also the *Disputatio cum Pyrrho*, which is probably not by the hand of Maximus but reflects his thought: Maximus the Confessor, *DP* 293BC; also in Marcel Doucet, "Dispute de Maxime le Confesseur avec Pyrrhus. Introduction, texte critique, traduction et notes" (Ph.D. thesis, Université de Montréal, Institut d'Études Mediévales, 1972), 548–49; *DP* 332A (Doucet 587), 340D (Doucet 596–97).

28. Maximus expresses an antidialectical view in *QThal* 44.43-54; *AI* 7, 1069C. See also *DP* 349CD (Doucet 606-7).

29. According to Maximus, God has three modes of willing. The first is the good will (εὐδοκία) that is closer to the notion of *logos*. The other two are the "economical will" and the will "according to concession" (κατὰ συγχώρησιν), which are closer to the notion of the economical mode since they are making use of evil inside History in order to save man from the fallen state he has reached: *QD* 83.2-7, "Τρία θελήματα ἐπὶ Θεοῦ χρὴ ὑπολαμβάνειν, κατ᾽ εὐδοκίαν, κατ᾽ οἰκονομίαν, κατὰ συγχώρησιν. Καὶ τὸ μὲν κατ᾽ εὐδοκίαν δηλοῖ τὰ κατὰ τὸν Ἀβραάμ, λέγοντα πρὸς αὐτόν, 'ἔξελθε ἐκ τῆς γῆς σου'· τὸ δὲ κατ᾽ οἰκονομίαν δηλοῖ τὰ κατὰ τὸν Ἰωσὴφ οἰκονομηθέντα πρὸς τὴν τῶν μελλόντων ἔκβασιν· τὸ δὲ κατὰ συγχώρησιν δηλοῖ τὰ κατὰ τὸν Ἰὼβ γενόμενα."

30. For a use of Maximian thought on History as a means to avoid totalitarian historicism see Nicholas Loudovikos, Ὀρθοδοξία καὶ ἐκσυγχρονισμός. Βυζαντινὴ ἐξατομίκευση, κράτος καὶ ἱστορία, στὴν προοπτικὴ τοῦ εὐρωπαϊκοῦ μέλλοντος [Orthodoxy and Modernization: Byzantine Individualization, State and History, in the perspective of the European Future] (Athens: Armos, 2006).

31. For the distinction between shadow, image, and truth see *CGn* 1.90, 1120C; *AI* 21, 1253CD; *AI* 37, 1293-96.

32. For an ontology based on an eschatological Christology see John Zizioulas, *Communion and Otherness: Further Studies in Personhood and the Church*, ed. Paul McPartlan (London; New York: T & T Clark, 2006).

33. For this triple schema see the following passages: *QThal* 2, 60.115-30, 61.328-40, 64.755-812; *AI* 7, 1073D; *AI* 65, 1392D; *CChar* 3.24, 4.11, 4.13; *CGn* 1.35, 1096C; 1.51-67, 1101C-8B; 2.88, 1165D.

34. For the notion of *dromos* or *odos* in Maximus see *QThal* 30.37-45, 47.68-227, 48.21, 51.16, 59.255-83, 64.745-54, 65.476; *PN* 721-54; *LA* 1023-33; *CGn* 2.25, 1136C; 2.68-69, 1156B; *AI* 7, 1084; *AI* 10, 1105A, 1113A, 1128CD, 1141B; *AI* 21-22, 1256; *AI* 37, 1292C, 1296D; *AI* 41, 1308A; *AI* 42, 1329.

35. For the relation of the many *logoi* with the One *Logos* see: *QThal* 35.6-24, 40.87-102; *AT* 2, 1037AB; *AI* 6, 1068AB, *AI* 7, 1077C-80A; *AI* 10, 1156AB, 1205C; *AI* 33, 1285C-88; *PN* 521-38; *CGn* 2.10, 1129AB; *Myst* 486-95, 682-91; 997-1009.

36. For the terms *logos*, *tropos*, and *telos*, see, for example, *Myst* 1134-65.

37. *CChar* 3.3, 4.15, 4.44, 4.80.

38. *QThal* 60.1-62. For the relevant Pauline expression see Col 1:26.

39. See *AI* 42, 1345A-C: "πᾶσα φύσις τῷ οἰκείῳ λόγῳ διαπαντὸς ἔχει τὸ τέλος."

40. For the soteriology of adoption by grace in Maximus, see *QThal* 15.28-40, 23.66-84, 61.216-44, 64.155-57; *AI* 10, 1140B, 1156A; *AI* 31, 1280D-81B; *AI* 42, 1348; *PN* 97-106, 258-69; *CGn* 1.77, 1112B; *Myst* 685-91, 752-59, 868, 928-29, 1048-56.

41. Inside History there is a dialogue between man and God. When man denies the divine will, then God might "modify" His own plan in order to save man by taking into account this denial and its results. The primordial will of God, which is also a sort of divine *logos*, is termed "θέλησις κατ᾽ εὐδοκίαν." The economic modes of the

divine will which do not annul but simply modify the primordial divine will are called "θέλησις κατ' οἰκονομίαν καὶ κατὰ συγχώρησιν." See *QD* 83.2–7.

42. See *QThal* 59.165–170.

43. For the Maximian treatment of the relation between image and resemblance, see *AI* 7, 1092B, 1096A; *AI* 10, 1140B; *CChar* 3.25; *CGn* 1.11, 1088A; *TP1* 9A–12A. See also the *DP*, which is probably not by the hand of Maximus but reflects his teachings, 304C (Doucet 561), 324D (Doucet 581).

44. See *TP15* 157A; *TP25* 276B–77B. See also the *DP* 301B–4C (Doucet 558–61).

45. *CGn* 1.3, 1084BC; *AI* 65, 1392AB.

46. For a comprehension of God's *logoi* as God's propositions for nature see Nikolaos Loudovikos, Ἡ κλειστὴ πνευματικότητα καὶ τὸ νόημα τοῦ ἑαυτοῦ. Ὁ μυστικισμὸς τῆς ἰσχύος καὶ ἡ ἀλήθεια φύσεως καὶ προσώπου [Closed Spirituality and the Meaning of the Self: Christian Mysticism of Power and the Truth of Personhood and Nature] (Athens: Ellinika Grammata, 1999), 191.

47. For this subject see the excellent works: Philipp Gabriel Renczes, *Agir de Dieu et liberté de l'homme. Recherches sur l'anthropologie théologique de saint Maxime le Confesseur*, Cogitatio fidei 229 (Paris: Cerf, 2003); David Houston Bradshaw, *Aristotle East and West: Metaphysics and the Division of Christendom* (Cambridge; New York: Cambridge University Press, 2004); Torstein T. Tollefsen, *The Christocentric Cosmology of St. Maximus the Confessor*, Oxford Early Christian Studies (Oxford; New York: Oxford University Press, 2008); Torstein T. Tollefsen, *Activity and Participation in Late Antique and Early Christian Thought* (Oxford: Oxford University Press, 2012).

48. An interesting example of the relation between *hexis* and *energeia* in the domain of human will is given in *TP1*, 17C.

49. See, for example, *QThal* 29.21, 59.28–66.

50. For the relation between essence, movement, and *energeia* see, for example, *CGn* 1.3, 1084BC.

51. See *CGn* 1.35, 1096C–7A.

52. For the particularly Christian conception of the Judaic Sabbath by Maximus see *CGn* 1.35.

53. *CGn* 1.67, 1108B: "Τὰ φαινόμενα πάντα δεῖται σταυροῦ, . . . τὰ δὲ νοούμενα πάντα χρήζει ταφῆς."

54. See the analysis in François-Marie Léthel, *Théologie de l'agonie du Christ. La liberté humaine du Fils de Dieu et son importance sotériologique mises en lumière par saint Maxime le Confesseur*, Théologie historique 52 (Paris: Beauchesne, 1979); Demetrios Bathrellos, *The Byzantine Christ: Person, Nature, and Will in the Christology of Saint Maximus the Confessor*, The Oxford Early Christian Studies (Oxford; New York: Oxford University Press, 2004), 140–47.

55. See Vasilios Betsakos, Στάσις ἀεικίνητος. Ἡ ἀνακαίνιση τῆς Ἀριστοτελικῆς κινήσεως στὴ θεολογία Μαξίμου τοῦ Ὁμολογητοῦ [Ever-Moving Repose: The Renewal of Aristotelian Movement in the Theology of Maximus the Confessor] (Athens: Armos, 2006); Sotiris Mitralexis, *Ever-Moving Repose: A Contemporary Reading of Maximus the Confessor's Theory of Time* (Eugene, OR: Cascade/Wipf & Stock, 2017).

56. For an eschatological twist of Aristotelian teleology see *QThal* 60.1–62; *AI* 7, 1069D.
57. See *CGn* 1.35, 1096C: "Ὅσα δὲ κατ' ἀρετὴν ἐπιστήμη Θεοῦ κατεργάζεται, τελειωθέντα πάλιν κινεῖται πρὸς αὔξησιν. Τὰ γὰρ τέλη αὐτῶν ἑτέρων ἀρχαὶ καθεστήκασιν."
58. See *TP8* 92B; *TP14* 152C; *PN* 721–54.
59. *Myst* 919–21, 950–59.
60. This ideal is expressed in *QThal* 64.747–54: "ὧν δὲ διάθεσις ἡ αὐτή, καὶ ὁ κατ' ἦθος τρόπος καὶ ὁ τοῦ βίου δρόμος εἷς ὑπάρχειν προδήλως πέφυκεν· ὧν δὲ τρόπος ἠθῶν καὶ βίου δρόμος ἐστίν ὁ αὐτός, εἷς δηλονότι καὶ ὁ αὐτὸς κατὰ τὴν γνώμην τῆς πρὸς ἀλλήλους σχέσεως ὑπάρχει δεσμός, κατὰ μίαν τὴν γνώμην ἄγων τοὺς πάντας πρὸς τὸν ἕνα λόγον τῆς φύσεως, ἐν ᾧ παντελῶς οὐκ ἔστιν ἡ νῦν κρατοῦσα τῆς φύσεως διὰ τὴν φιλαυτίαν διαίρεσις."
61. For the relevant eschatological vision of Maximus, see *Myst* 729–37.
62. See, *QThal* 59.159–70.

Chapter Four

The Liturgy behind Liturgies
The Church's Metaphysical Form
David W. Fagerberg

An addiction of the academy is to subdivide for the sake of analysis. I do not condemn this; I do want to complement it. Partitioning is done in order to achieve a certain kind of excellence, and so science apportions its organisms, history its eras, psychology its functions, humanities its arts, philosophy its phenomena, and theology its doctrines. My own field of liturgical studies is no different, having devised assorted ways of examining the little blue liturgy marble as it rolls along through history (or "marbles," plural, as a colleague once corrected me so that he could apply both a diachronic division across eras and a synchronic separation between traditions at any given point.) Liturgy is approached from the perspectives of speech-act, symbol-act, semantics, a history of formularies, cultural artifacts, ritual dynamics, rubrics, chant, art and architecture, sacramentaries, structural comparison, the reception of rites, philology, pagan and Jewish sources, text-context-pretext, linguistics, ecumenism, sacraments, hierarchy, interdisciplinarity, sociopolitical forces, cultural milieu, uncodified rituals, parallel secular rituals, cultural anthropology, practical-pastoral concerns, and probably two or three more have been created since I began writing this sentence.

As I said, I do not condemn this, but I do want to balance it. Specialization within liturgical studies is not my worry; isolation is.

I suggest for our consideration, therefore, that there is something that stands behind these specialty studies and that it also deserves our attention. I will call it the Liturgy behind liturgies. We could equally change the spatial metaphor from "behind" to "under"—there is an under-standing, a substance, a metaphysical form. In the words of the *Catechism of the Catholic Church*, offered here with my emphases added, "If from the beginning Christians have celebrated the Eucharist and *in a form whose substance has not changed* despite the great *diversity of times and liturgies*, it is because we know ourselves to be bound by the command the Lord gave on the eve of his Passion: 'Do this in remembrance of me'" (¶1356). The Liturgy behind liturgies is the metaphysical work and activity of God standing behind the historically contingent units. (The attentive reader will notice the contrast between plural and singular, and the use of capitalization in one case and not the other.) In addition to scrutinizing the diversity of times and liturgies, the evolution of rites, the empirical symbols, we should be interested in understanding the substance of the liturgy.

To develop this thought I will put three people into conversation with each other: two Orthodox writers and one Pope emeritus. Pavel Florensky will speak to us about metaphysical form, Joseph Ratzinger about the ontologically prior Church, and Alexander Schmemann about the living norm or logos of Liturgy.

PAVEL FLORENSKY ON METAPHYSICAL FORM

Fr. Pavel Florensky (1882–1937) produced a series of lectures on the relationship of theology and science, published under the title *At the Watersheds of Thought: the Elements of a Concrete Metaphysics*. An English translation has been made of those lectures that contain his central theological content, published as *At the Crossroads of Science and Mysticism*. Here Florensky seeks to prove that science is compatible with Christian theology and mysticism, a fact appreciated during the Medieval epoch, but forgotten by Renaissance rationalism. Therefore, he borrows the names of these two epochs as names of contrasting world-understandings.

> Every world-understanding has a center of treasure, of the spirit that is more ontological than we ourselves are. Our heart remains with it and begins to receive from it juices of life or death. It determines the main lines of the behavior of our reason, the main angles of our vision; that is, from a certain point of view spiritual objects toward which we orient ourselves are the primary categories according to which our thought is organized, just as a drop has the same composition as the source from which it comes.[1]

A Hegelian reader might automatically think that a movement from one epoch to another is irreversible, but Florensky does not. He speaks of history as having days and nights, neither of which are permanent or irreversible. Russian culture had been through a Renaissance epoch, but in the 1920s Florensky thought "we are now at the threshold of a new Middle Ages. In its depths the Christian world-understanding is medieval."[2] Florensky witnessed this revolution in the scientific thinking of his day and contributed to it by his ideas of discontinuity in science and mathematics.[3] But we do not have to understand this in full in order to look at the contrast he is proposing between the two world-understandings.

The Renaissance worldview tries to establish the rights of man and nature through an autonomy of reason that no longer looks at the whole world's mysteries, it only looks at particular specifics. It operates by fragmentation and isolation. "Biology was rushing toward protoplasms, chemistry toward elements, physics toward atoms. All complex processes were fragmented into parts that were not capable of causing wonder—the most boring of world-views."[4] This approach has been described by others as positivistic, mechanistic, and closed; Florensky describes it as "the *destruction of form* as a real principal."[5] Form is destroyed when one thinks that a thing, and in this case every thing, is only a collection of separate elements. Florensky offers the example of chopping up a curved line into such small parts that each fragment appears straight instead of curved. With divisions made small enough we lose the curve. Then, when we approach the units again, we find ourselves dealing with a broken line instead of a curve and are tricked into thinking that we can reconnect those units in any new way we like. The Renaissance worldview has done this with its study of motion, with its concept of time, with its theory of evolutionism, and more. "Some sort of process is occurring, and we stop it and break it up into a series of instants and see it as if in sectional view."[6] A worldview that wants to nullify form will fragment the whole into parts, leaving no room for anything outside the system, allowing no discontinuous motion, outlawing leaps and creativity. Florensky thinks this is not true to reality.

Therefore, Florensky welcomes a return to a Medieval world-understanding in sciences, ranging from mathematics to biology to physics. "Form is emerging more and more as something that has reality."[7] "Form is the principle that produces the whole diversity of different aspects. The whole precedes the parts, and the parts develop out of the whole."[8] The two world-understandings are contrasted precisely in the relationship they assume between the form and its parts. On the one hand, for Renaissance culture "to be able to negate a form, it is necessary to show that everything consists of separate elements or, in other words, that if we gradually attach some elements to others, a new form will appear."[9] Having lost the curve, and no longer restrained by ontology, we are at liberty to reshuffle the now discontinuous segments into whatever shape we want. On the other hand, Medieval culture understands the addition of elements to bring the form into view. There are parts, yes, but the parts do not *produce* a form, they *reveal* the form. The addition of elements is the condition under which the form can appear, but the form precedes the parts, and determines the parts. In a telling analogy, Florensky describes how a form appears. "For example, Pushkin's poem *Eugene Onegin* precedes its letters and appears in the case of a certain selection of letters, but not in the case of a random collection of letters."[10]

Let me make my application of Florensky forthrightly. I do not oppose specialization in liturgical studies, I only caution against any sort of isolation such as would come from a Renaissance world-understanding. Do not abandon the form for the elements. Just as we should not ignore the curve by breaking the line into tiny pieces that appear straight, and then reorganize them without attention to the curve's metaphysical form, neither should we ignore the Liturgy by breaking it into liturgies with units tiny enough to be studied, and see them without connection to Liturgy's metaphysical form. A Medieval world-understanding would instead start with the belief that the poem precedes the letters, the form controls the elements, and the Liturgy stands behind liturgies. God's Liturgical poem precedes the liturgical elements in it. To understand the parts of liturgy, it is necessary to understand the whole (form) of Liturgy. Liturgical theology seeks to know the substance, the form, that which is ontologically prior to our performance, the metaphysical form of the liturgy, the reason why any parts are connected at all—be they letters in a poem or structural units in a liturgy. Mrs. Murphy could be called a liturgical theologian for being able to read God's poem, even if she cannot make a structural analysis of liturgies. The Liturgy's meaning precedes our analysis of liturgies and should control it.

I am the one to have applied Florensky's Medieval worldview to Liturgy, but he applies his thought to a closely related case. He writes,

> Another example: the Church. Contemporary tendencies aver that the Church is we, the believers. But this is a Protestant opinion. The Church does not exist because we are members of her; she does not owe her existence to us. On the contrary, *she is a metaphysical form*, and we can be members of her or not members of her; the Church's metaphysical reality does not suffer any loss from this.[11]

What is true for Liturgy (vis-à-vis liturgies) is true for Church (vis-à-vis individual Churches). The whole precedes the parts; form determines diverse aspects; Liturgy is the metaphysical form of liturgies; and the Church is ontologically prior to her members. So, we are led to Ratzinger's discussion of the universal Church being ontologically prior to particular Churches.

JOSEPH RATZINGER ON THE ONTOLOGICALLY PRIOR CHURCH

Ratzinger's ecclesiology can be found in many of his writings, but there was a controversy at the turn of the century which prompted him to make explicit defense of ontological ecclesiology. This defense is found in three documents, and it is on these we will concentrate. In 1992, while Ratzinger was Prefect, the Congregation for the Doctrine of the Faith (CDF) issued a "Letter to the Bishops of the Catholic Church on Some Aspects of the Church Understood as Communion" (hereafter Letter). It brought forth some responses by theologians, which in turn led Ratzinger to want to again defend its content. Ratzinger writes, "Since it seems nowadays to have become a veritable duty, for theologians who have any self-confidence, to deliver a negative judgment upon documents issued by the Congregation for the Doctrine of the Faith, such a storm of criticism was unleashed upon it that one could scarcely admit there being anything good in it."[12] In 1999 Walter Kasper published an opinion piece in German asking some questions of clarification, so Ratzinger summarized the Letter's arguments in 2000 in "The Ecclesiology of the Constitution on the Church, Vatican II, 'Lumen Gentium'" (hereafter Ecclesiology Lumen Gentium), and again in 2001 in "The Ecclesiology of Vatican II" (hereafter Ecclesiology Vatican II). In that same year, Kasper repeated his questions for English-speaking audiences in *America* magazine in April, and Ratzinger responded in November.

If we return to the starting document, we find the relevant phrase in the last sentence of paragraph nine of the Letter (italicized below).

> In order to grasp the true meaning of the analogical application of the term communion to the particular Churches taken as a whole, one must bear in mind above all that the particular Churches, insofar as they are "part of the one Church of Christ", have a special relationship of "mutual interiority" with the whole, that is, with the universal Church, because in every particular Church "the one, holy, catholic and apostolic Church of Christ is truly present and active". For this reason, "the universal Church cannot be conceived as the sum of the particular Churches, or as a federation of particular Churches". It is not the result of the communion of the Churches, but, in its essential mystery, it is *a reality ontologically and temporally prior* to every individual particular Church.

The CDF letter concerns the term "communion," which had been somewhat marginal in the texts of the second Vatican Council but was more deliberately used in the 1985 Synod of bishops, and so its use could now benefit from some clarification. The Letter highlights the relationship between the universal and the particular, the whole and the parts, the one and the many, form and diversity. Does the Church universal exist because particular Churches enter into communion with each other? Which takes precedence over which? Is "communion" a juridical, social, political concept, or is it a theological concept?

Ontological ecclesiology had been affirmed before this Letter appeared. Eighteen years earlier (1973) the CDF said in *Mysterium Ecclesia*,[13] "The followers of Christ are therefore not permitted to imagine that Christ's Church is nothing more than a collection (divided, but still possessing a certain unity) of Churches and ecclesial communities. Nor are they free to hold that Christ's Church nowhere really exists today and that it is to be considered only as an end which all Churches and ecclesial communities must strive to reach" (¶ 1). Four years before the Letter (1988) *Christifideles Laici* had said, "The particular Church does not come about from a kind of fragmentation of the universal Church, nor does the universal Church come about by a simple amalgamation of particular Churches. But there is a real, essential and constant bond uniting each of them and this is why the universal Church exists and is manifested in the particular Churches" (¶ 25). In other words (mine), the Church is *neither fractionated nor federated*. Rather, the universal Church is fully present in each particular Church.

Ratzinger acknowledges that this ecclesiology of communion is profoundly Eucharistic, and "it is thus quite close to the eucharistic ecclesiology that Orthodox theologians have so impressively developed in the twentieth century."[14] But they applied it to another purpose. "The idea of eucharistic ecclesiology was stated first of all in the Orthodox theology of exiled Russian theologians and, furthermore, was set in opposition to the alleged Roman centralism."[15] A word of clarification is therefore in order at the outset. Whereas some theologians (Kasper) were objecting that the CDF Letter was covertly identifying the universal Church with the Church of Rome; whereas this is a central ecumenical sticking point between Churches of the East and West; and whereas I am engaging Ratzinger as a conversation partner with two Orthodox theologians, I should let Ratzinger forestall any misunderstanding. In his reply to Kasper in *America* he insists: "The letter from the congregation never dreamt of identifying the reality of the universal church with the Pope and curia." "The assertion of the inner precedents of God's idea of the one church, the one bride, over all its empirical realizations in particular churches has nothing whatsoever to do with the problem of centralism." "If one strips away all the false associations with church politics from the concept of the universal church and grasps it in its true theological (and hence quite concrete) content . . . then one can no longer also say that the 'universalistic view' of the church is 'ecumenically off-putting.'"[16]

If not covert papal centralism, then what is the purpose of saying the universal Church is ontologically and temporally prior to particular, local Churches? I suggest the purpose is to see the Church as a work of God instead of a work of man. Of course, human agency cooperates, and in that sense the Church may be compared "by no weak analogy," says *Lumen Gentium*, to the mystery of the incarnate Word. "As the assumed nature inseparably united to Him, serves the divine Word as a living organ of salvation, so, in a similar way, does the visible social structure of the Church serve the Spirit of Christ, who vivifies it, in the building up of the body" (LG ¶8). The Church is spiritual, heavenly, divine, and is vivified by the Spirit of Christ; the Church is also visible, earthly, human, and exists on a social plane. The latter serves the former, as the assumed nature serves the divine Word, but the former needs the latter in order to have its impact. Speaking of the Church, Ratzinger therefore affirms both sides: "This Word is set above the Church, and yet it is within her and is entrusted to her as a living agent. In order to be present and effective in history, the Word of God needs this agent, and yet the agent for her part cannot exist without the life-giving power of the Word—indeed, it is this that makes her a living agent."[17] Speaking of the Liturgy, we shall say that to be effectively present in history Liturgy needs liturgies, but liturgies on their part do not subsist without the vital life-giving force of the Word, making Liturgy an *opus Dei* that flows within the historical liturgies. The human being knows he is receiver and not initiator of either Church or Liturgy. One does not make the Church, one receives her; one does not produce the Liturgy, one receives it. In my search for a definition of Liturgy that would indicate this ontologically prior status, I have arrived at defining liturgy as "perichoresis of the Trinity kenotically extended to invite our synergistic ascent into deification."[18] Membership in particular Churches gives one membership in the universal Church; celebrating particular liturgies is celebrating the Liturgy. Yes, there is a synergy between the divine-human elements in Church and Liturgy, but in this cooperation God energizes and man synergizes. God's work is prior, ontologically and temporally.

So when Ratzinger re-explains the CDF's Letter, he begins with the image of the Church as mystical body, which brings him directly to the Eucharist. "*The liturgy is her form*—this means that within her there is a proper relation between multiplicity and unity that occurs nowhere else. In every celebration of the Eucharist, the Lord is entirely present. . . . He always gives himself whole and undivided."[19] The Letter upholds the patristic notion that God was forming the mystical body from the beginning of creation; in fact, the Church is the reason for creation—that is how prior she is! "Indeed, according to the Fathers, ontologically, the Church-mystery, the Church that is one and unique, precedes creation, and gives birth to the particular Churches as her daughters."[20] Ratzinger repeats this point in both of his talks, nearly word for word:

> Since the Fathers were fully persuaded that Israel and the Church were ultimately identical, they could not regard the Church as something that came into being at a late hour, by chance, but recognized in this gathering of the nations under the will of God the inner goal of creation. . . . [History] is interpreted . . . as a love

story involving God and man. God finds for himself a bride for the Son, the one bride who is the one church. . . . The one body of Christ is prepared for him; Christ and the Church will "become one flesh", will be one body, and thus God will become "everything to everyone".[21]

The Church is a divine artifact, and creation itself was for the purpose of bringing this bride into being. This is so obvious to Ratzinger that he says he finds it difficult to understand the objections being raised against it. "They seem to me to be possible at all only if one refuses to see God's great idea, the Church."[22]

I propose the following parallel to Liturgy. It, too, is a great work conceived by God, a divine artifact—an *opus Dei*.[23] Liturgy is not a species in the genus of human religions; Liturgy is the cult of the new Adam perpetuated in his Mystical Body. That is why baptism is required in order to commit Liturgy. What Ratzinger fears could happen to ecclesiology if the universal Church loses its ontological priority could equally happen to liturgical theology if Liturgy loses its metaphysical form. We can observe the parallelism by quoting what he says about the Church and inserting brackets to provoke us into thinking about Liturgy alongside his comments. The Church [Liturgy] then appears

> as the product of a fit of theological enthusiasm, and all that remains is the empirical structure of the Church [Liturgy empirically studied], her elements side-by-side in all their confusion and contradiction [conflicting liturgies]. Yet that means that the Church is [Liturgy is] ruled out as a theme of theology at all. If you can no longer see the Church [Liturgy] except as existing in human organizations [human ritual liturgies], then hopelessness is in fact all there is left.[24]

If Liturgy as a theological subject is obliterated, such that all remains is the empirical study of liturgies, then we would only be left with human organization. If Liturgy's theological dimension is cancelled, then we are left with an empirical image of mutually related liturgical activities, perhaps in conflict from one century to another, from one tradition to another. If there is no One behind the many, an orthodoxy behind diverse worship practices, a Liturgy ontologically prior to liturgies, then form would be destroyed as a real principal and the elements would lose their control, as Florensky feared could happen. Minus theology, ecclesiology would become ecclesiasticism; minus theology, Liturgy would become ritualism.

A mother is prior to the children she births; the universal Church is prior to Churches and individual believers; and the Liturgy is the prior metaphysical form of all liturgies. The Church transacts Liturgy and coming into the one Church is to come into the one substance of that Liturgy, despite the great diversity of times and liturgies (CCC ¶1356). This accounts for a recommendation Ratzinger has to offer to liturgical studies today.

Theology and liturgy each suffer if isolated from the other, a problem, Ratzinger admits, sometimes found in the Western Church. On the one hand, "medieval theology had already detached the theological study of the sacraments to a large extent from their administration in divine worship,"[25] with the result that sacramentology occupied itself with institution, sign, effect, minister, and recipient, paying little attention to the liturgical celebration. On the other hand, "'liturgics' (to the extent that one could speak of such a thing) became the study of the prevailing norms in divine worship and thus came close to being a sort of juridical positivism."[26] Ratzinger experienced the Liturgical Movement as an attempt to overcome this mutual isolation. It sought to think of liturgy as something more than an accidental collection of ceremonies; liturgy was, rather, the "organically developed and suitable expression of the sacrament in the worship celebration. The Constitution on the Sacred Liturgy of Vatican II set forth this synthesis in an impressive, albeit very concise, manner."[27] He also sees the *Catechism* as resolving to move from liturgies to the Liturgy behind them. "A catechism that intends (as ours does) to be 'catholic' in the strict sense, a catechism that is addressed to the one Church with her many rites, cannot give a privileged place to one rite exclusively" and that is why it took into consideration "the entire breadth of tradition."[28]

Alas, we are still quite far from the synthesis of liturgy and theology that the Council and the Constitution desired. "Liturgical studies once again have tended to detach themselves from dogmatic theology and to set themselves up as a sort of technique for worship celebrations. Conversely, dogmatic theology has not yet convincingly taken up the subject of its liturgical dimension, either."[29] Neither liturgy nor theology pay heed to each other, and, interestingly, this complaint finds a parallel in one of Florensky's descriptions. For him, the truths of Liturgy are formal theological truths, deriving from the Church herself as metaphysical form. We could see these truths if our eyes looked at the poem instead of the individual words: we could read dogma in liturgies. But, he laments,

> At present, we still do not have a liturgical theology, that is, a systematization of the theological ideas contained in our liturgy. But the Church's living self-consciousness is precisely there, for the liturgy is the flower of Church life and also its root and seed. What richness of ideas and new concepts in the domain of dogmatics, what abundance of profound psychological observations and moral guidance could be gathered here even by a not very diligent investigator! Yes, liturgical theology awaits its creator.[30]

The metaphysical form of Christian identity, Florensky will go on to say, is the Church's living self-consciousness, and the Church's own consciousness of that "living norm" of Liturgy is what Schmemann sought to find.

SCHMEMANN AND THE LIVING NORM OR LOGOS OF LITURGY

Schmemann also sees Church as ontologically prior to her ministries and liturgies. He expresses the thought in an essay concerning the temptation to slide into juridical definitions.

> The Church cannot be reduced to "jurisdiction." She is a living organism and her continuity is precisely that of life. The function of the Episcopate and of "power" in general is to preserve, defend and express this continuity in fullness of life, but it is a function *within* and not *above* the Church. The ministry of power does not *create* the church but is created by God within the Church, which is ontologically prior to all functions, charisms and ministries.[31]

The ministry of power is easier to see (as are liturgies), but the living Church is ontologically prior to it and gives form to ministries (as Liturgy gives form to liturgies). In this sense, the Church is sacramental for having both a visible dimension and a spiritual dimension.

> On the one hand the Church is certainly structure and institution, order and hierarchy, canons and chanceries. Yet this is only the visible structure. What is its content? Is it not also, and primarily, that which is to change and to transfigure life itself? Is it not the anticipation, the "Sacrament" of the kingdom of God? Yes, the Church is structure, but the unique purpose of that structure is to be an "epiphany," to manifest and to fulfill the Church as expectation and fulfillment.

In this sense, Liturgy is sacramental for having both a visible dimension and a spiritual dimension.

> It is, of course, in worship that this experience of the Church is given. It is in her *leitourgia* that the Church transcends herself as institution and structure and becomes "that which she is": response, adoration, encounter, presence, glory, and, ultimately, a mystical marriage between God and his new creation. It is precisely here that Mary stands at the center—as the personification, as the very expression, icon, and content of that response, that the very depth of man's "yes" to God in Christ.[32]

When I have wanted to distinguish the metaphysical form from contingent liturgies I have used Liturgy (singular, capitalized); Schmemann often resorts to the Greek *leitourgia*. "If Christian worship is *leitourgia*, it cannot be simply reduced to, or expressed in terms of, 'cult.' The ancient world knew a plethora of cultic religions or 'cults'. . . . But the Christian cult is *leitourgia*, and this means that it is *functional* in its essence, has a goal to achieve which transcends the categories of cult as such."[33] *Leitourgia* should extend beyond our fascination with liturgies. "One may be deeply attached to the 'ancient and colorful rites' of Byzantium or Russia, see in them precious relics of a cherished past, be a liturgical 'conservative'; and, at the same time, completely fail to see in them, in the totality of the Church's *leitourgia*, an all-embracing vision of life, a power meant to judge, inform and transform the whole of existence."[34] *Leitourgia* transcends the categories of cult as such, but how? Liturgy, in its essence, is eschatological, and liturgical theology is the discovery of that transcendent fact.

> *This* is the essence of Christianity as Eschatology. The Kingdom of God is the goal of history, and the Kingdom of God is already now *among us, within us*. Christianity is a unique historical event, and Christianity is the presence of that event as the completion of all events and of history itself. . . .
> Here is, for me, *the whole meaning of liturgical theology*. The Liturgy: the joining, revelation, actualization of the historicity of Christianity (remembrance) and of its transcendence over that historicity.[35]

This Liturgical woof is woven into the warp of every liturgy. The metaphysical form runs through every liturgical, cultic act. *Leitourgia* stands behind every liturgical action, and Schmemann was attentive to it from his first book onward.

In *Introduction to Liturgical Theology* he states that he wants to find the living norm or logos behind the worship activities.

> To find the Ordo behind the 'rubrics,' regulations and rules—to find the unchanging principle, the living norm or 'logos' of worship as a whole, within what is accidental and temporary: this is the primary task which faces those who regard liturgical theology not as the collecting of accidental and arbitrary explanations of services but as the systematic study of the *lex orandi* of the Church. This is nothing but the search for or identification of that element of the *Typicon* which is presupposed by its whole content, rather than contained by it.[36]

He advocates a search for the Ordo behind the rubrics, the Liturgy behind the liturgy, the logos behind what is accidental, the living norm behind the developing cult, the metaphysical form behind the diversity of expression, the *lex orandi* that is the ontological condition for theology. "Liturgical tradition is not an 'authority' or a *locus theologicus;* it is the ontological condition of theology, of the proper understanding of *kerygma,* of the Word of God."[37]

Liturgy is the ontological condition of theology "because it is in the Church, of which the *leitourgia* is the expression and the life, that the sources of theology are functioning as precisely 'sources.'"[38]

The Church is expressed and lived in *leitourgia*, and this is the subject matter of liturgical theology, which explores in depth the connection between liturgies, theology, and piety. Readers of Schmemann often misunderstand this (and mistakenly suppose he only wants to talk about worship, instead).

> Finally one may ask: but what do you propose, what do you want? To this I will answer without much hope, I confess, of being heard and understood: we need liturgical theology, viewed not as a theology of worship and not as a reduction of theology to liturgy, but as a slow and patient bringing together of that which was for too long a time and because of many factors broken and isolated—liturgy, theology, and piety, their reintegration within one fundamental vision. In this sense liturgical theology is an illegitimate child of a broken family. It exists, or maybe I should say it ought to exist, only because theology ceased to seek in the *lex orandi* its source and food, because liturgy ceased to be conducive to theology.[39]

The isolation he bemoans is not the result of a subdivision of academic labor, it occurs on a more fundamental level. If liturgy is isolated from theology and piety, then it can be kept in the laboratory for examination and be divorced from theology and piety. Here is a repeated description of the problem:

> The goal of liturgical theology, as its very name indicates, is to overcome the fateful divorce between theology, liturgy and piety—a divorce which, as we have already tried to show elsewhere, has had disastrous consequences for theology as well as for liturgy and piety. It deprived liturgy of its proper understanding by the people, who began to see in it beautiful and mysterious ceremonies in which, while attending them, they take no real part. It deprived theology of its living source and made it into an intellectual exercise for intellectuals. It deprived piety of its living content and term of reference.[40]

It can happen, and it has happened, that liturgy, theology, and piety twirl in their own spheres without touching each other. Then each of them deteriorates. Separate *liturgy* from theology and piety, and believers expect nothing but a mysterious ceremony that they cannot understand and in which they take no real part; separate *theology* from liturgy and piety, and it becomes an intellectual exercise for a privileged group of academics; separate *piety* from liturgy and theology, and it loses its living content and term of reference. It can happen, and it has happened, that liturgy becomes an object of historical and ritual investigation, theology becomes the province of academic sacramentology, and piety gets along without either of them as easily as the academics get along without piety. The three spin under centripetal force, but what counterforce could unite them?

Schmemann has called that unifying counterforce "liturgical theology" and by this he does not mean information (of history, of ritual phenomenology, of symbol performance, etc.). He means "a return to that vision and experience that from the beginning constituted the very life of the Church."[41] I conclude that understanding Liturgy is not so much a cogitation as it is a vision. In his *Journals* Schmemann asks himself what is absolute in Orthodoxy, and he answers himself, "I always come to the same conclusion: it is first of all a certain *vision*, an experience of God, the world, the man. The best in Orthodox theology is about that vision."[42] To understand the Liturgy behind liturgies is to be "given the vision of the Kingdom of God, as fulfillment in Him of all that exists, of all that He has created for Himself, and also we are made partakers of that new Reality. And having seen and tasted of the 'heaven and earth as full of His glory' we are then to relate all life, all activity, all time to this vision and experience, to judge and to transform our life by it."[43] Seen and tasted, it does not need didactic explanation.

> Pascha. Holy Week. Essentially, bright days such as are needed. And truly that is all that is needed. I am convinced that if people would really hear Holy Week, Pascha, the Resurrection, Pentecost, the Dormition, there would be no need for theology. All of theology is there. All that is needed for one's spirit, heart, mind and soul. How could people spend centuries discussing justification and redemption? It's all in these services. Not only is it revealed, it simply flows in one's heart and mind.[44]

CONCLUSION

Is there justification for associating the ontologically prior status of Church with the ontological-metaphysical form of Liturgy? I conclude with a category from Florensky that seems to do so.

Florensky's other classic work is titled *The Pillar and Ground of the Truth*. It consists of twenty-three letters (chapters), and the first is addressed "To the Reader." In the first sentence of the book he explains his project to the reader: "Living religious experience as the sole legitimate way to gain knowledge of the dogmas—that is how I would like to express the general theme of my book or, rather, my jottings."[45] Lived religious experience is prior to knowledge of dogmas, therefore with trepidation he asks, "Who am I to write about what is holy?"[46] Instead he chooses to bring us nourishment from our Mother's hand. The Holy Church is a treasure house, and in her, our

Mother, has been deposited over the centuries secret yearnings, joys of communion, torments of ardent repentance, the fragrance of prayer, quiet longing for heaven, and eternal seeking and eternal finding. Florensky has a name for this treasure house: "Ecclesiality—that is the name of the refuge where the heart's anxiety finds peace, where the pretensions of the rational mind are tamed, where great tranquility descends into our reason."[47]

The Russian word is *tserkovnost*, but it is not easy to translate. (Some have rendered it as *church-mindedness*, and the translator of this book, Boris Jakim, skilled as he is, resigns himself to expressing it as a mathematical formulation: "Ecclesiality = spiritual life."[48]) Florensky admits that it is not easy to define even in the Russian tongue.

> Let it be the case that neither I nor anyone else can define what ecclesiality is! . . . Indeed, do not its very indefinability, its ungraspableness in logical terms, its ineffability prove that ecclesiality is life, a special, new life, which is given to man, but which, like all life, is inaccessible to the rational mind? . . . How then can this "fullness" of Divine life be packed into a narrow coffin of logical definition?[49]

Its indefinability means it cannot be listed among the subdivisions in liturgical studies. Yet even if ecclesiality cannot be conceptualized, it is the most definite thing that every living member of the Church knows. "Orthodoxy is shown, not proved,"[50] and Florensky has in mind what we are shown by spiritual elders who are the masters of the "art of arts" (asceticism).[51] He finally blurts out, "What is ecclesiality? It is a new life, life in the Spirit. What is the criterion of the rightness of this life? Beauty. Yes, there is a special beauty of the spirit, and, ungraspable by logical formulas, it is at the same time the only true path to the definition of what is orthodox and what is not orthodox."[52]

Clement of Alexandria said understanding is the sight of the soul—and I propose this is the requirement placed upon liturgical theology if it is to catch sight of Liturgy in liturgies. It is a vision of Church in Liturgy behind the liturgies done by Churches. Ecclesiality is a form of life—a metaphysical form—that comes to appearance in historical vicissitudes. Ecclesiality "is prior to all its separate manifestations. . . . it is the Divine-human element out of which the sacraments, the dogmas, the canons, and even to some degree the temporary, everyday routine of the Church has been crystallized in the course of Church history."[53] The many crystallizations are studied by academic theology, but they come out of a whole, a form, a Divine-human element. We do not analyze ecclesiality, footnote or compare or scrutinize it; we must die and be reborn into it. The Liturgy behind all liturgies is where we imbibe of ecclesiality. When the ecclesiality of Liturgy has been grasped, then the meaning of liturgies will become evident.

NOTES

1. Pavel Florensky, *At the Crossroads of Science and Mysticism* (New York: Semantron Press, 2014), 120. In addition to the two works we will examine more closely, the reader is directed to *Iconostasis* (Crestwood, NY: Saint Vladimir's Seminary Press, 1996) and a collection of essays edited by Nicoletta Misler, *Beyond Vision: Essays on the Perception of Art* (London: Reaktion Books, 2002). See also a recent biography by Avril Pyman, *Pavel Florensky: A Quiet Genius* (New York: Continuum Publishing, 2010) and a study by Robert Slesinki, *Pavel Florensky: A Metaphysics of Love* (Crestwood, NY: Saint Vladimir's Seminary Press, 1984). He is described as "a mathematical genius who became famous in the fields of astronomy, physics and electrical engineering; a gifted poet, musician and art historian; a linguist and etymologist who mastered Greek, Latin, most of the modern European languages and those of the Caucacus, Iran and India; as well as an original theological thinker and metaphysician" by Abbot Herman and Fr. Damascene in their introduction to Florensky's book, *Salt of the Earth* (Platina, CA: St. Herman of Alaska Brotherhood, 1999), 9.

2. Florensky, *At the Crossroads*, 7.

3. His 1904 thesis had been titled, "On the Peculiarities of Flat Curves as Places of Interrupted Discontinuity."

4. Florensky, *At the Crossroads*, 21–22.

5. Florensky, *At the Crossroads*, 23, emphasis added.

6. Florensky, *At the Crossroads*, 29.

7. Florensky, *At the Crossroads*, 33.

8. Florensky, *At the Crossroads*, 24.

9. Florensky, *At the Crossroads*, 25.

10. Ibid.

11. Florensky, *At the Crossroads* 24–25, emphasis added.

12. Joseph Ratzinger, "The Ecclesiology of the Constitution Lumen Gentium," in *Pilgrim Fellowship of Faith: The Church as Communion*, ed. Stephan Otto Horn and Vinzenz Pfnur, trans. Henry Taylor (San Francisco: Ignatius Press, 2005), 133.

13. "Declaration in Defense of the Catholic Doctrine on the Church against Certain Errors of the Present Today."

14. Ratzinger, "Ecclesiology Lumen Gentium," 131.

15. Ratzinger, "The Ecclesiology of the Second Vatican Council," in *Church, Ecumenism and Politics: New Endeavors in Ecclesiology*, trans. Michael J. Miller et al. (San Francisco: Ignatius Press, 2008), 18.

16. All these quotations are from Ratzinger's reply to Kasper in *America* vol. 185, no. 16, Nov 19, 2001. I present them following their editor's practice of not capitalizing "church."

17. Ratzinger, "Ecclesiology Lumen Gentium," 142.

18. David Fagerberg, *On Liturgical Asceticism* (Washington, DC: The Catholic University of America Press, 2013), 9. It is conditioned by two other definitions that pay due attention to Liturgy's ontological status. The first is from Pope Pius XII. "The sacred liturgy is, consequently, the public worship which our Redeemer as Head of

the Church renders to the Father, as well as the worship which the community of the faithful renders to its Founder, and through Him to the heavenly Father. It is, in short, the worship rendered by the Mystical Body of Christ in the entirety of its Head and members" (*Mediator Dei* ¶ 20). The second is from the dean of the liturgical movement in America, Fr. Virgil Michel: "The liturgy, through Christ, comes from the Father, the eternal source of the divine life in the Trinity. It in turn addresses itself in a special way to the Father, rendering him the homage and the glory of which it is capable through the power of Christ. The flow of divine life between the eternal Father and the Church is achieved and completed through the operation of the Holy Ghost. The liturgy, reaching from God to man, and connecting man to the fullness of the Godhead, is the action of the Trinity in the Church. The Church in her liturgy partakes of the life of the divine society of the three persons in God" (*The Liturgy of the Church* [New York: The MacMillan Company, 1937], 40).

19. Ratzinger, Ecclesiology of the Second Vatican Council, 18. Emphasis added to suggest connection with Florensky's point.

20. The next subsection of paragraph ¶9.

21. Ratzinger, "Ecclesiology Lumen Gentium," 134.

22. Ratzinger, "Ecclesiology Lumen Gentium," 135.

23. Of course liturgies change, but the Liturgy does not if it is God's work. To suggest it changes is like asking what new *opus* the old *Dei* will be up to in this century.

24. Ratzinger, "Ecclesiology Lumen Gentium," 135.

25. Joseph Ratzinger, *On the Way to Jesus Christ*, trans. Michael J. Miller (San Francisco: Ignatius Press, 2005), 153. All these quotes appear in the context of Ratzinger discussing the presentation of sacramental doctrine in the Catechism.

26. Ratzinger, *On the Way*, 154.

27. Ibid.

28. Ratzinger, *On the Way*, 155.

29. Ratzinger, *On the Way*, 154.

30. Pavel Florensky, *The Pillar and Ground of the Truth* (Princeton: Princeton University Press, 1997), 217–18.

31. Alexander Schmemann, "Problems of Orthodoxy in America: The Canonical Problem," in *St. Vladimir's Seminary Quarterly*, vol. 8, no. 2, 1964, 71. I preserved Schmemann's upper and lower case use of Church and church.

32. Alexander Schmemann, *Celebration of Faith*, vol. 3, *The Virgin Mary* (Crestwood: St. Vladimir's Seminary Press, 1995), 64–65.

33. Alexander Schmemann, "Theology and Eucharist," in *Liturgy and Tradition*, ed. Thomas Fisch (Crestwood, NY: St. Vladimir's Seminary Press, 1990), 79.

34. Alexander Schmemann, "Liturgy and Theology," in *Liturgy and Tradition*, ed. Thomas Fisch (Crestwood, NY: St. Vladimir's Seminary Press, 1990), 51–52.

35. Alexander Schmemann, *The Journals of Father Alexander Schmemann 1973–1983*, trans. Juliana Schmemann (Crestwood, NY: St. Vladimir's Seminary Press, 1990; Crestwood, NY: St. Vladimir's Seminary Press, 2002), 234.

36. Alexander Schmemann, *Introduction to Liturgical Theology*, trans. Asheleigh E. Moorhouse (Crestwood, NY: St. Vladimir's Seminary Press, 1966), 32–33.

37. Alexander Schmemann, "Theology and Liturgical Tradition," in *Liturgy and Tradition*, ed. Thomas Fisch (Crestwood, NY: St. Vladimir's Seminary Press, 1990), 18.

38. Ibid.

39. Alexander Schmemann, "Liturgical Theology, Theology of Liturgy, and Liturgical Reform," in *Liturgy and Tradition*, ed. Thomas Fisch (Crestwood, NY: St. Vladimir's Seminary Press, 1990), 46.

40. Alexander Schmemann, *Of Water and the Spirit* (Crestwood, NY: St. Vladimir Seminary Press, 1974), 12. The reference he makes to "having tried to show elsewhere" is to his book, *Introduction to Liturgical Theology*.

41. Preface to Alexander Schmemann, *The Eucharist* (Crestwood, NY: St. Vladimir's Seminary Press, 1990), 9.

42. Schmemann, *Journals*, 89.

43. Schmemann, "Problems of Orthodoxy in America: II. The Liturgical Problem," in *Vladimir's Seminary Quarterly*, vol. 8, no. 4, 1964, 173.

44. Schmemann, *Journals*, 13.

45. Florensky, *Pillar and Ground*, 5.

46. Florensky, *Pillar and Ground*, 6.

47. Florensky, *Pillar and Ground*, 7.

48. Ibid., footnote d.

49. Ibid.

50. Florensky, *Pillar and Ground*, 9.

51. Florensky describes his relationship with the starets Isidore in his book, *Salt of the Earth, an Encounter with a Holy Russian Elder: Isidore of Gethsemane Hermitage* (Platina, CA: Saint Herman of Alaska Brotherhood, 1987).

52. Florensky, *Pillar and Ground*, 8.

53. Florensky, *Pillar and Ground*, 7.

Chapter Five

The Kantian "Two-Images" Problem, Its Lesson for Christian Eschatology, and the Path of Maximian Analogy

Demetrios Harper

As R. G. Collingwood demonstrates in his classic, *The Idea of History,* Immanuel Kant's expectant and forward-looking views of history conform to the inclinations of the post-Renaissance scientific perspective and the Rousseauian utopian vision, both of which regard past human events and civilizations with a critical eye, as bastions of irrationality and superstition.[1] While Kant cannot be regarded as a philosopher of history, having dedicated only one short essay to the topic, he concretizes many philosophical tendencies that inform his successor and critic, Georg Hegel,[2] and exemplifies early examples of philosophical presuppositions that are at work in the systems of an array of thinkers today, within both Christian and secular spheres. As I hope to show in this chapter, Kant's single work on history, *Idea for a Universal History with a Cosmopolitan Aim,* is driven by what thinkers like Robert Hanna refer to as the "two-images problem," an expression which is used to describe the seemingly perennial conflict between self-legislating subjectivity and the system of nature in Kantian thought.[3] This conflict, in the opinion of Robert Pippin, persists in various forms not only in philosophy but in the mind-set of the typical Westerner, if not between nature and subjectivity, then between general heteronomy and autonomous subjectivity.[4] Nevertheless, and despite this antinomy, Kant's *Idea of a Universal History* expresses the hope that a temporal "eschatological" state of utopia may be achieved in the distant future. This utopian ideal will come to pass if and only if human beings learn to overcome *autonomously* the despotism of nature,[5] a hope that is driven in Kant's third *Critique* by the regulative ideal which suggests that there may be unconditional truth lurking just beyond our immediate sphere of intuition.[6] Until such a time, however, this metaphysical or transcendental utopia is a mere aspiration, something that may encourage us to self-legislate *as though* it will happen, but which is no more certain than the noumenal realm from which we are so thoroughly and inextricably disconnected. If Kant proposes that we must orient ourselves as though there is ontological purposefulness in the movements of the cosmos, what he actually offers in relation to history and its purpose is quite modest. Perhaps Kant himself hoped for more, but all he proposes in relation to history is a temporal utopia, a party where the Creator still plays the role of *Deus Absconditus* (the hidden God). In an effort to offer an alternative perspective to the ontological void created within the flow of history by Kant's transcendental agnosticism, this chapter will briefly examine and comment upon the orientation of Maximus the Confessor's eschatological perspective with special reference to his use of *mimesis*. In so doing, it shall rely on a reading of the Confessor's work that affirms the inherent interrelatedness of nature's destiny to humanity's deified end and, consequently, the rather different way in which he conceived of ontology and history. Doubtless, this reading will be as unwelcome to some schools of thought as it will be welcome to others.

The manifestation of the inherent tension between the conflicting but apparently equally viable images of human subjectivity and natural causality in the mature thought of Immanuel Kant marks, in the views of some, the disruption of a previously harmonious but perhaps mistaken view of being. In particular, his philosophical critiques target the views of thinkers like Wolff and Leibniz, the views of whom accord the human subject a clear position of meaning in relation to the larger purpose of nature.[7] The conflict within the two-images problem arises from what Kant perceives to be an antinomy between necessitating forces of nature and the human subject's attempt to legislate him- or herself beyond its movements, expressing a continuous dialectical process in which the subject seeks to resist the heteronomy of animal impulses in favor of the establishment of autonomous rational ends.[8] On the one hand, the human subject's intellectual range is restricted to a scientific awareness of the phenomenal realm of Newtonian natural processes where he or she encounters natural law and its apparently inexorable determinism. On the other hand, Kant locates the hermeneutical precepts and structures for engagement within the transcendental capacity of the human subject himself or herself, securing, in his view, the metaphysical integrity of free, self-legislating human subjectivity beyond the necessitated movements of organic and inorganic natural forces.[9] These two competing systems of nature and freedom have quite naturally facilitated differing philosophical responses, encouraging, on the one hand, the tendency of thinkers like W. V. Quine or Bertrand Russell toward a strongly positivistic approach, but, on the other, simultaneously supporting what Robert Pippin describes as "persistent subjectivity" with an emphasis upon self-determining anthropocentricity.[10] As Pippin argues, this anthropocentric tendency emerges and is propagated in the Enlightenment by Rousseau, and it is concretized in the thought of Immanuel Kant, remaining an enduring feature of not only subsequent philosophical schools of thought but also of Western bourgeois culture in general.[11] It is noteworthy that Kant begins his devastating *Critique of Pure Reason* with an anthropocentric affirmation of belief, a feature of Kantian thought that is often overlooked. Scientific knowing (*Wissen*) has to allow room for belief (*Glauben*), which is what assists the human subject's attempt to establish natural superiority in the world and be distinctively human, distinguishing him or herself from both mechanical and organic causality.[12] In order to be consistent with the rest of the *Critique*'s epistemological restrictions, Kant grants that beliefs are only subjectively sufficient and unverifiable, but, nevertheless, provide the impetus for the human subject to not only strive for autonomous rational ends but also to explore the phenomenal world.[13] Put in another way, beliefs fall under the category of regulative ideals, precepts that enable the human being to live as though there is a Creator, as if we have immortal souls, and as though an intelligible realm lurks behind the veil of the phenomenal. More pertinent to the topic at hand, we also exist as if the realization of a universal human utopia is truly attainable.

The upshot of this antinomy between nature and subjectivity is that in order for the human subject to be free, he or she, guided by regulative ideals, must legislate ends that are distinct from those established by nature. As Kant argues in his third and final *Critique,* nature's impersonal ends are indifferent to human happiness and the human subject's particular realization, and, thus, cannot coincide with those of the self-legislating subject.[14] Metaphysical realization of the human subject is a transcendental reality, occurring outside the "domain of natural causation"[15] and transcendentally elevated beyond the nonrational movements of the natural aspect of the human being. This division of the human being into two distinct selves is a critical point and should not be passed over lightly. If, as Kant vociferously affirms in his third *Critique*, there is an insuperable gulf fixed between the realms of human freedom and nature and the human subject must learn to acquire an indifference to the "despotism of desire," the natural aspects of the human being must also be repudiated practically and regarded as having an end that is other than that of the metaphysical or noumenal self.[16] While it should also be noted that Kant holds out hope that there might be a way toward a certain complementarity between these antinomies, which is the stated purpose of his intellectually demanding third *Critique*, in practice this is a regulative ideal both epistemologically and morally speaking. A system of meaning that can lay claim to a coherent theory of everything remains elusive, and real human ends are restricted to the moral legislation of the noumenal self in opposition to the persistent nonrational drives of nature. This restriction of metaphysics to the rational movements of the human subject places morality in the seat of humanity's foremost philosophical concern at the expense, as Christos Yannaras has rightly noted, of humanity's participation in a larger ontological perspective.[17] Paul Guyer encapsulates this Kantian view well when he says that the structure of the human subject's self-legislation is teleological, but it is such in an entirely internalized and deontological sense as it can neither constrain nor be connected to nature's ends.[18] Moreover, and perhaps most significantly, human self-legislation does not and, indeed, must not respond to ontological or moral archetypes, a notion that is also particularly prominent in Kantian moral theory. The first and most obvious reason for the repudiation of archetypes is Kant's epistemological detachment of metaphysics and ontology, restricting the former to the domain of subjectivity while consigning the latter to the realm of the unknown or, perhaps, a place of relevance in the form of belief. As Kant argues in his *Groundwork*, "we cannot intuit God's [ontological or moral] perfection"[19] and must derive it from our own concepts, which we presumably achieve in conjunction with the encouragement of our belief that there really is some sort of ideal of divine perfection. The second but closely connected reason has to do with the fact that a response to an external paradigm would constitute a violation of the meaning-making subject's autonomy, or, his or her ability to legislate morals. Even "the Holy one of the gospel," the exemplar of moral perfection, Christ himself, is subordinate to objective moral principles and our autonomous ability to legislate them.[20] Imitation or *mimesis* of any virtuous paradigm, Kant tells us again in the *Groundwork*, has no place in morality and by extension no place in the meaning-making process other than, perhaps, to provide us with a measure of encouragement that there is some hope that we might be able to legislate our way to moral ends.[21] Determining a moral course of action on the basis of an external moral exemplar falls under the category of *heteronomy* and is equivalent to acting exclusively on the basis of a natural desire or urge.[22] The properly functioning human subject is wholly independent and self-sufficient in relation to *all* heteronomous influences, whether natural, social, familial, religious, or even divine. Indeed, there seems to be little that nature's laws (which Kant *believes* are organized and deployed by God), natural human relationships, or natural societal organization can offer us as free, autonomous subjects. To use Kant's own approach in the third *Critique,* these natural and heteronomous influences and realities might be able to provide us with a sense of systematicity outside ourselves.[23] Nevertheless, this intuition needs to be utilized as a regulative ideal toward the establishment of the autonomous subject and his or her rational capacity to self-determine.

Given Kant's views of autonomy and heteronomy, it is not really surprising that his philosophy of history is wholly forward-looking, partially foreshadowing the historically progressive and significantly more developed view of his successor and critic, Georg Wilhelm Hegel.[24] In short, Kant hopes that history will culminate in a freely formed "transcendental collective" or utopia of human subjects, who, having autonomously learned to ignore the irrational and animalistic urges of nature that have wrought such disaster and chaos throughout the historical process, establish a community that is based upon the self-legislation of transcendentally derived metaphysical principles. Kant fleshes out his approach in his rather brief essay, *Idea for a Universal History with a Cosmopolitan Aim.* As he opines in the introduction, it is not possible to contemplate "the great stage of the world" upon which human history has played out without feeling a sense of disgust.[25] When taken as a whole, he argues, we must regard humanity's collective activities as constituting a web of folly, a dark comedy of errors, and as manifesting a "rage to destruction."[26] Kant connects this rather dismal historical landscape to one of his more concise descriptions of the two-images problem, that is, to the fundamental antinomy between natural forces or laws and human autonomy or subjectivity. It often appears to us, Kant explains, as though we are free and that the processes of our historical life are brought about by the execution of freely determined decisions.[27] A scientific examination, however, reveals something else, namely that our actions are conditioned by natural forces and laws, and by the influence of others who are in turn necessitated by nature's compulsion, by heteronomous forces.[28] To use Kant's own criteria, we can say that the historical process prior to the attainment of the hoped-for utopia is one of heteronomous enslavement, of nature having its way with would-be autonomous subjects. Civilizations, social models, and human institutions, despite their seeming venerability, have thus far been primarily the product of unrestrained human desire, a move that arguably anticipates Nietzsche's discussion of the will-to-power and the ascetic ideal in his works. It is at this point in his essay that Kant introduces the regulative ideal of a complementarity between nature's laws and human autonomy, a notion he redeploys later in his *Critique of Judgment.* Though the source of heteronomy, nature also fulfills a purpose insofar as it drives human beings to seek transcendental autonomy, to rationally loose the bonds that have been imposed upon them and legislate rational alternatives to the natural systems and relationships dictated to them.[29] Put in another way, the chaos wrought by nature's compulsion provides autonomous freedom with its *raison d'être* and also enables the members of the seemingly meaningless process of human events to seek and achieve autonomous ends. As Kant clarifies in the last proposition of his essay, this is indeed a diachronic process according to which each subsequent generation of human beings gradually learns from the error of the foregoing and perfects the rational methods for achieving autonomy, culminating, *he hopes and believes,* in a utopian world of mutually recognizing autonomous beings.[30] It is important to emphasize that though nature provides a causal impetus and helps to enable this cosmic transcendental purpose, in the end, the natural aspects of the self must be left behind or set aside in favor of this higher end to history. As Kant dramatically affirms in the sixth proposition, "Out of such crooked wood as the human being is made, nothing entirely straight can be fabricated."[31] Universal hope for humankind lies exclusively in a transcendental and *meta*-physical τέλος (telos) of history that is truly distinct from natural causality and its purpose(s), a hope that functions as a regulative ideal along with the existence of a Creator, the Incarnate dispensation of Christ, and a belief in an immortal soul. Short of that, the maximum we can achieve in the here and now is a measure of subjective autonomy, free of the compulsion of nature and the clamoring "other."

It is interesting and relevant to the present topic to draw attention again to the fact that Kant indeed demonstrates his Christianity in the *Groundwork* by mentioning Jesus Christ and affirming his moral perfection. Nevertheless, he places the Christ event in the cherished but epistemologically inferior position of subjective regulatory ideal, a position that is more clearly demonstrated in his discussion of divine revelation in *Religion within the Boundaries of Mere Reason*.[32] The revelation of the Son of God through his assumption of human nature may hold particular significance for some human subjects, but it cannot be regarded as an ontological or epistemological touchstone and so must be treated as functionally secondary in comparison to our ability to self-legislate moral truth. The revelatory character of the Christological dispensation has relevance only to the extent that it inspires the human being to realize his or her subjective autonomy, which, in Kant's view, constitutes the only concrete and universal metaphysical ground. It is thus appropriate that history be realized on the basis of human transcendental autonomy as opposed to an unverifiable but *hopefully* true event embedded in humanity's dark past. In order to put this in perspective, it is helpful to briefly mention Paul Tillich's modification of Chalcedonian Christology in his *Theology of Culture*, which arguably reflects the logical development of this "regulatory" approach displayed by the Kantian view. Rather than affirming the dogmatic and ontological import of the historical Christ event, Tillich suggests that the truth of the Incarnation ought to be determined by the needs and criteria of human subjectivity. Humanity of today requires a different form of Chalcedonianism and a greater affirmation of the humanity of Christ. For this reason, Tillich argues, expediency demands that we abandon the doctrine of the virgin birth and affirm a conventional conception of Christ via a mortal father.[33]

With Kant's view of history in mind and especially the competing and antinomous systems that enable it, let us turn to the thought of the celebrated Byzantine monk, Maximus the Confessor. In comparing Kant's perspective to that of Maximus, the Kantian tendency to relegate the historical and ontological role of Christ to the subordinate position of regulatory ideal functions as an essential point of contrast. For our immediate purposes, there are two essential notions conveyed by Maximus's Christocentric synthesis that work to establish a substantially different vision of history and eschatology. First, as Maximus suggests in the twenty-second difficulty of the *Ad Thalassium,* "Our Lord Jesus Christ is the beginning, middle, and end of all past, present, and future ages (ἀρχὴ καὶ μεσότης καὶ τέλος ἐστὶ πάντων τῶν αἰώνων τῶν τε παρελθόντων καὶ ὄντων καὶ ἐσομένων ὁ Κύριος ἡμῶν Ἰησοῦς ὁ Χριστός),"[34] constituting in himself the fulfillment of divine intentionality for history,[35] kenotically introducing the potentiality or *δύναμις* for the Kingdom of Heaven into the mundane flow of spatiotemporality.[36] Maximus expresses this notion a bit more succinctly in his tenth *Ambiguum* when he says quite simply that Christ is the "successor," the διάδοχος of time and eternity,[37] thereby affirming the paradoxical convergence of the καὶ νῦν καὶ ἀεί ("both now and forever") in a concrete and living form. Second, and following logically from the first point, in kenotically introducing his own eternal existence into the becoming of human history and natural realities, the Incarnate Logos effects an ontological alteration of nature's laws.[38] He becomes in himself the manifest archetype and law of nature and, we might daringly affirm, the *natural* paradigm for human eschatological life.[39] Offering himself as a real and nonabstracted Archetype and disclosing "noumenal" realities through the phenomena with which he has clothed himself, Christ invites humanity to self-legislate through an analogous imitation of his own mode of existence, thereby merging ethical and ontological ends, something that is unthinkable from the standpoint of the Kantian. In this way, Maximus dissolves any potential two-images antinomies and, consequently, the pressing need for a transcendental flight from existence and history in order to encounter truth and rationality. This is not to dismiss the legitimacy of Kant's assertion regarding the persistent and sometimes dominant display of human weakness and, to wax Freudian, seeming manifestation of a death-drive throughout recorded human history. Rather, it is to suggest that the Maximian view presents an alternative in which the Christ event constitutes a vortex of ontological and epistemological legitimacy embedded into the sea of raging solipsism that is history, or rather would be history if taken independently of the real presence of the Incarnate Logos within it.

The presence of a form of "realized eschatology" in the thought of Maximus has been noted and affirmed by some Maximus scholars, though, to be fair, it is also disputed by some others. Perhaps the most recent affirmation of realized eschatology in the thought of the Confessor comes by way of Andreas Andreopoulos's essay, "Eschatology in Maximus the Confessor," in *The Oxford Handbook of Maximus the Confessor*. Arguing for an eschatological reading of Maximus's commentary on the Lord's Prayer and especially his use of the expression "our daily bread" (ἐπιούσιος ἄρτος), Andreopoulos says, "the boundlessness of God interjects itself into human history and is shared by many people in the Church."[40] To follow up his point, *ecclesiality* in the view of the Confessor is descriptive of an event in which the timeless and transcendent enters into communion with the spatiotemporal realm, when the barriers between the natural and the supernatural cease to function. The shared and communal life of the Church is not a metaphysically empty socioeconomic construct but constitutes the real manifestation and vitalizing presence of divine otherness. Paul Blowers encapsulates this reading of Maximus in his essay "Realized Eschatology in Maximus the Confessor," arguing that the Incarnation of the Logos results in the elevation of human nature and collapses "spatio-temporal extension," causing "activity and passivity [to] compenetrate."[41] In noting the perichoretic character of activity and passivity, Blowers comes very close to what Nicholas Loudovikos has described as "dialogical reciprocity" between created and uncreated, a reality that is contingent upon the Incarnate dispensation of Christ and enables a human being to have a "historical" dialogue with eternity in the here and now, making history itself eschatological.[42] This leads to an eschatological interrelatedness or, as Blowers terms it, the "eschatologically simultaneous" penetration of the divine into the supremely important historical event of Christ, the chronological conclusion of cosmos, and the life of the virtuous Christian. Though certainly implicit throughout the Maximian corpus, the Confessor's mentality is particularly evident in the aforementioned *Ad Thalassium* 22, where he declares that the Incarnate Christ himself is both the causal ground and consummation (τὸ τέλος) of the aeons.[43] This divine descent into history brings the "consummation of the predetermined ages upon us (Τῶν προωρισμένων αἰώνων εἰς ἡμᾶς τὰ τέλη κατήντησεν)" thereby giving created beings the δύναμις (potentiality) to realize and participate in a mode of life that was formerly enjoyed only by transcendent God.[44] Located within Christ and the work of his Incarnate dispensation is the complete and unadulterated potentiality for humanity's deification, and, a diachronic dialogue with eternity that takes place within the spatiotemporal and historical process.[45] When, therefore, we speak of realized eschatology in Maximian terms, we refer to what happened and continues to occur as a result of Christ and his earthly dispensation, in whom resides the eschatological potential for all particular instances of humanity to dialogically and diachronically realize, including that which will be actualized following his second advent—that is, the Resurrection. Nevertheless, insofar as ineffable eternity has truly come upon our human nature in Christ, the Confessor concludes in his *Capita Theologica et Oeconomica* that a partial realization of eschatological life, literally ποσῶς or ἐκ μέρους, is experienced prior to the Resurrection, within the *here and now* by those who avail themselves of the potentiality bestowed by the divine Archetype.[46] Indeed, such movement would have to occur in history. Insofar as Christ is simultaneously the successor of time and eternity, he has also become the paradigm and end of the spatiotemporal world, a point that we will we expand upon immediately below. If it is proper to describe Maximus's Christological viewpoint as constituting a realized eschatology, it is also appropriate to affirm that his anthropological perspective includes what we might refer to as a "partially realized eschatology."

Maximus extends Christ's assimilation of spatiotemporality to the laws and movements of nature itself, which, arguably, constitutes the starkest distinction between the views of the Confessor and those manifested by Kant's transcendental idealism. In his rather brief *aporia* 19 to Thalassius, Maximus provides us, perhaps, with his most unequivocal statement on the matter: "For the Logos of God is the author of every nature, of every law, regulation and order. . . . Apart from the Logos who promulgates it, there is no law."[47] In Maximus's view, there is no such thing as laws of nature that possesses a locus that is causally independent of the οἰκονομία (economy) of the Logos. There are, as Maximus indicates elsewhere, indeed τρόποι or modes of nature that constitute responses on the part of rational beings to divine laws and determinations, but these are not, properly speaking, indicative of natural "laws" in the same etiological sense.[48] However, the role of the Logos *qua* law is not one of mere causality. Rather, He is both the cause and the consummation, the latter of which occurs via his spatiotemporal and historical Incarnation. Interpreting the Apostle Paul's declaration in Romans 10:4 that "Christ is the end of the law," the Confessor says, "the natural law, the written law, and the law of grace converge (συνάγεται) in Christ, insofar as he is Creator, Provident, Lawgiver, and Redeemer."[49] The implication of this passage is indeed profound and should not be passed over lightly, echoing Maximus's affirmation in *Ad Thalassium* 22 that Christ is the consummation (τέλη) of all the *aeons*. In incarnating himself into historical and natural processes, the Incarnate Logos united natural and spatiotemporal ends with "transcendent" deifying ends, manifesting in himself a "focal meaning," a univocal relationship between both categories. This is why Maximus is very comfortable using seemingly paradoxical expressions like "transcendence according to nature" (ἔκβασις κατὰ φύσιν).[50] As a direct consequence of the Incarnation, a human being whose mode of life is expressed as existence "according to nature" (κατὰ φύσιν) diachronically comes into communion with his or her transcendent cause. Conversely, a παρὰ φύσιν mode of existence—a failure to live or actualize in accordance with natural and spiritual laws and purposes—constitutes a deprivation, a στέρησις of the grace offered and imparted by the Incarnate Logos in the here and now.[51]

This unification of hypernatural or deifying ends with natural τέλη in the Incarnate Christ eliminates the need to speak of two-images, as the human subject's end is now tied to its deified natural end. The historical process is infused with meaning and purpose that is distributed to all humanity through the historical presence of the divine and simultaneously natural Archetype. In the Confessor's opinion, the response to the Eucharistic distribution of the Archetype by the *logoi* and the realization of his divine life occur through *mimesis*. This is a self-acknowledged appropriation and augmentation of the Dionysian notion of "analogy," a Maximian development that has been noted and studied by Nikolaos Loudovikos.[52] Imitation of the divine Logos is neither a static mimicry nor a transcendental exercise but is a participatory action whereby the human subject voluntarily and diachronically seeks his deified natural end in the Incarnate Logos, which is an activity that is simultaneously ethical and ontological. This univocal relationship between ethical and ontological realities in the human subject's quest for the *imitatio Christi* is reflected particularly well in a passage from the Confessor's well-known *Ambiguum* 7: "The essence of the virtues is indeed our Lord Jesus Christ. Every man who by steadfast habit participates in virtue (ἀρετῆς καθ' ἕξιν παγίαν μετέχων), assuredly participates in God, the essence of all virtue."[53] Lest we be led to believe that this is purely a deontological or transcendental form of moral legislation, Maximus continues: "For he who has elected in accordance with the purpose of nature the seed of goodness (τὴν κατὰ φύσιν σπορὰν τοῦ ἀγαθοῦ), in this way indicates the end by the beginning and, conversely, the beginning by the end, or rather how the beginning and the end are the same (μᾶλλον δὲ ταυτὸν ἀρχὴν οὖσαν καὶ τέλος)."[54] This direct connection of ontology, virtue, and the imitation of Christ is further explored in the Confessor's *Ad Thalassium* 51, where he informs us that the intellect secures "the most uniform movement" (ὁμολωτάτην κίνησιν) of virtue through the "imitation of the heavenly natural law" (μιμούμενος τὸν κατὰ φύσιν τοῦ οὐρανοῦ νόμον) which, as we have seen, is paradigmatically represented by the Incarnate Logos himself.[55] The manifestation of virtue in human life is a phenomenal revelation of the human being's participation in Christ, a spatiotemporal demonstration of the diachronic realization of the human subject's deified and simultaneously natural end. In thorough imitation of the Incarnate Logos's mode of existence, the human subject habituates the divine virtues and demonstrates them in the seemingly mundane medium of human life and interaction, through other-directed acts of charity and virtue. This is expressed throughout Maximus's *Centuriae de*

Caritate, where, among other things, the simple act of giving alms is regarded as an imitation of God's own distribution of divine and heavenly blessings (Ὁ κατὰ μίμησιν Θεοῦ τὴν ἐλεημοσύνην ποιούμενος).[56] We might punctuate this discussion with a passage from Maximus's forty-eighth *Ambiguum.* Providing a quintessentially Eucharistic expression of mimesis and its indissoluble relationship to human ethical realities, the Confessor announces that the one who receives of the body of the Incarnate Logos, "shall by providence be inclined sympathetically toward those who have fallen and are sick in the faith, in this way imitating the Logos's own condescension towards us (τὴν πρὸς ἡμᾶς τοῦ Λόγου μιμούμενος συγκατάβασιν)."[57]

In conclusion, the transcendental and utopian vision of Kant and those of his ilk, founded as it is upon a persistent antinomy between subjectivity and the inexorable laws of nature, arguably leaves all those who do not live in the bright utopian future with nothing but a regulative ideal, subjective hopes and, to introduce a slightly Nietzschean slant, epiphenomenal dreams that the heteronomous and necessitating world of appearances is not all there is. It seems, that what there is—whether social institutions, like the family or the Church, or historical events—must be regarded with suspicion and as the product of heteronomous forces. The Christ event, for example, while perhaps functioning as subjective encouragement, contains no immediate ontological content, does not apparently alter history or nature, and is subordinate to our autonomous capacity to legislate. Indeed, if these are the circumstances, it is sorely tempting to follow Nietzsche and sweep these unverified regulative ideals and beliefs into the dustbin of history and embrace the necessitating world of the real. Standing as an alternative to Nietzsche, however, is not Aristotle but Maximus. According to the Confessor's vision, the Creator of the world, the living source of ontology, infuses our spatio-temporal world with his own eternal existence, visibly manifesting himself in and through the phenomena of nature, thereby disrupting our solipsistic and self-directed absorption by literally placing the end and purpose of history in front of us. In clothing himself in them, the phenomena of the created world acquire an ontological and historical purpose in Christ. To close with the words of Andreopoulos, "Christ draws into himself all possibilities of the human condition, all the accidentals of human nature" such that the "different conditions of the human being [. . .] converge around Christ."[58]

NOTES

1. R. G. Collingwood, *The Idea of History* (Oxford: Clarendon Press, 1946), 93.

2. Ibid., 114. Kant's utopian vision seems to reflect especially Jean-Jacques Rousseau's idea in *Discourse on Political Economy and the Social Contract,* trans.

Christopher Betts (New York: Oxford University Press, 1994), I.i–viii, of a transfer from a "state of nature" to the "civil state." See J. B. Schneewind, *The Invention of Autonomy* (New York: Cambridge University Press, 1998), 470–82.

3. Robert Hanna, *Kant, Science, and Human Nature* (New York: Oxford University Press, 2006), 8–10.

4. Robert Pippin, *The Persistence of Subjectivity* (New York: Cambridge University Press, 2005), 1–10.

5. Immanuel Kant, *Critique of Judgment*, trans. James Meredith (Oxford: Clarendon Press, 1952), 83, 5:432.

6. See Kant, *Critique of Judgement*, sections 76–77 and 84, 5:435. See also Immanuel Kant, *Religion within the Boundaries of Mere Reason*, in *Religion and Rational Theology: The Cambridge Edition of the Works of Immanuel Kant*, ed. and trans. Allen Wood and George Di Giovanni (Cambridge: Cambridge University Press, 1998), 6:138–39.

7. Robert Pippin, *The Persistence of Subjectivity*, 16. See also Michael Friedman, *Kant and the Exact Sciences* (Cambridge, MA: Harvard University Press, 1992), 11–13.

8. Immanuel Kant, *The Metaphysics of Morals*, trans. and ed. Mary J. Gregor (Cambridge: Cambridge University Press, 1996), 6:387, 6:392.

9. Kant provides one of his summaries of these two-images in the Introduction to the *Critique of Judgment*, II, 5:173–176. For Kant's assertion that he secures metaphysics through its restriction to the human subject, see Immanuel Kant, *Critique of Pure Reason*, trans. and eds. Paul Guyer and Allen Wood (Cambridge: Cambridge University Press, 1998), Bxvi and Bxviii.

10. Robert Pippin, *The Persistence of Subjectivity*, 1–5, 15–16.

11. Ibid.

12. Kant, *Critique of Pure Reason*, A822/B850 and A213/B260. I am indebted to Johannes Hoff for drawing this to my attention.

13. Ibid., A644–45/B672–73.

14. Kant, *Critique of Pure Judgment*, 83, 5:430–31.

15. I use J. B. Schneewind's expression here in *The Invention of Autonomy*, 515.

16. Introduction to the *Critique of Judgment*, II, 5:176 and 87, 5:450.

17. Christos Yannaras, *On the Absence and Unknowability of God*, trans. Haralambos Ventis (London: T&T Clark, 2005), 33.

18. Paul Guyer, *Kant's System of Nature and Freedom* (New York: Oxford University Press, 2005), 170–71.

19. Immanuel Kant, *Groundwork of the Metaphysic of Morals*, trans. H. J. Paton (New York: Harper Perennial, 1964), 443.

20. Ibid., 408.

21. Ibid., 406–9.

22. Ibid., 433.

23. Introduction to the *Critique of Judgment*, sections IV and V.

24. Emphasis should be placed on "partially" here, as Hegel sees history as culminating in the present and not in some future utopian existence. See Collingwood, *The Idea of History*, 114.

25. Immanuel Kant, "Idea for a Universal History with a Cosmopolitan Aim," in *Idea for a Universal History with a Cosmopolitan Aim: A Critical Guide*, eds. Amélie Oksenberg Rorty and James Schmidt (New York: Cambridge University Press, 2009), 10, 8:17.

26. Ibid., 8:18.

27. Ibid., 8:17.

28. Ibid.

29. Ibid. See the Fourth and Fifth Propositions, 8:20–22.

30. Ibid., 8:29 et. seq.

31. Ibid., 8.23.

32. Immanuel Kant, *Religion within the Boundaries of Mere Reason*, 6:153–55.

33. See Paul Tillich, *Theology of Culture* (New York: Oxford University Press, 1964), 66.

34. PG 90: 320B.

35. Ibid., 317BCD.

36. Ibid., and 320BC.

37. PG 91: 1164B.

38. *Ambiguum* 31, PG 91: 1276BC.

39. *Ambiguum* 10, PG 91: 1308D.

40. Andreas Andreopoulos, "Eschatology in Maximus the Confessor," in *The Oxford Handbook of Maximus the Confessor*, edited by Pauline Allen and Bronwen Neil (New York: Oxford University Press, 2015), 335. Andreopoulos also notes the inadequacy of the translation "our daily bread."

41. Paul Blowers, "Realized Eschatology in Maximus the Confessor, Ad Thalassium 22," in *Studia Patristica*, vol. XXXII, edited by Elizabeth Livingston (Leuven: Peeters, 1997), 262.

42. See Nikolaos Loudovikos, *A Eucharistic Ontology* (Brookline: Holy Cross Orthodox Press, 2010), 1–10.

43. PG 90: 320B.

44. Ibid., 317C.

45. Ibid.

46. II. 80, PG 90: 1161D and II. 87, PG 90: 1165BC.

47. This is Paul Blower's translation, taken from his *Exegesis and Spiritual Pedagogy in St. Maximus the Confessor* (Notre Dame: University of Notre Dame Press, 1991), 117. The original text can be found in the *Ad Thalassium*, PG 90: 308BC.

48. See *Opusculum* 1, PG 91: 24B.

49. This also taken from Paul Blower's *Exegesis and Spiritual Pedagogy in St. Maximus the Confessor*, 117. See *Ad Thalassium* 19, PG 90: 308BC.

50. *Ad Thalassium* 59, PG 90: 609B.

51. Ibid., 609C.

52. See Nikolaos Loudovikos, "*Eikon* and *Mimesis*: Eucharistic Ecclesiology and the Ecclesial Ontology of Dialogical Reciprocity," *International Journal for the Study of the Christian Church* 11, no. 2–3 (2011): 125–26.

53. PG 91: 1081CD.

54. PG 91: 1081D–1084A.
55. PG 90: 480CD.
56. I. 23–24, PG 90: 965A.
57. PG 91: 1365A.
58. Andreopoulos, "Eschatology in Maximus the Confessor," 337.

Part II

BEYOND BEING AND TIME: ESCHATOLOGICAL HERMENEUTICS

Chapter Six

Zizioulas and Heidegger
"Eschatological Ontology" and Hermeneutics
Matthew Baker

Recent criticisms of neopatristic theology have called for an Orthodox engagement of "contextual theologies" and have held the neopatristic movement and its chief inspirer, Georges Florovsky, responsible for an insensitivity to the historicity and contextuality of theology and for closing down the dialogue with modern philosophy opened by earlier figures such as Solovyov and Bulgakov.[1] Those criticizing the neopatristic model have called for a new attention to modern and postmodern hermeneutics. In the midst of these criticisms, however, no attention has been given to Florovsky's own engagements with Western historicism and a number of thinkers connected in crucial ways to philosophical hermeneutics: Wilhelm Dilthey, Josiah Royce, and R. G. Collingwood. It is the purpose of my dissertation to uncover these connections and their significance for understanding and further refining and developing Florovsky's program of neopatristic synthesis in response to present-day questions.[2]

Florovsky's core insights and questions concerning the nature of historical understanding and activity were not developed by the subsequent generations of Orthodox theologians impacted by Florovsky. The conversation with historicism and philosophical hermeneutics suggested by certain elements in Florovsky's work has not come to be characteristic of neopatristic theology as broadly developed and received. Some critics of neopatristic theology invoke the name of Hans-Georg Gadamer, calling for Orthodox appropriation of his thought. In histories of modern philosophical hermeneutics, a line is typically drawn from Dilthey to Heidegger to Gadamer, the first two names being major interlocutors in Gadamer's hermeneutics. If the significance of Florovsky's dialogue with Dilthey and Collingwood remains largely unnoticed, it is well known that the early work of Martin Heidegger has had a crucial influence on the thought of Christos Yannaras and John Zizioulas. The interest of these two Greek thinkers in Heidegger, however, is ontology, not hermeneutics. The crucial background of Heidegger's *Being and Time* in his study of Dilthey and his engagement with debates about the crisis of historicism and the humane sciences (*Geisteswissenschaften*) does not appear in the work of either Yannaras or Zizioulas. These elements, and the hermeneutic character of Heidegger's early ontological investigations—so crucial for Gadamer—are covered over and obscured, and the "existentialist" interpretation of *Being and Time* (so influential among theologians but eschewed by Heidegger himself) exercises a considerable influence, especially in the work of Zizioulas.

There are two parts to this chapter. In the first, I will expose the specifically hermeneutical character of key concepts from *Being and Time* appropriated by John Zizioulas in his own offerings to the program of neopatristic synthesis sketched by Florovsky: *ekstasis*, authenticity, and being-unto-death. As will be shown, although not explored by Zizioulas, these concepts are inextricable from Heidegger's critique of historicism and his account of historiography, tradition, and the uses of the past. Further, Heidegger's figuration of these ontological concepts bears a quasi-eschatological character, drawing from Heidegger's early study of Pauline eschatology. In response to historicism and its crisis of values, Heidegger suggests an eschatological approach to tradition—albeit a secularized and individualized eschatology, an eschatology of death.

In the second portion of the chapter, I will consider Zizioulas's use of the concepts of *ekstasis*, authenticity and being-unto-death, and the eucharistic-eschatological ontology which Zizioulas poses over against Heidegger's eschatological ontology of death. My interest here, however, remains in hermeneutics. Consideration will be given to Zizioulas's repeated (if undeveloped) criticisms of "historicism" in theology and the affinity of this critique with that of Heidegger. Having laid bare the hermeneutical shape of the Heideggerian concepts employed by Zizioulas, attempt will be made to draw out the implications of Zizioulas's handling of them for theological hermeneutics, a theme to which Zizioulas himself has given little concentrated attention.

HERMENEUTICS IN HEIDEGGER

Heidegger's posthumously published 1923 lectures *Ontology: The Hermeneutics of Facticity* give us a glimpse into the hermeneutics that led to *Being and Time*, submerged somewhat in that latter work in favor of other concerns. Heidegger developed his "hermeneutics of facticity" in the years 1919–1923 at Freiburg, shaped by early studies of Scotus, Aristotle, Luther,

Kierkegaard, Dilthey, and Emil Lask. *Faktizität*—a term first employed by Fichte, and reappearing in debates among post-Hegelian theologians concerning the historicity of the resurrection—denotes in Heidegger's usage historical existence in its utmost individuality.[3] Here Dilthey's concern with "life" and its expression (*Ausdruck*) is radicalized: "If we take 'life' to be a mode of being, then 'factical life' means: our own Dasein[4] which is there for us in one expression or another of the character of its being, and this expression, too, is in the manner of being."[5] Thus, Heidegger argues, the matter under concern here can never be an "object."

For Heidegger, hermeneutics indicates "the unified manner of the engaging, approaching, accessing, interrogating, and explicating of facticity."[6] The decisive epochs for hermeneutics were "the Patristic period and Luther." Heidegger is critical of the development from the seventeenth century to Schleiermacher, in which hermeneutics no longer meant interpretation itself but a formal methodology—a "disastrous limitation" even Dilthey was unable to overcome.[7] He seeks a return to what he takes to be the original significance of *hermeneuein:* not a doctrine about interpretation, but the unity of interpreting factical life itself. This presupposes not only that Dasein is a being capable of being interpreted, but also "that to be in some state of having-been-interpreted belongs to its being."[8]

Heidegger names two prejudices at work in contemporary philosophy and historical sciences that are obstacles to this "right path of looking at things": the subject-object schema and the demand for presupposition-free observation. Both obscure the character of Dasein as temporal-historical being-in-the-world. He objects to the view of Dilthey's student Edouard Spranger that the authentic tendency unifying contemporary philosophy (Rickert, phenomenology, Dilthey) is to be found in the struggle for the timeless in or beyond the historical, and a value-theory of objective validity. This desire to free philosophy of history is but "a Platonism of barbarians," and does not represent Dilthey's best insight. The entire framework underwriting such discussions—finite versus infinite, subject versus object, nature versus value—is a construct that must be questioned. Even the natural sciences are cultural products, having their starting point within culture.

Thus, for Heidegger, the quest for a kind of dispassionate metahistorical objectivity is illusory: "If the term is to say anything at all, *'freedom from standpoints'* is nothing other than an explicit *appropriation of our position of looking.* This position is itself something historical, i.e. bound up with Dasein (responsibility, how Dasein stands regarding itself), and not a chimerical in-itself outside of time."[9] Both historical and philosophical disciplines are modes of interpreting grounded in Dasein's own factical being as (already) having-been-interpreted.

Hermeneutics as a major concern for Heidegger needs to be emphasized as we turn to his magnum opus, *Being and Time*. In Division II of this work, the portion most associated with later existentialism, we find the core Heideggerian themes discussed by Zizioulas—being-unto-death, authenticity, *ekstasis*, and horizon. For our purposes, we must see how, quite apart from their popular existentialist interpretation, Heidegger's treatment of these themes extends his concept of hermeneutics sketched above.

In introducing his analysis of being-unto-death, Heidegger takes a lead from Dilthey: in order to understand historical life, we must understand its totality, and this requires viewing the whole from the perspective of its *end*. In the individual Dasein's case, this end is death. Yet I cannot access my own death phenomenologically, in *actuality*: being-at-an-end (*Zu-Ende-sein*) is never an actual vantage point. The "whole" must then be accessed by anticipation (*Vorlaufen*), as being-*toward* the end (*Sein zum Ende*), being-*unto*-death (*Sein zum Tode*). This is an orientation *toward* a *possibility* constitutive for Dasein—the *ultimate* possibility, incapable of being outstripped. This "not yet" is constitutive of the being Dasein is; when it ceases to be, Dasein ceases to be. Death as possibility brings Dasein face-to-face with its own being—as *finite*—and therefore with its freedom and its responsibility.

In spite of Heidegger's desire to present his fundamental ontology as a-theological, his analysis of being-unto-death has theological roots. Judith Wolfe has shown how Heidegger drew from his early study of Pauline eschatology (1918–1921) as well as such themes as time, suffering, sin, and affliction in Augustine, the young Luther, and Kierkegaard, in order to develop in the years 1921–1923 "an eschatological phenomenology without hope of salvation,"[10] in which "death and not eternal life becomes the authentic object of eschatology."[11] Heidegger's concept of anticipation (*Vorlaufen*) owes something to his analysis of the Pauline sense of Christian existence as eschatological expectation and wakefulness. This early "eschatology without eschaton" found its culmination in *Being and Time* in its analysis of being-unto-death. As Wolfe argues, while its religious sources have been obscured, "Heidegger's account of human existence in *Being and Time* is 'eschatological' because it envisions the possibility of authentic existence as dependent on a certain (existential) relation to one's future."[12]

Heidegger's notion of *authenticity* is closely tied to this "eschatology" of being-unto-death, as well as to freedom. Authenticity (*Eigentlichkeit*) concerns that which is one's own (*eigentlich*). Death individualizes. In inauthentic, "everyday" consciousness, one "falls" into being consumed with immediate concerns, loses oneself in the crowd, forgets one's own finitude, and fails to seize one's own ultimate possibility. Authenticity consists in winning oneself back in the seizure of this possibility, facing one's own death in anticipation (*Vorlaufen*), existing with "resoluteness" in the projection of one's finitude. This anticipatory resoluteness (*Ent-schlossenheit*) attends the disclosure (*Erschlossenheit*) of Dasein's own being, *as finite anticipation itself.* Authentic understanding understands itself as finite, and as possibility.

As projection, understanding is fundamentally future-oriented. In authenticity, Dasein has by anticipation an understanding of its existence as a whole through an apprehension of the possibility of its death. Only because of this fore-having of the whole can we inquire about what it means *to be*. There is thus an essential relationship between the eschatological ontology of *being-unto-death* and the "taking-as" structure of *interpretation* characteristic of all our involvements in the world. Interpretation is a constitutive feature of our existence because we are finite. An infinite being would understand without need of interpretation; as finite "being-there," we require the mediation of hermeneutics—taking *as*—to understand the world, others, and ourselves.[13]

This finite being takes the form of time. The taking-as structure of interpretation has its ground in *temporality,* as the *a priori* condition of intelligibility. This is similar to Kant's idea of time as the form of inner sense and the purest schema of understanding.[14] Heidegger, however, is concerned to avoid the "ordinary" idea of time as a linear sequence of past-present-future. Rather, Dasein itself is *ekstatic* temporality, a "standing out" or going out "toward." Temporality is a unified structure from which three ekstases "stand out," each toward their distinct "horizon": future, past as having-been, and present. "Horizon" indicates a finite vantage point within which beings are disclosed, and thus also an openness to being. Understanding and interpretation, with its as-structure, are grounded in this ecstatic-horizonal unity of temporality.[15]

Of the three ekstases or horizons, Heidegger asserts that the futural is the most determinative. Yet the possibility of being futural, or "existing," depends also upon facticity, or having-been.[16] As he notes, death marks only *one* of the "ends" of Dasein's totality. The wholeness of Dasein is a "stretching out" between birth and death. Recognition of futural being-toward-death is therefore one-sided without consideration of being-toward-the-beginning, relation to what has been. Heidegger is concerned to resist a "vulgar" linear interpretation of the constancy of self amidst always changing experiences, whether as a sum of successive moments appearing and disappearing or a framework existing somehow independently of these. Being-born is never simply past, dying never simply future; rather, both *are* as long as Dasein is. Self-constancy is grounded in Dasein's specific temporalizing of itself.

Heidegger seeks to draw from this analysis of authentic temporality an ontological understanding of historicity. Heidegger argues (again with a nod to Dilthey) that the presupposition for the possibility of "the foundation of the historical world in the humane sciences" lies in making explicit the interpretedness that belongs already essentially to historical being. At its most primordial level, history is not an object, but a past that is handed down, *überlieferte*—"traditioned"—whether explicitly or inexplicitly, and still having its effect (*Wirkung*). That is: not so much the past itself, as a "derivation" from the past—a heritage (*Herkunft*).[17] Earlier in *Being and Time*, tradition seemed to be associated mostly with "fallenness" and inauthentic being-with-others, losing oneself in the vulgar understanding of the crowd. But now Heidegger suggests that historicity at its most primordial, and the *a priori* condition of historical knowledge, lies precisely in tradition, with its inherited fore-structure of understandings—prior to any "critical" or "scientific" historiography.

Further, history as the derivation or heritage (*Herkunft*) of what is handed down has a fundamental relation to the future (*Zukunft*)—a relation that is *productive*:

> Whatever 'has a history' is in the nexus of becoming . . . [and] in this way can, at the same time, 'make' history. 'Epoch making,' it determines a 'future' [*Zukunft*] 'in the present'. Here history means 'an event nexus' that is a 'productive nexus' that moves through the 'past,' the 'present,' and the 'future'.[18]

Here Heidegger has introduced a concept of history of effects or productive history (*Wirkungsgeschichte*), which will later be crucial for hermeneutics as developed by Gadamer. Earlier, Heidegger suggested that authentic understanding takes the form of Dasein's confrontation with its own death—through anticipatory resoluteness—in order to seize its own existence and resolve upon the projection of its finite possibilities. Now, he clarifies: these possibilities of authentic self-projection, which death itself does not provide, are to be drawn precisely from the *heritage* into which Dasein is always thrown:

> The authentic existentiell understanding is so far from extricating itself from the way of interpreting Dasein which has come down to us, that in each case it is in terms of this interpretation, against it, and yet again for it, that any possibility one has chosen is seized upon in one's resolution. The resoluteness in which Dasein comes back to itself, discloses current factical possibilities of authentic existing, and discloses them *in terms of the heritage* which that resoluteness, as thrown, *takes over*. . . . If everything "good" is a heritage, and the character of "goodness" lies in making authentic existence possible, then the handing down of a heritage constitutes itself in resoluteness.[19]

In projecting on the future, authentic understanding grasps its possibilities from among the concrete cultural-historical determinations inherited by Dasein in its thrownness, freely appropriating these as its own. Authentic futurity depends upon this relation to tradition. Conversely, tradition depends upon resolute *ap-*

propriation in view of future possibility.[20] Finally, it is this specific mode of temporalizing future and past that makes possible an authentic *present*:

> Only an entity which, in its Being, is essentially futural so that it is free for its death and can let itself be thrown back upon its factical "there" by shattering itself against death—that is to say, only an entity which, as futural, is equiprimordially in the process of having-been, can, by handing down to itself the possibility it has inherited, take over its own thrownness and be in the moment of vision for "its time."[21]

Heidegger calls this authentic appropriation of the past *Wiederholung*— "repetition," or "retrieval."[22] In *Wiederholung*, Dasein "fetches back" from its heritage possibilities for its existence and projects them onto its future. Heidegger associates this with "choosing a hero" to follow and repeat in faithfulness. *Wiederholung* is no simple reactualization of the past, nor abandonment to it, but rather an act of *freedom* toward the past, insofar as its simple pastness is *renounced* and *Wiederholung* constitutes a *productive response* to previously unrealized *possibilities* inherent in what has been—an approach amply demonstrated in Heidegger's own reading of the tradition. It is precisely Dasein's *futurity* that throws anticipatory resoluteness back on its factical thrownness and gives the past its historical priority. Here being-toward-death provides the ground of authentic historicity, making the retrieval of heritage possible. Self-constancy, or cultural continuity, is not a linear diachronic succession of objectively graspable moments, but rather a "stretching along" and "handing down" between temporal horizons, by way of *Wiederholung*.

As can now be seen, the existential-ontological themes appropriated by Zizioulas from Heidegger—being-unto-death, authenticity, *ekstasis*—are, in context, *hermeneutical* in shape, having their function within a broadly encompassing account of history, understanding, and interpretation. When read in light of its theological sources, Heidegger's account of these themes suggests finally the idea of an *eschatological approach to tradition*. This eschatologically oriented return to heritage, which retrieves and productively appropriates an inheritance in view of its previously undisclosed possibilities, determines also the authentic relation to the *present*—a relation marked by *freedom*. In his 1924 lectures on *The Concept of Time*, Heidegger underscores this eschatological access to history as the very "first principle of all hermeneutics":

> The present generation thinks that it has found history and is even overburdened by it. It moans about historicism—*lucus a non lucendo*. It gives the name "history" to something that is not history at all. . . . The common interpretation of *Dasein* is threatened by the danger of relativism; but the anxiety concerning relativism is anxiety in the face of *Dasein*. The past as authentic history is

retrievable in "how" one exists. *The possibility of access to history is grounded in the possibility (according to which it understands the present as temporally particular) to be futural. This is the first principle of all hermeneutics.*[23]

Heidegger's suggestive eschatological-hermeneutical ontology[24] was offered in response to the "crisis of historicism" and its attendant anxieties regarding relativism. In his view, the debates surrounding historicism regarding whether historiography should be concerned with unique events or laws of development are meaningless, and a clear sign of alienation from authentic historicity; talk of "universal validity" in humane sciences is likewise out of place. The proper theme of authentic historiography is neither singular facts nor universals, but rather the thematization and retrieval from the past of *possibilities* that have become factically existent—and this retrieval, *contra* Rickert, is *already* a making-manifest of what is "universal" in the unique. Such possibilities are not grasped by imposing a supratemporal pattern, in anxious search for historical certainty or validity in escape from relativism, but are rather disclosed in time *in light of the future*.[25] It must be noted finally, however, that—as the readings of past texts in Heidegger's later work abundantly demonstrates—such creative retrieval of tradition in Heidegger's view requires an element of *Destruktion* of the tradition, and a "violent" interpretation.[26]

By his own admission, Heidegger's intent in *Being and Time* was to further certain basic hermeneutical-historiographical insights of Dilthey.[27] My larger project shows how Florovsky's engagement with Dilthey lay near to the conception of his neopatristic program. Thus, it is of particular interest to note the engagement with Heidegger on the part Florovsky's student, John Zizioulas, who has stated his intent to continue Florovsky's program. Zizioulas takes no note of the specifically *hermeneutical* shape and framework of the concepts he borrows from *Being and Time,* nor of their context and background in the debates about historicism and the methodology of the *Geisteswissenschaften* involving Dilthey and the Neo-Kantians. Yet Zizioulas also suggests an eschatological approach to tradition, and employs his own eschatological ontology in critique of what he calls "historicism." Like Heidegger, he associates this term both with a hopeless dialectic between relativism and the search for historical validity or security, and with the linear conception of history Heidegger saw issuing from the "vulgar" conception of time having its beginning with Aristotle and its last and greatest conceptualization in Hegel. Against this "historicism," Zizioulas poses an account of the Eucharist as an eschatologically mediated access to history, an *anamnesis* bearing some comparison with Heidegger's *Wiederholung*. Finally, a more substantial connection of Zizioulas's eschatological ontology with the debates concerning historicism and hermeneutics *à la* Dilthey can be established via Zizioulas's dialogue with the thought of Wolfhart Pannenberg, who engages directly with Dilthey, Heidegger, and Gadamer on these questions.

HERMENEUTICS AND THE ESCHATOLOGICAL ONTOLOGY OF ZIZIOULAS

The importance of hermeneutics is expressed but remains philosophically underdeveloped in Zizioulas's oeuvre. It emerges, for instance, in discussions of neopatristic synthesis, which he understands as a *hermeneutical* enterprise.[28] Theological hermeneutics he defines as "the task of re-stating Scripture and Christian doctrine." "All theology is a matter of hermeneutics, that is, of deciding how to receive and re-state the teaching of Scripture for the Church and the world."[29] This is a work of interpretation. Christian doctrine should be "approached as a tradition that comes to us from the past but which is *interpreted* in a way that answers the needs of human beings in our own time, particularly in the context of Western culture."[30]

For the process of interpretation and understanding, Zizioulas highlights the crucial role of *presuppositions,* as distinguished from sources or concrete theses.[31] Interpretation must lay bare these presuppositions: "Terms such as 'event' or 'institution' or even 'Church' can mean totally different things, depending on the theological presuppositions that lie behind them. After a rather long experience in ecumenical discussions, I have therefore come to the conclusion that instead of trying to agree on concrete theological theses we should try to agree on theological principles."[32] Though Zizioulas makes no reference here to philosophical sources, his idea of the primacy of presuppositions over concrete theses calls to mind Heidegger's fore-structure of understanding and its determinative role in interpretation, where truth-propositions occupy a strictly derivative place.[33] His concern to lay bare the hidden presuppositions driving interpretation likewise finds parallels in Heidegger and Gadamer's hermeneutics. The general insight of both into tradition as conditioning all thought is heard here too, justifying a historical approach to theology and ecumenical dialogue along the lines of Florovsky's "ecumenism in time."[34]

Most fundamentally, the question of hermeneutics is built in to Zizioulas's controlling concern: the Eucharist. In his dissertation on ecclesial unity in the pre-Nicene Church, Zizioulas stated his intent to work upward from "facts" to perennial principles.[35] In keeping with his own later expressed views, however, *choice* of facts would itself inevitably be predetermined by founding *presuppositions*. Here the key presupposition is not hard to pinpoint: it is the event of the Eucharist. As constitutive of the Church, "*the ecclesiological presuppositions of the Eucharist cannot be found outside the Eucharist. It is by studying the nature of the Eucharist that we can understand the nature of the Church that conditions the Eucharist.*"[36] The Divine Liturgy, as celebrated by the Orthodox Church, provides the hermeneutic framework out of which Zizioulas aims to draw the principles according to which other concrete doctrinal theses are to be interpreted.[37]

If this is so, then a major lacuna must be marked in Zizioulas's account of the two contexts of interpretation, past and present. For distinctive of Zizioulas's treatment of the Liturgy is his stress on its *eschatological* character. Reflecting critically on his own early work, *The Two Horizons*,[38] Anthony Thistleton, a leading British evangelical authority on theological hermeneutics, has commented on the need for hermeneutical theory "to move beyond the notion of 'Two Horizons,' to take account of the three horizons of 'past, present, and future', and thereby to ground hermeneutics more adequately in ontology and eschatology."[39] This remark is appropriate to Zizioulas. For while his *account* of interpretation above reflects only two horizons, past and present, in his own actual interpretive work, there is a "third horizon"—that of eschatology—that is in fact the most crucial in Zizioulas's theology and interpretive practice.[40] For Zizioulas, it is eschatology, imaged in the Eucharist, that determines the true identity of the Church and of the person, and stands as the ultimate determination of the truth of interpretation.

We have already noted the difficulties with speaking of eschatology in terms of horizon.[41] Understood as "pure presence," the eschaton would seem to spell an end to the ceaseless hermeneutics of historical experience,[42] thus placing a limit to the universality of the hermeneutic problem, and suggesting perhaps the possibility of a finality of certain interpretations already within history. Here again, eschatology serves to counter the threat of relativism issuing from the historicist search for certainty.

In his stress on cultural correlation and response to "existential" questions, Zizioulas reflects not only Florovsky, but equally another teacher from his Harvard years, Paul Tillich. This influence is suggested by other Zizioulian motifs as well: his critique of *auctoritas* (Tillich's "heteronomy"), insistence on ontology as the root question involved in all theological questioning, concern with finitude, and reliance on modern existentialism as voicing the problems of the age.[43] Apart from its own intrinsic significance, Tillich's influence forms one of multiple tacit links connecting Zizioulas to Heidegger.[44] Similar elements may have come from Zizioulas's reading of John Macquarrie.[45]

A basic difficulty in the theological appropriation of Heidegger concerns the question of whether the existence-structures analyzed in *Being and Time* ought to be understood as a phenomenology of man's fallen existence under sin (as Macquarrie argued), or whether it should be read as describing created existence proper (the view of Tillich). Zizioulas seems to take the latter view, in agreement with Tillich—thus inviting the criticism that he has confused creation and fall. Hermeneutically speaking, for Zizioulas as for Tillich, this meant taking Heidegger's analysis as stating the predicament of the creature, as a question which theology must then answer.

However, the form of the question has a way of determining the shape of the answer. Thus, in his apologetic use of Heidegger, Zizioulas establishes an equation of human "nature" with being-unto-death, which is then projected into his synthesis of Greek patristic theology, without sufficient revision by way of Christocentric correction or attention to the Fathers' own treatment of nature. This retention of a phenomenological conception of nature as being-toward-death results in a dualism between "nature" and "person," replicated on every level of Zizioulas's theology. Here Zizioulas could have been more consistent in maintaining his commitment to the resurrection of Christ as a hermeneutical starting point for Christology and therefore also anthropology,[46] revealing the authentic *telos* not only of person but of human *nature*. In spite of protests to the contrary, Zizioulas's recent clarification on the concept of *physis* constitutes a real about-face and self-correction which, while needed, also puts into question important dimensions of his earlier work, not only on person and nature but also his methodology and its implications for hermeneutics.[47] Here we hit up against the real problems in an adoption by Orthodox theology of Tillich's correlational model of doctrine.[48]

Zizioulas's straightforward reflections on interpretation and neopatristic synthesis are far from compassing all the contributions to hermeneutics suggested by his work. Crucial aspects of his own working "hermeneutic," significant for the theory of interpretation, are missing from his account of "hermeneutics."[49] To assess more fully Zizioulas's contribution to theological hermeneutics, and his response to historicism, and its relation to philosophical hermeneutics after Heidegger, we must now turn to his treatment of Eucharist and eschatology.

Florovsky named historical revelation and Church experience as the two key foundations of theology. The contrast in the opening to Zizioulas's dogmatics lectures is notable: "Theology starts in the worship of God and in the Church's experience of communion with God."[50] Zizioulas is critical of theologies that prioritize the concept of historical revelation. Conversely, while Florovsky stressed the need to root theology in liturgical experience, and also considered the Church as a mode of revelation, he gave little attention to the actual forms of the liturgy for their dogmatic significance. A nascent eucharistic ecclesiology is detectable in Florovsky, and he does suggest an understanding of the Eucharist as an eschatological event expressive of a theology of history. Only in Zizioulas, however, do these insights become foundational and pursued with systematic thoroughness. Zizioulas thus returns us to the tradition of patristic liturgical mystagogy—in the markedly philosophical mode of a Dionysius or a Maximus—as the very wellspring of systematic theology. Tellingly, he criticizes the tendency of systematic theologians to show no interest in the liturgical typikon.

"The sacraments witness to the indivisible and inexhaustible mystery of Christ, and cannot therefore be regarded as an individual topic, but rather as the hermeneutic by which we can approach ecclesiology as a whole."[51] It is out of this sacramental—and specifically eucharistic—"hermeneutic" that Zizioulas further attempts "to relate the theology of the Church to its philosophical and ontological implications."[52] Key here is his notion of the Church as a eucharistic "mode of being"—terminology we have already encountered in Heidegger, but with linguistic precedent in the patristic concept of *tropos hyparxeos*.[53] Heidegger's "ontology of understanding" took *Verstehen* as a founding "mode" of Dasein's being, and the self-interpreting being of Dasein as the "site" of its investigations into the truth of being. For Zizioulas, the Eucharist reveals the truth about "the being of man," "the being of the world," and "the being of God."[54]

Earlier we observed how Heidegger drew on theological resources in articulating his "eschatological" ontology of being-unto-death, a concept to which Zizioulas frequently makes reference, as expressing an accurate philosophical picture of the world "as it is." Thus, it is especially notable to find Zizioulas explicitly counterposing his own eschatological vision of the Eucharist against Heidegger's being-unto-death: "As an image of the Kingdom, the Eucharist makes us appreciate more deeply the contrast between the world as it is, and the world as it will be in the last times. What the Eucharist destroys is the 'being-unto-death' of existentialism, the ontological coupling of being and non-being, life and death, a coupling which leads either to despair or to indifference concerning the transfiguration of the world."[55] Having exposed the hermeneutical dimensions of being-unto-death as it relates to Heidegger's account of understanding, interpretation, and tradition, we are led to inquire what might be the corresponding dimensions of the eucharistic eschatology Zizioulas counters to it.

Like Heidegger, Zizioulas critiques historicism on the basis of eschatology, though to a far different end.[56] This eschatology, or rather synthesis of eschatology and history, is worked out chiefly through his interpretation of the Eucharist:

> The Eucharist is not a repetition or continuation of the past, or just one event amongst others, but it is the penetration of the future into time. The Eucharist is entirely live, and utterly new; there is no element of the past about it. The

Eucharist is the incarnation live, the crucifixion live, the resurrection live, the ascension live, the Lord's coming again and the day of judgment, live. . . . 'Now is the judgment of the world' (John 12.31). This 'now' of the Fourth Gospel refers to the Eucharist, in which all these events represent themselves immediately to us, without any gaps of history between them. . . . The eschaton means the end of all separate, disconnected times, the reconnection and reconciliation of our separate histories and the arrival of the future and fulfilment. All the continuity of our histories come from outside them, from the end times, so there cannot be any final reckoning of our history apart from the eschaton which gives it its coherence and future.[57]

Like Dilthey and Heidegger, Zizioulas regards the unity of historical interpretation as requiring eschatological perspective. This perspective, he holds, is granted in the Eucharist, as a penetration of the eschaton and thus also a gathering up of all time. "Christianity is founded on historical fact, and the Church Fathers were those Christians of their era who thought most along historical lines," he says. "Nevertheless,"

> history understood in light of Eucharistic experience is not the same as history as normally understood; it is conditioned by the *anamnetic* and *epicletic* character of the eucharist which, out of distance and decay, transfigures time into communion and life. Thus history ceases to be a succession of events moving from past to present linearly, but acquires the dimension of the future, which is also a *vertical* dimension transforming history into charismatic-pentecostal events.[58]

The Eucharist, as eschatological event, challenges the linear historicism in which time is broken up into the sequence of past-present-future, the "vulgar" conception of time which Heidegger regarded as characteristic of the Western tradition of metaphysics from Aristotle to Hegel. Key here are the *anamnetic* and *epicletic* dimensions of the Eucharist.

Just as Heidegger called for hermeneutics to shake off the historicist drive for certainty and method, so too Zizioulas:

> In an epicletical context, history ceases to be in itself a guarantee for security. The *epiclesis* means ecclesiologically that the Church *asks to receive from God what she has already received historically in Christ as if she had not received it at all,* i.e., as if history did not count in itself. . . . Just as in the eucharist the words of institution cannot be a guarantee in themselves without the Spirit, although what the Spirit does is nothing but prove true the words of Christ. . . . The epicletic life of the Church shows one thing: That there is no security for her to be found in any historical guarantee as such—be it ministry or word or sacrament or even the historical Christ himself. Her constant reliance on the Spirit proves that her history is to be constantly eschatological. At the same time the fact that the Spirit points to Christ shows equally well that history is not to be denied.[59]

Heidegger identified the "essence of truth" with freedom, and freedom with letting beings be. Zizioulas equally identifies truth with freedom, but the freedom of communion.[60] In the Eucharist, moreover, events and persons of the past and present are brought before God's remembrance, and draw their substance from the future Kingdom. The future is shown to be logically and ontologically prior, as the *cause* of these events. Not unlike the later Heidegger, Zizioulas associates protological ontology founded upon substance as productive of "metaphysics," whereas eschatological ontology, he argues, escapes this.[61]

On the grounds of an identification of the truth of being with eschatological communion, Zizioulas questions a chiefly epistemological conception of correspondence truth.[62] This is a move also evident in Heidegger, who questioned the notion of correspondence truth (*adaequatio intellectus et rei*) on the grounds that intelligibility presupposes a prior framework of readiness to hand, which further presupposes Dasein, as the transcendental condition to which the uncovering of being is related. As with Heidegger, this critique informs Zizioulas's view of propositional statements in doctrine. In the Eucharist, the Church's most perfect experience of truth, the Word of God comes as flesh and as communion—*as* a community. The truth of doctrinal formulations is determined by this context: dogmas are primarily soteriological and doxological statements, meant to free the icon of Christ from distortions, and have their truth only as received within communion. Likewise with Scripture itself, which Zizioulas conceives as a Word given from the future.[63] "Through its apocalyptic roots, iconological language liberates truth from our 'conception,' 'definition,' 'comprehension,' of it and protects it from being manipulated and objectified."[64] Like the Eucharist itself, they indicate an "*acceptance, sanctification,* and also *transcendence* of history and culture," in which certain historical-cultural elements become signs and instruments of communion and thus acquire permanence within the communion-event effected by the Spirit.[65]

As image of the *eschata*, the Eucharist is not only unity and communion, but also *judgment.*[66] Ecclesiastical structures, ministries, and doctrinal formulations are to be assessed in terms of whether they reflect or else distort the image of the Kingdom.[67] All the fundamental elements which constitute the Church's historical existence must pass through the Eucharistic gathering to be "sure" and "true."[68] As such, it is a hermeneutic criterion. Eschatology both guarantees the ultimate unity of interpretation *and* serves as a critical function by which to judge all historical formulations in theology, ministries, and so forth.[69] Here we see Zizioulas developing the theme of reception, as highlighted especially by Congar: reception takes place in the Spirit, in an event of communion, and concerns primarily the love of God, persons, churches, and the facts of salvation history; dogmatic formulations are received only as they existentially relate to these.[70]

Admitting this ultimacy of the eschatological, the relationship between history and eschatology still bears a clearly *circular* character. Zizioulas concedes that it is only from history—and indeed, from historical tradition—that the Church derives her image of the *eschata*. The Church, grounded in the Eucharist, looks both forward to the eschaton and backward to her historical past in order to maintain the integrity of truth, the person of Christ, present as the eucharistic synaxis, being the unifying horizon of all time. However, priority is given to eschatology, not as a future temporal moment, within an immanent frame, but the end of time itself. Zizioulas's eschatological ontology thus places a critical limit to historical hermeneutics, which, he says, "has been of little help in avoiding the danger of subjecting the eschaton to history."[71]

Zizioulas's eschatological account of tradition bears certain parallels with Heidegger's *Wiederholung,* a retrieval of past heritage in light of futurity. Yet, as we saw earlier, Zizioulas rejects Heidegger's radical temporalization of being. Further, in Heidegger's account, the end is never given as *presence*, but only as being-*toward*; arrival of the end would mean the annihilation of time, not its healing. The productive futurity of the past in Heidegger's account lies in its *possibility*; in Zizioulas, in contrast, it is the *actuality* of the future Kingdom that determines the meaning of the past.

Zizioulas thus more successfully overcomes "linear historicism" than either Heidegger or, for that matter, Gadamer. For Heidegger, priority is given to the futural possibility of the past existing in the present; for Gadamer, temporal distance as a medium of truth is likewise primary. Zizioulas admits that we require temporal distance in order to recognize things as distinct.[72] However, it is not temporal distance and its finite horizons which determine even temporal being, but the eschatological communion of all times:

> The Church is not an entity living outside time. Communion is not only a matter of the relatedness of each local Church with the rest of the Churches in space or with the rest of the world at a given time, but of *koinonia* with the communities of the past as well as of the future. As far as the past is concerned, the Church needs *Tradition* to exist as *koinonia*. When Tradition is itself affected and conditioned by communion, it ceases to be a formal transmission of teaching and life and becomes a re-interpreted and re-received reality in the light of the particular context in which it is transmitted. This makes Tradition acquire the form of *traditions*. . . . In this way diversity becomes part of the picture. . . . In an ecclesiology of communion, time is not broken into past, present, and future. The end of time is *time redeemed* from this kind of brokenness through the intervention of the Kingdom between the past and the present. The true criterion

of Tradition is, therefore, to be found in the revelation of what the world will be like in the Kingdom.[73]

It is their communion with the living Jesus Christ, and our communion with them, in the future Kingdom of God that finally makes any enclosure of the apostles or Fathers in the past, as implied by the proposal of a "post-patristic" theology, impossible. "If Christ is the eschatological man and our continuity with him is not determined by the time sequence which implies distance, but by a concept of time determined by an event of communion, the apostles themselves cannot be enclosed in a self-defined event, in a closed past."[74] As has been frequently remarked, the priority of tradition in both Heidegger and Gadamer provides little ground for criteria beyond particular cultures, and could underwrite simply a conservative affirmation of cultural tradition; reason remains regional, the framework radically immanentist, and in that sense, still "historicist."[75] Zizioulas's account reminds us that the tradition that matters to the Church is more than that: it is conditioned by the freedom of God, who is never imprisoned in history.

This fundamentally theocentric and epicletic vision of tradition and its reception is crucial to Zizioulas's contribution to theological hermeneutics. Florovsky also understood tradition as "the life of the Holy Spirit in the Church" and the "continual speech of God, apprehended in faith." Zizioulas gives this understanding a deeper grounding in the Liturgy and in his pneumatological Christology. Florovsky, however, also laid stress on the role of human subjects and their acts of interpretation. Zizioulas's account of tradition, in contrast, gives almost no account for the role of the subject and of human freedom in interpretation. For Florovsky, following Collingwood, events—among which he includes also interpretation—are fundamentally *actions* of free subjects. Zizioulas here resembles more Gadamer, for whom tradition and interpretation are fundamentally event or happening (*Geschehen*), only secondarily act (*Tathandlung*). As Zizioulas puts it: in the Eucharist, "the primary and decisive thing is the future event, not our actions."[76] Nevertheless, while Gadamer also decentralizes the role of the reflective subject and insists on the finitude of human thought, he does not neglect the role of consciousness, or of becoming.

These differences relate to creation and eschatology. While for Florovsky, creation *ex nihilo* means fundamentally contingency and the openness of history to new events, in Zizioulas's emphasis creation spells more the possibility of corruption, and history as necessity. Likewise, for Florovsky, eschatology serves to underwrite the permanent significance of human historical action—history determining eschatology. For Zizioulas, in contrast, the accent falls on the decisiveness of the end in determining and judging historical action, or freeing the creature from history. It is tempting, but perhaps unfair, to apply here to Zizioulas Florovsky's critique of a "realized eschatology" in which "meaning is shifted from the realm of history to the realm of sacramental experience, in which the *Eschaton* is present and re-enacted," with the implication that *"there is nothing else to be accomplished in history."*[77]

Yet in fact Zizioulas shows exceeding little interest in historical becoming. The "as" in "being *as* communion" is affected by eschatology, understood as *state,* not orientation; being-*toward* occupies only a negative place, as being-toward-*death*.[78] In spite of his stress on an "existential" theology, this inattentiveness to human becoming in fact *weakens* the "existential" character of his thought. Human freedom, as decision and growth, is left out of the account. Here Zizioulas may be contrasted not only with the ascetic tradition but also with other modern theologians impacted by Heidegger, who stress precisely the temporal dynamism of human becoming on the way to union with God. Zizioulas's critic and former disciple Nikolaos Loudovikos speaks of Maximus the Confessor's understanding of being as "being as a dialogical event of becoming-in-communion."[79] This theme of dialogue, as developed by Loudovikos as well as by Staniloae, holds much potential for a conversation with philosophical hermeneutics.

It would be remiss of us to proceed to a conclusion on eschatology, ontology, and hermeneutics in Hedeigger and Zizioulas without touching on a key figure linking the two: Wolfhart Pannenberg. Similar to both Heidegger and Zizioulas, Pannenberg finds in eschatology a way out of relativism, providing that Heidegger's limitation of wholeness to individual being-unto-death is set aside: eschatological truth, the presence of the whole, enters into the midst of historical relativity.[80] Precisely here, however, Pannenberg also differs from Zizioulas: in his emphasis, anticipation is only *mere* anticipation, not the whole itself. As he argues, "The category of fore-conception [*Vorgriff*] makes it possible to conceive the history of mankind as ordered toward a final destination without skipping over the unfinished character of the factual course of events."[81]

As we saw earlier, Zizioulas too makes a distinction between historical "image" and eschatological "truth." However, in his account of the Eucharist, stress falls much more on the identity of the two and the finality of what is given *already*. This difference is noted by Zizioulas himself in his distinction between Pannenberg's eschatology of orientation and his own eschatology of state. The result is that Zizioulas shows far less interest in the open-ended contingencies of historical events than Pannenberg, or for that matter, Florovsky, both of whom stress the unfinished character of history and its significance for epistemology, and understand eschatology as a culmination of contingent historical *process*.

Zizioulas derived a key inspiration from Pannenberg's notion of an eschatological approach to Church ministry, and more broadly, his idea of an eschatological ontology. Pannenberg's open debt to Heidegger on this point establishes a further connection between Zizioulas and Heidegger on the priority of eschatology. However, as we have seen, we find a very different development of this idea in Pannenberg's eschatology of process and orientation. In some ways, Pannenberg is closer to Florovsky, insofar as he sets much greater store by historical activity and its unfinished character, as well as the rational character of theology, than Zizioulas. Unique to Pannenberg, however, is the stress on the relationship of historical revelation to universal reason, and therefore its openness to probabilistic historiographical verification.

Pannenberg's claims for apologetic theological reasoning may be more robust than most modern theologians would find comfortably convincing, yet his eschatology is employed toward a *critical* historical realism—next to which the eschatological hermeneutics of Zizioulas may seem somewhat like a retreat from history and from reason. In any case, however, a common lesson may be gathered from Pannenberg and Zizioulas alike, as from Florovsky, in their dealings with hermeneutics: the hermeneutical problem, and discussion of contextuality, must find their ultimate reference point and limit with reference to eschatology, or the final *telos* of history, which is somehow already apprehended in Jesus Christ and in his Church.

CONCLUSION

As this chapter has shown, the conversation between Orthodox theology and modern historicism that lay at the roots of Florovsky's program of neopatristic synthesis is continued in the work of Zizioulas, albeit in far more tacit mode. The developments from Florovsky to Zizioulas keep pace with the movement from Dilthey and the "crisis of historicism" to Heidegger's radicalization of Dilthey and his ontological-eschatological deconstruction of historicism. For both theologians, the relationship with secular philosophy is that of a critical *ad hoc* appropriation.

Aside from his borrowing of certain concepts (*ekstasis*, etc.), Zizioulas is a debtor to Heidegger more generally, insofar as Heidegger restored questions of *being* and *truth*, rather than knowledge and method, to the center of philosophy. Heidegger's influence in putting eschatology at the very heart of twentieth-century theology is also key to Zizioulas's development of Florovsky's neopatristic program. Both Heidegger and Florovsky stressed immersion in history in their different ways, but questioned the priority of the past in historiographical interpretation. Florovsky criticized a "theology of repetition," and spoke of loyalty to tradition as "not only concord with the past, but, in a certain sense, freedom from the past, as from some outward formal criterion." Drawing from the Liturgy and St Maximus, but also in dialogue with Heidegger both directly and indirectly via Pannenberg, Zizioulas provides a clearer eschatological-ontological framework for this understanding, an approach to history characterized by freedom *toward* the past (always within the communion of the Church and in the one Spirit), thus placing a question mark beside any strict *limitation* of the truth of tradition to authorially intended meaning of texts, to be recovered naked from the past by way of historical-critical method. Equally challenged here is a triumphalist ecclesiastical conservatism that would confuse fidelity to the Church with a comforting repetition of formulas or mere maintenance of established forms.

Notwithstanding important critical questions regarding the status of nature, historical activity, and the correlational method in his thought, Zizioulas remains the most successful and compelling of all Orthodox theologians in carrying out the program of neopatristic synthesis suggested by Florovsky and demonstrating its broad potential for future theology. In keeping with our own reading, Zizioulas accurately recognizes the hermeneutical character of this program and its twofold orientation of ecumenical conversation with the Christian West and dialogue with philosophical culture, as conceived by Florovsky. Further, Zizioulas has placed the neopatristic program on a firmer foundation of liturgy and Church structures, crucial for Orthodox theological hermeneutics. Heidegger spoke of "interpretation in the 'Today.'" For Orthodox Christians, this "today" determinative for interpretation remains the σήμερον of the festal Liturgy, in which the events of salvation history are made present. In his limited dialogue with modern hermeneutical philosophy, Zizioulas also marks certain clear limits where Orthodox theology must differ critically. The eschatological finality of Jesus Christ and his presence in the Church marks a limit to the universality of the hermeneutic problem as conceived by philosophical hermeneutics, with its radical temporality and endless interpretation without *telos*.

NOTES

1. Due to his untimely passing, Fr Matthew Baker (1977–2015), much beloved husband, father, priest, and scholar, was unable to complete the paper he was preparing for the Delphi conference. It has fallen to some of his friends to put together (however imperfectly) the chapter that follows, compiled chiefly from his dissertation chapter on the figures of Heidegger and Zizioulas. While his dissertation remained unfinished at the time of his death, Fordham University has since posthumously awarded Fr Mat-

thew Baker with the degree of Doctor of Philosophy. May the memory of the Revd Dr Matthew Baker be eternal!—Editor's Note (Edited by Alexis Torrance).

2. This preamble is important to understand what follows: Fr Matthew Baker's work on Heidegger and Zizioulas was eventually intended to be read in the context of his larger project on the intricate philosophical underpinnings of Georges Florovsky's theological program and its relationship both to movements in philosophy and theology contemporaneous with Florovsky as well as to those of subsequent generations (especially with regard to hermeneutics). The draft from which this chapter is derived deals with part of this latter concern—Editor's Note.

3. On Fichte's usage, see Theodore Kisiel, "On the Genesis of Heidegger's Formally Indicative Hermeneutics of Facticity," in *Re-thinking Facticity*, eds. François Raffoul and Eric Sean Nelson (Albany: State University of New York Press, 2008), 61–64. More generally, see Scott M. Campbell, *The Early Heidegger's Philosophy of Life: Facticity, Being, and Language* (Fordham University Press, 2012).

4. Dasein ("there-being" or "to be there") is Heidegger's deliberately ambiguous term for the kind of being human beings are. Heidegger avoids any ready equation of Dasein with human being to resist association with humanism or an "ontically" understood definition of human nature (as rational animal, etc).

5. Martin Heidegger, *Ontology: The Hermeneutics of Facticity*, trans. John van Buren (Bloomington: Indiana University Press, 1999), 5.

6. Ibid., 5–6.

7. Ibid., 6–11.

8. Ibid., 11.

9. Ibid., 64.

10. Judith Wolfe, *Heidegger's Eschatology: Theological Horizons in Martin Heidegger's Early Work* (Oxford, UK: Oxford University Press, 2013), 75.

11. Wolfe, *Heidegger's Eschatology,* 72. Luther scholar Edmund Schlink early on claimed that Heidegger's existential analytic of Dasein was a radical secularization of Luther's anthropology.

12. Wolfe, *Heidegger's Eschatology*, 118. Commenting on his own early theological studies, Heidegger remarked: "Without this theological background I should never have come upon the path of thinking. But origin [Herkunft] always comes to meet us from the future [Zukunft]" ("Dialogue on Language: Between a Japanese and an Inquirer," *On the Way to Language*, trans. Peter D. Hertz [San Francisco: HarperSanFrancisco, 1982], 10).

13. For this interpretation, see Thomas Sheehan, "A Paradigm Shift in Heidegger Research," *Continental Philosophy Review* 32, no. 2 (2001): 1–20.

14. Immanuel Kant, *Critique of Pure Reason,* trans. Paul Guyer and Allen Wood (Cambridge: Cambridge University Press, 2000), A 136.

15. See Martin Heidegger, *Being and Time* trans. John MacQuarrie and Edward Robinson (Oxford: Blackwell, 2001), sections 65 and 69 for this whole discussion.

16. "Understanding is grounded primarily in the future. . . . All the same, understanding is in every case a present which 'is in the process of having been'. . . . Temporalizing does not signify that ecstasies come in a 'succession'. The future is *not later* than having been, and having been is not earlier than the present. Temporality

temporalizes itself as a future which makes present in the process of having been" (Heidegger, *Being and Time* [hereafter *BT*], 401 [68]).

17. Heidegger questions the priority given to simple pastness (*Vergangenheit*) in the common understanding of the historical, as distinct from the sense of having-been (*Gewesenheit*) characteristic of Dasein's ecstatic temporality. It is Dasein that is primarily historical, other entities only secondarily so. Museum pieces have the character of pastness because they originate in a world of a Dasein that has been. Yet the vulgar concept of history, Heidegger alleges, results from taking this secondary historicity as definitive.

18. *BT*, 430 (73), revised with reference to the translation by Joan Stambough of Heidegger, *Being and Time* (Albany: State University of New York Press, 2010), 361.

19. *BT*, 435 (74).

20. At this point Heidegger invokes the concepts of freedom, fate (*Schicksals*), and destiny (*Geschick*). Confrontation with death and the finitude of one's existence "snatches one back from the endless multiplicity of possibilities . . . and brings Dasein to the simplicity of its fate. This is how we designate Dasein's primordial historizing, which lies in authentic resoluteness and in which Dasein hands itself down to itself, free for death, in a possibility which it has inherited and yet has chosen" (*BT*, 435 [74]). This authentic temporalizing occurs not simply as individual fate but, in keeping with Dasein's being-with others, is always the destiny (*Geschick*) of a culture and a generation.

21. *BT*, 437, (74).

22. "Repetition" recalls to English-speaking readers the work of Kierkegaard, a key background here. Yet the sense of Heidegger's meaning is better captured as "retrieval," following *wieder holen*, "to fetch again." Kierkegaard's work *Repetition* (*Gjentagelse*, 1843) was translated into German in 1909 under the title *Wiederholung*, a translation Heidegger certainly knew. For discussion of Heidegger's *Wiederholung* in relation to Kierkegaard, see John D. Caputo, *Radical Hermeneutics: Repetition, Deconstruction, and the Hermeneutic Project* (Indiana University Press, 1988).

23. Heidegger, *Der Begriff der Zeit*, 25. [Baker does not provide full bibliographical information].

24. Later, in an essay published in the 1950 volume *Holzwege*, "Anaximander's Saying," Heidegger counterposes "the eschatology of being" explicitly against "historicism" which, he says, has not only not been overcome, but has entered into a new phase of domination through technology. Heidegger states that "being itself is eschatological," meaning "the eschatology of being in the sense in which the phenomenology of Spirit is to be thought, i.e., from within the history of being." Martin Heidegger, *Off the Beaten Track* (Cambridge University Press, 2002), 246–47.

25. It is precisely *because* of this pregnant character of heritage, and the fundamentally *concerned* interest of the historian, Heidegger argues, that relentless concern with facts is demanded of historiography. On the other hand, scientific access to facts is accessed always in the context of traditions of interpretation, prescientific and having a history of their own. Access to the past inevitably entails some kind of critical, appropriative, and productive relation to tradition.

26. "The authentic interpretation must show what does not stand there in the words and which is nevertheless said. For this the interpretation must necessarily use

violence. What is authentic is to be sought where nothing further can be found by scientific exegesis, which brands as unscientific everything that exceeds its domain." Martin Heidegger, *Introduction to Metaphysics*, trans. Gregory Fried and Richard Polt (Yale University Press, 2000), 173.

27. Heidegger's discussion of the correspondence between Dilthey and Count Graf von Yorck, found in section 77, was begun as a book review in 1924 and formed one of the first drafts of *BT*. See Theodore Kisiel, *The Genesis of Heidegger's Being and Time* (Berkley: University of California Press, 1993), 315–61.

28. John Zizioulas, *Lectures in Christian Dogmatics* (London: T&T Clark, 2009) [hereafter *LCD*], x.

29. *LCD*, 3.

30. *LCD*, x.

31. Ibid., 136: "When it comes to the Orthodox/non-Orthodox dialogue within the ecumenical debate, the important thing is always the *theological presuppositions, not the concrete theses. The latter are only logical developments of the former.*" In view of Florovsky's critique of logical theories of doctrinal development, with which Zizioulas seems to concur, one questions the choice of the term "logical" here.

32. Ibid., 137. Among such principles, he mentions, as characteristic of the Orthodox, the following: (1) ecclesiology situated within Trinitarian theology; (2) pneumatological Christology; (3) eschatological ecclesiology; (4) the cosmic dimension of ecclesiology.

33. This point is developed in different ways in the work of both Bultmann and Gadamer (*Vorverständnis*).

34. John Zizioulas, *The One and the Many: Studies on God, Man, the Church, and the World Today* (Alhambra, CA: Sebastian Press, 2010) [hereafter *OAM*], 128: "The tendency in most people in the ecumenical movement is to approach the existential problems of the Church today with no reference whatsoever to the inherited tradition of the Church. This is, in fact, an illusion, for none of us in the ecumenical movement, no Church whatsoever thinks, decides, and acts with regard to actual issues without being conditioned by some kind of tradition."

35. See John Zizioulas, *Eucharist, Bishop, Church: The Unity of the Church in the Divine Eucharist and the Bishop during the First Three Centuries*, trans. Elizabeth Theokritoff (Brookline, MA: Holy Cross Orthodox Press, 2001) [hereafter *EBC*], 19–21.

36. *OAM*, 69

37. This priority of the public liturgy explains in part also Zizioulas's singling out of Fathers who were heads of Eucharistic communities (Ignatius, Irenaeus, Athanasius, Cappadocians) in his intellectual genealogy of patristic thought, as opposed to lay intellectuals (Justin, Clement): see John Zizioulas, *Being as Communion* (Crestwood, NY: St Vladimir's Seminary Press, 1985) [hereafter *BAC*], 72–89.

38. See Anthony Thistleton, *New Horizons in Hermeneutics: The Theory and Practice of Transforming Biblical Reading* (Grand Rapids, MI: Zondervan, 1992), especially 10–16.

39. Thistleton, *New Horizons in Hermeneutics*, 337. Thistleton refers approvingly to a 1987 dissertation of James McHann, *Three Horizons: A Study in Biblical Hermeneutics with reference to Wolfhart Pannenberg*, for this insight.

40. Luke Ben Tallon hints at the suggestiveness of this eschatological element for hermeneutics: "Particularly interesting, if rather undeveloped, are the implications that Zizioulas' navigation of the difference-in-continuity between the historical events and the Church's *remembrance* might have for biblical interpretation beyond the accounts of the Last Supper. Even more interesting (and unremarked) are the implications of Zizioulas's account of *eschatological causality* for the study of scripture (and church history), given that such study generally assumes *protological causality*" ("Introduction," in Zizioulas, *The Eucharistic Communion and the World* [London: T&T Clark, 2011] [hereafter *ECW*], ix; *ECW*).

41. For Gadamer, horizon signifies a *finite* vantage point: "Every finite present has its limitations. We define the concept of 'situation' by saying that it represents a standpoint that limits the possibility of vision. Hence an essential part of the concept of situation is the concept of 'horizon.' The horizon is the range of vision that includes everything that can be seen from a particular vantage point" (*Truth and Method* [London: Bloomsbury Academic, 2004], 269).

42. On this point, see James K. A. Smith, *The Fall of Interpretation: Philosophical Foundations for a Creational Hermeneutic* (Intervarsity Press, 2000).

43. On all these themes, see Paul Tillich, *Systematic Theology*, vol. 1 (Chicago: University of Chicago Press, 1951).

44. See Martin Woessner, *Heidegger in America* (Cambridge: Cambridge University Press, 2010), 103. While Florovsky's affinities were decisively more with Barth than with Tillich, comments sprinkled throughout Zizioulas's work suggest little sympathy with Barth. Where Zizioulas speaks of the need for new terms and to re-interpret the tradition "in light of" the present, Florovsky tended to stress rather the necessity for moderns to learn the language of the Fathers, and to interpret the present cultural situation "in light of" the unchanging kerygma.

45. See *BAC*, 102n; John Zizioulas, *Communion and Otherness* (T&T Clark, 2007) [hereafter *CO*], 228.

46. *BAC* 55, fn 49: "All things in Christology are judged in the light of the resurrection. . . . This is the way in which Christology in the New Testament has developed—from the resurrection to the incarnation, not the other way around—and patristic theology has never lost this eschatological approach to Christology."

47. John Zizioulas, "Person and Nature in the Theology of St. Maximus the Confessor," *Knowing the Purpose of Creation through the Resurrection*, ed. Bishop Maxim Vasiljević (Sebastian Press, 2013), 85–113.

48. On this point, we need not be Barthians to take a wise caution from Karl Barth, here quoting his brother Heinrich Barth (speaking of Bultmann): "That theology should begin with a definition of existence, or man . . . is at root a piece of Liberalism" (Karl Barth, *Church Dogmatics* 1.1 [London: T&T Clark, 1975], 37). Likewise, Barth, *Church Dogmatics 1.2* (London: T&T Clark, 1956 [793]): "The Word of God is not the Word of God unless it precedes this question of man's existence, unless it is its origin even before it becomes its answer. And theology has ill understood its task unless it regards this question as one which . . . in the first instance is put by the Word of God itself."

49. Following other authors, I distinguish here between the singular sense of "hermeneutic," as the actual frame of reference of an interpretation or its working practice, and the plural "hermeneutics," referring to the science, theory, or philosophy of interpretation. See for example, John Robinson and John Cobb, *New Frontiers in Theology: The New Hermeneutic* (New York: Harper, 1964), ix–x.

50. *LCD*, 2.

51. *LCD*, 137—see further on 138 regarding eucharist.

52. *BAC*, 23. Anglophone reception of Zizioulas's work has tended to neglect Zizioulas's treatment of history and eschatology. Far more than the doctrine of the person or Trinitarian theology proper, however, it is this twofold theme, built out of his consideration of the Eucharist, that predominates in structuring Zizioulas's seminal work in the period up to the publication of *Being as Communion* (1985).

53. Yannaras credits the 1963 dissertation of Georgios Mantzaridis on Gregory Palamas for reintroducing this concept into modern Greek theology (Christos Yannaras, *Orthodoxy and the West* [Brookline, MA: Holy Cross Orthodox Press, 2006], 279–80); see Georgios Mantzaridis, *The Deification of Man: St Gregory Palamas and the Orthodox Tradition* (Crestwood, NY: St Vladimir's Seminary Press, 1984). Hans Urs von Balthasar had earlier drawn attention to this concept in his 1941 study of Maximus the Confessor, *Kosmische Liturgie,* a work cited by Florovsky and surely known to Zizioulas during the period of his Harvard studies.

54. *BAC*, 15. Reflecting on his own development, Zizioulas has recently commented: "Personally, I saw the Divine Eucharist as the key to understanding the early structure and ministries of the Church and then anthropology (with the concept of the person as communion and otherness), and, finally, the very mystery of the Triune God as essence and persons, communion and otherness" ("Orthodox Theology and the Challenges of the 21st Century," Address Delivered at the Reception of the Metropolitan of Pergamon as "Fellow" of the Volos Academy of Theological Studies, Volos, October 29, 2011, unpublished, 3–4).

55. *ECW*, 80.

56. This is somewhat in contrast to Florovsky, who drew his critique of evolutionary historicism primarily from his vision of contingency and of human freedom, marked by his apocalyptic sense of history.

57. *LCD*, 155.

58. *BAC,* 115–116.

59. Ibid., 185–186.

60. Ibid., 122: "Man is free only in communion. If the Church wishes to be the place of freedom, she must continually place all the 'objects' she possesses, whatever they may be (Scripture, sacraments, ministries, etc.) within the communion-event to make them 'true' and to make her members free in regard to them as objects, as well as in them and through them as channels of communion. Christians must learn not to lean on objective 'truths' as securities for truth, but to live in an *epicletic* way, i.e. leaning on the communion-event in which the structure of the Church involves them. Truth liberates by placing beings in communion."

61. John Zizioulas, "Towards an Eschatalogical Ontology," Resources for Christian Theology, accessed [by the Editor], May 16, 2015, https://www.resources forchristiantheology.org/towards-an-eschatological-ontology/

62. *BAC*, 103.

63. Ibid., 187–88, 89: "In the New Testament itself we can find an idea of *paradosis* or *logia* which are historically transmitted from place to place and time to time. And yet, it is the Spirit that vivifies the words, and it is only in the Spirit that the kerygma of Christ can make sense. . . . The spoken or written Word of God, as it is historically formulated and transmitted, becomes life and divine presence only in the context of the eschatological community of the eucharist."

64. Ibid., 100–101.

65. Ibid., 116–18.

66. *ECW*, 29–31, 36–37.

67. *BAC*, 207: "The Church relates to the apostles in and through the presence of the eschatological community in history. This is not a denial of history, for it is through historical forms that this presence takes place. But the ultimate criterion for unity is to be found in the question to what extent the actual form of the Church's ministry and message today—or at any given time—reflect the presence of this eschatological community." Cf. also *ECW*, 71.

68. Ibid., 21.

69. Ibid., 207: "The historical heritage of the past—on which the Churches have insisted for so long—as well as the historical needs of the present (concern with social problems, etc.)—which seem to preoccupy the ecumenical movement in our days—will both have to be judged by this ultimate, *final judgment* provided by the vision of the *eschata*, without which no real unity of the Church can exist."

70. *OAM*, 118–25; *LCD*, 161–64. See also *BAC*, 241–42.

71. *OAM*, 132.

72. *LCD*, 17.

73. *OAM*, 58.

74. *BAC*, 183.

75. See Carl Page, *Philosophical Historicism and the Betrayal of First Philosophy* (University Park: Pennsylvania State University, 1995); David Roberts, *Nothing But History: Reconstruction and Extremity after Metaphysics* (Berkley: University of California Press, 1995).

76. *OAM*, 133.

77. Georges Florovsky, "The Predicament of the Christian Historian," in *Collected Works of Georges Florovsky*, vol. 2, *Christianity and Culture* (Belmont, MA: Nordland Publishing, 1974), 61.

78. Here we may contrast Bonhoeffer's account, in *Act and Being,* of Christian life as martyric being-toward-death in Christ.

79. Nikolaos Loudovikos, *A Eucharistic Ontology: Maximus the Confessor's Eschatological Ontology of Being as Dialogical Reciprocity*, trans. Elizabeth Theokritoff (Brookline, MA: Holy Cross Press, 2010), 205.

80. Wolfhart Pannenberg, *Basic Questions in Theology*, trans. George H. Kehm (Philadelphia, PA: Westminster Press, 1969), 171.

81. Pannenberg, *Basic Questions in Theology,* 170.

Chapter Seven

What Does "Rising from the Dead" Mean?

A Hermeneutics of Resurrection

Maxim Vasiljević

In *Risen*, a 2016 American biblical drama film directed by Kevin Reynolds, the Resurrection story is recounted by a sceptic who finally meets Yeshua himself. The first forty days after the Resurrection of Jesus Christ is depicted through the eyes of an agnostic Roman Centurion, Clavius, authorized by Pontius Pilate to investigate rumors of a risen Jewish Messiah and find the dead body of Jesus of Nazareth to pacify a threatening rebellion in Jerusalem. During his mission, his suspicions of an enigmatic epiphany grow as he encounters the apostles and other historic biblical characters and bears witness to the great events that followed the Resurrection. As his quest to find the body takes him through paradox and disorientation, Centurion Clavius uncovers the verity that he has been pursuing. A great mystery unfolds, and he is intensely affected by his first-person investigation, as his previous beliefs on the matter are forever altered based on what he's now witnessed.

The responsibility of the theologian is to give an answer to John the Baptist's question: *Are you he who is to come, or shall we look for another?*[1] This question is not just for John to ask; this is the question for every generation and age. But that brings us to another question: how does a particular generation and culture recognize Christ as *their* Savior? All these issues can be reduced to the problem of understanding the starting point in theology, to the question of the universal person of Christ. What is it that makes him the only new thing that has ever appeared under the sun? Remember, even though the ancient world knew of the immortality of the soul, the angels, "sons of God," "redeemers," and so on, it had no precedent whatsoever for the mystery of the God-Man—the mystery that connects history with eternity and *immortalizes* not just his human nature, but also the entire universe and every individual being.[2]

The answer to the question of how a civilization relates to Christ is interwoven (contextualized) with the intellectual-cultural-ethical milieu of the people who will provide an answer to it. Hans-Georg Gadamer was right when he categorically stated that understanding always includes historical mediation.[3] However, the issue is not just ethical, intellectual, or aesthetic, but primarily *existential*. Only then is it able to provide responses to the highest pursuits, universal expectations, panhuman anxieties, and deepest requirements of the world, with which Christ is connected in the Spirit. But, first, one thing must be emphasized: Christ is not a *necessary* answer to *all* human demands. He is not even *that king* awaited by the Jews,[4] nor is God how *we* envision him. God in Christ and the Spirit is the One who in his manic love—even though we do not deserve it—meets us *unexpectedly* in our despair and embraces us when we fall into death.

In order to answer these questions, we begin with an examination of the relationship between the truth (ontology) and human culture (history). In this attempt we will be guided by considerations of modern Orthodox theology (especially George Florovsky, Wolfhart Pannenberg, John Zizioulas, and Matthew Baker), which introduces the element of futurity, an "eschatology with *eschaton*."[5] It seems that modern theology uses the resurrection of Christ as a hermeneutical starting point for Christology and anthropology.

THE RELATIONSHIP BETWEEN THE TRUTH AND HUMAN CULTURE

Let us begin by saying: in order for Christian culture to be an expression of the *ecclesial* ethos emanating from the experience of the Kingdom of God, it must reach beyond its context. Moreover, in a culture/civilization that is determined by rationalism and historicism, it becomes necessary, although extremely difficult, to allow an approach that confirms the factuality of truth by facts—by *events*, to be more precise—that go beyond ephemeral experience, and especially extend to the Future (*Eschaton*) which the eucharistic community experiences as the Supper of the Kingdom.

Here we become aware of one difficulty. The transcendent cannot be discerned by someone who asserts the truth *exclusively* as *adaequatio rei et intellectus* and never looks beyond the firm boundaries of this realm.[6] Philosophically, truth has traditionally been identified with "reality": what I say—or see—is true because it corresponds with experience. However, since reality is subject to change, corruption, et cetera, there is a fundamental and precisely framed question that emerges from such discourse: how can we know what the truth is? Obviously, the definition of truth depends on what you suppose your existence is like, or what your "beholder" eyes expect to see. If somebody told you that "you are dying *now*," you would say "that's nonsense." However, when an artist depicts you in a state of dying, he undoubtedly expresses an existential truth. This is exactly the point that the Eastern ecclesial art makes with its icon: things that contradict the mind could be more real than those corresponding to it.[7] The iconic ontology does not imply contradiction since it refers to the reality of the *future,* which is opposed to the reality of Plato for whom truth is not in the present or future reality but in the ideal world.[8] As modern science is becoming more aware, cosmic harmony and order are more and more revealed as objective, *unpredictable,* dynamic happenings that elude "synthetic conclusions" (ruling out definite prediction in the field of physical becoming) and whose workings are incomprehensible to us even though we can distinguish their outlines. It resembles mostly the matter in quantum physics that can be either a particle or a wave, or neither, or something which comprises both, depending how the *other* (observer) perceives it, and whether the other is capable of self-surrender.

Now, if the answers of philosophy, psychology, ethics, et cetera, would suffice as a reliable solution, a theologian would not have to turn to Christology. Yet, the context for theological reflection needs the element of *freedom* and of the *futurity*, and it can only arise as a result of an *event*. There is reason to believe that the logic hidden in the Resurrection of Christ *verifies* every Christological and ecclesial truth—not as a mere theological *truism,* of course, but as an ontological-hermeneutical answer to the problem of life and death. To understand this point more fully, we must remember that since birth (even from the mother's womb) each person is bestowed with life and awareness of a dialectic of life and death. A Christology of the Resurrection resolves this dialectic, as we will see explicitly later. The answer, however, is not readily available, but comes rather as a *surprise from the future*: when the case of "the deceiver"[9] was closed after Christ's suffering and death, the Resurrected entered through a closed door and proclaimed the good news that Life is stronger than death. This opens the door for the Christian epistemology that shows Christ's Resurrection as a *true* event, true precisely because it is so incredible and impossible that no one would dare preach it unless it *de facto* occurred.[10]

If this is proven correct, then we must accept that, for the Church, the context of the experience of that event is the divine Eucharist, as the *good news* of triumph over death and as an *icon* of the Kingdom. Philosophy, in this case, does not serve as a context but rather as a *tool* for extracting logical implications, while the eucharistic experience serves as the context for becoming cognizant of the existential consequences. The reason for this is that love, knowledge (logic), and faith—within the mystery of theology—cannot be separated.[11]

DOGMAS IN AND OF THEMSELVES AND THEIR RELATION TO US

While all theological musings on the Resurrection can be compelling, some of them lack a critical sharpness or clarity of description. (If someone uses words like "short," "close," or "excited," we all basically know what is meant, but with the word "resurrection," whose relation with psychological experience is less direct, there many possible interpretations.) There is an ultimate difficulty that arises from such conversation: should we ascribe a self-evident reality to the Resurrection, or should we take it as an *expected* event yet to be confirmed? Long before Gadamer, St Paul introduced the *future* as a hermeneutical tool: "For if the dead are not raised, then Christ has not been raised."[12] The reasoning behind Paul's conclusion is so subtle that even today it takes a lot of logical effort to appreciate it fully. Paul intended to indicate that the Resurrection of Christ would become pointless if it were not a collective realization—that is, if the whole body were not implicitly "pre-resurrected" with the Head. The "prehappening" of the future of the world in Christ's Resurrection speaks of the future's-work-in-progress. Obviously, as Pannenberg observes, "Paul's gospel, one must understand, is the exegesis of the appearance of the resurrected Jesus that he experienced."[13] This *a posteriori* verification of the past is almost forgotten in contemporary theology, so it is here that Gadamer steps in with his hermeneutics and dramatically changes the character of the debate. What is the contribution of hermeneutics to our subject? The answer emerges from a simple observation about the importance of the *future*. According to St Maximus the Confessor, who is keen to emphasize the *eschaton*:

> If . . . everything that was brought from non-being to being is moved because it tends toward some *end*, then nothing that moves is yet at rest. For movement driven by desire has not yet come to rest in that which is *ultimately desirable* (τῷ ἐσχάτῳ ὀρεκτῷ). Unless that which is ultimately desirable is possessed, nothing else is of such a nature as to bring to rest what is being driven by desire (οὐδὲν ἄρα κινούμενον ἔστη, ὡς τοῦ ἐσχάτου μήπω τυχὸν ὀρεκτοῦ).[14]

If we take hermeneutics[15] seriously and, to recall St Maximus's logic, we are surprised by the fact that there is nothing that is not *interpreted by the future,* then there is "nothing" behind; nothing is the past. This is a radically strange reality: it is only in the *distance of the future* that the mystery of existence (and, clearly, of salvation) will appear evident. Everything that is behind us, we have lived it as "today," and only by living it in that way, as today, does it receive its meaning. In other words, the future substantiates history in an ontological way. Only after the Resurrection, the disciples "remembered His words."[16]

The 'logic of the resurrection' differs from the classical scholastic approach in a number of essential ways, and foremost for us are the following three points.

The first point is related to the reality of *death*. Although the joy of life is truer than the agony of death that accompanies it, one cannot live the Resurrection without experiencing the tragedy of death. Even the saints die.

Secondly, the fact that there will be a resurrection of the body demonstrates that the *future* is quintessential. This dimension of the *future* has sadly disappeared from the horizon of contemporary theologians, as they consider everything to have been solved. Even within the Orthodox milieu people tend to take it for granted that the saints are fine *now*. However, when the Church sings, "death is trampled down by death," it points to the *future*, to something that *will* be revealed. So, we can only anticipate or eucharistically foretaste it.

The third point is related to *expectation*. This problem comes to the surface more and more because there is a great tendency today to replace the notion of "foretaste" with the idea of "realization" of the Eschaton. We do not deny that there is a "real presence" (for instance, Christ's presence in the Eucharist), but we have to add one caveat since we await that happening as a reality in the future. It does not take too much effort to recognize a paradoxical structure in history and, particularly, in biblical history: (a) the future *precedes* the past; (b) everything that happens is not completed in the moment of its happening but has its meaning in the future; (c) one must *wait* if one wants to see that which had happened; (d) if the future does not come to show what it was that had happened, then it (the past event) has no meaning and, literally, does not exist. From this perspective, the future is more than just an aspect of time; in the Bible time is the future's work in progress.

Unfortunately, this element of *expectation* (προσδοκία) and *prolepsis* has almost disappeared from contemporary theology,[17] as if we do not need to wait. This is an important topic in theology. In our modern debate, the notion of "realized eschatology" has to be corrected. But how can this be done? Oscar Cullman has a solution, and the answer he found is a logical yet profound extension of our discussion so far. The famous phrase that he invented to describe this dialectic is very important: the Kingdom is *already* here, but *not yet*. This concept has important implications. For example, we should not be satisfied by seeing a saint merely as a *relic* but should also desire to see the saint alive, which, again, leads us to the *future*. We should be concerned with death. When we stop being concerned with death—and with the expectation of its destruction—our creativity dries out. Precisely from the struggle with death springs love, sacrifice, art, et cetera.

To understand this point more fully, accept for a moment that dogmas are relevant only in the sense that their truth and validity is applicable *to us*. In this case, there is no danger, then, that the transcendent side of dogmas could be mistaken for their contextual expression as long as the transcendence of truth is a reality which is *yet to come* and be manifested in its fullness. Paradoxically, *the transcendent mystery of dogmas acts most powerfully not from the past* (for example, in the world of Ideas), *but rather from the future*.[18] By the power of the Holy Spirit, dogmas are exposed through anamnesis, but not merely in the "psychological-experiential" sense. The Holy Spirit actualizes the nonrepeatable and irreplaceable moments as a "prolepsis"[19] or an *enactment*, and not as an abstract, timeless *formula* that would contain them. Fr Matthew Baker's approach—in which he successfully encompassed Florovsky, Pannenberg, and Zizioulas, to mention a few—is one of the most attainable proposals concerning dogma that has been put forth in the last fifty years. Baker was vexed about the Tillichian echo that continued to sound in the discussion about the "existential concern."[20] We can add that dogmas, in fact, are genuine only in the sense that their truth and validity, which are truly *eschatological*, have always been active and present in the *mystery* (for the eschaton allows the human experience to take its course in history and does not deny it). In this context we are reminded of the unavoidable messianic *anticipation* of the dogmas of the Incarnation and the Resurrection of Christ in the Old Testament. Pannenberg rightly observed: "Why the man Jesus can be the ultimate revelation of God, why in him and only in him God is supposed to have appeared, remains incomprehensible apart from the horizon of the apocalyptic expectation."[21]

Once again, this idea of the "future's-work-in-progress" is strongly suggested by a number of well-reasoned considerations, and we should take a look at some of the most prominent. In the eucharistic experience of the Resurrection as the true judgment of this world, the Church validates dogmatic paradoxes, which no epistemology can comprehend without the element of *freedom* (freedom to *relate*), because these dogmas are a *remembrance of the future*. Thus, historically, dogmas are not "stages" of the Christological teaching that lead to an end (volition-creation-perfection); on the contrary, the *apocalyptic* nature of time, as the Church understands it, allows for, guarantees, and makes possible the *sudden* (ἐξαίφνης) penetration of the Truth "always and in all things."[22] So, the apocalyptic nature of ecclesial *kairos* breaks with the classic Greek tradition.[23] Zizioulas's arguments regarding a *remembrance of the future* considers some concrete forms of ecclesial communion that reflect this. Firstly, "remembering" something that has not yet happened (the Second Coming) cannot be explained unless it is transferred to an existential plane on which the fragmentation and necessary sequence of the three elements of time (past, present, and future) have been healed. Secondly, in the Kingdom everything is not turned into "present" but into the "future age which does not end or grow old," which being the state that ultimately prevails is logically prior, since it is this that gives "substance" and meaning to both past and present. Thirdly, according to St Maximus the end constitutes the reason for which both the past and the present subsist. In consequence, the future age that does not end, Zizioulas holds, becomes not an effect, like something that happens in time as we know it after the Fall, but the *cause* of all past and present events. Finally, *remembrance* of this "endless" future is not only possible but also ontologically definitive in the realm of the Eucharist as an icon of the Kingdom.[24]

In keeping with the futurity principle, though, is the Christological question the same for each age? According to epistemic contextualism, the answer is no. If, nonetheless, it goes beyond epistemology and includes the element of freedom, the Christological question is then *the same* for all ages, since it deals with *being* and *nonbeing*: Jesus Christ saves the world from nonexistence—and does it only as a perfect God and a perfect Man in the Person of the Logos Incarnate and Resurrected.

To one extent or another, this view of the Resurrection logic is one that many of us hold, if only implicitly. However, a necessary and important assumption of the existential significance of the Resurrection is that the Church "vivifies" dogmas, which implies that Christ becomes the way of being only *within* the ecclesial life. Outside the realm of the Church, teachings are mere dogmas, that is, mere semantic-logical propositions, surpassing all logic for those who believe and illogical for those who do not believe. Without freedom and outside the Church, Christological dogmas are applicable only to Jesus Christ, but they do not then have the power to raise the mortal to immortal. Florovsky developed this idea in particular:

> For the erring Christian consciousness, what is characteristic is precisely this striving for a logical exhaustion of faith, as if striving for a substitution of the living communication with God by religious and philosophical speculations about the Divine, of life—by teaching. . . . [I]n the need to fetter all the fullness of Church experience and hope into an infallible system of final dogmatic definitions, there is expressed a certain historical docetism, a derogation of the reality of time, a derogation of the mystery of the Church, derogation of the future Coming in glory—one might say, a bad remnant of time, in which the real deification of creation and development in grace is replaced by a logical unfolding of timeless and abstract principles.[25]

It turns out that the purification of all redundant contextual "deposits" for the sake of overcoming the naturalistic idolatry is necessary in order to gain the "one thing needful,"[26] which is knowledge of the Conqueror of death.

The Apostles passed on the truth of the Resurrection to the Church that, particularly during eucharistic gatherings, reveals and celebrates this greatest

Christological event. This event—the Resurrection of Jesus Christ, the God-Man and Savior of the world according to the faith of the Church—now, paradoxically, *precedes* all other events or doctrines, including the Incarnation. (The Cappadocian Fathers and St Maximus support this assertion.[27]) The Resurrection of the Messiah who rose from the dead *historically* (and not just rhetorically) precedes all other events that now become resurrectional projections and consequences.[28]

TRUTH AND THE RESURRECTION OF CHRIST

What, then, is the essence, basis, or *prototype* of dogma? Is it its theoretical or "logical" core, or is it something else? Gadamer gives a priority to the "original" vis-à-vis its interpretation.[29] But what solution to this dilemma is offered by Orthodox Christian tradition and theology?

The answer to this question comes from the event of Christ's resurrection and the human response to it. As seen in the light of the New Testament, the Resurrection of Christ is the foundation of all dogmas, and no dogma can be understood or explained *in itself*, outside of this *event* and its relation to *it*. Christology (and theology in general) is existentially irrelevant if death, as the basic problem of creation, is not *overcome*. Christology is about the following question: Who is Jesus Christ for every particular existential condition, for each epoch, and not just for the Apostolic Age? It is not possible to answer this question on the basis of ephemeral human desires and opinions, but only on the basis of soteriological expectations and resources (existential concepts, images, manners) available to the spiritual world in any given situation. Neither the *analogia entis* of the Scholastics, nor Spinoza's "intellectual love of God" can help in this matter. It requires an *event* that ontologically joins the created with the Uncreated, an *event* that breeds hope for overcoming death, the longing for true life, in all creation.

The opening of our eyes to the true nature of the Resurrection has always been one of the primary purposes of theology. Those who accept the logic of the Resurrection are, to paraphrase the words of Socrates in Plato's *Republic*, obliged to follow the argument wherever it leads. The Resurrection means and reveals everything the Holy Scripture says about it: that God the Father raised his eternal Son by the Holy Spirit; through this event, the ontology of the world and matter has experienced a radical change. Each movement of the paschal mystery thus attests to the mystery of Sonship.[30] As we shall discuss later, the existential-logical premise of the Christology of the Resurrection means that only the Life-creating Trinity can restore the original foundation of the person—that is, redeem existence. As Baker pointed out, "The Resurrection and the Kingdom of God form the chief context and condition for historical understanding," by adding a crucial (and in some way programmatic) assertion, "Christian theology is *a hermeneutics of resurrection*—the ever-new understandings of a cloud of witnesses in every age arising and entering permanently into the body of truth."[31]

In this sense, then, all other dogmas (truths) of Christianity are, simply, *reflections* or expressions of the dogma of the Resurrection. Thus, we can understand the overall mystery of existence only in retrospect, as the Cappadocians and St Maximus the Confessor emphatically claimed.[32] Not even a vision of the transfigured Lord was sufficient to fathom the mystery of Christ, and that is why the Evangelist wrote: "He charged them to tell no one what they had seen, *until the Son of man should have risen from the dead*. So they kept the matter to themselves, questioning what the rising from the dead meant."[33] The apostles had not yet become aware of the true problem. Only in the light of the Resurrection—which is the solution to the eternal life of creation—could they see the true *problem* of the created world.[34] Asserting the retroactive power of the Resurrection, Pannenberg states:

> Only an integrated view of the Easter event together with the coming end, a view originally based on the expectation of the eschatological imminent end, made it possible to understand Jesus' activity and fate as God's revelation. An individual event can say something about the one God only when it has in view the totality of reality. In the Biblical sense, however, *this totality as the totality of history is accessible only through the anticipation of the end of all events*.[35]

This is a deep and subtle suggestion. To really absorb it, we need to put ourselves into the example earnestly and fully imagine the experience of the Apostles. The testimony of the Apostles about the resurrected Christ is the first dogmatic formulation and verification of the truth about God: there is a God who is powerful enough to conquer death. For the Apostles, the Resurrection of Jesus was proof that he was the eschatological Messiah, the true *anthropos*, who, in contrast to the first Adam, took the world in his hands with thanksgiving and offered it back to God, freeing creation from the bondage of sin/death, thus setting not only the *end* but also the *beginning* (ἀρχή) of the world. The same is valid for St Paul. When he realized that Jesus—whom he persecuted—was no longer dead, his worldview was completely turned upside down: if Jesus was exalted by God in his resurrection, then his *death* must have had a *meaning* in God's economy. According to Pannenberg,[36] there are several points that summarize the immediate inherent significance of Jesus's Resurrection. First, if Jesus has been raised then the end of the world has begun. Second, if Jesus has been raised this can only mean, for a Jew, that God himself has confirmed the pre-Easter activity of Jesus. Third, through his Resurrection from the dead, Jesus so closely resembled the Son of Man that the insight became obvious to Paul: the Son of Man is none other than the man Jesus who will come again. If Jesus, having been raised from the dead, is ascended to God and if thereby the end of the world has begun, then God is ultimately revealed in Jesus. As a cultural implication, the transition to the Gentile mission is then motivated by the eschatological Resurrection of Jesus as Resurrection of the crucified one.[37]

This reasoning is sound, as far as it goes, since each age does *not* begin its search for God from some eternal principle (πρωταρχικὴ ἀρχὴ) that it tries to understand or interpret, but from the thirst for the resurrected life, from making the Resurrection present in the Church through the Eucharist. In the Eucharist Christians come to know God by fostering a *relationship* with him and not by grasping the meanings of some unalterable, abstract, divine concepts. Furthermore, every age interprets this experience (event) within its own context. The Greek Fathers interpreted this event with the assistance of the ontological questions of philosophy (i.e., the ontological problem). They received the Semitic (in this case, iconic) version of the truth of the Incarnation and the Resurrection, but they interpreted it ontologically by using Greek idioms. They are the ones who established the doctrines so that a *simple* (Semitic) religion might have a σύστασις, or ontological content.[38] With this approach, the Fathers brought a shift in perspective, enabling us to rediscover the true meaning of iconicity in history.

This leads us to the concluding point in our understanding of the problem. Since our civilization and culture are essentially still Hellenic, still based on the Greek philosophical heritage with its interest in ontology (the question, "What truly *is*?" originated in Greece), we can therefore say with Florovsky that the Hellenism of the Church is a diachronic, permanent category. Of course, it is not advisable to insist that the cultures of Africa, China, or any other, should adopt Hellenism, because these cultures express their interest in salvation through iconology and symbols different from those required by Hellenic terminology, which is based on the ontological questions of being, life, and death. What can and should be accepted by these or any other cultures is the event of the Resurrection, an event that is the basis for all cultural expressions of Christ. Thus, the folk art of those cultures will inevitably manifest the resurrected ethos, just as—following the logic of the Resurrection—Christian iconography from the beginning depicted a *risen* man, adding a crown of light as a sign of adoption and the "resurrectional" relationship with the transcendent God.[39] How did this happen? In contrast with natural art that idealizes the natural world and is therefore bound by time, the icon is the truth presented in a way that is not controlled by our senses or our mind. This encounter with the divine, in paradox and ambiguity, is a matter of *relation* rather than logical argumentation. Since our relation in history is also iconic, not direct (this perceived weakness of the icon is precisely its strength.), we cannot have logical proof; rather, there is a decision one makes to *relate*.[40]

In this sense, every culture, despite the ongoing cultural *constants* characteristic of all ages, has its own mind-set by which to evaluate the authority of the truth revealed to it. The reasoning of Florovsky, Pannenberg, and Zizioulas can easily be extended to the question of how does eternal *truth* become relevant for different mind-sets. As already noted, for Semitic culture, it is essential that the truth be revealed by someone who *lives (does) the truth*—πράττειν takes priority over εἶναι— hence the extreme asceticism of the Stylites, for example. Jewish culture expects the truth from someone who brings the judgment of history (hence, apocalypses as a test for the truthfulness of history), whereas Greek culture looks for someone who is eternal, who is verily the only truth. If there is *one* answer to all the searching found in every culture and age, it is the *Resurrection*. It is the *constant* and unchanging condition *sine qua non* of every soteriology. Upon hearing "Christ is Risen" from the myrrh-bearing women, the Jew understands it as the beginning of judgment upon all, the Greek as a victory over corruptibility, the Chinese as the eternal Tao, and a postmodern man—perhaps?—as his human *right* to deification. The point, however, is that this truth should not be merely proclaimed but lived in the faith, at which time our being will then resound as it shouts: "Christ is risen!" (This also eliminates the issue of the clarity of what we are proclaiming.) For Christ not only solves the problem of simple being (and its ethical-aesthetic or juridical dilemma) but gives an *eternal well-being* (ἀεὶ εὖ εἶναι), because he is the bearer of immortality, incorruption, and the perpetuation of existence.

IMPLICATIONS OF A HERMENEUTICS OF RESURRECTION

The neopatristic insights of the twentieth and twenty-first centuries have generated excitement because they have raised the possibility of a new answer—one in which Tradition plays a crucial role in interpretation, pointing back toward the Greek Fathers and their hermeneutics, and advocated by Florovsky, Zizioulas, Baker, and others. In this perspective, the preaching of the Resurrection is the nucleus of every dogma. "Christ is Risen" is the message for all people, but the Greeks give a reply that, "*Truly* He is Risen!" The incarnate Christ overcame death, thus showing the correlation between *truth* and *existence*, something that would be recognized by the apostles only *after* the Resurrection, not before. In his Person, the created lives forever, of which the Holy Eucharist is a guarantor as the "resurrectional" event *par excellence*.

This hermeneutic is among the most precious and monumental achievements of the Greek Fathers. It should be emphasized at this point that Hellenism is not some independent, eternal category, but one important, spiritual category that served as a key requirement for the *universality* of the Church. In relation to the Church, Hellenism is not an independent value uncritically inherited by the Church Fathers. Hellenism had to be transformed by the same Fathers.

We then reach the most important point of this argument. The essence of Christology is not in itself, but in its existential "transformation" and "*topos*," which is the Church. In itself (i.e., without ecclesiological realization), Christology is simply a dogma without existential significance: it explains something that is applicable to Jesus Christ (for example, the Incarnation), but not to all of us. Even for a believing Christian, separated from the Church's community, a dogma is a "supralogical" proposition that is believed without argument solely because it is a dogma. "In its ecclesiological significance, however," as Zizioulas remarked (after previously considering what the Chalcedonian terms "without division" and "without confusion" mean outside the experience of the Church) "this dogma expresses a way of being."[41] Only this relationship can indicate the logical or philosophical (primarily in the analytical sense) aspects of the dogma of Christ and the Holy Trinity, and never vice versa.

In conclusion, let us add the following to those considerations: What Christ reveals through his Person is an unprecedented way of two natures existing in his hypostases, a way which mysteriously leads into ecclesiology. St Maximus, along with the great Fathers of the monastic tradition, such as Macarius, demonstrated that the God-Man captivates with the countenance that reveals and radiates the unfathomable eschatological newness of Love who was once lifted up to the Cross, descended to Hades, and resurrected from the grave. Therefore, the Church has no definition of truth that simply satisfies intellectual curiosity; any aspiring definitions must describe a life experience, like the famous definition of Nicholas Cabasilas: "The Church is seen (present) in the holy mysteries" (and especially the Eucharist).[42]

Thus, we understand here that a dogmatic "gigantomachia" does not simply end in the agreement of words and formulas, but in the reality of the Mystery, recognized in the Image of the crucified and resurrected Christ.[43] Then, by his ethos, the Church can daringly struggle in history and, although realistically weak, be victorious; being defeated, crushed, humiliated, she is able to encourage the defeated, to resurrect the dead, and in the arena of history appear "in another form,"[44] and exist even where she phenomenologically is not. To this, as well as to the victory of dogmas, testify the Church Fathers who bear that name exactly because they help us be born again in the community of the Holy Spirit.

With these seemingly slight modifications, our understanding of theology's arena is transformed. The eternal truths of the Church come to us revived with a new infusion of creativity. The way is new but not the content; we are not talking about new things, but about the same in a new, different way. Christ asks us again: "But who do you say that I am?" The answer cannot but read exactly like Peter's: "You are the Christ, the Son of the living God."[45] The question is who will ask the question and who will provide the answer.

The mission and the calling of the Church is to foster the hermeneutics of the Resurrection as something that speaks to all people and all contexts. Our theology, a eucharistic vision of the world, has preserved and upheld this truth throughout history, but it has to continue to do so into the future, in our millennium. Only as such will it bring hope and life to the world.

NOTES

1. Lk 7:19.
2. "Neither Greco-Roman nor Jewish religious tradition knew about this 'myth.'" Martin Hengel, *The Son of God: The Origin of Christology and the History of Jewish-Hellenistic Religion* (Eugene, OR: Wipf & Stock Publishers, 2007), 76. That is why St. John of Damascus (*An Exposition of the Orthodox Faith* III, 1) said that Christ is "the only new thing under the sun," meaning: the only new event in a cyclical context or in the "multiverse." John of Damascus, *An Exact Exposition of the Orthodox Faith*, ed. B. Kotter (Berlin: Walter de Gruyter, 1973), 3.1. The God-Man became *history*, a thing unheard of in the entire ancient world, whose view of history has always been veiled in myth.
3. Hans-Georg Gadamer, *Truth and Method* (London: Bloomsbury, 2004), 165. This, however, does not imply that the meaning is produced exclusively by the reader in his interaction with the text.
4. Lk 24:21.
5. This is as opposed to Heidegger's phenomenology which seeks in the empirical end of our lives the one and only vantage point to conceive and understand the sense of our being; however, it is an "eschatology without eschaton," as Judith Wolfe points out in *Heidegger's Eschatology: Theological Horizons in Martin Heidegger's Early Work* (Oxford: Oxford University Press, 2013).
6. *Transcendental idealism*, a system developed by Kant, is based on the idea that, in order to understand the nature of reality, one must first examine and analyze the reasoning process that governs the nature of experience.
7. Cf. Fr Maximos Constas's remark: "Only things that contradict the mind are real, there is no contradiction in what is imaginary" (*The Art of Seeing: Paradox and Perception in Orthodox Iconography* [Los Angeles: Sebastian Press, 2014], 31).
8. See John Zizioulas's remark regarding the Eucharist: "The 'truth of what is now accomplished in the synaxis' is to be found not in a Platonic type of ideal reality but in a 'reality of the future,' in the Kingdom which is to come" (*Eucharistic Communion*

and the World [New York: T&T Clark, 2011], 44). Also, "The archetype, the cause of 'what is accomplished in the synaxis', lies in the future. The Eucharist is the result of the Kingdom which is to come. The Kingdom which is to come, a future event (the state of things to come), being the cause of the Eucharist, gives it its true being." Ibid., 45.

9. Cf. Mt 27.63.

10. "The resurrection of Christ must be a true event, because it is, considering ordinary human expectations, so improbable and impossible that none would have preached it if it had not actually (*de facto*) happened. In other words, if the Apostles had wanted to convince us of some fiction, then, this fiction would have to have been probable, i.e., acceptable to us, so that we could more easily believe in it (is it not the effort of every liar to make his lie seem as convincing as possible just so that the people would more easily believe in it?). But, since the resurrection from the dead is an *extremely improbable* event, and many had, in spite of that, testified about it, then they must have been confronted with irrefutable evidence, otherwise it would never have occurred to them to testify about such a 'foolishness' and 'insanity.'" Vladan Perišić, *Theological Disambiguations: An Unconventional Handbook of Orthodox Theology* (Los Angeles: Sebastian Press, 2012), 23.

11. Love does not classify the experience using some logical principles, because true love does not know the reluctance that is present in the epistemological process. "Phenomenology should not and cannot decide *a priori* (i.e., before my relationship with the other and the world) how to classify phenomena, as if it were some old librarian who orders books by their serial number" (John P. Manoussakis, *God after Metaphysics* [Bloomington: Indiana University Press, 2007], 55).

12. 1 Cor 15:16.

13. Wolfhart Pannenberg, *Jesus—God and Man* (Philadelphia: The Westminster Press, 1977), 73.

14. *Ambiguum* 7, 3, PG 91, 1069B. According to Maximus the creation occurs out of the future so that the beginning of creation is inconceivable without the future end. Maximus's interpretation is markedly different from that of Origen. See Maxim Vasiljević, "The Beginning and the End Are not the Same" in *Theology as a Surprise: Patristic and Pastoral Insight* (Crestwood, NY: St Vladimir's Seminary Press, 2018), 54, fn. 28. Gregory of Nyssa has a similar view to Maximus: "In the case of the first creation the final state was intertwined with the beginning (ἐπὶ μὲν οὖν τῆς πρώτης κτίσεως ἀδιαστάτως τῇ ἀρχῇ συνανεφάνη τὸ πέρας) and the race took the starting point of its existence in its perfection (καὶ ἀπὸ τῆς τελειότητος ἡ φύσις τοῦ εἶναι ἤρξατο)." See also, "It was the case for each of these that its start and its full actualization were achieved together (ἐφ' ἑκάστου τῶν ὄντων ἀδιαστάτως τῇ ἀρχῇ συναπηρτίσθη τὸ πέρας). . . . [F]or all that were brought from nonexistence to existence their perfection coincided with their beginning (πᾶσι τοῖς ἐκ τοῦ μὴ ὄντος εἰς τὸ εἶναι παραγομένοις ὁμοῦ τῇ ἀρχῇ συνανασχούσης τῆς τελειότητος) . . . from its first moment of existence it was formed simultaneously with its perfection (ἀπὸ τῆς πρώτης ὑπάρξεως συμπλασθεῖσα τῇ τελειότητι)" (Gregory of Nyssa, *Commentary on Song of Songs*, ed. Richard A. Norris Jr. [Atlanta: Society of Biblical Literature, 2012], 15:5, 6:486).

15. Hermeneutics here is not a process in which an interpreter finds a particular meaning but a creative effort to account for understanding as the ontological process of man.

16. Lk 24:8.

17. It is with a sense of relief that we come across a renowned Protestant theologian who identifies this problem and discusses it. "Where the tension between the present and the expectation for the future is lost, the occurrence of Jesus' resurrection loses the inherent significance that it originally had, that is, the significance that was inherent in it within its original context in the history of traditions, namely, in the horizon of the apocalyptic expectation for the future" (Pannenberg, *Jesus*, 66–67).

18. This approach is somehow at odds with the protological sentence in the well-known saying in the Epistle of Barnabas, "Behold I make the last things as the first things" (Barn 6.13). What is meant by this is that "only the one who has control over the beginning has the whole matter in his grasp. The beginning therefore had to be illuminated by the end, and ultimately the idea of pre-existence was a favorite means of bringing out the special significance of particular phenomena for salvation" (Hengel, *Son of God*, 69).

19. "The thing that often escapes us is that, in the New Testament, the Spirit is given after Christ's Resurrection (Jn 7:39), precisely because his coming into the world signals the coming of the 'last days' in history (Acts 2:17). It is no exaggeration to identify the Kingdom and the Holy Spirit: 'Thy Kingdom come: that is, the Holy Spirit.' So the linking of the Holy Spirit with 'holding together the whole institution of the Church' suggests that both the 'institution' of the Church and the framework within which it becomes a reality, the eucharistic synaxis in other words, derive their meaning from the Kingdom of God" (Zizioulas, *Eucharistic Communion and the World*, 74).

20. In his comments on the discussion of the answer and the concern, Matthew Baker wrote that it sounds very Tillichian, and insisted on the stability of the *content* of the message, which Florovsky so stressed. For Baker, "the concern is human, but the message is divine. And the condition for apprehending and understanding the message is not simply a universal human concern, but precisely *faith*—which again is a divine gift" (unpublished correspondence). According to Pannenberg, "The unity of event and word in the resurrection appearances is important for the question of how this event can establish faith. If the resurrection or the appearances of the resurrected Jesus were only brute facts without inherent significance, then, certainly, the origin of faith would not be understandable from this event. But that event had its own meaning within its sphere in the history of traditions" (Pannenberg, *Jesus*, 73).

21. Pannenberg, *Jesus*, 83.

22. "For the Word of God . . . wants always and in all things to accomplish the mystery of His embodiment." St Maximus the Confessor, PG 91, 1084CD.

23. Yet, we naturally ask, how can God possibly behave in such a strange manner? The answer is that in no way can we control or predict the outcome of any *spiritual* action. We cannot ever know the exact location of God's presence. We cannot predict with total certainty the outcome of even the simplest of spiritual moments.

24. See Zizioulas, *Eucharistic Communion and the World*, 59–60. Here Zizioulas claims that "this is attested both in the Gospel descriptions of the Last Supper and in the liturgical practice of the Church."

25. George Florovsky, "The House of the Father," in *The Collected Works of Georges Florovsky*, vol. 13, *Ecumenism I: A Doctrinal Approach*, trans. Roberta Reeder (Vaduz, Europa: Büchervertriebsanstalt, 1987), 75, 78.

26. Cf. Lk 10:42.

27. Cf. Gregory the Theologian, *Or*. 45, 22; Maximus, *Or. Dom.*, PG 90, 879d-880B, et cetera. The Resurrection clarifies, at least in Maximus's account, the exact ontological import of the Incarnation into the history of salvation.

28. "All things in Christology are judged in the light of the resurrection. . . . This is the way in which Christology in the New Testament has developed—from the resurrection to the incarnation, not the other way around—and patristic theology has never lost this eschatological approach to Christology" (John Zizioulas, *Being as Communion* [Crestwood, NY: St Vladimir's Seminary Press, 1985], 55, n. 49).

29. "Interpretation does not seek to replace the interpreted work. It does not, for example, seek to draw attention to itself by the poetic power of its own utterance" (Gadamer, *Truth and Method*, 418).

30. Anne Hunt, "The Trinity through Paschal Eyes," in *Rethinking Trinitarian Theology: Disputed Questions and Contemporary Issues in Trinitarian Theology*, eds. Giulio Maspero and Robert J. Wozniak (New York: T&T Clark, 2012), 480. "In and through the post-resurrection shock waves, the disciples recognize Jesus as Lord and God, the Father as author of this plan for our salvation, and the Holy Spirit as yet another divine power centre in their new God-consciousness, not merely a divine impersonal force but a distinct personal being, one in whom Father and Son are united in love" (Ibid., 486).

31. Fr Matthew Baker, "'Alles Verständnis ist Interpretation': Neo-Patristic Synthesis and Philosophical Hermeneutics—Georges Florovsky and Hans-Georg Gadamer in Conversation" (unpublished paper, 2012). Baker's paper can now be viewed as among the first to point out "resurrection hermeneutics."

32. "Moreover, the entire season of Pentecost is a reminder of the *resurrection* we expect in *the age to come*" (Basil the Great, *Basil the Great: On the Holy Spirit*, trans. David Anderson [Crestwood, NY: St Vladimir's Seminary Press, 1997], 66 [PG 27]; "Thus the honoring of the number seven brought with it the honor of Pentecost. For seven multiplied by itself generates fifty minus one day, and this we have taken from the age to come, which is at once the eighth and the first (Gen. 1:5; John 20:1,26), or rather one and indissoluble" (Gregory the Theologian, *Or*. 41, 2; SCh 358, 316–18; PG 36, 432AB). Maximus the Confessor adds: This "state *above nature* (καὶ γενέσθαι ἐν τῇ ὑπὲρ φύσιν) is identified with the Eighth day (ἥτις ἐστὶν ὀγδόη) and characterizes the future condition (καὶ τὴν μέλλουσαν χαρακτηρίζει κατάστασιν)" (*Quaestiones et dubia* 191, CChr series graeca 10:133,17–24. Cf. also *Letter to Marinos*, PG 91, 81D).

33. Mk 9:9–10.

34. "For Western theology as a whole, the resurrection of Christ is nothing more than a confirmation of the saving work of the cross. The essential part has already

been accomplished in the sacrifice on the cross" (Zizioulas, *Eucharistic Communion and the World*, 39–40).

35. Pannenberg, *Jesus*, 185 (my emphasis).

36. Ibid., 67–73.

37. In spite of the occasional inconsistencies in Pannenberg's priority of futurity (negligence of the *somatic* aspect as constitutive of the meaning of a person, insistence that the only divine Thou in Jesus's earthly life was the Father, etc.), his contribution to Christology is substantial.

38. "In simple words through the power of the Spirit, you *framed dogmas* (συνιστάτε τὰ δόγματα) set down earlier by the fishermen . . . indeed our plain faith needed a *consistency* (τὴν σύστασιν)" (Kontakion of the Holy Three Hierarchs, in Greek Menaion, kathisma after 3rd ode, PG 29, 369A).

39. Cf. Stamatis Skliris, *In the Mirror: A Collection of Iconographic Essays and Illustrations* (Los Angeles: Sebastian Press, 2007), 101.

40. Therefore, the iconic approach presupposes that one accepts a presence to which one can *relate*. This was the argumentation of the theologians (among them, Maximus the Confessor, John Damascene, and Theodore the Studite) throughout the history of Byzantium.

41. John Zizioulas, *Communion and Otherness* (New York: T&T Clark, 2006), 261.

42. "The Church is present in the Holy Mysteries (the Eucharist) not in symbols but as members of the heart. . . . For this is not a fellowship in name only, or some similarity by analogy, but this is the very same (identical) thing. For these mysteries are the Body and the Blood of Christ, and they are the real food and drink of Christ's Church. . . . And if someone could see Christ's Church through the extent of one's unity with Christ and through the communion with His Body, he would see none other than only the Body of Christ" (Nicholas Cabasilas, *Commentary on the Liturgy*, 38, 43, 45; PG 150, 452–53, 461–65).

43. An icon bridges the chasm between Creator and creation only through the intervention of the *person* of Christ as opposed to pagan symbolism which believes that the *nature* bridges the chasm on its own.

44. Mk 16:12.

45. Mt 16:15–16.

Chapter Eight

Ecstatic or Reciprocal Meaningfulness?

Orthodox Eschatology between Theology, Philosophy, and Psychoanalysis

Nikolaos Loudovikos

The modern secular *consensus* regarding eschatology is probably best portrayed in two recent films. The first of them is *Avatar,* a box-office success a few years ago, which is about the search for a lost earthly paradise and which reveals the glowing embers of a Neopaganism widely disseminated throughout the West today. This film is no more than the most recent manifestation of narcissism in Western culture, a tendency that Christopher Lasch has shrewdly noted. What it seeks is a return to the womb and its security, to a collective preservation of an unmitigated narcissism, either by the conquest and crude exploitation of the natural world or else by surrendering to this paradise of great mother nature, which simultaneously assuages the guilty feelings associated with the former mode of exploitive behavior.[1]

What is it, however, that has made a genuine Greek-Westerner and, of course, a Christian feel nausea at the prospect of living in such a paradise? It is the fact that this pagan paradise is only an eternal repetition of the "same." It constitutes the absence of a true and unexpected creativity with all its achievements and dangers, or, in other words, it is the absence of freedom and a "paradise" that lies beyond good and evil. Mimicking the submission of the *Star Wars* Jedi, it is the blind surrender to those hypothetically wise hidden cosmic powers which permanently and immutably preserve an *invisible harmony* in Heraclitean terms, even if Heraclitus's Logos, which effectively maintains this harmony and provides it with *dialectical* meaning and content, is utterly absent. Put in yet another way, what is absent from *Avatar*'s paradise is precisely the likelihood of any gradual and progressive movement toward creating meaningfulness—that is, any groundbreaking development or movement toward a higher level of existential perfection and understanding on the part of the world's rational beings that live bound together, as it were, in this self-sufficient natural Eden. According to theological criteria, *Avatar*'s paradise seems to be not so much a paradise as a hell, precisely because of this absence of creative meaningfulness.

For the Greek-Western Christian there is no paradise without hermeneutics—that is, the freedom to create meaning, a freedom which includes both the possibility of hell and its transcendence. Without an understanding of hell, paradise for creatures would be an asphyxiating repetition of a non-meaningful sameness, a reality captured so well in *Avatar*'s neopagan paradise-prison. Unless the attainment of wholeness and the transformation of nature is linked with continuous development, salvation is bereft of sense and meaning. The eschata, from this standpoint, relates to ontology and its dangers—that is, to the vicissitudes of a perpetual development of created nature's being or, conversely, of its fall from being. Eschatology is thereby unavoidably linked to ontology.

The struggle for eschatological meaningfulness has been preserved by Christian theology in two forms, that is, in two important ways of understanding the "last things": a legal (or even, at times, juridical) way and an ontological way. These two different forms appear in both the East and the West and, indeed, they are not always mutually exclusive. In the West, beginning with the so-called *Fides Damasi* in the fifth century, hell is defined as eternal punishment for sins (DS 72).[2] This teaching is simply repeated in the *Quicunque* (DS 76), also of the fifth century, at the Fourth Lateran Council of the eighth century (DS 852), and at the Councils of Florence in the fifteenth century (DS 1351) and Trent of 1547 (DS 1575). The recent, 1992 version of the *Catechism of the Catholic Church* also explicitly states that the souls of sinners "descend immediately after death to hell, where they suffer the punishment of hell, eternal fire."[3] Without requiring any further evidence, the legal dimension in this context can easily be taken as a sort of juridicalism, which constitutes the end of eschatological ontology since it represents the end of any creative meaningfulness, unless, of course, one thinks that this tug of war between sin and punishment alone can offer meaning to eternity. Some of the greatest Western Mystics have indeed tried to provide further "explanation." To what extent this *infernalisme*,[4] a disastrous expansion of the exclusively juridical understanding of so-called "original sin" (another invention of the West), rendered the Western Christian conscience guilt-ridden and melancholic, creating the presuppositions for an equally juridical understanding of inherited guilt and salvation, as well as the stimulus for modern atheism, can only, according to Delumeau, be evaluated in the light of the ontological teaching of the Greek Fathers on these matters.[5] This is not to suggest that there is not an inherent element of justice in Christian eschatology, which appears early on in the Gospels themselves. However, it is significant that some of the greatest Fathers of the Church do not simply attempt to combine this element with an ontological understanding of the Kingdom of God as the means to avoid juridicalism, and, in so doing, somehow transform the eschata into a meaningful existential/ontological reality. Moreover, as we shall see below, a juridical understanding of the "last things" was not absent in the East either, though an ontological understanding was developed parallel to it, stretching from Irenaeus of Lyons to Maximus the Confessor. This ontological understanding, however, has yet to fully supplant not only the juridical but also the Origenistic understanding of the "last things," which, although clearly not juridical, nevertheless inhibits any plausible development of an authentically ontological understanding of the eschata.

Before we turn our attention to the East, however, we must not neglect to emphasize that the high points of the Western juridical understanding of the last judgement lie without any doubt in the work of Augustine, on the one hand,[6] and of Thomas Aquinas,[7] on the other. Both regard the judgment simply as a work of *justice* and thus render God essentially a merciless judge who suddenly forgets his love, who, in a fashion wildly out of character for him, inflicts the precise punishment due for each sin. Fr Sergius Bulgakov likes to remind us how Augustine used to mock those who were opposed to this merciless legalism, calling them "the merciful ones" (*misericordes*).[8] It is evident that according to such a perspective hell must remain an eternal torment for the punishment of sinners and the great joy of the elect, on the one hand, while both condemnation and justification lie under the absolute authority of God, on the other. Here we have the appalling teaching on absolute predestination. In his important work, *Freedom and Necessity: St Augustine's Teaching on Divine Power and Human Freedom*, Gerald Bonner notes that Augustine, in a rather contradictory fashion and despite his respect for humanity's innate desire for God, cannot help regarding God as utterly transcendent, unaffected by humanity's desire and, consequently, utterly indifferent to it in predetermining on his own each person's eternally good or eternally bad destiny.[9] Understood in this way, absolute predestination creates the relentless legal arsenal on behalf of the eternity of hell that has marked Western theology up to our own day. The full reception of the above theses have been taken as a given, not only against Pelagius but even against John Cassian, by the whole of the West. This, of course, includes Protestant theology and especially Calvin. Only recently have theologians appeared, both Roman Catholics, such as von Balthasar,[10] and Protestants, such as Jenson,[11] who, along with Orthodox writers such as Evdokimov[12] have timorously attempted to recover the Origenistic line of *universalism*, the theory of the restoration of all things, in spite of all the difficulties that accompany it. The dominant trend today among Christian theologians of all denominations is to reject the eternity of hell. The problem is that usually the theological argumentation is lacking that would offer sound criteria for adopting one or the other position. Perhaps it is possible for this trend to be regarded as a desperate attempt to overcome the legalism that is innate to our understanding of the "last things," an argument that also attracts Orthodox theologians precisely because the aforementioned ontological understanding of the "last things" has not yet been sufficiently appreciated.

I have said that the juridical perception of judgment and hell is present even in the East. For reasons that are obviously pedagogical, the "eternal fire," the "deep pit, the inescapable blackness, the lightless flame in the darkness that nevertheless has the power to burn, and the privation of light," and the "worm of a poisonous and flesh-eating kind that eats voraciously and is never satisfied, inflicting unbearable pain as it devours" accompanies Basil the Great's descriptions of the eternity and horror of hell fire, which, according to John Chrysostom, "burns those it has seized hold of forever and never ceases, and that is why it is called unquenchable."[13] Similarly, teaching on the eternity of hell is a common feature from the *Martyrdom of Polycarp* and the *Epistle of Diognetus* up to the preachers of the Ottoman period. Nevertheless, alongside this line of thought there is also that of Irenaeus, Maximus, and John Damascene.

It is refreshing, after what has been set out in the previous paragraph, to encounter the assertions of John Damascene: "and you should also know this, that God does not punish[14] anyone in the world to come, but each person makes himself capable of participation in God. Participation in God is joy; non-participation in him is hell."[15] According to John Damascene, hell is made by created beings and especially by the devil. As such, in the familiar description of hell in the Gospel, "the eternal fire prepared for the devil and his angels" (Matt. 25:41), the dative (rendered in English as "for the devil") should rather be read as a dative of causal agency ("by the devil")! Even if the patristic tradition in its kerygmatic form usually regarded this expression as indicating a form of punishment for the devil, it is clear that, in keeping with the deeper criteria of Orthodox theology, the devil is the one who envies God's love and opposes it. Consequently, hell becomes the self-maltreatment of the creature, which is expressed in terms of refusal to participate in the Godhead on account of achieving its own satisfaction by turning itself into an idol, declaring the freedom of the creature in terms of a narcissistic enclosure within the self. Texts such as this one, perhaps, take their original impetus from the theology of Irenaeus of Lyons. The essential and noteworthy feature of this great father's teaching on the present topic is that, on the one hand, it connects judgment with the ontological renewal of creation and, on the other, it regards this renewal as a consequence of humanity's spiritual restoration and attainment of bodily incorruption. When this happens, humankind advances "towards incorruption, so that [the body] can no longer deteriorate, [and] there will be a new heaven and a new earth."[16] In short, heaven and hell occur through a *synergistic intermeaningfulness* between God and Man, not through a one-sided moral and juridical provision on the part of God. What we have here are processes of *reciprocal meaningfulness*, profound encounters of the freedom of God with the deiform freedom of rational creatures, God and man creating together the meaning of creation in the sense of an active and conscious human progress and fulfilment in divinity by grace. We shall see more of this below with the help of Maximus the Confessor and Gregory Palamas. The positions of John Damascene and Irenaeus signify above all that hell and heaven are inextricably related to ontology, to the full restoration of the created nature of beings and the never-ending evolution of that nature, or, alternatively, to its never-ending ontological fixity or nullification. The Western theologians who are perhaps closest to this perspective are Karl Rahner, for whom our eschatological future is salvation as *the fulfilment of the whole person*,[17] and Wolfhart Pannenberg, for whom it is essential to understand eschatology "in positive relation to the nature and the deepest yearnings of human beings and the world to which they refer. Otherwise we cannot see why we should understand what is said about the future as a promise and not as a threat."[18] However, as we shall see, Maximus and Palamas go even further.

The other recent film that represents well the secular Biblical/Neoplatonic version of eschatological ontology is Luc Besson's *Lucy*. There are two critical points that I want to make here. First, as is typical of the Origenist/ Augustinian/Thomist tradition, man's essence is portrayed as being *nous* or mind, which dominates everything that is not "spiritual." "I don't feel pain, fear, desire; it's like all things that make us human fade away," says Lucy. Even the by the expressions "brain" or "brain capacity," the characters of the film always mean simply "intellect," the *detached* intellect of the ancient and modern Western philosophical/idealistic dualism, which is a *disembodied mind,* as modern Cognitive Science and Neuropsychology have so successfully made clear. The other parts of *psyche*, since they are closer to the body, do not belong to the real human essence, a position that unconsciously follows the old Plotinian division between a higher "intellectual" soul and a "lower" bodily one, which is "body-like" (σωματοειδής) and contaminated insofar as it is attached to the body (ὡς ἐφαπτομένη σώματι).[19] Even the mysterious drug which upgrades Lucy's mind touches only her intellect, leaving all the other parts of her soul or brain, for some chemically inconceivable reason, untouched. Second, and connected to the first, an ecstatic and egocentric meaningfulness of domination or of will-to-power, seems to be subtly suggested in this movie as the only possible understanding of human nature and its way of relating to other beings. The *telos* of human existence is Lucy's final spiritualization-as-vaporization through which she escapes her material nature in an ecstatic deification-as-a-total-personal-meaningfulness, and, consequently, as spiritual domination/possession of being.

I think that it is highly unlikely that Luc Besson ever read Origen, but the themes present in *Lucy* are all too close to his eschatology. All the scholars of Origen agree that the identification of nature with the Fall was first made explicitly by him. It is extremely revealing that even some of the greatest modern defenders of Origen concur that he was the first to identify the nature of beings with the evil of a fundamental fall. H. Crouzel writes: "If the Devil is called [in Origen] the First Terrestrial, that is because he was the source of the Fall which caused the creation of the perceptible world[. . .]."[20] P. Tzamalikos, in his *Origen: Philosophy of History and Eschatology*, also writes something similar: "The 'Fall', on the one hand, coincides with the actual creation and marks the 'beginning' of space-time."[21] The problem with the Origenist view of eschatology—a difficulty that St Maximus alone resolved—is not that the spatiotemporal character of eternal life is not accepted, for it is indeed received at this stage. The problem is that the final Kingdom of God, which is distinguished from the initial eternal life after death, is precisely a transcendence of this spatiotemporal eternity. For Origen, eschatology ultimately means that beings transcend their nature when they enter the realm of God, since the world is by nature ontologically outside God. Heaven is the final abrogation of the nature of beings, of their spatiotemporal character, despite the restoration of all things through their relationship with God. Restoration is thereby connected with a return to pre-creational conditions,[22] which is like Lucy's return to the conditions before the *big bang*.

St Maximus the Confessor represents a different perspective. The most important discovery of this great theologian in the present context is not simply the distinction between the *gnomic* and the *natural* will but chiefly their deep connection. In order for the *gnomic* or *personal* will to "advance directly," it must listen to the uncreated *logos* or principle of nature, which, as an ecstatic *logos*-invitation of God, awaits an ecstatic answering *dia-logos*, expressed on the part of the creature as the personal or gnomic direction of his *natural will* toward God's ecstatic call, asking God for "its own natural and full onticity."[23] That is to say, the gnomic will does not seek deliverance from nature since this nature is created by God. On the contrary, it needs to "bow to the *logos* of nature" with the intention of being led toward the "good use" (*euchrēstia*) rather than the "non-use" (*achrēstia*) of the *logoi* of nature. In such a manner, every rational creature responds such that "either the *logos* that is in accordance with nature comes to subsist in it through being used well, or the mode that is against nature exists co-ordinately with it through not being used; the one is in accordance with nature, the other becomes the messenger of a free choice that is contrary to nature."[24] It is, in any case, for this reason that, on the one hand, "nothing belonging to the natural world ever conflicts with its cause, just as nature as a whole never conflicts with its cause"[25] and, on the other, "the natural things that belong to the intellectual beings are not subject to necessity."[26] Nature at its core is not necessity but the freedom invoked by the loving offering on the part of God and a reciprocal response in thanksgiving on the part of Man. Despite the Fall, nature remains a gift of God, whereas it is precisely the "censurable" sinful fall of the free will, which, according to Maximus, provoked the "noncensurable" fall of nature, not the other way round.[27] The following text from the *Ambigua* merits close study: "For the Word, who is beyond being, truly assumed our being for our sake and joined together the transcendent negation with the affirmation of nature and what is natural to it, and became man, having linked together the way of being that is beyond nature that he might confirm [human] nature in its new modes of being without there being any change in its *logos*, and make known the power that transcends infinity, recognized as such in the coming to be of opposites."[28] According to Maximus, there is no existential "*apo-stasis*" or "*ek-stasis*" or "freedom" from nature. Rather, there is its affirmation and its opening up to a mode that is beyond nature, not simply to the mode of the "person," but the mode of uncreated enhypostatic nature in Christ. This anthropology of a psychosomatic sanctification and participation in God, which flows from Chalcedonian Christology, remains a constant throughout Eastern theology, from Macarius to Maximus to Gregory Palamas.

What, then, is the meaning of *ecstasis* here? According to Maximus, *ecstasis* means dialogue. Consequently, what we call paradise here is the freely chosen continuation of the natural ecstatic and dialogical development of personal created nature by participation and effected in Christ, whereas hell is precisely the freely chosen refusal to allow personal nature to follow the path to its completion by participation through this ecstatic dialogue. I have called this double *ecstasis* or "analogical *ecstasis*" elsewhere.[29] What is important here in relation to our discussion of eschatology is that this kind of *ecstasis* enables both meaning and history. Real history is opened dialogically to a reciprocity of both created and uncreated meaning, a mutual "giving meaning" and "being given meaning." Even God himself is given human meaning insofar as he is "God-with-us," not simply as an *esse* but as a *possest*, to use Richard Kearney's fine expression.[30] In this way, divine selfhood and created selfhood exist in a state of *interhypostatic synenergetic* becoming, according to Palamite terminology, and, therefore, in Maximian terms, an ineffable *change of the mode of existence* of created beings in the Spirit is effected.

Eschatology is not merely the mystery of a presence, Eucharistic or spiritual, which rhythmically interrupts the dire necessity of fallen history. Rather, it is the mystery of a realistic *metamorphosis,* transformation/transfiguration, of existence and history, through this interhypostatic, synenergetic, and *reciprocal meaningfulness.*

If such a *metamorphosis* is truly impossible, then we must follow Origen toward this final swallowing up of created nature by God or, better, accompany Plotinus in his self-effacing dance around the indifferent One. This noble but desperate dance is not analogical, since no reciprocity is manifested on the part of the One. In Plotinus's words:

> The One, therefore, since it *has no otherness* always present, and we are present to it *when we have no otherness*; and the One does not desire us, so *as to be around us,* but we desire it, so that we are around it. And we are always around it but do not always look to it, it is like a choral dance: in the order of its singing the choir keeps round its conductor but may sometimes turn away, so that he is out of their sight but when it turns back to him it sings beautifully and is truly with him; so we too are always around him—and if we were not, we should be totally dissolved and no longer exist—but not always turned to him; but *when we do look to him, then we are at our goal and at rest and do not sing out of time* as we truly dance our god-inspired dance around him.[31]

The One "does not desire us," "it does not move towards us, it does not want to be "around us." There is no *ecstasis* of the One toward creation, but only this monological *ecstasis* on the part of the creature, which would seem to occur as the result of ontological or existential necessity, inasmuch as the soul originates from God. *Ecstasis* now is a necessary return to an indifferent and nonecstatic One, rather than a free loving choice of analogical response to a divine ecstatic call on the part of the creature.[32]

I have mentioned Plotinus not only because of his relation to Origen, but also because of a possible relation of this concept of *ecstasis* with that of Thomas Aquinas. Thomas, of course, is clearly not Neo-Platonic but Christian. Nevertheless, he describes this kind of created relationship of the creature with God as nonreal on the part of God: "Therefore there is no real relation in God to the creature, whereas in creatures there is a real relationship to God; because creatures are contained under the divine order, and their very nature entails dependence on God."[33] According to the terms that we have already elaborated, in Thomas we have a dictated monological meaningfulness on the part of God instead of reciprocal meaningfulness and an *ecstatic meaningfulness* as a response on the part of man. Thus, he goes beyond Plotinus in the sense that there is clearly a response on the part of God, but this response does not really seem to be *dialogical* in the Biblical sense of the term.

It is possible, however, to find a theory of participation in Thomas, especially if we read him in light of the Greek Fathers, as I have argued elsewhere.[34] Nevertheless, it seems that such an approach is only possible—as it is manifested in its modern secular form—after having been cut off from its initial theological context, namely, either the modern *detached self* (in Charles Taylor's terms) manifested from the Cartesians until Kant and, perhaps, Husserl and Heidegger, or the modern narcissistic *self-referring subject*, which might call it in light of modern Depth Psychology.[35] In terms of our discussion here, these approaches appear to be the modern versions of the Origenist/Plotinian transcendental subject who, by escaping his perpetually fallen nature, assumes or even becomes in himself the ultimate divine meaning *in person*, within or without history but always at the level of an ultimate myth-ontological fantasy of ecstatic meaningfulness. In psychoanalytic language, this fantasy is neurotic, or even at times psychotic, a fantasy of existential amalgamation of the self with the *Thing* (the Other or the One) without the recognition through the Symbolic Law of both the existence and the definite distance of the Thing/Other/One from the subject. According to Lacan, it is the presence of this Symbolic Law and the need of an embodied mind for the self's dialogical transformation through a real, diachronic, and challenging encounter with the other that signals the need for an immediate separation of the subject. The subject needs to be separated from the illusionary holistic, imaginary, mystical, and mythical immediate merging with the absolute Other in order to find the way to the real Other, with the limitations that such a relationship entails. The only way for this *transubstantiation* to occur, according to psychoanalysis, is by an act through which the subject elevates the object of his love to the worthiness of the Thing/Other. The other option is the repulsion/negation of the real Other for the sake of the narcissistic merging with the false Otherness of the One, which ignores any subjective deficiency or finitude, and it is neurotic precisely for this reason. In other words, *transubstantiation,* in theological terms, means to create meaning-in-synergy. It means that the subject does not either project meaning upon the Other or have meaning projected upon him by the Other, while adoring a fugitive presence before or without it being actualized into a real transformative relationship of dialogical reciprocity in the here and now.

Psychoanalysis is useful in our theological discussion of eschatology for other reasons too. First, psychoanalysis is paradoxically Biblical in its roots, as I have asserted elsewhere.[36] In a way, it is eschatological inasmuch as it is founded upon a belief that man *can become different*, can take part in the formation of his fate, can *lay claim* to a future instead of just passively endure or suffer it. Second, as Wittgenstein, Ricoeur, and Castoriadis have shown in different ways, psychoanalysis represents the most convincing Western discipline because it regards the absolute necessity of any meaning to be reciprocal insofar as it is not neurotic or even psychotic. The very reality of my unconscious needs always has to be discussed with or scrutinized by another, as Ricoeur insists, and it is only through my persuasion by the analyst that an interpretation can be accepted, as Wittgenstein has claimed. Although the Other is never completely reachable in psychoanalysis, due to the games of narcissism (and this is precisely the limit of psychoanalysis), it is important to note that only a meaning-in-synergy can possibly heal a neurosis. As such, neurosis is always manifested in terms of ecstatic or solipsistic meaning.

This last term brings to mind Ludwig Wittgenstein, perhaps the most significant modern philosopher, who demonstrated the spiritual impasse of the self-referring subject. It is probable that Wittgenstein can help us to understand some of the eschatological views of Maximus's most genial Greek student, to wit, Gregory Palamas. As I have claimed elsewhere,[37] the most important thing concerning the Palamite concept of deification is its absolutely *relational* and, ultimately, *ecclesial* character. The energies themselves are "relational and participational"—that is, dialogical and analogical. Let us investigate further. Palamas identifies the divine energies with the Dionysian and Maximian divine "processions" and "participations" and, in the end, with the Maximian "divine logoi of beings." For Dionysius as well as for Maximus, the divine processions/participations/logoi/energies, insofar as they are manifestations of the benevolent divine will, are deeply connected to the concept of *analogy*. This is a term which signifies a dialogue of *synergy*, or, better, *synenergy,* since *analogy* for the above authors refers not to a similitude of essences but to an analogous action between different agents in order for them to achieve union. Thus, divine energy as a participable manifestation of divine will is *dialogical* in the sense that it calls for an energetic/active response on the part of its recipients. Energy/will begs for synenergy, a reality that finds its ultimate confirmation in the Incarnation. But if energies are dialogical/synenergetic events of analogical participation, and participation is an analogy of dialogical synenergy, then eschatology is essentially no different from the same common meaningfulness we met in Maximus.

This is precisely what the mature Wittgenstein claimed when he replaced all remnants of philosophical metaphysics with a deeper intersubjectivity,[38] thus supplanting metaphysics with the study of everyday conditions where common meaning is created in mutual understanding and responsibility beyond any sort of ecstatic solipsism. If Wittgenstein could discuss eschatology with us, deliberation would perhaps start as a common consultation on the use of language/meaning and probably end up as a synenergetic analogical/reciprocal meaningfuless, approaching Palamas's claim about the way in which the energies, divine and human, function; and this similarity is due to the two authors' common antimetaphysical persuasion.

It has been made apparent from our brief foregoing investigation that this understanding of Christian eschatology as reciprocal meaningfulness, a reality that manifests itself in the Church "here and now," can also have a corrective impact upon modern thought. In this common modern battle against the Western ahistorical or hyperhistorical self-referring subject, it can rectify this ecstatic meaningfulness upon which this subject relies.

It is now time to shift the discussion to an examination of the ways in which my aforementioned positions both converge with and diverge from the eschatological views of certain other Orthodox thinkers, such as J. Zizioulas, C. Yannaras, and J. Romanides. Concerning Zizioulas, it is obvious that we share the term "eschatological ontology" and that I affirm his conception of eschatology as a Eucharistically realized "eschatology of presence." Concerning ways in which we diverge, they have been excellently described by the late Fr Matthew Baker in his chapter on "Zizioulas and Heidegger," which was widely distributed by him a little before his premature death. I will let him speak in my place here:

> Yet in fact Zizioulas shows exceeding little interest in historical becoming. The "as" in "being *as* communion" is effected by eschatology, understood as *state,* not orientation; being-*toward* occupies only a negative place, as being-toward-*death*. In spite of his stress on an "existential" theology, this inattentiveness to human becoming in fact *weakens* the "existential" character of his thought. Human freedom, as decision and growth, is left out of the account. Zizioulas' critic and former disciple Nikolaos Loudovikos speaks of Maximus the Confessor's understanding of being as "being as a dialogical event of *becoming-in-communion*." [. . .] As Loudovikos rightly stresses, the dialogue of human becoming also includes *knowledge,* as an encounter with God. Zizioulas has reiterated Florovsky's criticism of Lossky's exaggerated apophaticism, yet Florovsky's caveat that "life" in Christ also includes knowledge stands as a corrective to Zizioulas as well. [. . .] Yet so intent is he on resisting the Parmenidean equation of thinking and being and the priority of the subject, that he says little to relate his ontology to epistemology. In this perspective, Zizioulas's dismissal of the "intellectualist" tradition of Justin, Clement and Origen—a tradition more present in later Fathers like the Cappadocians and Maximus than he admits—appears too hasty. For Maximus also, communion involves knowledge of the *logoi* or reasons of things, a point not unrelated to his theology of the Eucharist (as Loudovikos claims).[39]

The underplaying of history as *dialogical becoming* along with knowledge, as well as *consciousness* as an element of this becoming—which Baker also rightly claimed,[40] following my thread of thought—is succeeded by the hasty near identification of nature with fall. In Zizioulas's recent work, this same nature must be possessed by person in order to be given existence and meaning while, conversely, nature offers nothing meaningful to person.[41] This weakens any potential eschatology of presence, whether Eucharistic or not, because it leaves little room for a genuine reciprocal meaningfulness. As Baker correctly argues and which I have also affirmed,

> While for Florovsky, creation *ex nihilo* means fundamentally contingency and the openness of history to new events, in Zizioulas' emphasis creation spells more the possibility of corruption, and history as necessity. Likewise, for Florovsky, eschatology serves to underwrite the permanent significance of human historical action—history determining eschatology. For Zizioulas, in contrast, accent falls on the decisiveness of the end in determining and judging historical action, or freeing the creature from history.[42]

In this way, as Paul McPartlan writes, the Eucharistic presence remains a "rhythmical outlet from history" for Zizioulas,[43] and it is for this reason that I prefer to use the expression "eschatology of *metamorphosis*" instead of "eschatology of presence." An "eschatology of *metamorphosis*" includes an eschatology of repentance and ascetic life, philokalic knowledge, a change of consciousness and human creativity, as well as the possibility of changing the mode of existence of living things, all of which presuppose a transformation perspective. The Eucharist then becomes the sacrament of an eschatological dialogical reciprocity, an analogical *mimesis* of the divine act of offering, distributing, and receiving back being, and not simply as a means for transcending createdness and history. Such an outlet of escape, by the way, represents the greatest spiritual drama of the modern narcissistic self-referring subject, and the latest transformation of his modern will-to-power.

Concerning Yannaras, I would argue that his 1977 book, *Truth and Unity of the Church,* is valuable insofar as it is the first ecclesiological work in recent years in which the ecclesial event is directly connected with the very ontology—that is, with the possibility of a change to the mode of existence of beings. Nevertheless, and despite this excellent perspective, Yannaras's identification of nature with fall does not allow him to make full use of this perspective. Indeed, the Fall never happened precisely because *nature means fall.* The Fall never occurred historically due to nature already being in a state of evil and decay. Yannaras regards the instincts—that is, the instincts of self-preservation, domination, and pleasure—as the primary content of nature, which exist already in the prelapsarian period in a state of "functional independence from the reason and will of the human subject, an independence that is experienced empirically by us as more or less a state of existential schizophrenia: a splitting of our reason and will from the biological demands of our nature."[44] In the face of this dangerous nature, all that is available to us as human beings is "resistance to, control of and suspension of the necessities that the mode of nature imposes on us," and, in the author's view, this is precisely "the possibility of *ek-stasis* from nature: a possibility that a rational (personal) hypostasis should exist *ex-istamenē* ('standing out' in existential 'apartness') from the necessities given in nature (urges—instincts—reflexes) that determine the common mode of homogeneity."[45] Finally, Yannaras offers the following clarification: "*ek-stasis* from nature is a linguistic expression that permits the ontological content of the word *freedom* to be signified and communicated."[46] As we saw in the above discussion regarding the Maximian views of these matters, created nature remains a divine work even in its postlapsarian state. Salvation, in the view of the Confessor, consists in our following Christ and correctly using the divine logoi of nature. Though the Fall consists precisely in a *personal* misuse of the logoi, they remain unaffected in themselves.

But, given these assertions by Yannaras, can we speak of the possibility of transforming such a nature at all—that is, of changing its mode of existence? Moreover, what then is eschatology? Yannaras writes the following, again clearly identifying creation with fall: "Man is created, and his given *mode* of existence (his nature or essence) is by necessity that of individual onticity, of the instinctive urges of self-preservation, domination, perpetuation. It is that of self-completeness at the opposite pole to the *good*; that is, it is *evil*," an evil "which destroys a *personal* human being with the same even-handed indifference with which it destroys any animate existence [. . .]."[47] Finally, the author asserts that eternal life in God—that is, eschatology—means nothing other than that "human beings [should] exist, after the death of their physical being, by hypostasizing existence as grace, without the mediation of created nature."[48] But then nature has no future in eternity and remains soteriologically unaffected, simply checked and controlled like an infection. In the end, it is thoroughly abrogated through an *ecstasis* wherein the created being hypostasizes the natural energies of God without nature. However, in such a scenario, the creature is simply flooded by divinity, thereby catastrophically losing its natural otherness. So, while I agree with Yannaras's ecclesiology, I disagree with his eschatology.

There is little space left for Romanides in this chapter. I will limit myself to two points only: Romanides is prophetic in his theological articulation concerning the need for the incorporation of spiritual life into theology. But, as I have claimed elsewhere,[49] his views led him to a sort of devaluation of the Sacraments and ecclesiology. His tendency to transfer the entire eschatological event into the human spiritual experience of the "here and now" results in the elimination of the historical expectation of the eschata, a position that is rather reminiscent of Bultmann and early Barthian eschatology.

CONCLUSION

My final position is that there are essentially two poles in Orthodox eschatological theology. On the one side stands Origen and the residual elements of Plotinian Neo-Platonism, which is enabled today by modern transcendental subjectivism in its many forms and manifested in thinkers from Kant to Heidegger. On the other side is Maximus the Confessor and his disciple, Gregory Palamas, whose thought can perhaps be made more accessible by thinkers such as Wittgenstein and, despite its shortcomings, some of modern psychoanalysis. It would be unfair to argue that any of the three aforementioned Orthodox theologians are clearly on the side of Origen. There are indeed certain aspects and different parts of their thought wherein they come close to Origen's position. Nevertheless, all three seem to want to move toward the positions of Maximus and Palamas. Thus, even if their initial tendency is toward ecstatic meaningfulness, they still try to orientate themselves toward reciprocal meaningfulness. This is demonstrated by Zizioulas's *being as communion,* Yannaras's *ontology of relationship,* and, finally, Romanides's emphasis on the need for *selfless love.* On the other hand, the Origenist element in Romanides is manifested by his embrace of a "spiritual" church/communion and the near rejection of the "external" historical church/communion; the Origenist tendency in Yannaras shows itself through his arguments for the control or even abrogation rather than transformation of nature, and the ultimate "personal" escape from it; the Origenist tendency in Zizioulas emerges in his eradication of history and, again, via his emphasis on the repression if not complete escape of a thoroughly passive nature together with his conviction that otherness is something passively given/dictated to a fellow subject. These Origenist characteristics result in an overexaltation of person at the expense of nature and history, the overstressing of the monarchy of the Father over consubstantiality, an overestimation of the role of ecstatic spirituality, an overemphasis upon the dictation of the other's otherness, et cetera, all of which work to prevent us from creating real dialogical reciprocity and the reciprocal meaningfulness of all creation as described in this chapter.

To conclude, according to the Greek patristic tradition, heaven and hell are born of the personal and free choice of creatures alone, "in accordance with nature" or "contrary to nature," while created nature is universally resurrected. It is precisely for this reason that heaven and hell are active realizations of freedom of creative reciprocal meaningfulness and not merely decisions of passive reward or punishment on the part of God. Heaven is the free determination "in accordance with nature" of the dialogical and participatory development of created nature in Christ for all eternity, an "ever-moving stasis," according to Maximus, of the creature within God. Conversely, hell is the free determination "contrary to nature" to refuse the dialogical liberation of nature achieved in the absolute meaning of the Incarnation. Here, God is encountered with malicious envy and hostility, "in knowledge but not by participation," as Maximus argues.[50] This constitutes a peculiar refusal of the Resurrection through a rejection of the participation that would have allowed the Resurrection to be transformed into a full and conscious intermeaningfulness in cooperation with God. If heaven also appears to be a supernatural reward, this is because of God's limitless response to the human desire for participation. If hell also appears to be a punishment, this is on account of the intense bitter resentment that lies in the denial of knowing God *through participation.*

To be sure, patristic theology testifies that the Kingdom of God, and heaven in particular, are ontologically iconized in the Holy Eucharist. Saint Symeon the New Theologian, an ascetic writer of great authority and stature, describes the good things of the Kingdom "which God has prepared for those who love him" as follows: "Among the good things stored in heaven are the body and blood itself of our Lord Jesus Christ, which we see every day and eat and drink. These are acknowledged to be those good things; without them you will not be able to find any of the things mentioned, not even one, even if you go through the whole of creation." This scholion, clearly based on the sixth chapter of John's Gospel, is astonishing precisely because it removes any kind of ecstatic or monophysite temptation. Saint Symeon continues: "You have heard that communion of the divine and spotless mysteries is eternal life and that those who have eternal life are the ones the Lord says he will raise on the last day, not like the others at all events abandoned in the tombs, but like those who possess life, raised from life to eternal life, while the rest are raised to the death of eternal punishment."[51] Eucharistic participation in Christ is the foundation of a freely willed movement toward God, and is the present realization of the personal choice "in accordance with nature" of that dialogical reciprocity that saves and perfects nature, whereas its denial kindles the "contrary to nature" self-loving necrosis within the very abundance of life itself. In each case, freedom according to the image of God remains. We have, then, either freedom as a dialogical and reciprocal meaningfulness out of love that liberates nature in a Eucharistic relationship, or freedom without love or, rather, an ecstatic meaningfulness, which imprisons nature in malicious self-will and self-activity. Thus, the question of the eternity of hell does not ultimately affect God and his love, because hell will end when the devil wants it to end, when he ceases his malice against God. If hell is the absolute narcissistic enclosure within oneself in an imaginary superiority that denies the reality of corruption and the need for the transformation of the created, then this situation constitutes the soul's ultimate blindness in the end, its self-condemnation to hell.

Hell, then, is the denial of the Eucharist, the tragic freedom of absolute narcissism—that is, the supreme self-torture of a freely chosen enmity against love. At the frontier of heaven, hell is lit dimly by heaven's light, and this minimal gleam of rationality that is shed on it besieges the abyss of its irrationality with the compassion of the saints of God. But the battle against this hardened self-deification is indescribably frightening and inauspicious.

The rest is known to God . . .

NOTES

1. See Christopher Lasch, *The Culture of Narcissism* (New York: Norton, 1978). See also the addendum to his first book-length work, *The Minimal Self* (New York: Norton, 1984).

2. Heinrich Denzinger and Adolf Schönmetzer eds., *Enchiridion Symbolorum* (Fribourg: Herder, 1976).

3. See paragraph 1035.

4. To use J. Delumeau's expression.

5. Jean Delumeau, *Sin and Fear: The Emergence of a Western Guilt Culture* (New York: St Martin's Press, 1990), 244–65.

6. Augustine, *De Civitate Dei* XXI, 72.

7. Thomas Aquinas, *Summa Theologica,* Ia q. 20–25; Ia IIae, q. 87; *De Malo*, q. 5.

8. Sergius Bulgakov, *The Orthodox Church* (Crestwood, NY: St. Vladimir's Seminary Press, 1988), 185.

9. Gerald Bonner, *Freedom and Necessity: St Augustine's Teaching on Divine Power and Human Freedom* (Washington DC: The Catholic University of America Press, 2007), 34–35.

10. Hans Urs von Balthasar, *Kleiner Diskurs über die Hölle* (Einsiedelen: Johannes Verlag, 2007).

11. Robert Jenson, *Systematic Theology,* vol. 2 (Oxford: Oxford University Press, 1999), 359–68.

12. See Paul Evdokimov, *Orthodoxie* (Neuchatel: Delachaux Niestlé, 1959). I use the Greek translation here, Ορθοδοξία (Θεσσαλονίκη: Ριγόπουλος, 1972), 445–47.

13. Basil the Great, *On the Psalm 33,* 8, PG 29: 372. John Chrysostom, *On the Epistle to the Romans,* homily 5, PG 47: 288–289.

14. Note that the author uses the verb κολάζει here, from which κόλασις originates, which means hell.

15. John Damascene, *Against the Manicheans,* PG 94: 1545D–1548A.

16. Irenaeus of Lyons, *Against Heresies V,* 36.1, PG 7:1545D–1548A.

17. See Karl Rahner, *Theological Investigations IV,* 323 et. seq.

18. Wolfhart Pannenberg, *Systematic Theology,* vol. 3, trans. G. W. Bromiley (London: T&T Clark, 1998), 541.

19. *Enneads,* I.1.3.

20. Henry Crouzel, *Origen: The Life and Thought of the First Great Theologian*, trans. A. S. Worrall (Edinburgh: T&T Clark, 1989), 215.

21. Panayiotis Tzamalikos, *Origen: Philosophy of History and Eschatology* (Leiden: Brill, 2007), 354.

22. See Tzamalikos, 156, 273–74, 293.

23. Maximus the Confessor, *To Marinus*, PG 91: 12 CD. All my arguments relating to Maximus that follow have been discussed at length in the English translation of my *Eucharistic Ontology: Maximus the Confessor's Eschatological Ontology as Dialogical Reciprocity*, trans. Elizabeth Theokritoff (Brookline, MA: Holy Cross Orthodox Press, 2010) as well as in some of my other works in Greek, namely, *Closed Spirituality and the Meaning of the Self* (Athens: Ellinika Grammata, 1999), 189–204; *Terrors of the Person and the Torments of Love* (Athens: Armos, 2009), 19–31.

24. Maximus the Confessor, *Opuscula*, PG 91: 28D-29A.

25. Ibid., PG 91: 80A.

26. Maximus the Confessor, *Disputation with Pyrrhus*, PG 91: 293BCD.

27. Maximus the Confessor, *To Thalassius*, PG 90: 405BC.

28. Maximus the Confessor, *Ambigua*, PG 91: 1053BC. I use Louth's translation here.

29. See my *Eucharistic Ontology*, especially the sixth chapter.

30. See Richard Kearney, *The God Who May Be* (Bloomington: Indiana University Press, 2001), 2001.

31. *Enneads*, VI.9.8.

32. It is not difficult here to discern a deep similarity between Neo-Platonism and Hinduistic or Buddhistic *meditation*, which has been described as "an application of a technique without interlocutor," since "the Absolute, on its part, shows a very little interest for humans" (see the twenty-third chapter in Klaus Kenneth's *Götter,Götzen,Guru:* Östliche *Mystik und Meditation. Heil oder Unheil?* [Maranatha: Verlag, 2011]; see also Sir Norman Anderson, *Christianity and World Religions* [Leicester: IVP, 1984], 84).

33. Thomas, *Summa Theologica*, I. 28.1, response to objection 3.

34. See my "Striving for Participation: Palamite Analogy as Dialogical Synenergy and Thomist Analogy as Emanational Similitude," in *Divine Essence and Divine Energies: Ecumenical Reflections on the Presence of God in Eastern Orthodoxy*, eds. C. Athanasopoulos and C. Schneider (Cambridge: J. Clarke, 2013), 122–48.

35. See my forthcoming essay, "Consubstantial Selves: A Discussion between Orthodox Theology, Existential Psychology, Heinz Kohut, and Jean-Luc Marion," *Personhood in the Byzantine Christian Tradition: Early, Medieval, and Modern Perspectives*, eds. Alexis Torrance and Symeon Paschalidis (New York: Routledge, 2018), 182–96, and "Being and Essence Revisited: Reciprocal Logoi and Energies in Maximus the Confessor and Thomas Aquinas, and the Genesis of the Self-referring Subject," in *Revista Portuguesa de Filosofia* 72, 1 (2016): 117–46.

36. See the third chapter of my work in Greek, *Psychoanalysis and Orthodox Theology: One Desire, Catholicity, and Eschatology* (Athens: Armos, 2003).

37. See my "Striving for Participation: Palamite Analogy as Dialogical Synenergy and Thomist Analogy as Emanational Similitude."

38. See my "From the Daydreams of a Private Religious Language to Its Ecclesiology: Wittgenstein and Maximus the Confessor," in *Church in the Making: An Apophatic Ecclesiology of Consubstantiality* (New York: St Vladimir's Press, 2015), where the relevant bibliography is discussed. See also my "Δι-εννοημάτωσις or Inter-meaningfullness: Reading Wittgenstein through Gregory Palamas' and Thomas Aquinas' readings of Aristotle," in *Ludwig Wittgenstein between Analytic Philosophy and Apophaticism*, ed. Sotiris Mitralexis (Newcastle Upon Tyne: Cambridge Scholars, 2015), 151–65.

39. Matthew Baker, unfinished PhD diss. (Fordham University, 2015), 62.

40. Ibid., 63.

41. See my "Possession or Wholeness? Maximus the Confessor and John Zizioulas on Person, Nature and Will," *Participatio*, no. 4 (2013): 258–86.

42. Baker, 61.

43. Paul McPartlan, *The Eucharist Makes the Church: Henri de Lubac and John Zizioulas in Dialogue* (Edinburgh: T&T Clark, 1993), 270.

44. Christos Yannaras, *Six Philosophical Sketches* (Athens: Ikaros, 2011), 90.

45. Ibid., 128–29.

46. Ibid., 129.

47. Christos Yannaras, *The Enigma of Evil*, trans. Norman Russell (Brookline: Holy Cross Orthodox Press, 2012), 35–37.

48. Yannaras, *The Enigma of Evil*, 136. See also Christo Yannaras, Το ρητό και το άρρητο [The Effable and the Ineffable] (Athens: Ikaros, 1999), 209: "The created hypostasis of every human being also exists after death by hypostasizing no longer its created nature but the uncreated vivifying energy of divine love" since human beings after death are changed into an empty, nonsubstantial hypostatic shell, "an existential mould" according to Yannaras (214). It is doubtful whether such views allow us to expect the survival of even the soul after death. The problem then, at least according to Gregory of Nyssa, is how the resurrection of the dead is possible under such circumstances. Without the soul acting as a "natural mould" for each of us, the Resurrection would then be the resurrection of the people themselves and not a new creation.

49. See chapter 2.1 of my, Ἡ κλειστὴ πνευματικότητα καὶ τὸ νόημα τοῦ ἑαυτοῦ. Ὁ μυστικισμὸς τῆς ἰσχύος καὶ ἡ ἀλήθεια φύσεως καὶ προσώπου [Closed Spirituality and the Meaning of the Self: Christian Mysticism of Power and the Truth of Personhood and Nature] (Athens: Ellinika Grammata, 1999).

50. PG 90: 796ABC.

51. Simeon the New Theologian, *The Discourses*, trans. C. J. De Catanzaro (New Jersey: Paulist Press, 1980), 3, 167.

Part III

PERSONHOOD BETWEEN ONTOLOGY AND HISTORY

Chapter Nine

The Ontology of the Person—An Outline

Christos Yannaras

I. COMMON PLACES (in the manner of Wittgenstein)
- The limits of my language are the limits of my world.
- That which cannot be put into words (the ineffable) certainly exists. It is that which is only experienced and shown—the experiential element.
- The sense of the world must lie outside the world. In the world everything is as it is, and everything happens as it does. *Within* the world there are no values; and if there were, they would have no value. If there is any value that does have value, it must lie outside everything that happens and is the case. For everything that happens and is the case is accidental. What makes it nonaccidental cannot lie *within* the world, since if it did, it would itself be accidental.

   It must lie outside the world.
- What we call the "sense" of the world, that is, the "sense" of existence and of existents, is their *cause* and their *end*. We understand cause and end only as relational givens. Irrationality cannot constitute the *sense* of what exists.

II. THE PLATONIC PROPOSITION
- The sense of the world (the cause and end of existents) is realized in (unexplained given) *ideas*. The ideas (the models, the *logoi*-modes-blueprints of existents) pre-exist, are given, and have no causal explanation. They constitute the primary starting point and final end of existents. The existence of every existent presupposes its *idea* and refers to its *idea*.

- The word "idea" is derived from the verb *orō* ("I see,"–second aorist *eidon* from *idein*) and indicates the cognitive result of a particular sensory experience, that of *seeing (orān)*.
- The Platonic *ideas* are not products of the intellectual capacity of human beings. We do not recognize *ideas* thanks to our power of reasoning, or by ways of mysticism and ek-stasis. We recognize them by the sensory experience of vision, as a vision-*contemplation* of the real—as the *recollection* (*anamnesis*) of the vision-*contemplation* which has been granted to us as a result of the "pre-existence" of our souls.
- The value and significance of Platonic ontology is not to be located in its hermeneutic adequacy. Its hermeneutic adequacy is limited by the a priori assumptions which it presupposes. The most important thing about Platonic ontology is its reliance on the experiential starting point of the *knowledge* of the *sense* (cause and end) of existents in *recollection*.
- The empiricism of *recollection* (*anamnesis*) is probably Plato's chief contribution to ontology. After Plato it was Christian Hellenism's philosophical discourse that was to rely consistently on the empirical clarification of ontological questions. When the post-Roman West began to be capable of articulating philosophical questions (chiefly from the twelfth century onward), trapped as it was in the individualistic character of the Augustinian paradigm, it was also to imprison ontological argumentation in "correct" reasoning (in an autonomous intellectualism) or in "mystical" investigations that were by definition incommunicable.
- Two and a half thousand years after Plato comes Heidegger, who was to venture to pose the problem of existence in terms of, and in accordance with the requirements of, empirical assertions.

III. THE HEIDEGGERIAN PROPOSITION
- The existence of existents is their phenomenicity. They *are* what they appear to be and *because* they appear to be such. Nothing else.
- Phenomenicity, identified with existence, is an empirical given. It is the experience of time; we experience the appearing of existents as time. Time is the empirical horizon of the rising up of existents into disclosure.
- Without time there is no *Being* and without *Being* there is no time. Existents exist as a result of their property of "persisting in time," that is, of being manifested by constituting time, of being phenomena in time.
- Human beings are the only existents that not only have the passive property of "persisting in time" but also have the awareness-cognition of doing so. They are aware of temporality as a rising up of existents into phenomenicity.

- We recognize existents as phenomena in time. That is to say, we recognize the essence (the *ousia*—the mode of participation in Being) of existents either as presence (*par-ousia*—temporal phenomenicity) or as absence (*ap-ousia*—the nullifying of manifestation). We recognize Being (*einai*) either as being-present (*par-einai*) or as being-absent (*ap-einai*). Being-absent (nothingness) is contained within Being, constituting one of the two empirical confirmations of Being.
- Presence as phenomenicity (a rising up into temporality, in relation to absence, that is, to nothingness) is the empirical knowledge of that which exists. That which exists is known in relation to nothingness, not through a hermeneutic intellectual analysis, but through experience—experience of the anxiety (*Angst*) of existence as ephemerally "thrown down" in the world, experience of care (*Sorge*) for the "fall" into temporal "with-one-anotherness" (*Miteinandersein*) as an awareness of finite "being-thereness" (*Dasein*), as an experience of the given mortality of inexorably approaching death (*Sein zum Tode*).

IV. THE PROPOSITION OF THE "ONTOLOGY OF THE PERSON"

1. The existence of existents is an active *how*, not a phenomenal *what*. The existence of every existent is in a state of activity, a state of becoming. The becoming of existence constitutes *relations*; it is the reality of relations.
2. The "world" (the totality of existents) is a reality of active relations, not a totality of given (perfected) entities. Even the smallest unit (atom) of any material element is constituted by the relations of specific tiny active quanta—of electric charges, impulses, et cetera. The initial givens of matter are energy. They constitute an existential event because they are correlated (because they are-in-relation). The confirmation of their existence (observation) is also a function of relation. If observation ascertains "position," then what is observed behaves (is manifested) as a *particle*. If observation ascertains "motion" (velocity), then it behaves as a *wave*. What is observed constitutes a particle or a wave according to the relation which observation seeks to establish (wave-particle duality).
    2.1 An isolated atom of any material element cannot by itself realize and manifest the specific difference of matter, its existential alterity. Only the coexistence of more than one atom (a different number for each material element) realizes and manifests the specific difference of each material. The specific difference arises both from the particularity of relations of active quanta in each

atom and from the particularity of relations between the atoms of each material element.

3. A human being is the only existent which is not only constituted as an individual existence by active units of perfected relations (bioparticles)—relations between primordial active givens, structured constituents of the cell—but also has the power, as an active individual totality, to *establish* relations with other (opposite) active totalities.

   3.1 To "establish" relations means to bring about new unforeseen relations not predetermined by natural-biological necessity, the necessity that is constitutive of the relations by which existents operate.

   3.2 The ability of human beings to establish relations, to participate in an unforeseen and undetermined manner in active relations with what is opposite them, we call a rational capacity, a capacity of reason. "Reason" is what we call an active event of disclosure, of becoming apparent, of coming *into the light*. Such a disclosure is always a referential event; it presupposes a "horizon," a *where*, a recipient of the disclosure. We confirm as the horizon of the disclosure of existents (the presupposition for them to be existential *phenomena*) the *rational* capacity that human beings possess, their capacity to "apprehend mentally" (*noein*), to receive into the mind (*en no*[*i*]) the images (ideas, from *idein*) of beings and to make them concepts (*ennoies*).

   3.2.1 We call *nous* (noetic energy-capacity, usually rendered in English as "mind") the exclusively human capacity to put together or synthesize the information (in Greek *eidēseis*, from *eidon*, "I saw") that is offered by the phenomenicity of phenomena. The mind assembles information (*syn-eidēsis*, or "shared knowledge") about existents: the interconnection, correlation, and correspondences of whatever information is conveyed to the mind by the senses.

   3.2.2 The rational capacity of human beings (the mind) is the power to receive information (*eidēseis*—images, ideas) regarding existents *consciously*, that is to say, correlating each item of information not simply with the quantitative totality of sensible things but chiefly with the *modes* (the *how*) of coming together, the coordinates of form, size, dimensions, distances, temporality, causality, and purpose. The conscious (*en-syn-eidētē*) apprehension of the reality of existents is a work of the human mind (*nous*) and constitutes the event of apprehension (*kata-noēsis*—mental perception) of reality, which means: in accordance with reason (*kata-logon*), with an active *relation* or engagement.

3.3 The power of human beings to realize their *relation* with existents as an event of mental *perception* of existents—the apprehension of forms-ideas (of the phenomenicity of existents) as mental images, as concepts—is a rational capacity. Also rational is the power of the mind to "make symbols" of concepts, to connect-identify optical images with "acoustic images" (images acoustiques—Saussure) so that by the production of vocal sounds it (the same mind, but also the mind of all who share in the same phonetic code, in the same "language") recalls the same concepts, and consequently accomplishes a common mental perception (*kata-noēsis*) of reality.

    3.3.1 Phonetic signifiers refer to what is *signified* mentally, to the sensory-empirical *relation* of the rational subject to the existents and processes of becoming that are opposite it, a relation that is formulated in the mind.

4. Also empirical is the relation that arouses and coordinates the cognitive powers of human beings, the infinite parts of the soul (Aristotle, *On the Soul* III, 9, 432a24)—sensation, intellection, imagination, judgment, perception, memory, discrimination—in the confirmation, recognition, and notation of sensible representations of the existent and the real.

    4.1 Irrational animals also apprehend sensible images, *but* without the capacity to turn them into concepts and symbols. They recognize the same image when it is repeated. They have the same reflexive responses on the recognition of repeated images (Pavlovian conditioning). They distinguish between pleasant and unpleasant images. But they are unable to assemble a *relation* that coordinates more elements than sensation and memory: they have no cognitive powers.

    4.2 Human beings are the only existents that have the power to establish rational relations not subject to the necessity of relations that constitutes the reality of the natural world, both animate and inanimate. (The *uncertainty principle* and the *theory of relativity* refer to the mode by which human beings recognize the reality of the natural world, not to a power of matter-energy to choose behaviors.) The power of human beings to establish relations or to reject a relation, to realize or to avoid relations by judging the result to be either positive or negative, to submit to or to resist relations that are dictated by natural necessity—all these are a mark that is exclusively human. We signify this mark by the word *freedom*.

5. Freedom is the power of human beings to resist natural necessities (laws of nature), to create relations that are not subject to predeterminations, to choose and decide about what they do by their individual thought and judgment.

   5.1 Human beings gain knowledge-awareness of the reality of existents and of events in virtue of having the power-freedom to bring about a relation with what belongs to their environment—that is, to recognize their uniqueness (existential otherness) with regard to beings and events opposite them, to recognize it in a manner that is unique, dissimilar, and unrepeatable for every human being. The cognitive relation is the event of realizing and manifesting the inner principle (*logos*), the otherness, of the knowing subject and the known objects.

      5.1.1 Every existent possesses a morphic otherness as a given or as something that has come about. Only human beings also possess an *active* otherness-power to bring about or establish *relations* that realize and manifest the existential otherness of both terms of the *relation*. Through the articulated word (*logos*) and the multiformity of the language of the arts, human beings realize and manifest this double alterity.

      5.1.2 A Beethoven sonata or a painting by Van Gogh establishes a *relation* between the hearer or beholder and the specific work of the composer or artist, a relation cognizant of the existential otherness of the creator and his work. We say: this music *is* Beethoven; this painting *is* Van Gogh.

6. We characterize human beings as *personal* existences so as to indicate that human beings are and are known only as events of *relation*. The Greek word *pros*-ōpon ("person") is constructed from the preposition *pros* ("toward") and the noun ōps (ōpos in the genitive), which means: I have my face turned toward someone or something. I am opposite, I am known only as the term of a relation, as an experience of relation.

   6.1 We say in everyday speech, "Do you know so-and-so?—No, I've heard about him—So you don't know him," because knowledge consists only of the experience of direct relation, of personal encounter, not of information passed on.

6.2 The experience of an interpersonal relation is knowledge that is actualized dynamically. It is accomplished continuously, without ever being accomplished fully and definitively. A collaboration, a cohabitation, a friendship, a love affair confirm this ever more perfect but never fully accomplished knowledge of the other, along with the dynamics of self-knowledge that are generated by the relation.

6.3 The cognitive dynamics of a relation are an expression of the degree of freedom which each term of the relation achieves. Relation means: the other interests me; I wish to know this person. The primordial desire is usually instinctive need, a product of the necessities which govern my natural hypostasis. The other is useful to me, is necessary to me—for the services which they can furnish me with, for their agility of mind which delights me, for the pleasure which they can probably supply, for the protection which perhaps they can grant me.

6.4 In all these cases the desire for relation is tied to the law of natural necessity. It is a nonfree dependence, an egocentric quest, not a relation. A relation comes about when the other interests me for that which they are, without ulterior motives. Consequently, knowledge of the other presupposes my own withdrawal from the necessities of my self-centered urges; it presupposes an acquired freedom from impersonal instinct. The more I free myself from the demands of nature, which are impersonal, the more fully (without ties of submission to self-interest) I can recognize the otherness of the other.

    6.4.1 At the summit of freedom from subjection to the necessities of nature is love, eros. Eros is an ek-static event: people who fall in love "stand out" (*exo-istantai*) from themselves; they stand outside their egoistic self-centeredness, outside their imprisonment in instinctive self-interest. The other interests them more than their very selves do. Erotic love is the only possible experience of freedom from nature's inexorable necessity for self-centeredness and self-interest.

    6.4.2 The knowledge of the other, freed from the subjection of their image to self-interested motives, is increasingly nearer to that which really *is*. Because this liberation is accomplished within the bounds of nature, it is realized as a continuous dynamic becoming. We know the person we love in a continuous manner, without ever arriving at perfected knowledge, at knowledge possessed as a "thing" that has been acquired, the acquisition having annulled the adventure of relation.

7. The chief question of ontology, the central issue of every philosophical question, concerns the *causal principle* of what exists: What is it that makes beings be? Heidegger rejected the specific formulation of the question, the logic of its construction, with the observation that it binds us to the "ontification" of the causal principle, to conceiving of it as a being. With this question we presuppose the causal principle of Being as an individual entity ("that" which makes beings be), as "something," as a transcendent entity, a *supreme, divine, and most venerable class of being*. Heidegger himself based his empirically coherent nihilistic ontology on posing a question not about the *relation* between beings and Being but about their *difference*. Beings *are disclosed*; they are phenomena. Being *loves to hide* (Heraclitus), to conceal itself in the presence/absence of beings, in their phenomenicity/nothingness.

   7.1 Heidegger did not suspect that the definitive (with a definition) location of the causal principle ("*what* it is that makes beings be") may reveal not an ontic *what* but a modal *how*, that the causal principle of existence and of existents can be a mode of existing, that the mode *hypostasizes* the existence (constitutes it as a *hypostasis*, as an existent fact) and not that the existent entity defines the *mode*.

   7.2 From the first moment that the ecclesial event appeared on the historical scene, it referred to the Causal Principle of what exists not by the word *God* but by the word *Father*. The word "God" defines a *what*, an existent whose onticity (his existential identity) is given-predetermined as a result of his *essence* (the divine essence, his *Godhead*). He cannot *be* or *become* anything other than that which the *logos* (the rational blueprint) of his essence prescribes-determines. Thus, it is the *logos* of his essence, an a priori necessity not existential freedom, that is the causal principle of existence and of what exists. If the Causal First Principle of all things is a God predetermined by his essence, there is no existential room for alterity, for the unexpected, for the new, for history.

   7.2.1 The word "Father" reveals an existence which draws its identity from the freedom of *relation*, not from the necessity of *being* and *cause*. The word "Father" refers not to an individual entity (as the names Zeus, Apollo, and Poseidon do) but to an existence that exists *as-toward*, that exists *in-relation*—its hypostatic alterity is realized and manifested thanks to relations which it forms existentially: "begetting" the Son and causing the Spirit to "proceed."

7.2.2 This is the only way in our language, limited as it is by the boundaries of the given and the *caused*, that we can "say" the reality of the *cause* identified with freedom. The Father exists as cause-in-itself: the cause of existence and of everything that exists. He exists because he freely wills to exist, and he wills to exist because he loves. His love is not simply a fact of volition or behavior. It is the mode by which he exists: he "begets" the Son and causes the Spirit to "proceed"—he hypostasizes his *being* (makes it a hypostatic reality) as freedom of personal-existences, which exist because they will to exist, and they will to exist because they love. The only definition of the Causal Principle of all things, within the context of the experience of the ecclesial event, is that it "is love." It is the "real eros," the triumph of freedom.

Chapter Ten

Berdyaev's Solution to History
Redeeming Persons in Historical Love
Daniel S. Robinson

From its methodological starting point in the personal revelation of God, contemporary Eastern Orthodox theology has greatly emphasized the epistemological, ontological, and ethical primacy of personhood over essentialist notions of being. In many ways this method of Orthodox theology, termed here "Orthodox Personalism," is rooted in the early centuries of patristic theology. But in its contemporary articulation, this theological idiom emerges from the nineteenth century milieu of Westernization in pre-revolutionary Russia. As the Enlightenment and its aftermath led to great strides in Western European science, as well as significant social changes, these developments made their way into Eastern European culture as conspicuously foreign elements. In both Russia and Greece, the importation of "Westernism," "Modernism," "Scientism," et cetera, was embraced by some and rejected by others precisely in virtue of its break with the traditional "Orthodox" past. As these foreign ideas were incorporated into the social institutions of Eastern Europe, Orthodox thinkers were presented with a challenge and an opportunity: Orthodox theology had come face to face with modern Western thought and was now forced to articulate itself in a Western philosophical idiom.

In consideration of Orthodox theology's adoption of a Western idiom we would benefit from posing the following question: What can a philosophical discourse in terms of personhood contribute toward our understanding and solving of the problem of history? Within that general question, this chapter will focus on the theory of personhood developed by Nikolai Berdyaev (1874 Kiev–1948 Paris). Berdyaev is a good place to start on this question for two reasons. First, Berdyaev is of tremendous importance to the later trajectory of twentieth and twenty-first century theology, both Orthodox and Roman Catholic. This importance is seen in his personal influence on his fellow Russian thinkers, especially on Fr. Georges Florovsky, as well as in his personal interactions with both the Neo-Thomist and the Ressourcement schools in France.[1]

Berdyaev is not the most prominent of the émigré theologians in contemporary English-speaking Orthodox scholarship. He is, however, rightly recognized for his prolific philosophical writings which center on the freedom of personality from natural determinism and the various temptations to slavery through objectivization. Berdyaev's early career was sufficiently relevant for him to be exiled from the Soviet Union soon after the Russian Civil War (1917–1922). He eventually found himself at the Institute St. Serge in Paris, teaching alongside Georges Florovsky, Sergei Bulgakov, and others (including Vladimir Lossky who, though writing in Paris, was not affiliated with St. Serge for various reasons). Berdyaev lectured and published in Paris until his death in 1948.[2]

The second reason for focusing on Berdyaev in regard to this general question of personhood and history concerns the specifics of Berdyaev's own thought. In fact, his approach to personhood was explicitly addressed toward making sense of a period in history that was excessively problematic:[3] the overthrow of the Russian Empire, the subjugation and dispersion of the Russian Church, Stalin's slaughter of dissidents, Hitler's extermination of Jews, the Allied obliteration of German and Japanese cities, et cetera. In the context of the early twentieth century, and in the shadow of Idealist theories of historical progress, Berdyaev identified the problem of history with the recognition that historical change does not in fact lead inevitably to ever greater syntheses of consciousness, freedom, Spirit, et cetera. Against the Idealist background of the nineteenth century, the fact of historical suffering and the failure of progress led to an acute problematizing of history. The problem can be put this way: if the march of history brings with it all the suffering and injustice which it surely does, all this suffering must be somehow justified in the name of historical inevitability; but such a justification could never be regarded as truly just by those human beings who must endure the criminality of historical suffering. As Berdyaev explained it, the temptation to ascribe historical change to the activity of an all-controlling divinity enslaves human beings to the false idea of a monstrous God.[4]

As a solution to this problem, I will argue that Berdyaev's approach to ontology through personhood establishes a way of properly correlating ontology along with our experience of history that avoids a self-contradictory and oppressive account of God's action in the world. Approaching ontology in terms of personhood rather than essentialism, or "objectivization" as Berdyaev termed it, can reorient our thinking about divine activity away from a model of cosmic control and toward one of personal cosuffering and liberation. With this approach History is transformed from the object of divine sovereignty—in other words, an idealized harmonious world order to which all persons must submit themselves—into the arena of divine suffering and love, through participation in which human persons are liberated from history and made capable of loving in history.[5]

Berdyaev's personalism was formulated as a diagnosis and refutation of Russian Communism as an erroneous religious system. In his view, the objectivization of God through monistic metaphysics left Christianity with an unresolvable theodicy leading to the atheism and totalitarianism of the Soviet Union. Against this attempt to forcibly eliminate suffering through oppressive conformity, Berdyaev articulated his view of Christian personalism as a means to redeem human suffering through the voluntary love of persons acting in history.

Berdyaev and his fellow émigrés left Russia in the wake of revolution and civil war. They then journeyed across a continent devastated by "the war to end all wars" and settled in France just in time to watch as the Second World War brought even greater sufferings to even more human beings. Along with many others of his day, Berdyaev was well aware that the Idealist/Hegelian dialectic of history was supposed to usher forth in heightened cosmic freedom as Spirit unfolded its self-understanding through the inevitable rationality of historical progress. Or, if one opted against German Idealism in favor of a more traditional Christian providence, God was supposed to be taking care of His people and establishing the Kingdom of God through the one Holy Russian Church.[6] But the twentieth century brought forth nothing of the sort. So Berdyaev informs us that the problem of history is essentially the problem of theodicy. Human beings are lured into worshipping historical developments as though they are the handiwork of God, but we humans are then scandalized and horrified by the recognition that history is in fact full of cruelty, suffering, oppression, and injustice.[7] How, then, can we reconcile the terrors of history with our notions of a providential divinity?

Of Berdyaev's impressive corpus, three works will be dealt with here. Two of these are his historical analyses of Russian Communism, *The Russian Revolution*, and *The Origins of Russian Communism*; the third, *Slavery and Freedom*, was written as a sort of culmination of Berdyaev's personalist thought. In these works, one can see Berdyaev's synthesis of Russian social and intellectual history. In his historical works, he clearly diagnoses the Russian Revolution as a spiritual crisis, and in *Slavery and Freedom* he explains the philosophical dangers of the rationalism incorporated into Russian history.

Berdyaev's explanation of Russia's spiritual crisis centers around his concepts of personality and objectivization. Personality is the source of reality as the center of freedom and of life. Objectivization, in Berdyaev's thought, is every reductionist temptation to enslave the subjective world of the person to the world of natural determinism. In this construct, Berdyaev resists all categories of thought that reduce the person's capacity for freedom to any determinate constraints. Slavery to Nature, Being, God, et cetera are all rejected as fundamental temptations to objectivize the person. All are considered enslaving due to the logical necessity required for conclusive knowledge of them; and all are implicated directly in the establishment of totalitarian regimes, including most specifically for Berdyaev, the Soviet Union.

Berdyaev's analysis of the revolution's origins focuses on four historical periods that ultimately led to a change in Russian religious sensibility which itself beckoned the Communist Revolution. According to Berdyaev, the beginning of the Muscovite state under the ideology of the Third Rome fused the eschatological promise of the Kingdom of God with the particular dynastic aspirations of the Russian state.[8] Secondly, the reforms of Patriarch Nikon and the resulting "Old-Believer" schism significantly weakened the people's confidence in the institutions of church and state as harbingers of the eschatological kingdom.[9] Thirdly, the program of Westernization conducted by Tsar Peter and especially his reduction of the Russian Church to a department of state finalized and enforced a total break in the people's trust of the Church as an independent spiritual authority and as an advocate for justice in this world.[10] Finally, Berdyaev understands the nihilists and socialists of the late nineteenth century to be the direct inheritors of the latent *raskolnik* (schismatic) hope for the establishment of eschatological justice within Russian society, as preserved throughout the preceding centuries in opposition to these official state policies.[11] According to Berdyaev, the atheism of Soviet Communism is therefore itself a deeply religious expression of the traditional Russian calling to usher in the Kingdom of God.[12] It has simply been transposed from Russian Orthodoxy through the religious reforms of Nikon and Peter into Marxist atheism. But at its root, it is still a religious striving to attain the Kingdom of God by alleviating suffering. Because the church had been so successfully absorbed by the state, dominated by civil concerns and controls, institutional Christianity was powerless to speak for justice. Consequently, the nihilist socialists, the inherent *raskolniki* of the intelligentsia, were the clear seekers for justice, and Russian socialism settled on an atheistic foundation for the pursuit of the Christian ideal of the Kingdom of God.[13]

THEODICAL ORIGINS OF RUSSIAN SOCIALISM

Berdyaev's philosophical explanation for atheistic socialism is just as involved and important as his historical analysis. The Russian Church under

Peter's reign simply could not sufficiently answer the problem of suffering. This problem of suffering, so acutely felt by the compassionate Russian socialists, especially during the debates surrounding the emancipation of the serfs, provides the centerpiece to the Marxist utopianism which the Bolshevik Revolution attempted to embody. Both proceed from a classical notion of theodicy. The one omnipotent, benevolent God must be somehow responsible for evil. Therefore, either evil is somehow justified by the ultimate value of God's will, or God's benevolence must be admitted to be rather, in actuality, malevolence. Petrine Orthodoxy simply affirmed that God's benevolent will was enough to justify suffering. But the Russian socialists considered this solution reprehensible. "Russian atheism rejected every kind of God, because to admit God was to justify evil, injustice and suffering and give in to them."[14] The socialists were too aware of suffering in the world and committed themselves to its eradication. For them, the existence of a sovereign God could only serve to justify and prolong suffering. Paraphrasing Bielinsky, Berdyaev explains, "God created an unjust world full of suffering, and therefore He must be rejected for moral reasons."[15]

Russian socialism, after this atheistic turn, developed into nihilism, which as Berdyaev characterizes its "main themes," is essentially materialist utilitarianism.[16] This utilitarianism set as its goal the creation of a perfect society which would eliminate all material suffering. But paradoxically, the creation of this society would require a great deal of sacrifice and suffering on the part of its citizens. "Nihilism, at its sources and in its purest form, is asceticism without grace; asceticism not in the name of God, but in the name of the future welfare of mankind, in the name of a perfect society."[17] The nihilists, especially as the revolutionary movement in Russia gained momentum, recognized the suffering that would be necessary in order to achieve their utopian elimination of suffering.

Berdyaev notes the contradiction of this Revolutionary strategy to end suffering and recognizes it as a theodicy parallel to traditional Christianity. It is in his analysis of this "nihilist theodicy" that Berdyaev engages his philosophy of Personality to demonstrate the failure of Communist ideology.[18] Socialism's desire to eliminate suffering quickly became Nihilism's willingness to destroy the failed society and sacrifice individuals for the sake of a perfected utopian vision.

In the end, Russian atheism tried to solve theodicy by justifying suffering for the sake of what Berdyaev terms the "world order," which is itself constructed on supposedly scientific principles in order to banish suffering. Marxism gained popularity in Russia, particularly after the failure of the Nicholaevan reforms and the disastrous defeat of the Crimean War in 1856.[19] Its economic materialism provided a theory with which to build a world order that could parallel and trump Christianity's theodicy. Materialist utilitarianism would establish a utopian world order that would justify the suffering and sacrifice of individuals. In this utilitarian utopia, suffering would be abolished through the provision of all material necessities. Marxism was here vastly superior to Christianity because its justification of suffering was only for the sake of eliminating that suffering, not prolonging or redeeming it. Any meaning for suffering was still rejected. Berdyaev notes that this rejection results from forgetfulness of Christ's redemption of suffering.[20]

BERDYAEV'S DIAGNOSIS OF THE PROBLEM

Berdyaev explains that the atheistic utopian dream rests on a monistic view of reality. The world must be a unified whole and subject to deterministic laws in order for a perfect society to be scientifically constructed. His critique of such a utopian worldview is its valuing of the world whole higher than its parts, actual people. He sees the monistic systems of Marxist utopianism and Christian theocracy as essentially the same in their determinism and objectification. They both subject the value of the person to the ultimate value of the cosmic order. He equates the theodicies of institutional Christianity and Marxist materialism because they both are willing to justify suffering in favor of the monistic world order they imagine. The unity of this world order establishes a monistic system of logical necessity to which all individuals must conform. Personal deviation from this system threatens the cohesion of the world order, and deviation must be suppressed. In Berdyaev's view, this explains both traditional theocratic morality and the oppression of the Soviet state. In short, monistic systems believe the utilitarian or righteous unity of the world order to be more valuable than particular persons. Therefore, sacrificing personal freedom for the sake of the world order is justified, and in the case of dissidents is necessary.

We must turn to Berdyaev's *Slavery and Freedom* for a more thorough treatment of his theodical analysis of Russian Communism. In Berdyaev's words, his work *Slavery and Freedom* "is the outcome of a long philosophical journey in search of truth, of a long struggle on behalf of a transvaluation of values."[21] The work is a sort of *Summa* of Personalism, laying out all the ways in which personality is lured into objectivization and slavery to various constructs. Berdyaev devotes his second chapter to the objectivization of God, in which he discusses the theocratic slavery that results from classical theodicies. He provocatively agrees with Feuerbach (1804–1872) that humans do create God according to their own conceptions, and that this false, objectivized God is at the root of all social domination and injustice.[22]

This objectivized God is conceived along a sociomorphic analogy to human relationships of dominance and subservience. In this objectivized form, God is thought to be the dictator of the universe, causing suffering and demanding worship from his subjects, all for the sake of his "righteous" world harmony.[23] Berdyaev links his criticism of Russian socialism to that of all monistic systems. He sees all monistic systems, whether classical philosophy, institutional objectivized Christianity, or Soviet Communism as essentially the same in that their foundations are philosophical determinism and objectification. Thus, Berdyaev equates the theodicies of objectivized Christianity and nihilist utopianism because they both justify the undeserved suffering and slavery of the person to society in the name of the monistic world order that they envision.

FROM MONISM TO TOTALITARIANISM

The hoped-for world order of utopianism enthrones the "lure of sovereignty," in Berdyaev's terms, and is the primary instance of objectivization. "The greatest temptation of human history is the temptation to exercise sovereignty and in it there is concealed a most powerful enslaving force."[24] The monistic view of reality and the dream of building the perfect society with the unified laws of the monistic universe lead humanity to yearn for a universal sovereign state.[25] With a single stroke, Berdyaev characterizes all of human history with this quest for universal sovereignty. It is all firmly rooted in the inherent dream of perfecting society to alleviate suffering, in the flawed religious instinct to attain the Kingdom of God on materialistic terms.[26]

Berdyaev condemns this temptation precisely on personalistic grounds. The supreme value of the world order in the quest for sovereignty decenters the person as the ultimate ethical end. The person is no longer of any inherent value but receives value only in its function as a means toward the attainment of sovereignty.[27] Berdyaev sees this epitomized in the words of Caiaphas, "'It is better for us that one man should die for the people than that the whole nation should perish.'... The state always repeats the words of Caiaphas; it is the state's confession of faith."[28] When societies seek universal sovereignty, they are forced to sacrifice personhood to the "lure of sovereignty"; real people are no longer ends, but mere steps on the path to world order. The supreme valuation of the world order commandeers humanity's instinct for ultimacy. It steals all value away from personhood and places it rather on the utilitarian functionality of utopia. The lure of sovereignty usurps the value of a person's own worth and renders the person a simple object for the sake of the world order. Because the world order is of ultimate value, the lure of sovereignty transforms our ethical sensibilities into overt patriotism, whether for church, state, or nation. What is clearly sinful for the person becomes virtuous for the sake of the idol of society.[29] Coercion, dishonesty, and war all become heroic actions for the sake of the world order. Thus, Berdyaev explains the horrible failure of the utopian experiment of the Soviet Union.

The monistic view of reality, permeating European philosophy especially since Parmenides, led to an impossible theodicy.[30] The implication of God in the fact of evil forced the Russian socialists to become atheists, to pursue a nihilist utopia on materialist, Marxist grounds. This utopianism could not but rest on the equivalent monism of scientific determinism. Only from this objectivized, deterministic framework could such a utopia be constructed. And so the same impossible theodicy remained in force, albeit in antireligious terms. The utopia retained its rights over personal freedom, its rights to justify the sacrifice of citizens to the totalitarian state. Now, instead of the sovereign will of God justifying suffering and demanding conformity to the theocratic state, the sovereign will of the Soviet Union would justify oppression and enforce totalitarian conformity to the atheistic state. Berdyaev sees the monistic frameworks of both theocracy and Communism as equally depersonalizing. It is precisely this failure to uphold the primacy of personality that has abandoned the world to totalitarianism.

Berdyaev further explains that the very possibility of society's subjugation to a totalitarian regime derives from a false theodicy underlying the philosophy of history. According to him, humans are all too often seduced by the sheer inevitability of historical processes, by history's all-encompassing power to determine the events of human life.[31] Through this seduction humans worship the unfolding of history as though it were God's own activity in our midst.[32] When we credit God with the unfolding of history, we quickly face the uncomfortable realization that much of history is filled with oppression, violence, and meaninglessness. How is it that God is responsible for this criminality in history? The pervasive habit of objectivization tempts people to conclude that the criminality of history must be justified as the operation of the all-powerful and all ruling God. In this view, people conclude that the victors of history, the empires, the churches, the institutions, no matter how oppressive, must be venerated by their victims as the agents of God. The view of God that results from this mistaken worship of history is monstrous. It is a God who sanctifies the slaughter of human dignity, of personal value, for the sake of the objectivized ideals of progress. It is a God who forces and constrains human beings into conformity rather than liberating and redeeming His children into His Life of Freedom.

This monstrous God of historical veneration was not only unacceptable to Berdyaev, it is an entirely imaginary and therefore false concept. Berdyaev argued that such a God simply does not exist; this concept of God, derived from an erroneously monistic concept of being, remains only an abstract object of thought in the minds of real existing human beings. As such, the oppression that this concept of God justifies has no philosophical foundation in anything real. It must be rejected as simply a false idea. "The so-called ontological proof of the existence of God is only the play of abstract thought."[33] Consequently, "Slavery to being is indeed the primary slavery of man."[34]

In Berdyaev's observation, this objectivized ontology perpetuates a dialectic of revolution. The Russian Marxists were right to reject the unjust deity presented by this ontology. The God who justifies the suffering of the poor in the name of well-ordered world harmony should be rejected, even as Dostoevsky has Ivan Karamazov bitterly return his ticket for entry into such an unjust world.[35] But without an ontology of personhood the Soviet program for revolution could only replace the world-controlling God with an equally unjust world-controlling state, political party, and dictator. In fact, operating from this ontology, every revolution, every war, every act of treason and terror can be justified and yet will fail in its aspiration for justice. Berdyaev asserted that the whole history of human interaction is witness to the intractable failure of this historical dialectic based upon an ontology of objectivization. All states and all institutions coerce, subjugate, and enslave the very people whose suffering they are sworn to alleviate.[36] For Berdyaev, this is the problem of history: the necessary enslavement of objectified human beings to a quasi-divine master. It is inescapable even through revolution, as long as one proceeds from an ontology of object rather than an ontology of person.

BERDYAEV'S CORRECTIVE: AN ONTOLOGY OF PERSONHOOD

We can now turn to Berdyaev's understanding of personhood, which he articulated precisely as the antidote to the spiritual crisis of Revolutionary Russia. An ontology of personhood denies the ontological ground of the abstracted ideas of being, history, world order, et cetera. "Being does not exist."[37] Instead of these ideas, which ironically exist only in the subjective consciousness of individuals, Berdyaev posits the primacy and ultimacy of particular beings, of persons over and above the common and universal. Proceeding from this ontology, there is no such thing as being, no thing called world order, no thing called history, nature, or the rest. Rather there are only particular existents, persons who act and interact. Because this ontology denies the proper existence of the world and of history as abstracted objects, it is no longer correct to say that God is in charge of the world or that He directs history.

Astutely distinguishing between "God and the human idea of God," Berdyaev writes,

> The base human category of domination is not applicable to God. God is not a master and He does not dominate. No power is inherent in God. . . . He determines nothing. . . . God is certainly not the cause of the world. . . . God is the liberator. Theology has made a slave of him. . . . God understood as an object with all the properties of an objectivized world has become a source of slavery. God as object is only the highest natural force of determination made absolute.[38]

He continues against this false thesis:

> But God is not world providence, that is to say not a ruler and sovereign of the universe, not pantokrator. God is freedom and meaning, love and sacrifice; He is struggle against the objectivized world order.[39]

Starting with an ontology of personhood, the action of God is not deduced from the false premise that being exists. Instead, the action of God is observed in the particular actions of Jesus. God is revealed to us as a cosufferer and liberator, not as the world-controller in charge of historical providence and cosmic harmony:

> Christianity is not the revelation of God as an absolute monarch. The Christian revelation of the Son of God Who sacrificed Himself, suffered and was crucified, saves us from that. God is not . . . monarch. God is a God Who suffers with the world and with man. He is crucified Love; He is the Liberator . . . not as power, but as Crucifixion.[40]

It is the incarnation of the personal God that ultimately invalidates both the utopian and the theocratic theodicy. The suffering God, the particular person, Jesus Christ, demonstrates that God is not the world-controller, "God is certainly not the constructor of the world order, or an administrator of the world whole."[41] Rather, "God is in the child which has shed tears, and not in the world order by which those tears are said to be justified."[42] From this theological position, any attempt to justify suffering for the sake of some more ultimate social or cosmic end is invalid. The problem of suffering "is only solved on the existential plane where God reveals Himself as freedom, love and sacrifice, where He suffers for man and strives together with man against the falsity and wrong of the world. . . . We have no right to justify, all the unhappiness, all the suffering and evil in the world with the help of the idea of God as Providence and Sovereign of the Universe" (*Slavery and Freedom*, 89). The Incarnation of Jesus Christ is for Berdyaev the ultimate refutation of Russian utopianism.

Berdyaev's refutations of the objectivized, "world-controlling" concept of God are worth quoting here in such volume in order to show the prominence of Christology in his metaphysical rejection of objectivized, causative theism. In other words, Berdyaev's overall response to Russian Communism proceeds directly from his understanding of the Incarnation as demonstrating the primacy of God's personhood. Having first established the religious nature of Russian Communism, Berdyaev's thought continues on to explain how the religion of Russian Communism is, at root, a misunderstanding of the Personalist significance of Jesus Christ. The significance of Berdyaev's rejection of theodicy is that what he sees as traditional Christian theology—the objectivization of God as cause of the universe, rooted in Aristotle, not the freely suffering personhood of Jesus Christ—comes to bear primary culpability for the atheistic and oppressive conclusions of Russian Nihilism. It was this unjust theodicy, perpetuated by institutional Christianity's failure to uphold the personhood of God, that prompted the socialists to reject the divine autocrat for their own "idol of sovereignty," that changed the socialists into nihilists and brought about the Russian Revolution.

FROM DIVINE SOVEREIGNTY TO THE COSUFFERING CHRIST

It is in Berdyaev's view of God that his thought is at once most scandalous and most deeply Christian. From his rejection of an objectivized ontology Berdyaev rejects the concept of God that is deduced from the necessity of a first cause of the cosmic order. Berdyaev's beginning point is the particular revelation of Jesus, not the universal deduction of a first cause. The revelation of God in Christ's incarnation shows us that God is not the world controller, but the personal cosufferer. This view of God as a person who is not in control of the world, but who suffers and loves within the world certainly appears scandalous, but at the same time it immediately defuses the dialectic of revolution. Here, there is no world-controlling God to dethrone and replace. There is no need for the false dichotomy of either submitting to or rejecting the providence of God. While an objectivized ontology must always replace the unjust God with an unjust divine placeholder, this personalist ontology replaces the deducible God of control over history with the observable God of personal action within history. This God is not to be worshipped through the veneration of history, but instead He witnesses alongside us to the injustice and meaninglessness of historical crimes. This is the scandalous and revolutionary core of Berdyaev's understanding of the gospel.

Berdyaev's denial that God controls history, his denial that God is παντοκράτωρ, is certainly eccentric within the Christian tradition. Can it really be accepted that God is not in control of the world, but only suffers within it? Does not the Christian tradition require that God is affirmed as the creator of all things? To answer these questions, the significance of Berdyaev's personhood is paramount. God is indeed the creator of persons, but never the controller of persons as objects, nor therefore the controller of history. Christ reveals God to us even as he reveals humanity to us: not as the controller of historical events, but as the passionless sufferer who loves within and throughout history. Thus, God's action is revealed as love, not historical determination.

From this perspective, history is no longer the oppressive tool of God that humans need to steal and coopt, but it is now the record of God's suffering alongside and within human beings. This historical struggle of God among us is now the primary revelation of God's action and so also the model of our own deification. If history is not an idealized object of control, but a record of personal action, it serves theologically as the arena of both divine and human struggle against injustice, for love, forgiveness, and liberation.

To return to the chapter's initial question: How can a philosophical discourse in terms of personhood contribute toward our understanding and solving the problem of history? Berdyaev's personalism as a solution to the connected problems of history and theodicy offered a strong precedent for subsequent Orthodox thinking on the subject. In Berdyaev's model, divine providence does not work for the well-ordering of historical progress, but for the liberation of human persons from the constraints of historical inevitability. History is no longer conceived as the universal trajectory of cosmic harmony, controlled by God, to which all humans must submit. Rather, history becomes a series of particular circumstances enabling us to choose particular acts of love just as Christ did. Far from action in control of objects, Christ reveals to us the action of freedom in forgiveness and love; and through His incarnation, He reveals this action to be as much human as divine. In Berdyaev's account, history is transformed from the manipulated object of a criminal God into the field of opportunity for free acts of historical love.

NOTES

1. See Andrew Louth, "French Ressourcement Theology and Orthodoxy: A Living Mutual Relationship?" in *Ressourcement: A Movement for Renewal in Twentieth-Century Catholic Theology*, eds. Gabriel Flynn and P. D. Murray (Oxford: Oxford University Press, 2012), 495–507. Cf. Georges Florovsky and Andrew Blane,

Georges Florovsky: Russian Intellectual and Orthodox Churchman (Crestwood, NY: St. Vladimir's Seminary Press, 1993).

2. Florovsky and Blane, *Georges Florovsky*. Manfred S. Frings includes Berdyaev among the correspondents of Max Scheler, with whom his philosophy bears marked agreements (*The Mind of Max Scheler: The First Comprehensive Guide Based on the Complete Works* [Milwaukee, WI: Marquette University Press, 1997], 16).

3. Nikolai Berdyaev, *Slavery and Freedom*, trans., R. M. French (San Rafael: Semantron Press, 2009), 7–19. See also Nikolai Berdyaev, *The Russian Revolution* (Ann Arbor: University of Michigan Press, 1961); and Nikolai Berdyaev, *The Origin of Russian Communism* (Ann Arbor: University of Michigan Press, 1960).

4. Berdyaev, *Slavery and Freedom*, 255–57.

5. It may be noted at this point that, in developing his ontology of personhood, Berdyaev was a very early critic of ontotheology. In fact, the core of Berdyaev's response to the problem of history and theodicy is a rejection of the adequation between God and being. I will further develop this theme below, but it should be pointed out here that Berdyaev developed this line of thinking already by 1923 with his book, *The Meaning of History*, four years before Heidegger's publication of *Sein und Zeit* in 1927.

6. See Berdyaev, "The Religion of Communism," in *The Russian Revolution*; Berdyaev, *The Origin of Russian Communism*, 37–57.

7. Berdyaev, *Slavery and Freedom*, 256, discussed below.

8. "The doctrine of Moscow the Third Rome became the basic idea on which the Muscovite state was formed. The kingdom was consolidated and shaped under the symbol of a messianic idea" (Berdyaev, *Origins*, 10). Berdyaev explains this type of spiritual fallacy as the seduction of the "Lure of Society": the exchange of an objectified social identity for the immediate personal calling of God (*Slavery and Freedom*, 102–16).

9. This identity between the Russian state and the Kingdom of God was deeply shaken by Patriarch Nikon's campaign to reform the Russian liturgical practices along Greek lines. Russian Christianity could not be the real Kingdom of God if it required an external Greek authority for its verification. "The question was this: is the Russian kingdom a true Orthodox kingdom, i.e. is the Russian people fulfilling its messianic vocation? . . . A suspicion awoke in the people that the Orthodox kingdom, the Third Rome, was being impaired, that a betrayal of the true faith was taking place. Antichrist had seized on the hierarchy of Church and State alike. Popular Orthodoxy broke with both. True Orthodoxy retired underground" (Berdyaev, *Origins*, 11). By supporting this false church, the Russian state had abdicated its calling as the Kingdom of God; and Russian civilization, the would-be savior of the world, was now cut off from grace. The *raskolniki* withdrew in suspicion from official society, and rejected history, politics, and culture as betrayals of the Orthodox Empire. This rejection of history and culture, of church and state, is Berdyaev's *sine qua non* of the Revolution. "Russians are, by their very psychology, inclined to become raskolniki (schismatics)" (Berdyaev, *Revolution*, 2). Nikon's reforms caused "a divorce between the Church's people and her rulers, between the common people and the cultured class" (Berdyaev, *Revolution*, 4).

10. A century later, Peter's reforms increased the suspicion of the Russian people for both church and state. "The schism gave the first blow to the idea of Moscow as the Third Rome. It showed that all was not well with the Russian messianic consciousness. The second blow was given by the reform of Peter" (Berdyaev, *Origins*, 12). Peter's reforms were "an act of violence against the people's soul" (Berdyaev, *Revolution*, 4). "An attitude of aloofness and suspicion towards the authorities grows up. The Russian religious messianic idea remains, but it settles into a profound divorce from its actual surroundings" (Berdyaev, *Revolution*, 5).

11. Consequently, "the Russian *intelligentsia* of the nineteenth century was a class of intellectual schismatics, an intellectual *Raskol*" (Berdyaev, *Revolution*, 5–6; Berdyaev's italics). Cf. "Russians were true to type, both in the seventeenth century as Dissenters and Old-ritualists, and in the nineteenth century as revolutionaries, nihilists and communists. The structure of spirit remained the same. The Russian revolutionary intelligentsia inherited it from the Dissenters of the seventeenth century" (Berdyaev, *Origins*, 9).

12. Because Russian messianic hopes had despaired of expression through the institutions of church or state, they were directed rather to immediate social experience, to the problems of suffering and justice. "Socialism, broadly speaking, was the dominant religious faith of most of the nineteenth-century Russian intelligentsia . . . was essentially a non-acceptance of suffering . . . a refusal to admit that there was any meaning in it" (Berdyaev, *Revolution*, 8). Berdyaev credits Dostoevsky with the most profound realization and expression of Russian socialism as "not a political but a religious question. . . . Dostoevsky revealed the religious psychology and religious dialectics of Russian Nihilism and revolutionary Socialism. And once one has understood the basis of Russian Nihilism, and recognised it as an original product of the Russian spirit, one is able to grasp the source and basis of the militant atheistic element in Russian Communism" (Berdyaev, *Revolution*, 8–9).

13. "A typical intellectual raskolnik, Bielinsky searched for truth throughout his life and became a Nihilist and an atheist for love of justice and the welfare of the people and of humanity" (Berdyaev, *Revolution*, 9).

14. Berdyaev, *Revolution*, 12.

15. Ibid.

16. "The Nihilism of the 'sixties had already brought forth the main themes that operate and triumph in the Bolshevik Revolution: hatred of all religion, mysticism, metaphysics and pure art, as things which deflect energy from the creation of a better social order; substitution of social utilitarianism for all absolute morality; exclusive domination of natural science and political economy, together with suspicion of the humanities; recognition of the labourers, workmen and peasants, as the only real men; oppression of interior personal life by the social principle and social utility; the Utopia of a perfect social structure" (Berdyaev, *Revolution*, 17).

17. Berdyaev, *Revolution*, 18. Berdyaev continues, "Russian atheism, in its most profound forms, may be expressed in the following paradox: God must be denied, in order that the Kingdom of God may come on earth. . . . That atheism comes, above all, from having forgotten that Christ, our God, Himself suffered and was sacrificed for us" (*Revolution*, 26).

18. "Nihilism is torn by a fundamental contradiction: it begins by wanting to emancipate personality and free it from the slavery of social surroundings . . . and yet it finally enslaves the human person to social utility. . . . And it is obliged to do so, because it considers human personality to be a mere product of social surroundings, and denies its spiritual nature" (Berdyaev, *Revolution*, 18–19).

19. Georges Florovsky, *Ways of Russian Theology*, vol. 2 (Belmont, MA: Buchervertriebsanstalt, 1987), 53–54.

20. As above, "That atheism comes, above all, from having forgotten that Christ, our God, Himself suffered and was sacrificed for us" (Berdyaev, *Revolution*, 26).

21. Berdyaev, *Slavery and Freedom*, 7.

22. Ibid., 82.

23. This "makes God appear always as an autocratic monarch, making use of every part of the world, of every individuality, for the establishment of the common world order, for the administration of the whole to the glory of God. This is held to be a justification of every injustice, every evil, every sorrow, of the parts of the world" (Berdyaev, *Slavery and Freedom*, 86). "All these doctrines are founded more or less on the principle of the domination of the universal common over the individual singular" Ibid., 87).

24. Berdyaev, *Slavery and Freedom*, 139.

25. "The Empires of the ancient East, the Roman Empire, Papal Theocracy, the Holy Byzantine Empire, the Tsardom of Moscow, the Third Rome, the Empire of Peter, the Communist State, the Third German Reich. . . . In his search for sovereignty man expresses his passion for the universal. He identifies his longed-for kingdom with world unity, with the final unification of humanity" (Berdyaev, *Slavery and Freedom*, 139).

26. "That weird and horrible phenomenon of human life which today is called the totalitarian state, is certainly not a temporary and accidental phenomenon of a certain epoch. It is a revelation of the true nature of the state, of sovereignty. The totalitarian state itself wishes to be a church, to organize the souls of men, to exercise dominion over souls, over conscience and thought, and to leave no room for freedom of spirit, for the sphere of the Kingdom of God" (Berdyaev, *Slavery and Freedom*, 140). It is important to note that Berdyaev does not focus his condemnation on the West or on the East, but on this common human temptation.

27. "The temptation of sovereignty is one of the temptations which Christ rejected in the wilderness" (Berdyaev, *Slavery and Freedom*, 139).

28. Berdyaev, *Slavery and Freedom*, 144.

29. "That which has been considered immoral for a person has been considered entirely moral for the state. The state has always used evil means . . . these methods . . . have always been justified by a good and exalted end in view." "No-one can ever clearly explain and justify the fact that undoubted vices and sins in an individual person . . . should assume the appearance of virtues and a gallantry in the state. . . . No-one has ever in any way justified on metaphysical and religious grounds the ethics of the state." "If the state and nation be regarded as a person and to this personality a different and non-human code of ethics is applied, then man is not personality, man is a slave" (Berdyaev, *Slavery and Freedom*, 132–33).

30. Berdyaev, *Slavery and Freedom*, 73–81.

31. "The greatest of all forms of the seduction and slavery of man is connected with history. The solidity of history and the apparent magnificence of the processes which go on in history impose upon man and overawe him to an unusual degree. He is crushed by history and consents to be a tool for the accomplishment of history, to be made use of by the artfulness of reason" (Berdyaev, *Slavery and Freedom*, 255).

32. "Man not only accepts the burden of history, not only carries on a conflict with it, and realizes his destiny, but he has a tendency to deify history, to regard the process which takes place in it as sacred. And here begins the lure and slavery of history. Man is ready to bow the knee before historical necessity, historical fate, and to see in it divine activity" (Berdyaev, *Slavery and Freedom*, 256).

33. Ibid., 81.
34. Ibid., 78.
35. Ibid., 266.
36. Ibid., 140–42.
37. Ibid., 78.
38. Ibid., 82–83.
39. Ibid., 89.
40. Ibid., 85.
41. Ibid., 87.
42. Ibid., 88.

Chapter Eleven

Joseph Ratzinger's *Imago Dei* Anthropology

The Reconciliation of Ontology and Salvation History

Isabel C. Troconis Iribarren

One of Joseph Ratzinger's main theological questions concerns the role that history plays in salvation.[1] The reason for this is because of the significant implications that this question has for theological methodology and for ecumenism. His reflections on this matter are an answer to the issues raised by what he calls a "discontinuous Christianity," which is a particular interpretation of the Christian faith that eliminates any permanent relationship between salvation and history.

According to Ratzinger, this interpretation originated from the Protestant Reformation's fear that the acceptance of a historical or created mediation of salvation undermines God's transcendence.

This chapter seeks to show that by giving origin to a relational and open ontology, Ratzinger's *Imago Dei* Anthropology can pave the way for the possibility of a created and historical salvific mediation that does not jeopardize God's infinite transcendence and, because of that, makes possible a reconciliation of ontology with salvation history.

"The defense of the inseparable link that ties . . . the Historic-salvific dimension of the Christian message with the ontological level, constitutes one of the central aspects of Ratzinger's theological thought."[2] This affirmation of A. Bellandi represents the opinion of a significant group of scholars who believe that one of Joseph Ratzinger's main theological concerns is how to reconcile time and being within Christian faith.[3]

For Ratzinger the importance of this problem comes not only from the fact that it forms part of the cultural context of his time,[4] but also because he considers it to be the "essential problem which underlies all the difficulties of dogmatic theology today."[5] Interested in this question since the beginning of his academic life, Ratzinger has written on the topic from different points of view: exegetical,[6] liturgical,[7] and systematic.[8] In the present chapter we aim to offer his understanding of the problem in the context of his ideas about Christian salvation.

THE ECUMENICAL RELEVANCE OF THE PROBLEM

When examining the various writings that Joseph Ratzinger has dedicated to the question of how to reconcile time and being, one immediately discovers that Ratzinger's interest in the matter is a consequence of a deep ecumenical concern, that of uncovering the fundamental factors that drive apart Protestant and Catholic theological perspectives.[9]

Following in the footsteps of his mentor and friend Gottlieb Söhngen, Ratzinger has examined the question since his first writings[10] while maintaining a dialogue with some outstanding contemporary Protestant theologians such as Karl Barth, Oscar Cullmann, Rudolph Bultmann, and also taking into account some important theological movements such as Political Theology and Liberation Theology.

The temporal and spatial limitations of this chapter do not allow us to enter into a detailed analysis of Ratzinger's views on each one of these authors, so it shall be enough to say that he divides them into two different groups in accordance with whether they consider our problem from a "conventional" point of view (Barth, Cullmann, and Bultmann) or from a "revolutionary" one (J. B. Metz). The "conventional" approach seeks to explain how history can serve as a medium for the development of human being. The revolutionary point of view instead tries to solve this dilemma by denying the existence of human essence and thus understanding History no longer as a means, but as an end, as salvation itself.[11]

Going beyond these differences, Ratzinger believes that there is common ground that unifies these two positions. This common ground is what he calls the "discontinuity principle." In order to understand the "discontinuity principle," let us start by reviewing Ratzinger's reflections on the conditions on which History has traditionally been considered a means of salvation. In his 1970 text *Heil und Geschichte*, Ratzinger explains that many civilizations have viewed history as a salvific force to the degree that it provides human individuals with social, cultural, and technological structures to help them manage their daily existence and their understanding of self.[12] In many civilizations these structures were usually considered divine gifts (as supernaturally founded), thus determining that the salvific force of History always had a transcendent origin and destiny.[13]

Among the wide spectrum of religious interpretations of history, in Ratzinger's view Christian faith gives rise to a particular reading of History's salvific potential. The "particularity" of the Christian reading of History lies in the fact that it is salvific in an eschatological manner, in the fact that it is *already* salvific but *not yet fully* so.

It is already salvific because, living "in a world formed by and filled with faith," the Christian finds "a firm basis that gives his life meaning, salvation and shelter."[14] However, it is not yet fully so because these historical forms that give freedom to his life do it by giving him hope: by directing him to a realm that transcends secular history. In Ratzinger's words thanks to faith "while remaining in history, one nevertheless always transcends history but in such a way that this 'transcending' actually enters into history as source and hope."[15]

Ratzinger goes on to explain that with the passing of time this original salvific model—characterized by the continuous (already salvific) and at the same time discontinuous (and not yet fully so) relationship between salvation and history—was watered down due to an excessive identification of salvation history with secular history (i.e., a radicalization of the continuous aspect).[16] When this Christian-secular history passed through moments of moral decadence, it stopped being perceived by people as salvific and was instead felt as oppressive. In this moment new proposals, like the one by Martin Luther, appeared that strived to save Christianity from such decadence by placing it completely outside of history (i.e., a radicalization of the discontinuous aspect).[17] This is what Ratzinger means by the "discontinuity principle": an interpretation of Christianity that eliminates any permanent relationship between salvation and history, an interpretation that no longer understands Christendom as a "salvific history," but only sees it as a promise of salvation that acts in history without giving origin to any historical form capable of communicating salvation.

By placing salvation outside of history, this "discontinuous Christianity" paradoxically did not end up becoming an exclusively ontological doctrine of salvation but, on the contrary, it gradually moved toward the refusal of any ontological objectification of God's salvific action, and this refusal affected many essential and basic elements of the faith:

> In place of *successio*, the expression and safeguard of continuity, there appears now the charismatic power of the Spirit that acts here and now; in place of typology, which pointed to the continuity of history in promise and fulfillment, there appears now the spoken appeal to what was in the beginning; history, once understood as the union of promise and fulfillment, is interpreted now as the contradiction between law and gospel. Because ontology is the basic philosophical expression of

> the concept of continuity, it is opposed first as a Scholastic and later as a Hellenistic perversion of Christianity and is contrasted with the idea of history. . . . Finally, since the concept of Incarnation is the real anchor-point of ontology in theology, it is opposed antithetically by emphasis on the Cross as the real axis of the Christ-event—the Cross as the expression of radical discontinuity, as the permanent escape from organized historical forms (even if they are Christian) into the *extra portam* of a faith that is ultimately not to be institutionalized.[18]

This leads us to the core of the "discontinuity principle." As we can see, the ultimate discontinuity is not so much between salvation and history, but above all between God's salvific action and created being.

This idea also appears in the introduction of Ratzinger's *Habilitationsschrift* on Bonaventure's comprehension of Revelation and History. Speaking about God's self-revelation, Ratzinger not only mentions this deeper level of the "discontinuity principle," but he also manifests his belief that this refusal to admit any objectification of God's action is the consequence of a sincere concern for defending God's infinite transcendence, the result of a real interest in safeguarding God's being and God's salvific work from all possible human manipulation:[19]

> In relation to the being of Creation, this act [Revelation] remains as a pure act that can never curdle into "being". . . . Revelation is neither an objective doctrine nor an objective being, it is a personal act, inseparable from God's person, in which He reveals Himself to the *person* of a man. With this it has already been said what matters here: Protestant theology rejects the objectification of the salvific event; because it sees there the danger that this event, that is God's alone, might be wrested from His hands and fall into the disposal of men, who could handle it however they please, a danger that, in the opinion of Protestantism, has become real in the Catholic Church's magisterial teachings and concrete sacramental praxis. When they refuse to interpret Revelation as sacred doctrine and when at the same time they refuse to understand it as an ontological elevation, in both cases they are referring to the same: to the rejection of an objectification of God's personal acts.[20]

Ratzinger is also concerned about upholding God's infinite transcendence, but in his opinion such a defense does not necessarily entail a total rupture between God's salvific work and the created and historical realm. In addition, he is conscious of the fact that a certain kind of Catholic Theology has not sufficiently respected this fundamental aspect of the faith.[21] He therefore presents his own proposal as an alternative both to this kind of Catholic Theology as well as to the discontinuous interpretation of Christianity, which tends to be predominant in the Reformed Tradition.

RATZINGER'S PROPOSAL

It is clear that for Ratzinger salvation has a strong ontological component. This aspect of his thought appears patently in his frequent characterization of salvation in terms of "the return to one's self or essence" (*zu sich selbe/ Wesen kommen*),[22] "becoming, finding or receiving oneself" (*wird er selbst;*[23] *sich finden;*[24] *sich zurückzuerhalten*[25]), or "the liberation of man's being" (*Entschränkung des Seins*).[26]

This is not a marginal aspect of his soteriology; on the contrary, it is central. In fact, we find these kinds of descriptions in most of his theological writings. It is already present in some of his earliest works, such as *Einführung in das Christentum* (1968),[27] and it still appears in his most recent ones, such as the second part of *Jesus von Nazareth* (2011).[28] The fact that he sustains such an ontological approach to salvation does not mean that he considers salvation to be a merely natural process or as something that humans can obtain by their own effort. Actually, he is critical toward authors like Karl Rahner[29] whose proposals move in that direction.

Ratzinger's consideration of salvation avoids this interpretation. His approach to the human being is biblically grounded—that is, he normally describes and understands the human as an "image of God" (cf. Gen. 1.27) which, for the German author, means fundamentally two things.

First, it means that the human has an open existence and an innate tendency toward God. This is the interpretation we find, for example, in his *Habilitationsschrift* on Bonaventure's theology (1959).[30] With reference to the difference between men and irrational beings, he explains that being an "image of God" means that the human is the only creature capable of establishing a relationship of knowledge and love with God:

> For [the beings that are] "trace" and "shadow," God is only "cause"; for [the beings that are] "image" God is also "object of knowledge" (*obiectum*).[31] So similarity with God means being directed towards God, having knowledge of God. It does not mean a state or range of a being closed in itself, but the openness of a being towards God, a relation of knowledge and love of God. This is expressed in the frequently repeated Augustinian definition of "image": Man's being an image of God consists in the fact that he is capable of grasping God through knowledge and love.[32] The result of this is the powerful dynamism that breathes in Bonaventure's concept of *imago*: "image" means not only a relation, but—as long as this relation is broken and incomplete here on earth (as it was already in Paradise)[33]—it means a movement, a yearning for the full unity with God. In this measure, the doctrine of the divine likeness of man is identical to the doctrine of man's natural desire for God.[34]

We find this same idea again in *Gratia Praesupponit Naturam* (1962, 1973).[35] The thesis of this text, written in the occasion of the seventieth birthday of his mentor Gottlieb Söhngen, is that the human spirit cannot be put under the category of "nature," because the human spirit is not a substance or a part of the human *physis*, but of human openness toward God, "the yearning cry that arises out of its nature."[36] He stresses this auto-transcendent aspect of the spirit to such an extent that sometimes he declares that "spirit surpasses pure nature."[37]

Another text that testifies to Ratzinger's understanding of the human's being *imago Dei* as the human desire for God is *Zum Personenverständnis in der Theologie* (1966, 1973).[38] Referring to the struggle of the Fathers of the Church to defend the integrity of Christ's human nature against the multiple heresies that threatened to diminish it, Ratzinger puts forward an idea that perfectly suits what we indicated in *Gratia Praesupponit Naturam*. He says that personhood is something that should not be explained in terms of substance, but rather from an existential point of view[39]; and further on he presents human beings' relational condition (that is, their personal condition) in terms of "spirit," which he again characterizes as our open existence, and as our tendency to self-transcendence:

> The essence of mind or spirit in general is being-in-relation, the capability of seeing oneself and the other. Hedwig Conrad-Martius speaks about the "retroscendence" of the spirit, the fact that the spirit is not only there but, as it were, investigates itself and knows about itself, presenting a double existence that not only *is* but also *understands* itself and *possesses* itself. Accordingly, the difference between matter and spirit would consist of the fact that matter is what is "thrown upon itself", while spirit is what "designs itself", that it is not just there but is what it is in surpassing itself, in looking out to something else, and in looking back to itself.[40] Whatever the details of that may be—we do not have to examine it more closely here—*openness, relatedness to the whole, is an essential element of spirit*. And it comes to itself, precisely by the fact that it not only *is* but also reaches beyond itself. In going beyond itself, it *possesses* itself; only by being with the other does it become itself and come into its own. Or, to put it yet another way: Being with another is its form of being with itself.[41]

So, once again, we find that Ratzinger considers the human not only as nature (or substance) but also as spirit, and that he defines spirit as the relational tendency of human beings. As explicated, Ratzinger understands our being as an image of God in two ways. The first one consists in our *desire* for God. The second one, refers to our *similarity* with God.

This second sense of our being *imago Dei* appears, for example, in the paragraph quoted above in which Ratzinger characterizes the human as a "being-in-relation," which is a characteristic that previously he had indicated as distinctive of the Trinity. In *Einführung in das Christentum* (1968) Ratzinger goes into more detail about the similarity between the Trinitarian God and the human creature by establishing an analogical comparison between the Second Person of the Trinity and man, but from the point of view of their origin, between the human's creation and the Son's generation:

> Let us round off the whole discussion with a passage from St Augustine which elucidates splendidly what we mean. It occurs in his commentary on St John and hinges on the sentence in the gospel which runs, "*Mea doctrina non est mea*"— "My teaching is not my teaching, but that of the Father who sent me" (7.16). Augustine has used the paradox in this sentence to illuminate the paradoxical nature of the Christian image of God and of the Christian existence. He asks himself first whether it is not a sheer contradiction, an offence against the elementary rules of logic, to say something like "Mine is not mine". But, he goes on to say, digging deeper, what really is the teaching of Jesus which is simultaneously his and not his? Jesus is "word", and thus it becomes clear that his teaching is he himself. If one reads the sentence again from this angle it then says: I am by no means just I; I am not mine at all; my I is that of another. With this we have moved on out of Christology and arrived at ourselves: "*Quid tam tuum quam tu, quid tam non tuum quam tu*"—"What is so much yours as yourself and what is so little yours as yourself?"[42] The most individual element in us—the only thing that belongs to us in the last analysis—our own "I", is at the same time the least individual element of all, for it is precisely our "I" that we have neither from ourselves nor for ourselves. The "I" is simultaneously what I have completely and what least of all belongs to me. Thus here again the concept of mere substance (= what stands in itself!) is shattered and it is made apparent how being that truly understands itself grasps at the same time that *in* its self-being it does not belong to itself; that it only comes to itself by moving away from itself and finding its way back as relatedness to its true primordial state.[43]

This text is interesting because it not only illustrates Ratzinger's second interpretation of the human as *imago Dei* (i.e., his likeness with God), but also because it reveals the foundation of his first interpretation of the term (i.e., the human's longing for God). Here we see that our tendency toward God is the consequence of *our creatural condition*, of the fact that we have received our being neither from ourselves, nor for ourselves ("our own 'I', is at the same time the least individual element of all, for it is precisely our 'I' that we have neither from ourselves [*von uns*] nor for ourselves [*für uns*]"). Secondly, it is the consequence of *our spiritual condition*. That is, it is our capacity to understand ourselves, to understand that "*in* its self-being it does not belong to itself."

With this note about the human's creatural and spiritual condition as the foundation of our relational being, we have completed the picture of Ratzinger's anthropology, a picture that we find confirmed in the rest of his works.

In *Glaube als Umkehr–Metanoia* (1972),[44] for example, talking about the difference between the Greek idea of conversion and the Christian one, Ratzinger affirms that the human tendency toward God is the other face of being a created spirit:

> Man is oriented, not to the innermost depths of his own being, but to the God who comes to him from without, to the Thou who reveals himself to him and, in doing so, redeems him. Thus metanoia is synonymous with obedience and faith. ... From this fact, it is immediately clear that metanoia is not just any Christian attitude but the fundamental Christian act per se, understood admittedly from a very definite perspective: that of transformation, conversion, renewal and change. To be a Christian one must change not just to some particular place but without reservation even to the innermost depths of one's being.[45]

In *Eschatologie Tod und ewiges Leben* (1977),[46] the same idea appears in the context of Ratzinger's explanation about the source of the immortality of the human soul. There he explains that this immortality must not be understood as the consequence of the indivisibility of the spiritual substance of the human soul (that is, it must not be understood in substantial terms),[47] but as a consequence of the fact that for the human, being a spiritual creature means that for the individual the "relationship to God can be seen to express the core of his very essence." He continues,

> Being referred to God, to truth himself, is not, for man, some optional pleasurable diversion for the intellect. When man is understood in terms of the formula *anima forma corporis*, that relationship to God can be seen to express the core of his very essence. As a created being he is made for a relationship which entails indestructibility. ... We can describe man as that stage of the creation, that creature, then, for whom the vision of God is part and parcel of his very being. Because this is so, because man is capable of grasping truth in its most comprehensive meaning, it also belongs intrinsically to his being to participate in life. We agreed earlier that it is not a relationless being oneself that makes a human being immortal, but precisely his relatedness, or capacity for relatedness, to God. We must now add that such an opening of one's existence is not a trimming, an addition to a being which really might subsist in an independent fashion. On the contrary, it constitutes what is deepest in man's being. It is nothing other than what we call "soul".[48]

In Ratzinger's small collection of homilies on Creation and Sin *Im Anfang Schuf Gott* (1986),[49] we find again the explanation of the human's *imago Dei* both as our relatedness to God and as our similarity with Him (as our "divine capacity"): "*To be image of God implies relationality. It is the dynamic that sets the human being in motion toward the totally Other*. Hence it means the capacity for relationship; it is the divine capacity of man [*Gottfähigkeit des Menschen*]" [emphasis is added].[50] Ratzinger comments on this idea further using the metaphor of a painting, which is something that refers to an object that is beyond itself, but to which it is similar.[51]

This affirmation about relationality as the human's principal similarity to God is also the subject of another of his texts: *Freiheit und Wahrheit* (1995).[52] Here Ratzinger explains it using the phenomenological consideration of the human's situation in the world as his departure point. By doing so, Ratzinger manages to draw with more detail the contours of his relational idea of humanity, because it lets him characterize the human as the creature that "can only exist/be with the other person [*mit dem anderen*] and from him [*von ihm*] and is thus forever dependent on this being-for [*Für-Sein*]":

> In this particular example [a baby in the womb of his mother] the basic shape of human freedom, its typical human character, becomes clear. For what is at issue here? The being of another person is so closely interwoven with the being of this first person, the mother, that for the moment it can only exist at all in bodily association with the mother, in a physical union with her, which nonetheless does not abolish its otherness and does not permit us to dispute its being itself. Of course, this being itself is, in quite radical fashion, a being from the other person, through the other person; conversely, the being of the other person—the mother—is forced through this coexistence into an existence-for-someone that contradicts its own self-will and is thus experienced as the contrary of its own freedom. Now, we have to add that the child, even when he is born and the outward form of being-from and of coexistence changes, remains even so as dependent, just as much in need of someone being there for it. Of course, you can push it away into a home and assign someone else to be there for it, but the anthropological figure stays the same; it remains the derived being, demanding someone be there for it, meaning an assumption of the limits of my freedom, or rather the living of my freedom, not in competition, but in mutual support.
>
> If we open our eyes, we see that this is not only true of a child, that the child in its mother's womb just makes us most vividly aware of the nature of human existence as a whole [*das Wesen menschlicher Exitenz im ganzen*]: it is also true of the adult that he can only exist/be with the other person [*mit dem anderen*] and from him [*und von ihm*] and is thus forever dependent on this being for [*Für-Sein*] that he would most of all like to eliminate.[53]

In this way Ratzinger sets down the basis for a closer similarity between the human and God: The true God is, of his own nature, being-for (Father), being-from (Son), and being-with (Holy Spirit). Yet, the human is in the image of God precisely because the being for, from, and with constitute the basic anthropological shape. Whenever people try to free themselves from this, they are moving, not toward divinity, but toward dehumanizing, toward the destruction of being itself through the destruction of truth.[54] Through the exploration of man's filial condition, Ratzinger leads us to a more detailed and complete consideration of the human's likeness with God, because it is a similarity with each one of the Divine Persons.

CONCLUSION

Ratzinger's soteriology successfully maintains the ontological dimension of salvation without undermining God's transcendence. He manages to do so by characterizing it as the "return to" or the "fulfillment of" one's essence. Thus, the human's essence remains throughout the salvific process, from its starting point (the sinful condition) to its final stage (the saved condition). This continuity does not entail the enclosure of the created being in itself. The German theologian avoids such a risk by comprehending the human's *imago Dei* relationally. That is, the human is a being who has analogical similarity with God, which consists in an open and relational existence. This means that we can only reach the fulfillment of *our own* essence by entering in relation with someone *different from ourselves* and who *transcends us*—that is, the Trinitarian God, toward whom our creaturely condition "pushes" us. In other words, for Ratzinger salvation implies not only a continuous element (the constant existence of a human essence and its yearning for fulfillment), but also a discontinuous element (the fact that this essence can only reach its fulfillment through communion with another). Or, in Ratzinger's words, "only by being with the other does it [man] become itself and come into its own. . . . Being with another is its form of being with itself."[55] In this way Ratzinger maintains an open and relational ontology that paves the way for an interpretation of the created and historical salvific mediations that do not jeopardize God's infinite transcendence. This could help diminish the gap between Catholic and Protestant understandings of salvation.

NOTES

1. Revised version of Isabel Troconis, "L'antropologia ratzingeriana dell'Imago Dei come via di uscita dallo storicismo teologico," in *Storia e mistero. Una chiave di acceso alla teologia di Joseph Ratzinger e Jean Daniélou*, eds. Giulio Maspero and Jonas Lynch (Roma: Edizioni Santa Croce, 2016).

2. "La difesa del legame inscindibile tra fede cristiana e verità, tra dimensione storico-salvifica del messaggio cristiano e livello ontologico rappresenta uno dei cardini dell'intera riflessione teologica di Ratzinger, presente fin dalle prime opere (cf. *Der Gott des Glaubens*), ripreso in *Introduzione al cristianesimo* e affrontato poi dettagliatamente in diversi articoli riuniti successivamente nella *Theologische*

Prinzipienlehre" (Andrea Bellandi, *Fede cristiana come "stare e comprendere". La giustificazione dei fondamenti della fede in Joseph Ratzinger* [Roma: Editrice Pontificia Università Gregoriana, 1996], 105–6, n 17). The translation is mine.

3. Andrea Bellandi is Professor of Fundamental Theology at the *Facoltà Teologica dell'Italia Centrale*. Some of the authors who share this opinion are: Pablo Blanco, *Joseph Ratzinger. Razón y Cristianismo. La victoria de la inteligencia en el mundo de las religiones* (Madrid: Rialp, 2005); Robert A. Krieg, "Kardinal Ratzinger, Max Scheler und eine Grundfrage der Christologie," *Theologische Quartalschrift* 160 (1980): 106–22; Tracey Rowland, *Ratzinger's Faith: The Theology of Pope Benedict XVI* (New York: Oxford University Press, 2008); Jacek Wojciech, "Katholische Theologie," in *Die Religion in Geschichte und Gegenwart VI*, ed. K. Galling (Tubingen: J.C.B. Mohr, 1962); Jacek Wojciech, *La foi comme dialogue. Une introduction à la théologie de J. Ratzinger* (Paris: Institut Catholique, 1991).

4. As Blanco indicates, "Seguramente se trata tan solo de una coincidencia, pero Ratzinger nació en 1927, el mismo año en que Heidegger publicaba su *Ser y tiempo*" (*Joseph Ratzinger. Razón y Cristianismo*, 132).

5. "In Ratzinger's view, there is one essential problem which underlies all the difficulties of dogmatic theology today. That problem is the nature of historical process, in relation to the transcendence of God and his truth." (Aidan Nichols, *The Theology of Benedict XVI* [London-New York: Burns and Oats, 2007], 160).

6. Cf., for example, the prologue to the first volume of Joseph Ratzinger, *Jesus of Nazareth: From the Baptism in the Jordan to the Transfiguration*, trans. Adrian J. Walker (New York: Doubleday, 2007) and "L'interpretazione biblica in conflitto: problemi del fondamento ed orientamento dell'esegesi contemporanea," in *L'esegesi cristiana oggi*, eds. Luciano Pacomio and Ignace de La Potterie (Casale Monferrato: Piemme, 1991). This exegetical question is also present in many of his systematic works such as: *Eschatology: Death and Eternal Life*, trans. Michael Waldstein (Washington: CUA Press, 1988); and *In the Beginning. A Catholic Understanding of the Story of Creation and Fall*, trans. Boniface Ramsey (London: T&T Clark, 1995).

7. Cf., for example, Joseph Ratzinger, *The Feast of Faith: Approaches to a Theology of the Liturgy* (San Francisco: Ignatius Press, 1986); and *Milestones. Memoirs 1927–1977* (San Francisco: Ignatius Press, 1998), 56–57.

8. Some of his principal systematic works on the subject (chronologically ordered) are: *Das Offenbarungsverständnis und die Geschichtstheologie Bonaventuras* (published for the first time in 2009 [Freiburg im Breisgau: Herder] but written in 1957); *Der Gott des Glaubens und der Gott der Philosophen* (München-Zürich: Schnell & Steiner, 1960); *Grace Presupposes Nature*, in *Dogma and Preaching* (San Francisco: Ignatius Press, 2011), 143–161 (German original edition: Freiburg: 1962); *Introduction to Christianity*, trans. J. R. Foster (San Francisco: Ignatius Press, 1990; German original edition: München: Kösel, 1968); *Salvation History, Metaphysics and Eschatology*, in *Principles of Catholic Theology*, trans. Mary Frances McCarthy (San Francisco: Ignatius, 1987); 171–90 (German original edition: München: Erich Wewel Verlag, 1982, 180–99); *Salvation and History*, in *Principles of Catholic Theology*, 153–71 (German original edition: 159–79); *Eschatology: Death and Eternal Life* (German original edition: Regensburg: Pustet, 1977); *The Nature and Mission of Theology* (San Francisco: Ignatius, 1995; German original: Einsiedeln–Freiburg:

Johannes Verlag, 1993); *The End of Time? The Provocation of Talking about God*, ed. and trans. Matthew Ashley (New York: Paulist Press, 2004; German original edition: Mainz: Matthias Grünewald Verlag, 1999).

9. The following phrase is a good expression of this concern: "The division of Christianity is inseparably linked to a division in the relationship to history and finds its principal expression in the opposing forms of historical consciousness" (Ratzinger, *Principles of Catholic Theology*, 155).

10. His *Habilitationsschrift* on Saint Bonaventure's understanding of revelation and history reflects this interest: "Das Offenbarungsverständnis und die Geschichtstheologie Bonaventuras," in *Joseph Ratzinger Gesammelte Schriften*, vol. 2, *Offenbarungsverständnis und Geschichtstheologie Bonaventuras* (Freiburg im Breisgau: Herder, 2009), 53–662.

11. Cf. Ratzinger, *Principles of Catholic Theology*, 158–60.

12. When it "provides him with the external means of mastering that existence and, in the structuring of marriage and family as well as in the ordering of social relationships in general, supplies him with the answers to the question about his own existence; that enables him to form and interpret in terms that are essentially human the open riddle of existence" (Ratzinger, *Principles of Catholic Theology*, 153).

13. Cf. Ratzinger, *Principles of Catholic Theology*, 154.

14. Ibid.

15. Ibid., 156. The eschatological character of Christian salvation has also been the central topic of some of his magisterial writings as pope (cf. his encyclical letter *Spe salvi*, November 30, 2007).

16. For more on this subject see also: Ratzinger, *Das Offenbarungsverständnis*, 567–71.

17. "Such an experience produced genuinely historical change only with Luther, who considered this heavenly-earthly, Christian-secular history no longer as salvation-bringing and Christian but as anti-Christian, and who sought Christianity, not in it, but against it, even though he remained imprisoned in it in all his thinking" (Ratzinger, *Principles of Catholic Theology*, 157).

18. Ibid., 157–58.

19. This idea is also present in his work *Eschatology*.

20. Ratzinger, *Das Offenbarungsverständnis*, 61–62: "So wie zunächst das 'Wort' Gottes ganz 'Tat' ist, Akt, der nicht oder nur sekundär gegenständlich erfasst und zum (stehenden) Lehrgegenstand erhoben werden kann, so bleibt nun dieser Akt auch im Verhältnis zum Sein der Schöpfung reiner Akt, der nie zum 'Sein' gerinnen kann (. . .). Die Offenbarung ist weder gegenständliche Lehre noch objektives Sein, sie ist ein von der Person Gottes unablösbarer, *personaler* Akt eben dieses Gottes, in dem er sich der *Person* des Menschen erschließt. Damit ist zugleich auch schon ausgesprochen, worauf es hier ankommt: Die protestantische Theologie lehnt die Objektivierung des Heilsereignisses ab; sie sieht darin die Gefahr, dass dieses Ereignis, das allein Gottes ist, den Händen Gottes entwunden wird und in die Verfügung des Menschen gerät, der damit nach seinem Belieben zu schalten beginnt, eine Gefahr, die nach Auffassung des Protestantismus im Lehramt der katholischen Kirche wie in ihrer Sakramentenpraxis konkrete Gestalt gewonnen hat. Wenn also abgelehnt wird,

die Offenbarung als heilige Lehre aufzufassen, und wenn gleichzeitig abgelehnt wird, sie als eine Seinserhebung zu verstehen, geht es beide Male um dasselbe: eine Vergegenständlichung der durchaus ungegenständlichen personalen Gottestat zuruckzuweisen." The translation is mine; as of yet there is no English edition of this work.

21. Cf. Ratzinger, *Principles of Catholic Theology*, 162; and *Dogma and Preaching*, ed. Michael J. Miller, trans. Michael J. Miller and Matthew J. O'Connell (San Francisco: Ignatius Press, 2011), 143–44.

22. Cf. Ratzinger, *Introduction to Christianity*, 181 (German edition: 224), 196 (German edition: 239), 213 (German edition: 257); Ratzinger, *Principles of Catholic Theology*, 187 (German edition: 196), 161 (German edition: 168). In other parts of *Principles of Catholic Theology*, Ratzinger exposes this same idea in a negative way, when speaking about man's condemnation or when criticizing contrary positions: 154 (German edition: 161), 159–60 (German edition: 166–67), 160 (German edition: 167), 161 (German edition: 168).

23. Cf. Ratzinger, Joseph, *Jesus of Nazareth: Holy Week. From the Entrance into Jerusalem to the Resurrection* (San Francisco: Ignatius Press, 2011), 192 (German edition: 561).

24. Ratzinger, *Eschatology*, 101 (German edition: 119).

25. Ratzinger, *In the Beginning*, 48 (German edition: 40).

26. Cf. for example: Ratzinger, *Eschatology* (German edition: 237).

27. For example: "The future of man hangs on the cross—the redemption of man is the cross. And he can only come to himself [*kommt er zu sich selbst*] by letting the walls of his existence be broken down, by looking on him who has been pierced (John 19.37), and by following him who as the pierced and opened one has opened the path into the future" (*Introduction to Christianity*, 181; German edition, 223–24). "To the Bible, the limits of human righteousness, of human power as a whole, become an indication of the way in which man is thrown back upon the unquestioning gift of love, a gift which unexpectedly opens itself to him and thereby opens up man himself, and without which man would remain shut up in all his 'righteousness' and thus unrighteous. Only the man who accepts this gift can come to himself [*zu sich selbe kommen*]" (*Introduction to Christianity*, 195–96; German edition: 238–39).

28. Some examples: "Man becomes true [*wird wahr*], he becomes himself [*wird er selbst*], when he grows in God's likeness. Then he attains to his proper nature [*kommt er zu seinem eigentlichen Wesen*]. God is the reality that gives being and intelligibility" (Ratzinger, *Jesus of Nazareth: Holy Week. From the Entrance into Jerusalem to the Resurrection*, trans. Vatican Secretariat of State (San Francisco: Ignatius Press, 2011), 192; German edition: 561). "The kingship proclaimed by Jesus, at first in parables and then at the end quite openly before the earthly judge, is none other than the kingship of truth. The inauguration of this kingship is man's true liberation [*die wahre Befreiung des Menschen*]" Ibid., 194; German edition: 563.

29. Whom he reproaches for talking of the Revelation as something already present in the human race as a whole: "If revelation history is not to be understood as categorically extrinsic but refers, rather, to the human race as a whole, Rahner argues, then it must also be present in the human race as a whole" (Ratzinger, *Principles of Catholic Theology*, 163).

30. Ratzinger, *Das Offenbarungsverständnis*.
31. Cf. Bonaventure, *Sc Chr* q.4 c (V 24a).
32. Cf. Augustine, *Trin* XIV, 8, 11 (PL 42, 1044).
33. Cf. Bonaventure, *II Sent* d.23 a.2 q.3 c (II 543 b).
34. Ratzinger, *Das Offenbarungsverständnis*, 320–21: "Für 'Spur' und 'Schatten' ist also Gott nur 'Ursache', für das 'Bild' auch 'Erkenntnisgegenstand (obiectum)' (Bonaventura, *Sc Chr* q.4 c [V 24a]). So besagt also Gottebenbildlichkeit Zugewandtheit zu Gott, Erkenntnis Gottes. Sie bedeutet nicht einen Zustand oder eine Ranghöhe eines in sich geschlossenen Seins, sondern sie bedeutet die Offenheit eines Seienden auf Gott hin, sie besagt eine Beziehung des Erkennens und des Liebens zu Gott. Das spricht sich aus in der immer wieder in den verschiedensten Formen wiederholten augustinischen Definition des 'Bildes': Das Bild-Gottes-Sein des Menschen besteht darin, dass er fähig ist, Gott in Erkenntnis und in Liebe zu erfassen (AUGUSTINUS, *Trin* XIV, 8, 11 [PL 42, 1044]). Daraus ergibt sich aber nun ganz von selbst die gewaltige Dynamik, die in Bonaventuras imago-Begriff lebt: 'Bild' besagt nicht nur eine Beziehung, sondern—sofern nämlich diese Beziehung hienieden (auch schon im Paradies) gebrochen und unerfüllt ist (Bonaventura, *II Sent* d.23 a.2 q.3 c [II 543 b])—eine *Bewegung*, eine Sehnsucht nach völliger Einheit mit Gott. Insofern ist die Lehre von der Gottebenbildlichkeit des Menschen identisch mit der Lehre von der natürlichen Sehnsucht des Menschen nach Gott." The translation is mine.
35. See Ratzinger, *Dogma and Preaching*, 143–61.
36. Ibid., 161. An example of this comprehension of man's spirit: Following saint Bonaventure's answer to the question on whether human will could have lifted itself out of guilt without divine grace, Ratzinger says: "It is instructive (. . .) how Bonaventure argues in favor of this No against the objection that the body can overcome sickness by itself, and so the spirit, which after all belongs to a higher order than the body, should also be able to overcome its sickness, sin. The saint replies that the comparison falls short, or, rather: there is no real comparison at all. For the principle of bodily healing is nature, while the principle of spiritual healing is something 'above nature' (*supra naturam*): grace. Nature is still preserved in a case of bodily sickness and, therefore, can bring about a recovery, whereas grace is lost through sin, so that a fresh infusion of divine love is needed in order to restore the original life of the soul. The importance of such a statement is difficult to overestimate. For it means that in Bonaventure's view, the human soul is entirely beyond the realm of mere nature. A merely natural soul is inconceivable; an essential feature of the soul is that it cannot subsist in itself alone. It must be preserved by something that is greater than itself, by something 'supernatural'. This 'supernatural' thing does not thereby cease to be a freely given grace (. . .); it does not cease to be 'supernatural' and, thus, something that cannot be derived from mere nature. But just as real at the same time is the unique structure of the soul: the immediacy of its relation to God is so intimately essential to it that it cannot exist properly except in being preserved immediately by God: at every moment, spirit surpasses pure nature." It "can exist only in the manner of dialogue and freedom" (Ratzinger, *Dogma and Preaching*, 153).
37. Ibid., 153.
38. Ibid., 181–96.

39. Cf. Ratzinger, *Dogma and Preaching*, 190–91. In these pages Ratzinger explains that the problem of most Christological heresies is that they thought they had to take away some aspect of Christ's psychology in order to defend the fact that he only had one personhood: the divine one. In that context he affirms the following: "All of these are attempts to situate the concept of person somewhere in the inventory of the mind. One error after the other has been refuted, in order to determine that the statement is not meant in that way; there is absolutely nothing missing; there can be and there was no subtraction from his humanity. I think that when we trace the course of this struggle, in which Jesus' humanity had to be, so to speak, stocked up and formally declared bit by bit, we see what a tremendous effort and intellectual transformation there was behind the elaboration of this concept of person, which in its approach is quite foreign to the Greek and Latin mind: it is not understood substantially but existentially."

40. Cf. Hedwig Conrad-Martius, *Das Sein* (Munich: Kösel, 1957), 133.

41. Ratzinger, *Dogma and Preaching*, 193. The emphasis is mine.

42. Augustine, *In Ioannis Evangelium tractatus* 29, 3 (on John 7.16), in CChr 36, 285.

43. Ratzinger, *Introduction to Christianity*, 136–37.

44. In Ratzinger, *Principles of Catholic Theology*, 55–67.

45. Ratzinger, *Principles of Catholic Theology*, 60 (German edition: 62). The translation of this last phrase is mine, for here the English translation doesn't respect the exact (and for our argumentation, important) significance of the original text: "Um Christ zu werden, muß der Mensch sich ändern, nicht bloß an irgendeiner Stelle, sondern ohne Vorbehalt, bis in den letzten Grund seines Seins hinab."

46. Ratzinger, *Eschatology*.

47. Cf. Ratzinger, *Eschatology*, 151.

48. Ibid., 154–55.

49. Ratzinger, *In the Beginning*.

50. Ibid., 47 (German edition: 40). Here again we translate directly from the German edition, for in this point the English translation does not do full justice to the original meaning of the phrase.

51. Cf. Ratzinger, *In the Beginning*, 47.

52. In Joseph Ratzinger, *Truth and Tolerance: Christian Belief and World Religions*, trans. Henry Taylor (San Francisco: Ignatius Press, 2004), 231–58.

53. Ibid., 246–47 (German edition: *Glaube–Warheit–Toleranz. Das Christentum und die Weltreligionen* [Herder: Freiburg im Br., 2005], 199).

54. Ibid., 248.

55. Ratzinger, *Dogma and Preaching*, 193.

Chapter Twelve

Praying and Presence
Kierkegaard on Despair and the Prolepsis of the Self

Chris Doude van Troostwijk

Should we consider Kierkegaard's *Sickness unto Death* (1849) as the *summit*, if not the *summa* of his work, notwithstanding the fact that its pseudonymous author was called Anti-Climacus?[1] Concluding a period of mere philosophical writings to engage in more direct spiritual reflections, this "edifying discourse" indeed appears as the intermediary apex of previous dialectic arguments, and, at the same time, sums up many themes already treated in earlier texts. However, a closer look at its structure immediately shows the difficulty of this thesis. The book consists of two parts, the first of a philosophical, the other of a theological character. In this respect, *Sickness unto Death* is indeed a rather paradoxical summit: at its core it displays the turning point between the two orientations of Kierkegaard's thought, but the turning point as such is a void. But is this sudden paradoxical collapse from philosophical and existential reflection to theological considerations not precisely what summarizes Kierkegaard's dialectics? Is the core of this dialectic not precisely the refusal of continuity between the historicity of existence (the finite) and the essentiality of salvation (the infinite)?

If this is the case, we may see the structure of the book as an image of Kierkegaard's conception of the Self. As is well known, he defines the Self in terms of an impossible synthesis:

> A human being is spirit. But what is spirit? Spirit is the self. But what is the self? The self is a relation that relates itself to itself or is the relation's relating itself to itself in the relation; the self is not the relation but is the relation's relating itself to itself. A human being is a synthesis of the infinite and the finite, of the temporal and the eternal, of freedom and necessity, in short, a synthesis. (SD, 13)

The inherent incompatibility of the human Self and the subsequent discontinuity between thinking and faith could summarize Kierkegaard's entire thought in *Sickness unto Death*. Faced with his relation to himself, a relation of despair that is the theme of the first part of the book (*The Sickness unto Death Is Despair*), man cannot but recognize his reflexive and volative shortcomings. We have only to recall Kierkegaard's dictum about the "leap into faith"—borrowed from Lessing—to make this clear. The human's relation to God, the theme of the book's second part (*Despair Is Sin*), is thought in the light of divine grace that echoes human absurdity. Abraham, the hero of faith, was not justified in deciding to sacrifice on ethical grounds; however, he was justified on "absurd" grounds; in other words, he was justified by faith. What is absurd, from a human point of view, becomes wisdom for God.

Hence, we might conceive *Sickness unto Death* as a book that marks the incommensurability and the paradoxical transition between two spheres of "givenness." Kierkegaard rejects the pretentions of his Hegelian era that believed in the all-pervading power of the Absolute Spirit. He defends the Kantian standpoint of the nondeducibility of being. The existential experience is the experience of reality that trespasses the rational, of the interruption between the inner and the outer realms of being. The onto-logical gap between *einai* and *logos* is rationally insurmountable. Analogically, he rejects those Hegelianizing pretentions that identify the divine with the Absolute Spirit. He adopts a radical Lutheran position, departs from the *sola fide* postulate, and defends the grace character of faith. Downward and upward, human experience is faced with the double conundrum of "knowing beyond its epistemic capacities." Being human is being aware of the dual gift, of *being* on the one side and of *faith* on the other. The *datum* of being and faith precedes the *factum* of historical constitution. In other words, not only *l'existence precède l'essence*, as Sartre would have it, but, more profoundly, the existential experience is the very experience of *original receptivity*.

It is through the awareness of this double-sided gift that *prayer* enters the stage of Kierkegaard's reflection. "To pray is the highest pathos of the infinite," he writes in his *Concluding Unscientific Postscript*.[2] Prayer is possible in so far as the God-Man, Jesus Christ, has been a real possibility—and for the believer still is. Prayer reconciles the historical and the eternal, the negative experience of human ontological insufficiency and the positive possibility of faith. Christ's *presence* is more important than the outcome of the discussion about his historical life:

> Believe that Christ is God—then call upon him and pray to him. The rest comes by itself. When the fact that he is present is more intimately and inwardly certain than all historical information, then you will come out all right with the

details of his historical existence. [. . .] The historical details are not nearly so important simply because Christ is Christ, the eternally present one who is true God and true man.[3]

In what follows, I will concentrate on the problem of prayer that emerges from the incompatibility of *logos* and being, of historical existence and divine eternal being. After a short sketch of Kierkegaard's dialectics of despair, considered as the sin of not being one's self, I will follow him in the transformation of sin into a *felix culpa*. True and pure prayer accompanies this transformation: what is a paradox for reason appears to be, in the light of faith, the miracle of possible impossibility. The paradox includes also a promise: what was lost in despair, the Self, is regained through faithful prayer. The human being, as will be shown in the last part, is endowed with the paradoxical faculty of Self-perfection, which consists of the readiness of being helped by God.

THE FRUIT OF DESPAIR

Although Kierkegaard characterizes the human's subjectivity as "spirit," this spirit is far from Hegelian. It does not embrace the totality of being and history. Rather, it is the existing, subjective spirit that drives a wedge between the two. Bound to existence, the "I" resists every kind of reduction to speculative *Logos* (and subsequently to onto-logy). In an act of subjective *anamnesis*, he discovers his incapacity to follow the Delphic commandment: "Know thyself." Man did not create himself *ex nihilo*; he cannot derive his *being* from his thinking. Against Hegel's *self-extensification* of the objective Spirit that includes even human interior subjectivity in the historical process of self-redemption of Being, Kierkegaard posits inwardly directed self-reflection.

> There are two ways of reflection. For objective reflection, truth becomes an object, and the point is to disregard the knowing subject (the individual). By contrast, in subjective reflection truth becomes personal appropriation, a life, inwardness, and the point is to immerse oneself in this subjectivity.[4]

This *anamnestic* immersion is reflexive *intensification* of the human spirit to the point where it meets is own inadequateness and irreconcilability. In contrast to Hegel's threefold method, Kierkegaard develops his own subjective dialectics, characterized by Ricoeur as a "broken dialectics . . . without resolution, a dual dialectics: *either* too much of possibility, *or* too much of actuality; *either* too much of finitude, *or* too much of infinitude."[5]

Kierkegaard's spirit discovers the inadequateness of the relation of the Self-to-the-Self.[6]

Kierkegaard's dual dialectical method amounts to the postulate of an *archi-position* of the Self, an *ex-istence* that precedes—always already—any Self-determination. Ontology is secondary to this gift of being, that is, to existence. The *archi-position* of the Self literally "ex-ists," in the sense of having its seat outside of the realm of rational conceptuality. Nonetheless, not being accessible to reason (*logos*), the original, singular *exteriority* of the Self-to-itself does signal itself. Subjective insufficiency becomes perceivable in the pathos of despair. Despair pushes man to the point where he risks falling in something such as the death of his Self: either he is not conscious of having a self, or he does not will to be himself, or a third, and most desperate option, he really wants to be himself, but he does not know how. Not being able to grasp his origins, the Self of man evaporates and despair becomes indeed a *Sickness unto Death*.

Yet, despair is only the pathetic expression of the fact that the being of the Self resists the thinking of this Self-being. Kierkegaard's dialectics of reflexive, inward intensification, in the end, takes a positive twist. The fallibility of the Self is fortunate.[7] From *for-tviv-lel-sen*, from the desperate inability of only *having* a Self instead of *being* Himself, from the desperate insight in the impossibility of original Self-positing, a miraculous possibility emerges: the possibility of faith.

THE NEED FOR PRAYER: FROM CRY TO CALL

"It's me, it's me, it's me oh Lord, standing in the need of prayer," sings an old Spiritual song. Kierkegaard's treatise on despair explores this need. It describes, dialectically, how the need for prayer is driven by a double force. The need originates firstly, as we saw, in the experience of the impossible *anamnesis* of the Self. Discovering its own insufficiency, the human subject discovers his tragic, existential condition, discovers the asymmetry of his constitution. Not having created himself, man cannot redeem himself. From this recognition grows fear, anxiety, absurdity, despair. The need of prayer is a *cry,* a cry of despair.

But, the darkest hour is just before dawn. The fact that the subject is not self-positing is at the same time the condition of the possibility of his standing in relation to himself. From the failure of self-constitution, the Self—this Being-in-relation that exists onto itself only in relation—opens itself up to a third possibility that appears as the possible being of the One that did establish the Self in his uniqueness.

Such a relation that relates itself to itself, must either have established itself or have been established by another. [The Self is] relating itself to itself [...] willing to be itself [...] rest[ing] transparently in the power that established it. (SD, 1–4)

The Self that relates to itself, wants to be itself, and finally becomes transparent to itself. This Self discovers its creational condition: Man is not man-made, nor self-made. He grounds himself in the energetic origin through which he was brought into being. Being-in-relation, the Self is destined to relate to this third instance, to God. From the desperate relation of man to himself emerges the positive desire to enter into relation with his Creator. The gift of Being collapses into the Gift of Faith, when man, in prayer, recognizes the possibility of his rebirth. This is the second driving force of the need for prayer: it becomes a *call* for help. Praying is crying and calling. From despair about the Self emerges the longing for the source of the Self. From historical finitude emerges the desire for Eternal Being. From the negativity of despair emerges the positivity of prayer.

THE PRAYER PARADOX: THE INVERSED ARISTOTELIAN GOD

In his *Sickness unto Death* Kierkegaard reflects, in his well-known ironic tone of voice, on the impossible possibility of prayer. He imagines someone who utters the following words to the Eternal:

> God in heaven, I thank Thee that Thou hast not required it of man that he should comprehend Christianity; for if that were required, I should be of all men the most miserable. The more I seek to comprehend it, the more incomprehensible it appears to me, and the more I discover merely the possibility of offense. Therefore I thank Thee that Thou dost only require faith, and I pray Thee to increase it more and more. (SD, 150)

The offense Kierkegaard's prayer refers to, is the *skandalon* of faith. The scandal of God becoming human. Prayer mirrors, in an inverse direction, the dynamics of incarnation. Wanting to address the Infinite Being from within historical finitude is ridiculous and makes prayer a sheer impossibility. At least, from a rational point of view, the pretention that prayer reaches the divine ear does not make sense. Human praying implies something like the injection of a morsel of mortal life into His eternal Being. Yet, faithful and pure inwardness does have this pretention. Therefore, Kierkegaard concludes that true prayer would correspond perfectly to orthodox theology, and it would be, at the same time, a performative dismantling of speculative,

Hegelian rationality. "This prayer would from the point of view of orthodoxy be entirely correct, and, assuming that it is true in the man who prays, it at the same time would be correct as irony upon speculation as a whole. But is faith, I wonder, to be found on earth?" (SD, 150).

This last exclamation points to the paradox of prayer and is expressed in one of Kierkegaard's famous prayers "God's unchangeability" (1851)—famously put to music by the American composer Samuel Barber. In it he proposes a concept of the divine that echoes, in a reverse version, the Aristotelean *unmoved mover*. Praying to God presupposes the engagement with an immutable God that is nonetheless compassionately moved in His inner essence. For Kierkegaard, the idea of God equals *moved immovability*.

> O Thou who are unchangeable, whom nothing changes! [. . .] Not art Thou like man; if he is to preserve only some degree of constancy he must not permit himself too much to be moved, nor by too many things. Thou on the contrary art moved, and moved in infinite love, by all things. Even [. . .] the need of a sparrow, even this moves Thee; and what we so often scarcely notice, a human sigh, this moves Thee, O Infinite Love! But nothing changes Thee, O Thou who art unchangeable![8]

God being moved in His immovability is the kernel of Kierkegaard's paradox of the prayer. If God is eternal he is immutable. But if God is immutable how could our prayer interest him? Evidently, if he responded by some miraculous upending of natural laws, he would short-circuit finitude and infinity. But it is not God's answer alone that would be paradoxical. The same interference of historicity and eternity occurs with only the slightest divine openness to human crying and calling. God's simple willingness to hear the prayers of men and women alone disrupts his eternal transcendence. The problem for reflection is to stick to God's immutability without paying the price of losing His compassion.

Kierkegaard shares the anguish of those miserable souls whose prayers are not fulfilled. Nevertheless, he notes that this anguish must find an echo in God himself. In a diary entry from 1851, he argues that even if God cannot answer to human wishes—in the sense of fulfilling them—He is nonetheless touched by the cries and exclamations.

> Your sigh, your prayer, etc. are heard: O, in grace they have touched Him, moved Him deeply, Him who is infinite love. But it does not follow from this that your desire is fulfilled. . . . But it touches and moves him. Both your prayer and that he must deny it—for nothing changes him.[9]

God's faithfulness surpasses his nonchangeability. God is touched by the "cry of all creatures," but His will cannot be commanded by the wishful call of human beings.[10]

THE PRAYER MIRACLE: THE POSSIBLE IMPOSSIBILITY

Kierkegaard leaves his prayer paradox in faithfulness and without recourse to any metalogical or dialectical solutions. They would not make sense:

> Every external reflection *eo ipso* nullifies prayer, be it reflection squinting at the temporal advantage or be it reflection on the individual himself and his relation to others, as if a man were so earnest that he could not pray within himself and alone but had to step forward and benefit the whole congregation with his intercession and his example as one who prays.[11]

The only aim of Kierkegaard's work as an author, the central focus of his *dialectics of intensification,* is to attain the stage that confronts the believer with the incomprehensibility of the fact of prayer. For human beings, prayer means encountering divine Being and thus engaging immediately with the One who has brought them into existence. To argue in favor or against the utility of prayer would signify the lowering of prayer to the sphere of the world, to exteriority and to negativity. In that case prayer would be the effort to repair or to complement a lack. Its meaning would reside not in itself, but in its effects. Prayer would be only secondary, only a passage to something more important, and a way to accomplish desire. But this is what prayer is precisely not. It is not an instrument for pious pragmatism. Therefore, in contrast to Lutheran theologians around him, Kierkegaard refuses to justify prayer on a rational—Hegelian or Kantian—basis. Such a justification would be an invitation to existential and spiritual nihilism. True prayer on the contrary is the experience of an impossibility that has become possible.[12] The fact and the act of prayer must be on its own the fulfillment of prayer. True prayer is self-sufficient. If I am able to pray, my prayer is fulfilled.

Father Taciturnus, in *Stages on Life's Way*, confirms this view.[13] Not without humor, he declares not to want to criticize the reasons a person could have for praying.[14] He compares praying to the original astonishment that set Aristotle and Plato on their philosophical journeys. Is it not an amazing prerogative to believe that God is listening to human beings?[15] But the amazement goes deeper. It is the astonishment expressed in Leibniz's fundamental question why there *is* something rather than nothing. Astonishment before the fact—the *gift*—of being.

Prayer—that is, relating to the infinite from within the historical—provokes for Kierkegaard an astonishment analogous to that with which philosophy begins. But more than this, prayer, true prayer, if it exists, is the impossible turned into reality. It would be a miracle. How could it not be miraculous that the Eternal Being permits historical human beings to pray and to be moved by them, even if He, in His eternal being, in His omniscience and all-encompassing love, knows already how man will pray and how He will answer? But this wondrous phenomenon, commanded by Christ, this amazing *possibility of the impossibility*, only achieves actuality through faith, and faith is never provoked, but only given. The "holy wonder of prayer," as Kierkegaard calls it, is self-sufficient in the sense that the believer takes it, in itself, as the act and the presence of the divine love he was longing for. Because, on a profound level, prayer is not simply a miraculous faculty, but rather, as the Danish vocabulary "forundering" suggests, it is an incomprehensible *consent* and a *permission to pray* received by man out of God's hands.[16]

> God in heaven is the only one who does not become weary of listening to a human being. And this holy wonder in turn will keep the one who is praying from thinking whether he receives what he is praying about. But if one understands to the point of wonder—indeed, to the point where wonder shipwrecks one's understanding—that it is a favor, then arguments are perceived to be not necessary, either, for it is only the problematic that is commended by arguments.[17]

If Kierkegaard's existential dialectics of despair push reason to and beyond its speculative limits, it is for the sake of opening up a space for the scandal of faith. Is this not pushing Lutheran orthodoxy—*soli Deo gratia* and *sola fides*—to its apogee? A faith that, according to the believer's existential despair, "cannot be found on earth!" Consequently, according to Kierkegaard, prayer is a highly tense paradoxical exercise of the type "Lord, I believe; help thou mine unbelief" (Mk 9:24).

The essay *Sickness unto Death* discovers prayer as an *impossible possibility*, as a "double bind": praying for faith presupposes the faith that it is praying for. Thus, Kierkegaard approaches prayer in what we would call today a deconstructive mode of thinking. The prayer phenomenon is conditioned by the same thing that obstructs its possibility. "Prayer is the daughter of faith, but the daughter must support the mother."[18] It is only through faith that we can pray, but it also faith that is given as the answer to, or better, the performative effect of praying. Nonetheless, this does not chase reflection away. Rather it implies a radical modification of reflexive pretentions. Reflecting on prayer has no intention of justification; religious reflection implies understanding prayer in its incomprehensibility and therefore the opening up of the reflecting subject to the miracle of pure positivity. The positivity of the Self, the Gift of being human.

THE PRAYER PROMISE: INVERSED MYSTICISM OF THE NOBLE SOUL

If we do not pray for the effects of praying, does it mean that praying as such does not have any effect? Rationally speaking, praying does not make sense.

The Addressed knows better than we do ourselves what we are praying for. The only effect of prayer is its affect. Its only "product" is pathos. The sentiment of sacred amazement in front of the divine paradox is a sign both of God's Being surpassing human comprehension and of His paradoxical *presence* in human, historical reality. If true prayer implies its immediate fulfilment, the effect of it is not a "result," but a radical, abrupt modification of human existence. The sense of praying is not to be found on the side of the *moved immutability*. The deeper meaning of prayer is not the incomprehensible change that it provokes in God, the compassionate but yet immutable. Its meaning is the change prayer effectuates, thanks to God, in the praying person.

> O Thou who in infinite love dost submit to be moved, may this our prayer also move Thee to add Thy blessing, in order that there may be wrought such a change in him who prays as to bring him into conformity with Thy unchangeable will. Thou who are unchangeable![19]

It is in this sense that Kierkegaard, in one of his famous edifying discourses, explains true prayer as a struggle with God—not *against* God—in which the victory of God is at the same time the victory of the praying subject.[20] True prayer is a combat with God in which man triumphs thanks to the triumph of God over him.

Praying means being changed in front of God. The corollary phenomenon of the *leap into faith* is the radical event of subjective conversion—rebirth, as Christian tradition has it. In the already quoted *Stage on a Life's Way* (1845), Kierkegaard explains this anthropological change as follows: "Prayer was certainly not devised in order to rebuke God but is a favor that is graciously granted to every human being and that makes him more than a nobleman."[21]

The aristocrat, *adelsmand* in Danish, is a noble person. Prayer transposes the Self to a higher level and thus transposes it from an initial, desperate acceptance of his insufficiency into a positive yet unjustifiable being. From despair to nobility; this is the path Kierkegaard sketches in his disparate reflections on prayer. Despair opens up a person to prayer, prayer gives access to the nobility of the Soul, in a way that recalls Master Eckhart's conception of the soul-beyond-the-ego, the soul in his "citadel," encountering the god-beyond-trinity, the Deity. Nonetheless, an important difference separates Kierkegaard from the negative theological and mystical tradition.[22] Where Eckhart's neo-Platonic and ontological paradigm considers the destruction of the Self as the necessary condition of returning to Oneness, to the ultimate and original source of Being, Kierkegaard thinks the inverse.

The reflexive subject discovers through despair the impossibility of *being* a Self, the impossibility of self-coincidence. The encounter with God in prayer, on the contrary, pushes him into the acceptance of a Self from God's hands, immediately, as through a second original act of creation, and for that reason, incomprehensibly. Instead of dissolving the human subject *in* the divine unity—*unio mystica*—Kierkegaard allows the human subject to be born, born-again-and-again, in an as it were Buber-like face-to-face relation with God. Becoming oneself is possible only through the encounter with divine Presence, which is the only originating force of bringing humans into being. This miracle of coming-to-be-oneself takes place, time and again, in true prayer. What has been lost in despair, the Self, has been regained in prayer. In the face of the possibility of the unthinkable, the human subject receives his eternity. Or rather, he receives it back from the hands that created him.[23] That makes the event of prayer into something of a *flash forward*, a *prolepsis* that anticipates, from within history, what will be the real possibility of God's eternal being. In the pathos of prayer, the believer receives confirmation that his *Sickness unto Death* is on an absolute level *Sickness unto Life*. But this demands that he is ready to make—and in a sense already made—his *salto mortale* or better *salto vitale* into faith!

HUMAN WISDOM AND DIVINE INTERVENTION

Existence is the *pathos* of desiring to become oneself on the deepest level of who one is. This longing of the Self for becoming the Self is tragic—that is, is the endless *regressio ad infinitum* that does not have an end because, not being self-positioning, the human subject always already presupposes itself. It is only through faith in the *Archi-positioner* that man finds his answer to this Baron Munchhausen syndrome.

In a diary note he later elaborated on in one of his *Edifying Discourses*, Kierkegaard gives an insight into what might have been his own most intimate piety. "To need God is man's highest perfection. [. . .] If man did not have absolute need of God he could not (1) know himself—self-knowledge, (2) be immortal. Man's highest achievement is to let God be able to help him."[24] This spiritual intuition has a philosophical echo. Nothing went more against the spirit of Kierkegaard's modernist days than this acceptance of insufficiency, this allowance for a lack of human autonomy. Against this view, Kierkegaard describes human insufficiency in terms of something that could be called a paradoxical human faculty. From a divine point of view— one that is humanly speaking impossible to take—this human incapacity for self-sufficiency becomes the acknowledgment of the need for help. This is the highest and most eminent capacity of man. Losing one's pretention to self-sufficiency equates to winning the assistance of the Absolute. "God in heaven, let me rightly feel my nothingness, not to despair over it, but all the more intensely to feel the greatness of your goodness."²⁵ The elevation of man consists in his absolute diminution before God.

Prayer is the practical affirmation of human (in-)capacity to allow himself to be helped by God, despair and sin—and despair is sin—are expressions of his essential incapacity. But, one might ask, once imprisoned by despair is there a way out? Yes, there is. The inversion—in religious terms: the conversion—from despair into prayer relies on the dialectical dynamics of human existence, of which God is the *archi-original* creator. In this sense we have always been, so to speak from the beginning of existence, helped by God, even if we refuse his help and stick, sinfully, to despair. The art of praying is only to open up once again to this most simple and eternal truth.²⁶

CONCLUSION

For Kierkegaard, living in and by prayer is not a guaranty for happiness. The *face-to-face* with God presupposes the sickness unto death. Yet, this Sickness is wholesome, as the parable in the gospel of John from which Kierkegaard derived the expression shows (the resurrection of Lazarus in John 11:4). The struggle with God in which man wins by losing is the struggle in which the Eternal demands us to accept his help. This is authentic prayer: the moment when man is ready to be helped in his historical, existential condition by the Eternal, the moment in which he no longer resists the grace and mercy, but, by his prayer, proves paradoxically that he is ready to make, and has made already, his leap into faith. Prayer is the moment when man finds himself in his loss.

Two roads lead Kierkegaard to this paradoxical human capacity. The first consists of a, so to speak, dorsal, backward approach; the other of a frontal approach. Either man approaches God through his refusal to go to this encounter: he is the Lutheran archetype of historical man as being *incurvatus in se*, enrolled in himself, unconsciously or consciously, but finally engulfed by despair. Theologically speaking, Kierkegaard identifies this desperate refusal to face God with *sin*. Or, as we saw, man chooses prayer in which he seeks God and goes for the encounter with Him. The two dynamics, the negative one of desperate sin and the positive one of faith-seeking prayer, are mutually complementary. The *anamnesis of* self-discovery, which is the discovery of insufficiency, despair, and sin, prepares man for the dialectics of prayer that consists of the acceptance of God's assistance, and, in an eschatological sense, a *prolepsis* of the Self. In his historical existence, the human being experiences the impossible possibility of not yet being, and nonetheless, of already being the one who he is in his deepest Self.

NOTES

1. Søren Kierkegaard, *Sickness unto Death*, ed. and trans. Howard V. Hong and Edna H. Hong (Princeton: Princeton University Press, 1980). Quoted as SD, followed by page-number.
2. Søren Kierkegaard, *Concluding Unscientific Postscript to the Philosophical Crumbs*, eds. and trans. Howard V. Hong and Edna H. Hong (Cambridge: Cambridge University Press, 2009), 76.
3. Søren Kierkegaard, *Søren Kierkegaard's Journals and Papers*, vol. 1, *A–E*, eds. Howard V. Hong and Edna H. Hong (Princeton: Princeton University Press, 1967), 133–34.
4. Kierkegaard, *Concluding Unscientific Postscript*, 192.
5. Paul Ricoeur "Kierkegaard et le mal," in *Lectures 2. La contrée des philosophes* (Paris: Seuil, 1999), 22.
6. This subjective dialectics is inherent to the experience of despair, as the original Danish word for despair—*for-tviv-lel-sen*—shows. The word embraces the root *tviv*, etymologically close to *two* (German *zwei*, retraceable in *Verzweiflung*) and expresses thus the fundamental existential *incompatibility* that traverses human subjectivity.
7. Jason A. Mahn, *Fortunate Fallibility: Kierkegaard and the Power of Sin* (Oxford: Oxford University Press, 2011).
8. Søren Kierkegaard, *The Prayers of Kierkegaard*, ed. and trans. Perry D. Le Fevre (Chicago: University of Chicago Press, 1956), 9.
9. Søren Kierkegaard, *Soren Kierkegaard's Journals and Papers*, vol. 4, *S–Z*, eds. Howard V. Hong and Edna H. Hong (Princeton: Princeton University Press, 1975), 506–7 (X4-A-305, *n.d.*, 1851).
10. "Thou who bearest the weight of the stars and who governest the forces of the world through immense spaces [. . .], Thou hearest the cry of all the creatures, and the cry of man whom Thou hast specially formed. . . . Man cries to Thee in the day of distress and he gives thanks to Thee in the day of joy. . . . More blessed though it is to give thanks when the heart is oppressed and the soul darkened, when reason is a traitor in its ambiguity and memory is mistaken in its forgetting . . . for the one who thus is thankful truly loves God." Kierkegaard, *Prayers of Kierkegaard*, 16.
11. Søren Kierkegaard, *Stages on Life's Way*, eds. and trans. Howard V. and Edna H. Hong (Princeton: Princeton University Press, 1991), 348.
12. "The more a person prays, the more certain his final consolation is that God has commanded that we *shall* pray; for God is so infinite that many times a person would otherwise hardly dare to pray, however much he wanted to. Søren Kierkegaard, *Søren Kierkegaard's Journals and Papers*, vol. 3, *L–R*, eds. Howard V. and Edna H. Hong (Princeton: Princeton University Press, 1975), 568 (IX-A-192, *n.d.*, 1848).
13. Kierkegaard, *Stages on Life's Way*, 347–48.
14. Kierkegaard's himself was much less tolerant! "Christ wept blood when he prayed—nowadays the preachers give three reasons to prove that it is expedient to pray." Kierkegaard, *Kierkegaard's Journals and Papers*, vol. 3, 564 (N° 3414, VIII-A-304, *n.d.*, 1847).
15. "How often have I reflected on what pests we men must be to God inconveniencing him with all our little griefs and little joys, wanting him to rejoice with us when we

thank him for the good. What is a man, after all, that you are mindful to him. There is a lot of preaching about our duty to pray to God, but would it not be more correct to point out to men the prodigious prerogative of being able to talk with God." Kierkegaard, *Kierkegaard's Journals and Papers*, vol. 3, 563 (N° 3412, VIII-A-159, *n.d.*, 1847).

16. The verb *forundre* links etymologically speaking to *vor-wundern* (to wonder beforehand), whereas the root *wunder* is derived from the *althochdeutsch* "wuntar," which means "longing for" or "desiring." Wanting is wondering, wondering is wanting: prayer gets in advance what it wants only by wanting it.

17. "God in Heaven is not disgusted with what is boring [prayers]. It is supposed to be a duty to pray, it is supposed to be beneficial to pray, there are supposed to be three reasons, perhaps even four, for praying. I have no intention of depraving anyone of his reasons; he is welcome to them, if only I may keep *daring* to pray as something so inspiring that in a far deeper sense than Plato and Aristotle one can say that wonder [*Forundring*] is the starting point of knowledge" (Kierkegaard, *Stages on Life's Way*, 348).

18. Kierkegaard, *Søren Kierkegaard's Journals and Papers*, vol. 3, 577 (N° 3456, X3-A-531, *n.d.*, 1850).

19. Kierkegaard, *Prayers of Kierkegaard*, 9.

20. The discourse has a programmatic title: "One Who Prays Aright Struggles in Prayer and Is Victorious—in That God Is Victorious (1844)," in Søren Kierkegaard, *Eighteen Upbuilding Discourses*, ed. and trans. Howard V. Hong and Edna H. Hong (Princeton: Princeton University Press, 1990), 377–401.

21. Kierkegaard, *Stages on Life's Way*, 348.

22. Kierkegaard's private opinion about mysticism merits further exploration. Roughly speaking, we might say that he venerates suspicion toward the mystical tradition that annihilates the paradox of human existence, as becomes clear in this diary entry: "Mysticism does not have the patience to wait for God's revelation" (*Kierkegaard's Journals and Papers*, vol. 3, 234 [III-A-8, July 11, 1840]).

23. "The Church Fathers were right in observing that to pray is to breathe. Here we see the stupidity of talking about a *why*—for why do I breathe? Because otherwise I would die—and so it is with praying. Nor do I intend to change the world through my breathing—I simply intend to replenish my vitality and be *renewed*—it is the same with prayer in the relation to God" (Kierkegaard, *Kierkegaard's Journals and Papers*, vol. 3, 568 [IX-A-462, *n.d.*, 1848]).

24. Kierkegaard, *Kierkegaard's Journals and Papers*, vol. 1, 1967, 22 (respectively V B-196, *n.d.*, 1844, and V B-198, *n.d.*, 1844). The abovementioned discourse is: "To need God is a Human Being's Highest Perfection," in Kierkegaard, *Upbuilding Discourses*, 297–326.

25. Kierkegaard, *Kierkegaard's Journals and Papers*, vol. 3, 550 (II-A-423, May 14, 1839).

26. "The spontaneous, immediate person believes and imagines that when he prays the main thing, the thing he has to work at especially, is that *God hears* what it is *he is praying about*. And yet in truth's eternal sense it is just the opposite: the true prayer-relationship does not exist when God hears what is being prayed about but when the *pray-er* continues to pray until he is the *one who hears*, who hears what God wills" (Kierkegaard, *Søren Kierkegaard's Journals and Papers*, vol. 3, 1975, p. 558 [N°3403, VII-A-56, *n.d.*, 1846]).

Part IV

POLITICS BETWEEN BEING AND TIME

Chapter Thirteen

Mapping the Theo-Political

Metaphysical Prolegomenon for Political Theology

Jared Schumacher

Following a rough outline provided by Adrian Thatcher, this chapter develops a genealogy of the modern concept of ontology, the purpose of which is to demonstrate the polysemy of the term. Exposing this plurality is crucial to clarifying the manner in which the term has been equivocally used in the historical discourse concerning being. Tracing the trajectory of ontology from its birth as a neologism synonymous with metaphysics through to its usage in modern anti- and postmetaphysical discourse, I argue that the project of ontology, in contradistinction to metaphysics, rejects philosophical realism. This rejection forces the discourse of being into either a rationalist or an idealist track, neither of which can be fully satisfying to theology. Indeed, without a map of reality such as classical metaphysics produces, theology cannot be coordinated with experiential reality in such a way that basic doctrines of Christianity might be understood, let alone have any practical consequence upon human realities, ruling out of court as impossibilities theological ethics in general and political theology in particular short of a secularist reduction.

In what follows, the theological and political consequences of the transition from metaphysics to ontology will be discussed, and two particularly modern theo-political forms rejected: ideological secularism and religious fundamentalism. If theology is to have anything substantive to say in the political realm, it will require the recovery of metaphysical realism, at the philosophical level, and an incarnational politics, at the practical level. However, what this means in terms of particular political contexts remains beyond the scope of the chapter and is therefore deferred to future research.

THE THEOLOGICAL RELATION TO METAPHYSICS AS ONTOLOGY

In the first few pages of his investigation of *The Ontology of Paul Tillich*, Adrian Thatcher rehearses several prominent historical definitions of ontology with a view to comparison with Tillich's own idiosyncratic usage of the term. I begin by following the broad strokes of Thatcher's definitional list, supplementing it where out of date or insufficient for my purposes, and developing it into a genealogy of my own in order to establish a range of meanings for the term. As is the case in all genealogy, exposing and highlighting the practical significance of the divergent meanings will be my main goal.

According to Thatcher, the term *ontology* first appeared in the work of Joannes Claubergius (1622–1665), where it receives the following formulation: "Just as theosophy or theology is said to be a science about God, it seems we might be able, quite appropriately, to call that science which does not deal with this or that being . . . but with being in general, ontosophy or ontology."[1] Thatcher notes two things that are of particular relevance from this initial definition. The first is that such a definition puts ontology in the semantic range of the classical understanding of metaphysics. "Ontology" thus operates as a rough equivalent for the philosophical discipline of metaphysics, which discipline, it is well known, had its definitive inauguration in the work of Aristotle known by that name.

The second is that there is what Thatcher calls a strong "parallel" between "ontology" and "theology" internal to Claubergius's definition. Unfortunately, he fails to explicate the exact nature of this relationship, implying only that both can be construed as "science" of a similar type.[2] We might add to Thatcher's observations by remarking that what makes Claubergius's definitional parallelism between ontology and theology so keen is its recognition of the fact that both sciences investigate objects that transcend direct experience. Ontology is not conceived simply as the science about being as Thatcher seems to suggest,[3] but is rather the science of being *in general*, the generality of such an account of being necessarily transcending the directly experiential. In the same way theology, whose object of contemplation is the transcendent God, is a science that lacks experiential immediacy. It is this similarity, rather than the mere fact that both are "sciences," which establishes the definitional parallelism between ontology—understood as synonymous with metaphysics—and theology.

As a result, the import of Claubergius's parallel is to be found in its establishment of a structural *analogy* between theology and ontology at the level of definition. What one means by "theology" and its relation to its object, "God," thus has consequences for how ontology relates to its object, "being in general." This analogy takes on greater importance when we consider that Aristotle, whose *Metaphysics* set the standard for the discipline, did not call the science by that name at all, but rather called it "first philosophy," or simply "theology."[4]

THE ONTOLOGICAL SHIFT TOWARDS INTELLIGIBILITY AND THE SUBTLE SLIP OF TRANSCENDENCE

In point of fact, *pace* Thatcher, Claubergius was not the first to use the word ontology. Recent research into the etymology of the term has uncovered its earlier coinage in the work of Jacob Lorhard (1561–1609). In his *Ogdoas Scholastica* (1606), Lorhard, like Claubergius, uses the term "ontology" synonymously with metaphysics, but provides an additional gloss. He defines ontology as "the knowledge of the intelligible by which it is intelligible."[5] Thatcher did not have access to this definition of ontology; he therefore misses the subtle shift in subject that this definition manifests from the point of view of classical metaphysics. Whereas metaphysical investigation dealt with "being in general," ontology can be understood to focus on being as it can be understood, that is, with the intelligibility of being. The possible consequences of this modulation will be made clear below.

Despite this subtle difference, what remains consistent in both Lorhard and Claubergius is the clear theological underpinnings in their conception of ontology. While this is not as obvious at the definitional level for Lorhard as it is in Claubergius, several authors have convincingly argued that Lorhard nevertheless maintains an overall "religious approach to ontology according [*sic*] which the world as a whole from the very beginning has been under divine supervision and according to which worldly things have been permanently under divine management."[6] Theology for both thinkers constitutes an *essential* structural element in the science of ontology, as the things in the world of being are presumed to bear an essential relation to God.

The recognition of the essential link between theology and ontology/metaphysics calls forth the complexity of the relationship, especially as it relates to the ultimate purposes for which the metaphysical enterprise is undertaken, which is to create a comprehensible, if not comprehensive, account of the things of reality. As Peter Øhrstrøm, Henrik Schärfe, and Sara L. Uckelman cited above note in reference to Lorhard's teleology, which remains clearly indebted to Aristotelean philosophy, the schematic use of the language of "[a] final cause (*telos*) implies an assumption of a purpose. However, according to Lorhard 'purpose' does not have to refer to human intent. Teleological causes may also be found in nature. There can be little doubt that this approach to purpose (*telos*) in nature should be interpreted in light of the religious assumptions incorporated in Lorhard's ontology."[7] The authors correctly see the link between the theological assumptions of Lorhard and his conceptualization of final or ultimate purposes in his ontology, which is to say, seeing teleology in nature is a correlate of Lorhard's religious assumptions and those of the classical metaphysical tradition as a whole.

It will become important to our discussion later to see here that, at least from the perspective of classical metaphysics, this theological addendum is not detachable from ontology without compromising its metaphysical purpose; and this for the reason that Thomas Aquinas mentions in his famous "proofs" of the existence of God: the category of "the self-caused cause" is a logical impossibility.[8] Thus, the rational recognition of immanent "nature" as a realm of causation vectorally directed to some end or ends is already the holding of a worldview, if not fully "religious," at least amenable to the imputation of primary and ultimate causation and the existence of divine transcendence, of a "first cause" (with respect to material causation) or "final cause" (with respect to existential purpose).[9]

This point applies to my argument, as we will see, in that the rejection of transcendent causation or denial of anything other than immanent material causality relies upon an unstated presumption of a "self-caused cause," which is, from the perspective of classical metaphysics, logically absurd. The absurdity manifests itself in the performative contradiction of the moral discourse of immanantist philosophies, which on the one hand maintain a vision of the good in their use of moral injunctions (without which vision their "ought" discourse is referentially meaningless), while contradicting that performance of moral discourse in their view of a necessary rejection of any ultimate or transcendent teleology. This constitutes a performative contradiction because the substance of their speech act—denial of final or theological meaning—is contradicted by the speech act itself, in its deployment as a species of moral discourse, under the presumption that it matters ultimately and morally that this fact be recognized and future decisions modulated with it in view. The existential urgency driving these immanentist claims betrays a transcendental viewpoint, despite having formally ruled out transcendence, and creates an ontology of uncaused-causation.

Put in another way, all moral arguments must address the potential conflict between the language of "is" and "ought" in a way which recognizes the teleological purpose of moral discourse, which presumes the directing of a rational agent to an end required by an extrinsic agency, law-giver, or moral order (ultimately, God), while at the same time recognizing the contingency of the moral actor's decision-making—that is, the fact that they might not choose to follow such a directive. On purely immanent grounds *alone*, there is no reason for stipulating the existence of such contingency, since whatever the person chooses to do *will have been*, post facto, the manifestation of a purely immanent causality—and this point is key to recognize, *even if* such a decision was made on the putatively mistaken ground of belief in divine transcendence. A reduction of moral discourse to pure immanence creates a self-referential discourse loop, but precisely for that reason, cannot manifest any meaningful distinction between "is" and "ought" to make sense of the urgency of its own moral claims. Moral discourse as such is meaningless in this case, as whatever will be, will be, as it in fact will always have been.

A robust immanentist who denies any causality beyond the immanent cannot in principle justify "ought" language apart from the assumption of a viewpoint other than pure immanence, which viewpoint, I argue with the metaphysical tradition, is required for the derivation of the existential meaning of moral argument and its demands on the *vita activa*. At best, moral language in a purely immanentist schema is fully reducible to the level of a personal preference, of merely solipsistic significance.[10]

The move toward intelligibility in ontological discourse in itself does not require the loss of transcendence, as the work of Lorhard shows. His understanding of ontology is not hostile to the possibility of divine causation in experiential reality, given that the human recognition of the idea of "final cause" and a teleological view of nature can be taken as evidence of the existence of the possibility of divine causation within the immanent, at least as a "first cause." However, a move away from transcendence as a category in relation to ontology *does* require a loss of intelligibility, as "first cause" is replaced by "self-caused cause," and an infinite regression of immanent causation becomes the new "ground" for a different conception of morality. But given the logical meaninglessness of such a regression, a loss of transcendence presages a loss of intelligibility, as the loss of transcendence *necessarily* results in the loss of first and final causality, and thus the loss of a teleological view of reality as whole. This is because the cause-effect view of natural reality is wedded to a metaphysical view of nature, as Aquinas argued, which is oriented toward the divine as its origin and end.[11]

ONTOLOGY LOSES ITS RELIGION

Returning to Thatcher's list, the religious approach to ontology was not to last long, and the theological insights of Claubergius's analogical definition and Lorhard's transcendently referential teleology quickly erode in subsequent historical reiterations. Gottfried Leibniz (1646–1716), writing in the generation subsequent to Claubergius, defines ontology as a "general science," which is to say, a "science about something and nothing, being and non-being, entities and their modes of existing, substance, and accident."[12] While Thatcher simply lists this definition, before passing on to others, a comparison of this rendition with Claubergius's makes manifest three key changes upon which it is worthwhile to reflect. The first is that the theological link has been severed, at least nominally.[13] No longer is the science of being conceived as a science whose general nature is substantially related to theology; rather, it becomes a theologically independent endeavor.

Secondly, with the structural analogy between theology and ontology displaced, the general account of being is reoriented by a different logical contrast point: the relation of being to nonbeing. Whereas the object of ontology for Claubergius was "being in general," for Leibniz it is "being and non-being," a change which, when coupled with a belief that ontology specializes in "intelligibilities," has substantial repercussions for just what it was possible to claim that the human mind might know.[14] We might say that such a reorientation of ontology is achieved through immanentization, as the being of experiential reality loses its ecstatic grounding, becoming a self-enclosed and immanent-to-itself whole. Nonbeing can be said to gain a more positive characterization as a result of this immanentization, as being and nonbeing are contrasted as putative "things" of a similar kind, whose "intelligibility" is brought within the purview of the science so conceived.

Relatedly, the third key difference between the ontological definitions of Claubergius and Leibniz concerns its *general* nature. As mentioned, Claubergius's definition focuses on "being in general," while Leibniz makes the generality of ontology's investigation concern the science itself. It is a "general science," rather than a science concerning general being. I see this difference as bearing the potential to render unnecessarily abstract the object of ontology (being in general), while simultaneously privileging the method of our intellectual encounter with that object (knowing in general). Making the point in a more phenomenological vein, no longer is "being" taken as generally "given," but science becomes the means through which "the given" can be said to arise as a phenomenon for our general consideration. In my view, this subtle redefinition harbors the potential for a move away from epistemological realism toward the various modern rationalisms and idealisms that historically succeeded it.[15]

THE KANTIAN REVOLUTION IN ONTOLOGY

This drift away from realism reaches a critical level in the metaphysical concepts of Immanuel Kant (1724–1804). Thatcher gives us two definitional glosses from Kant concerning ontology:

Kant ... called ontology 'the science of the general attributes of all things' or the science of 'the possibility of our knowledge of things a priori, i.e. independent of experience.' Ontology, [Kant] wrote, 'can teach us nothing about things as they are in themselves, but only the a priori conditions under which we can know things in our general experience, i.e. principles of the possibility of experience.'[16]

But apart from this, Thatcher tells us nothing about how Kant's understanding relates to other conceptualizations of ontology. We should thus take a moment to grasp Kant's understanding more clearly, as his position becomes decisive in the history of the concept.[17]

As is well known, Kant envisioned his whole rational-critical project as an attempt to save the venerable enterprise of metaphysics from what he considered to be the "superstition" of its dogmatic special-pleaders, and this through a critical analysis of reason's limits. Only an account of reason that first had been purified by critical investigation, he argued, would be capable of metaphysical and ethical thought devoid of the prejudice of tradition. For the "dogmatic" tradition Kant was taking upon himself to critique—which included the aforementioned Leibniz, Christian Wolff, and Alexander Gottlieb Baumgarten—"ontology" was conceived as a synonym for "metaphysics in general," which these figures contrasted with the "special metaphysics" of psychology, cosmology, and theology.[18] Kant saw this "dogmatic" definition of ontology as the attempt to give "synthetic a priori cognitions of things in general in a systematic doctrine," which, however, failed by the light of his own critical methodology and epistemology; he thus thought that the metaphysics of the dogmatic tradition "must [now] give way to the modest mere analytic of pure understanding," Kant's own sort of ontology.[19] Because Kant famously denies the possibility of the knowledge of the existence of "things in general," as Thatcher's quotation shows us, we see him here make good on the radical potential of Leibniz's definition of ontology, even as he critiques it: Kant inflates the systematizing impulse of modern science, while also seeking to temper the mind-external objectivity of its referential claims. This double move has the net result of further abstracting metaphysics from a realist investigation of being, while sublating ontology into an all-consuming transcendental idealism. Martin Heidegger seems to notice this exchange when he argues that "Kant gives the name transcendental philosophy to that ontology that, as a result of the transformation effected by the *Critique of Pure Reason*, considers the being of beings as the objectivity of the object of experience."[20] Reason *creates* the intelligibles, which are then posited as "being" on the basis of their rational objectification; the objectivity of being is subjectively constituted. Kant's transcendental methodology, his rationalistic ontology, was thus posited as a replacement for metaphysics in general, one which abolishes the need for any "special" metaphysics and thus for theology (at least as it was conventionally understood) as well.[21]

In sum, Kant's "modest" proposal was to save metaphysics from dogmatic superstition by making ontology about the analytic of pure understanding in the faculty of reason (or to be more technically correct: by recognizing the synthetic unity of apperception as the ground for the positing of "being," at least on Heidegger's reading), instead of about substantial claims concerning the being of things as they are in themselves, how they *are* or *aren't* in a world beyond the rational subject.[22] According to him, we can have no true knowledge of this world of things in themselves, no knowledge of being in general, only knowledge of sense phenomena which may or may not correspond to a reality "out there."

But Kant's ontological "modesty" had unintended consequences. For the classical tradition, ontology was useful because it produced an operational map of reality; which is to say, its purpose was to provide humanity with an ordered picture of its place in a larger world, a picture according to which moral action might be organized and undertaken. Kant's own critical ontology had the (perhaps unintended) effect of picturing humanity at the center of a metaphysical world that humans construct through the rational-critical process. With him, ontology becomes the conceptualization and artefaction of the world, with the Enlightenment subject at its center. This rendering of ontology, I argue, is the final result of Kant's so-called "Copernican Revolution" in thinking, in which objects of thought are presumed to conform to our cognition of them, rather than the other way around.[23] Be that as it may, something of a definitive subjectification of the language game of "being" happens here. Now, in addition to the loss of the theological point of reference, ontology loses contact with the external world as its object of investigation. Or differently put, we lose direct contact with the externality of being through our depiction of thought as a subjective "positing," knowledge of mind-externals having been judged impossible a priori.[24]

HEIDEGGER AND THE POLITICAL PROBLEM OF THE METAPHYSICS OF MODERN SUBJECTIVITY

When reflecting on the history of ontology, Thatcher correctly claims that all "[p]hilosophers who produced ontology in the three centuries before our own can fairly be called either rationalists or idealist."[25] Kant gives evidence of both of these modern tendencies, as does Thatcher's own subject of research, Paul Tillich. However, what can be adduced on the basis of Thatcher's claim—but which he himself declines to explore—is that, from Aristotle until the modern turn four centuries ago, metaphysics as an activity of science held different—what can aptly be called "realist"—presuppositions than those currently en vogue among modern ontologists. It is not mere coincidence then that contemporaneous with the rationalist and idealist reconception of metaphysics comes a neologism, initially used synonymously with, but growing ever more divergent from, classical metaphysics: the new science named ontology. Seen from this perspective, the term does not seem simply to be the application of poetic license to metaphysics, but a concrete lexical development in view of a fundamental change in the conception and practice of the discourse concerning being. What Thomas Kuhn would later call "a paradigm shift" in the broader philosophical worldview has taken place, as evidenced in the arising of ontology as a distinct conceptualization concerning the question of being.[26]

To grasp the full scope of this change, the final of Thatcher's ontological precursors to Tillich should be mentioned. Thatcher cites Martin Heidegger (1889–1976) as producing the most formative modern account of ontology—at least as it relates to the development of what he calls a "fundamental" or "existential" ontology, to which Tillich's own is near kin. In his groundbreaking work *Being and Time*, Heidegger states that "all ontology, no matter how rich and firmly compacted a system of categories it has at its disposal, remains blind and perverted from its ownmost aim, if it has not first adequately clarified the meaning of Being, and conceived this clarification as its fundamental task."[27] On this definition, ontology finishes its subjectivist turn. Since "meaning" is a relational concept—something means something to someone—the investigation of the question of the meaning of being, which Heidegger believes to be at the core of ontology, inevitably becomes relative to the subject (rather than the object) under investigation. The subject who pursues ontology no longer investigates "being in general," a world order in which he is enmeshed and which supersedes himself; rather, he investigates the "meaning of being," the subject's quest becoming focused on his own understanding, or at most, the collective understanding of *Dasein*, Heidegger's technical term for "the being of man."[28] Ontology thus becomes anthropocentric at best and subjectivist at worst as a result of the shift of focus in ontology from "being in general" to the "meaning of being."

I hasten to add, however, that such a definitional shift to a single word is not in itself problematic. It is manifestly possible to hold an existentialist definition of ontology as a consideration of the meaning of being to humanity in tandem with philosophical realism, but then the problem of how the human way of being differs from or is fundamentally related to "other-being" and "being in general" again resurfaces. This is to say, ontology can continue its investigation of the meaning of being just so long as being is prior to meaning;

which is also to say, just so long as metaphysics and ontology are not identical activities. In such a rendering—where ontology is focused on the meaning of being as it is related primarily to the human situation—ontology must remain a special mode of a more general metaphysics to avoid becoming fully anthropocentric and, when relativized by the experiential meaning of the ontological investigator, metaphysically subjectivist. The problem of the subjectivization of ontology arises when ontology's original function as a synonym for metaphysics remains despite the modern shift in subject matter, where the difference between the questions concerning the quiddity of being and the meaning of (human) being is elided. Such is the case with Kant as we have seen, but arguably also with Heidegger, whose ontological considerations contain just such an elision.

Does Heidegger succumb to this negative potential? In one sense, Heidegger seeks to uphold metaphysics as an inquiry into being itself. "In such an impartial inquiring, determining, grounding," he maintains of metaphysics, "a peculiar submission to beings themselves obtains, in order that they may reveal themselves."[29] This humbleness of the subject before the object of his inquiry opens up space for being in general to reveal itself, on Heidegger's terms, and is, I would suggest, a hallmark of classical metaphysics. In this sense, Heidegger seeks to locate humanity by placing its scientific and metaphysical inquiry within a world of other-beings and ultimately into a horizon where being is prior to human existence.[30] Humanity does not stand over all being, but, by virtue of its proper nature, has its being as a being-in-the-world. His rejection of "humanism" is consistent with the humility concomitant with the enterprise of traditional metaphysics, which is why he speaks so vociferously against "the modern metaphysics of subjectivity,"[31] and sees his own work as carrying on the broader metaphysical tradition of Western philosophical thought.[32]

However, Heidegger also betrays a conflation of the question of being and the question of the meaning of being, confusing metaphysics and ontology, strictly understood. This tendency is revealed when we consider another of the fundamental definitions he offers for ontology. "Ontology," he says, is "the science of being."[33] It differs in kind from what he calls the "ontic" or "positive" sciences—in which he places theology and the other technical endeavors of knowledge—because these others have discrete and given objects, while ontology deals directly with being as such, in general, prior to its objectification in a techno-scientific thinking. On this understanding, metaphysics as he defined it above (recall: a "submission to beings") must also count as an "ontic" science, given that the objectification of Being into beings has already occurred when metaphysics takes up its investigation. Moreover, he repeatedly stresses that the nature of the difference between ontic and ontological thinking is "absolute,"[34] which means that ontology then becomes the most "original" or primordial kind of thinking, because it thinks of the ground of everything, the ground of thingness itself (i.e. Being) prior to its givenness or thematization as an object of investigation—prior, that is, to its instantiation as *a* being. It is on this more primary ground that all of the positive sciences must be built, at least if they *care* to be sciences concerned with *Dasein*, the human's being in the world. Here ontology has a suprametaphysical character, dealing not with "beings as a whole," as was the case in metaphysics, but with Being as such. Thus, ontology replaces classical metaphysics as the most primary and fundamental science, and metaphysics becomes a kind of subdiscipline of ontology concerned with beings as a whole, underneath an architectonic of ontology understood as the consideration of being in general.[35]

Despite all of his manifest antihumanism and antisubjectivism, Heidegger seems to reinscribe, at a higher level, precisely those things that his philosophy of being was meant to reject.[36] By conflating the question of being itself with the question of the meaning of being within the singular field of ontology, necessary distinctions that would disallow modern subjectivism from gaining an upper hand cannot be made. The problematic can be seen to arise when we ask: if the human being is already posited such that it is capable of thinking being in itself prior to division, then in what "field" can such a mind already exist but in the field of being itself?[37] He has posited a division in the field of being between "being as such" and a human being whose existence is a letting-being-be, but somehow, impossibly, prior to division. His desire to secure for humanity a thinking which is untainted by a subject-object distinction posits a nevertheless *human* being standing before, or at least within, the field of being prior to ontic fracturing. The only possible way this is logically consistent is if human existence becomes synonymous with being in itself, or if human thought is capable of witnessing the being of beings prior to their manifestation, contrary to Heidegger's intentions.

As problematically, the arc of Heidegger's narrative is one of declination, meaning that the story he tells concerns the fall of *Dasein* into a confusion of tongues, where the language of being is misspoken and needs to be purified. He speaks of "the rapidly spreading devastation of language" which represents a "threat to the essence of humanity."[38] But, given that language is precisely the means Heidegger posits through which being reveals itself, he cannot account for this corruption of being's proper abode. If language is, as Heidegger claims, "the house of the truth of being,"[39] what then justifies his claim that this house needs a "liberation . . . from grammar"?[40] Isn't grammar essential to language, and hasn't truth *already* taken up its abode within it? Why does it need liberation from itself? Put differently, if the subject-object division is problematic, why can it be manifest in language at all? If language is the house of the truth of being, then why, within this home, does there arise the speaking of a "should" be? If being *is*, then why does it presence itself as a *should be* in language, as if it *might not be*? This is, in a subversive way, to ask of Heidegger's conception of Being the question of theodicy.

Regardless of how he might answer this cluster of questions, for the purposes of my genealogy we have seen enough to observe a paradigm shift in the language of ontology, whose demonstration was the point of my initial investigation. From its origin as a modern synonym for metaphysics, ontology slowly becomes a distinct understanding of the field of being juxtaposed with classical metaphysics. This divergence becomes programmatic when it is coupled with a belief that the basic conception of being in classical metaphysics has been tainted by a naïve realism that needs to be critically purified in some way, whether by a rationalism, modern idealism, or (post) modern existentialism. Ontology becomes the name for a new, presumably more "critical," science of being whose focus remains the clarification of the meaning of being, and in some renditions, the clarification of the meaning of being *and* nonbeing, where nonbeing attains a more positivistic characterization.[41] While Heidegger arguably succumbs to the subjectivist problematic, he is nevertheless an important figure for my purpose because he correctly sees the problem subjectivism poses at the metaphysical level, which is its resultant positivistic—and thus uncritical—humanism, one which reduces the plentitude of being to merely human "meanings."

The political consequence of his recognition of the problem of ontological subjectivism is also worthy of note. Heidegger correctly sees that metaphysical subjectivism necessarily results in "the dictatorship of the public realm,"[42] as manifest in political ideologies competing for control of the social whole. When technological-subjectivist thinking is applied to human social being, individual existence is extruded into a "privatized" substance, to be socially conglomerated through political ideologies, what he calls "-isms."[43] These "-isms" claim to represent the totality of "the public." The individual loses any intrinsic or personal or nonreducible value, and any value it does have is only attributed to it through a politics of recognition in which the public dictates and distributes value to the individual. As such the very modes of thought and language of the individual are co-opted and colonized by such "-isms." What Heidegger calls "the dictatorship of the public realm" I will later refer to as ideological totalitarianism.

THEOLOGY AND METAPHYSICS: A NECESSARY RELATION

The impact of this mottled genealogy is ostensible in the systematic structure of Paul Tillich's own theology, as Thatcher's analysis shows; and while it is beyond my present concern to elaborate the nature and system of Tillich's specific ontology, what is pertinent to mention is how Thatcher understands the import of ontological analysis for theology in general. According to Thatcher, Tillich uses "ontology" and "metaphysics" in a range of essential ways, on some occasions rendering the terms as synonymous, and other times loading the terms with distinct meanings, meant to serve different, sometimes contradictory functions. In the end, Thatcher argues that Tillich equivocates on the terms at different points in his career.[44] While at some level this is to be expected of a theologian whose distinguished literary corpus spans decades (especially in consideration of a subject matter as definitionally diverse as my genealogy suggests), it becomes problematic when occasional writings over a career are synthesized into a theological system; and precisely because Tillich was a concerned systematician who understood the need for consistency, the charge of incoherence in basic concepts threatens his project more than other less-systematic theologians.

In the end, one's ontology establishes the basic framework or worldview under which a thinker labors. Accordingly, Thatcher calls ontology a "universal frame of reference."[45] To be charged with ontological equivocation is therefore to be charged with what amounts to basic or fundamental incoherence, similar to the architectural judgment that one's building is structurally unsound (i.e., insufficiently "grounded"). If the foundation and framework are compromised, the whole will collapse when pressured. This is precisely Thatcher's claim concerning the ontology of Paul Tillich. He argues, "The major criticism we have more than once launched against him is that of philosophical eclecticism, whereby basic ontological concepts and ideas have become almost indistinguishably merged together, sometimes with the result that quite incompatible meanings are fused together beneath a single general term."[46] This is to say, for Thatcher, ontological discourse vocalizes the basic (i.e., load-bearing) terms of a conceptual system, and any equivocation at such a level is impermissible because it violates one of the essential laws of speculative reason, noncontradiction: something cannot both be and not be with respect to the same thing at the same time. No determinate knowledge is possible if this rule is broken. Hence, ontological "eclecticism" at the very least obfuscates the clarity of a system and at worst causes the system to fail due to inadequate grounding. Given that the role of metaphysics is to provide an operational map of reality with the goal of grounding concrete moral projects, such opacity risks compromising its constitutional purpose.

However, Thatcher is shrewd to insist that, despite the structural failure inherent in Tillich's own systematic theology, the enterprises of ontology and theology themselves remain valid and, when brought together, mutually enriching. His conclusion reads as a persuasive defense of ontology (understood in its original sense as a synonym for metaphysics), both in its own right as a philosophical discipline and also as an aid to theology. This defense is required, he is aware, because of the broadly antimetaphysical posture of the postmodern academy.[47] He thus provides a cluster of compelling links in the structural relationship between ontology and theology that justify their mutual and overlapping engagement, links which incline us to recover the original meaning of ontology and its "parallel" relation to theology.

The first is that, from a theological perspective, certain biblical passages are impossible to comprehend apart from ontological thinking. Thatcher focuses on the Johannine prologue as one obvious text which is impossible to apprehend apart from seeing it as establishing an ontological framework both for the gospel itself and for the subsequent Christian theological tradition as a whole. We might add to this all those metaphysically implicated passages which Etienne Gilson discusses in his *Christian Philosophy*, none more metaphysically primary than the proper name God gives himself in Exodus 3:13–14—"I am."[48] To be understood rightly, all such passages require what Thatcher calls "ontological sensitivity," a sense for understanding what can be posited as really existing in and beyond the world.[49]

Another link is established between the two disciplines when it is observed that ontology provides an "other mode of expression" for theological concepts, functioning as a kind of "alternative theological language."[50] Here Thatcher accesses the structural analogy between theology and ontology/metaphysics to argue that the latter can be of service to the former because "the very emptiness and colourlessness of ontological concepts is a distinct advantage" in speaking of God, a "trans-empirical reality."[51] What Thatcher calls the "descriptive neutrality" of ontological discourse presents theology with the ability to put in language something which is believed to transcend confinement in human language, but which is nevertheless believed to be communicable in some of its multitudinous aspects. This is why Thatcher believes that "ontological concepts are the most suitable kind of linguistic currency for speaking about what cannot be contained by any words at all,"[52] something essential to the theological enterprise for those who believe in the Christian doctrine of creation *ex nihilo*, that God is the transcendent source of all that exists. Drawing upon earlier observations, what makes this synergy between theology and ontology possible is the "general" nature of their respective objects, although I hesitate to follow Thatcher in thinking of this generality in terms of "descriptive neutrality." Rather, an analogy of being is established such that correspondences and essential structures observable in our language concerning ultimate reality are truly and really deemed capable of adequate, if limited, theological reference. Without ontological discourse, theology is bereft of a means through which it might communicate divine reality as it impinges upon experiential reality, while at the same time preserving the mysterious sense of a divine surplus both in our use of the language about being and in our direct experience of reality itself.

In other words, without recourse to a metaphysical language that makes possible the allocution of being in a nonreductive way, theology is subjected to a twofold threat, one internal and one external. On the one hand, it may decay internally into what Gilson calls "theologism"—a form of irrational fideism in which God's transcendence is marshaled to denigrate human reason, rendering meaningful (from the perspective of linking human motivations up to divine intentions) action in history impossible. The danger here is that theology is used to justify its own exclusion from social and political matters, on the presumption that human history is ultimately or essentially meaningless. On the other hand, there remains the external problem of political legitimation once the political realm is shorn of its theological referentiality. In the history of political thought, this problem arises as the issue of political theology, which is, summarily, the problem of justifying a political regime through appeal to transcendence. In the face of the manifest need to integrate diverse social phenomena into a systematic whole—but one foreclosed to the possibility of metaphysical and theological knowledge—modern political ideologies are generated to fill the referential void created by the sequestering of theology. Each ideology relies on some immanent principle that must be taken in a strictly univocal way (e.g., reason *alone*, class struggle, human freedom, etc.) such that it is capable of serving as the final grounding for sociopolitical action as a whole. From the perspective of theology, this threat manifests itself as a secularist recuperation of theological language by purely materialist and immanentist philosophies that provide secular interpretations of "religious" phenomenon.[53] Theology and religion become stripped of meaningful reference to divine transcendence, tolerated only as a functionalistic means of justifying the political whole as an object of human striving.

Without recourse to a language that makes some sense of the divine-human relationship such as ontology provides, a language at once capable of meaningful reference to divine realities but limited by the contingencies of creaturely being, theology becomes either meaningless to human existence or fully reducible to it, neither of which is satisfactory to the faith revealed in the historical existence of the Incarnate Son of God.[54] Short of such a realist metaphysical language, theological problematics—like how Christ manifests himself as "King," though paradoxically "not of this world"—become insoluble.[55] Moreover, the ability of theology to limit totalitarian political ideologies becomes impossible, as these latter have already dictated the meaning of terms such that theology only makes sense within a hermeneutical range determined by the political authority itself—that is, as a religious activity whose sole purpose is to justify the political discrimination of things. Negotiating this biblical and existential tension without falling either into sectarianism or secularism requires a robust metaphysical insight.

AVOIDING THE SECTARIAN AND SECULARIST TEMPTATIONS

This last point deserves further elaboration as a prolegomenon to political theology just because maintaining this metaphysical tension is necessary to prevent against two practical temptations inherent in negotiating our understanding of the relationship between theology and politics. One is the so-called "sectarian temptation,'" which is constituted in the belief that Christian faith is a private affair and should eschew engagement in material and political realities. A theology built on an (anti)metaphysics which denigrates the human capacity to meaningfully and rationally relate to God in this world (i.e., theologism) lies behind a wide swath of escapist and sectarian political theologies, all of which assume either on principle or in practice the incommensurability of faith and reason, and thus the impossibility of drawing meaningful moral judgments about political realities on the basis of God's existence or the perceptible natural order. Indeed, knowledge of revelation itself becomes a sketchy affair. Here, theological *irrelevance* to practical human life is the concern.

The other temptation is that of theological *cooption* or *reduction*, in which theological language comes under the control of political and immanentist secular ideologies, who instrumentalize god-talk to license political regimes that are established prior to or apart from meaningful theological appeal. In these types of political theology, immanentist totalitarian ideologies dress themselves in god-language, with the state coming to subsume the role of the Church as the supreme object of human striving, the ultimate form of human integration.[56] This can be called "the secularist temptation."

I have argued that a philosophical realism was implied in the enterprise of classical metaphysics, a reality-mapping project open and amenable to the enterprise of theology, but was subsequently lost with the ascendancy of modern rationalist and idealist epistemologies; which is to say, as metaphysics became the new science of ontology, philosophical realism was swept into the dustbin of history. Recovering this realistic framework—whether under the nomenclature of metaphysics or ontology—is necessary to the perseverance of theology as a meaningful discipline, as well as a means for preventing the venerable enterprise of metaphysics from corroding into subjectivism, something which Heidegger himself correctly saw as the greatest modern metaphysical threat. Without holding forth the possibility of metaphysical realism, theology cannot justify itself as a meaningful discourse concerning the relationship of God and man, having cut itself off from the existential realm where such justification could have any practical bearing; nor can theology prevent its own subjugation to positivistic philosophies, other human sciences, or political ideologies without a robust metaphysics. This is the backside of Thatcher's claims "that any theology whatever which regards belief in God as in some sense factual and cognitive, and which also takes seriously the doctrine of creation, needs an ontology to make any sense of its *own* account of the relationship between God and the world."[57] Theology *itself* demands metaphysics for its own internal coherence, for adequately grasping standard Christian dogmas like the doctrine of creation, indeed anything dealing with God's activity in the world; this must also include the doctrine of the Incarnation, that point in theological thinking most in need of Thatcher's "ontological sensitivity."

Failure to maintain such a metaphysical possibility would thus constitute a betrayal of theology. As R. W. Hepburn has said, "If this metaphysical task (i.e. that of delineating the transcendent) is altogether rejected by the theologian, the only account of Christianity that is still open to him is an account in terms of a pattern of human living here and now. . . . Theology becomes 'anthropology.'"[58] It is just this reduction of theology to mere anthropology that enables the co-option of theology by immanentist philosophy. Without a metaphysical realism open to theological transcendence, there is nothing to prevent a Feuerbach or a Freud from offering purely psychological or socio-political interpretations to theological phenomena, foreclosing the possibility of a realm of meaning beyond the material.[59] This foreclosure is crucial to secularist and totalitarian ideologies that seek to instrumentalize theology in service to their preferred political programs.

Far from being an act of epistemological hubris,[60] metaphysics performed in a realist key is the very means through which totalitarian ideologies are prevented from gaining hermeneutical traction; this happens through the dogmatic perseverance of a divine surplus in the recognition that "being" is ecstatically grounded. This divine surplus in turn establishes an articulation of the essential possibilities of, and natural limits to, human reason; however, far from denigrating the material, these limits remain porous to transcendence in a nonreductive and noncompetitive relation, as a fecund tension is maintained between the contingent and the necessary, between the human and the divine, such that reason and faith mutually coinhere.[61] Seen in such a metaphysical light, theologism is as reprehensible to a right understanding of faith as it is repugnant to right reason; religious zealotry is no less problematic to the joint testimony of faith and reason than is ideological totalitarianism, manifesting itself in a dogmatic, or metaphysically agnostic, secularism.

CONCLUSION: RETRIEVING REALISM FOR AN INCARNATIONAL POLITICS

The history of twentieth-century political affairs can be read as a dire warning against the loss of metaphysical realism and the acceptance of ideologies cut loose from theological critique. As *Gaudium et Spes* reminds us, "When God is forgotten... the [human] creature itself grows unintelligible."[62] In the face of the unintelligibility that necessarily results from a loss of sight of the divine in modern ontology, modern politics has been seduced by partial truths concerning human nature into political absolutism, the investiture of ultimate human meaning in political authority.

Realist metaphysics is therefore a necessary correlate for the establishment of a theological anthropology, an account of human being and his political projects that includes relationship with God as an essential structural element. Without this element in place, human striving can only be meaningful as the achievement of some immanent or self-referential purpose, whether political or biological, chosen either randomly or on the basis of some irrefrangible political ideology.

Once modern ontology replaces classical metaphysics, even the social and philosophical sciences themselves become incapable of meaningful external reference. This is because the "realm of meaning" becomes locked in a Cartesian mind, increasingly closed off from external reality the more that "meaning" is relativized and the more that "the world" is conceptualized as an artifact of human consciousness.[63] In this way, some come to despair even of the possibility of political absolutism, which requires at the very least belief in human intersubjectivity. A healthy theology and philosophy, even a healthy politics, therefore depend on the realist assumptions embedded in classical metaphysics for their internal coherence and mutual enrichment.

The transition from medieval metaphysics to modern ontology signified a foundational change in worldview. Kant's own metaphor of the Copernican Revolution is indicative of this fact. The revolution from geocentric to heliocentric views of the world had an unintended cascading effect in metaphysics, calling into question the received classical categories, none more primary than the medieval conceptualization of "nature." Romano Guardini grasps the essential difference this way: "For medieval man nature was the creation of God; classicism was a foreshadowing of Revelation. For modern man both nature and classicism became means for severing existence from Revelation. Revelation had become empty of meaning and hostile to life."[64] The metaphysical revolution sought by Kant was not a simple change in whether the sun orbited the planet or the reverse (i.e., the change in a fact about nature) but was more fundamentally a revolution *against* the theological conception of what it meant "to be," what was or wasn't "natural." The change in understanding one natural relation—namely which celestial object rotated around the other—was (mis)taken to mean a change in everything that had a nature. In seeking a Copernican revolution in metaphysics, Kant was attempting a total revolution, and those who continue to rely on Kant's modern subject necessarily do the same in appropriating his ontological epistemology.[65]

With this cosmological reconceptualization came the first unintended—and then increasingly programmatic—metaphysical revolution now understood as modern ontology. But its consequences are not limited to purely conceptual or speculative matters; this is because man really is a being-in-the-world, as Heidegger understood, and thus a change in how reality is "mapped" necessarily has consequences for ethical life. Here is the last point I will make concerning the need to recover classical metaphysics as necessary for theology, especially moral theology, of which the study of political theology is a subdiscipline: a metaphysical map is not morally or politically neutral. Charles Taylor gets at this point obliquely through his critical realization that modernity does not simply have a new metaphysical worldview, but a "modern moral order," the structure of which determines and is determined by the modern social imaginary of that metaphysical worldview.[66] As such, the practical life and our understanding of its language of "the good" is implicated in the transposition from classical metaphysics to modern ontology. Realization of this fact is absolutely crucial to understanding, for example, Alasdair MacIntyre's claim that there is not one but at least three rival versions of "the good" at large today, each of which is underwritten by a distinct (anti-)metaphysical worldview.[67] However, far from being a pluralistic or subjectivist claim that resigns the theological tradition to postmodern despair in the face of such plurality, MacIntyre's description of the current field of moral discussion highlights the need for truly theological insights into human nature and its political consequences, as a nonreductive means of integrating the seemingly divergent moral traditions of (post)modernity, even as the realist belief in the possibility of this enterprise is maintained.

This chapter serves to confirm the work of others who have investigated the historical link between metaphysics and theology.[68] What Louis Dupré called "the passage to modernity" indeed involved not simply development or continuity of the preceding classical tradition, but a rupture of paradigmatic proportions.[69] This does not mean, however, that this rupture was in fact "real," nor does it serve to invalidate the preceding philosophical and theological tradition against which the whole of modern thought can, from the perspective of this chapter, be seen as a reaction. In fact, and with a certain amount of perceptible irony, the rejection of metaphysical realism at the heart of the modern ontological worldview is the very means through which its rationalistic and idealistic critiques of the classical tradition fail to be determinative, fail to be "real."[70] This does not mean that developments within the larger moral, metaphysical, and theological tradition have not happened in the time of Enlightenment modernity, only that the very means of judging those advances *as advances* will have to move back through a historical and theological critique of Enlightenment reason itself, which is to say, back through a recovery of "the real" against which modernity tried to actualize itself.

At the political level, such a critique will necessitate the suspension of Enlightenment political ideologies (and their postmodern epigones) and the convenient political mythologies upon which they are based[71]; equally problematic would be any recourse to theology approaching theologism, in the form of fideistic appeals to revelation incapable of rational assent. The categorical imperatives derived from such a move will entail the avoidance of absolutist totalitarian political theologies just as much as naive religious fundamentalisms.

Charting a course between the postmodern Scylla and Charybdis of totalitarianism and fundamentalism remains the task of an incarnational politics, a politics which maintains belief in the reality of the Incarnation and in the possibility of meaningfully participating in that reality through the goods common to human life. It has not been the goal of this chapter to detail what such an incarnational politics might look like in a specific historical context, only the negative interdiction of political and metaphysical forms which reject its possibility *a priori*. One can easily imagine that such a recovery will include reimagining "the political" as a site of spiritual conflict. But precisely because there is believed to be a *spiritual* realm nonidentical to the material realm, this conflict need not devolve to physical violence. Seen in this way, a theologically robust metaphysical map will manifest the best of the theological wisdom of the Christian tradition: "For our struggle is not against flesh and blood, but against the rulers, against the powers, against the world forces of this darkness, against the spiritual forces of wickedness in the heavenly places" (Eph. 6:12 [NASB]). The temptation to absolutize the political can be overcome in the recovery of a realist metaphysical discourse which does not reduce transcendence to human agency, even as it leaves open the possibility that such absolutism is itself a secular and fallen sign of a distinctly theological truth: God became man that Man might become God. The Divine and human are not in competition, even if there is a spiritual battle raging for the soul of the world.

NOTES

1. Adrian Thatcher, *The Ontology of Paul Tillich* (Oxford: Oxford University Press, 1978), 1.
2. Ibid.
3. In his conclusion, Thatcher comes much closer to grasping the general nature of ontology when claiming that it remains useful to theology (in the latter's attempt to speak meaningfully about a transcendent God) because ontological concepts have the "distinct advantage" of being "general in character." See Thatcher, *The Ontology of Paul Tillich*, 165.
4. Aristotle, *Metaphysics*, 6:1.
5. Jacob Lorhard, *Ogdoas Scholastica*, as cited in Peter Øhrstrøm, Henrik Schärfe, and Sara L. Uckelman, "Jacob Lorhard's Ontology: A 17th Century Hypertext on the Reality and Temporality of the World of Intelligibles," in *Conceptual Structures: Knowledge Visualization and Reasoning*, eds. Peter Eklund and Ollivier Haemmerlé (Berlin: Springer, 2008), 76. Lorhard relies on the work of Clemens Timpler, who first "proposed that the subject-matter of metaphysics is not being, but rather the intelligible, παν νοητον" (p. 75). According to the authors, Lorhard reproduces Timpler's system but is the first to introduce "ontology" as a semantic equivalent to metaphysics so conceived.
6. Øhrstrøm et. al, "Jacob Lorhard's Ontology," 82.
7. Ibid.
8. The argument for pure immanence succeeds or fails on the rational intelligibility of an infinite regress of causes without beginning (and so, it would seem without necessary end), while yet remaining intelligible as a ground for the meaning of moral language. Following Aristotle, Thomas deems this a rational impossibility, on the grounds that the infinite regression removes the possibility of any explanatory power, as the failure to specify a beginning redounds to a failure to choose an end rationally consummate with its beginning; which is to say, the "self-caused" as a category is inherently contradictory and lacks explanatory power. It is precisely the concept of the "self-caused" that any consistent doctrine of pure immanence utilizes as ultimate ground for its moral injunctions; precisely for this reason, it is illogical, or at least an indefinite deferral of warranting ground. Immanence as a category of rational thought derives its intelligibility from its relation to transcendence, which is Thomas's main point in denying immanent "nature" self-referentiality. See Thomas Aquinas, *ST* I, Q.2, Art.3, ad. 2.
9. Ibid.
10. Here my argument finds confirmation in George Santayana's claim that solipsism, while undisprovable at the level of mere "theory," is in fact contradicted *in practice*, as such practice presupposes the existence of an objective world of self-externals in which the solipsistic self is in meaningful enough relation to describe their thought in this "world" as *action*. Action exposes the absurdity of solipsism through its tacit presumption of the real existence of things external to the self, toward which the self directs its own action, a realm as putatively real and objective as the very self

takes itself to be. My argument is that, just as the solipsist contradicts itself in the realm of action, so too pure immanentism is exposed as contradictory in the activity of its moral declamations. See George Santayana, *The Letters of George Santayana*, vol. 5, bk I, ed. William G. Holzberger (Cambridge: MIT Press, 2001), 47–48.

11. Aquinas, *ST* I, Q.2, Art.3.

12. Thatcher, *The Ontology of Paul Tillich*, 1.

13. My emphasis here is on the lack of a definitional linkage. Leibniz remains consistent with the larger philosophical tradition of his time, which integrated theology into philosophical speculation. This is especially evident in his *Monadology*, where it becomes clear that his understanding of divinity controls his account of existence and causation, most especially his understanding of the Creator's "pure love" for his creation indicating that we must live in "the best of all possible worlds."

14. Of course Leibniz did not invent the opposing of being with nonbeing. Aristotle's *Metaphysics*, for example, initially assumes such a juxtaposition. The point here is that with Leibniz the subject which "ontology" attempted to define was a different kind of "being-in-general," no longer understood on analogy to God or theology, but as the dialectics of being and nonbeing as intelligible entities in the ontological language game. I do not mean that Leibniz necessarily thought of nonbeing positively— that is, as a substance of its own—but merely that, at the definitional level, there is sufficient ambiguity to make this rendering a future possibility.

15. Here my insight has been tutored by Charles Taylor and Hubert Dreyfus, who have argued that the modern epistemological tradition is premised on a dualistic "framework mistake," which depicts knowledge as an inner (self-)representation rather than—as it was in the premodern tradition—a grasp, however partial, of a greater reality. The consequence of this shift from premodern to modern epistemology is that reality became a mind-dependent thing, as "epistemology dictates ontology" (Hubert Dreyfus and Charles Taylor, *Retrieving Realism* [Cambridge: Harvard University Press, 2015], 23–24). Such "ontology" as rationalism and idealism still permit is one subordinate to how the human mind functions; thus, the mind becomes the limitless or transcendent source of "being," while "the real" becomes limited to its function in relation to the all-determining mind.

16. Thatcher, *The Ontology of Paul Tillich*, 1–2.

17. In a genealogy with similarities to my own, James Richmond argues that Immanuel Kant and Martin Luther are the two most formative metaphysical figures in the history of modern European thought (*Theology and Metaphysics* [London: SCM Press, 1970], 6).

18. Paul Guyer and Allen Wood, "Introduction to the *Critique of Pure Reason*," in Immanuel Kant, *Critique of Pure Reason*, trans. Paul Guyer and Allen Wood (Cambridge: Cambridge University Press, 2000), 5, 14. This way of imagining the relationship between metaphysics and theology, as "general" in relation to "special," already demonstrates the degradation of the theological object, subordinating God's being to a special case of being in general.

19. Kant, *Critique of Pure Reason*, A247/B303.

20. Martin Heidegger, "Kant's Thesis about Being," in *Pathmarks*, ed. William McNeill (Cambridge: Cambridge University Press, 1998), 350.

21. Guyer and Wood, "Introduction," 5. Special metaphysics could again be undertaken only once it had been tutored or purified through Kant's critique of reason. His well-known treatise *Religion within the Boundaries of Mere Reason* demonstrates what the deforming effect such a rationalistic limiting of theology would produce. Perhaps its most important consequence is the relegation of the deity to the realm of the "noumenal," which assumes God cannot be experienced in the world of human experience. Theology in such a worldview is reduced to grounding a moral system and can speak to nothing concerning the nature of divine things. See Robert Merrihew Adams, "Introduction," in Immanuel Kant, *Religion within the Boundaries of Mere Reason*, trans. Allen Wood and George Di Giovanni (Cambridge: Cambridge University Press, 1998), x.

22. This is, in fact, Martin Heidegger's critical interpretation of Kant—that is, that he fully subjectivizes "being." As he sees it, Kant's notion of "being as positing is situated, i.e., is located in relation to the structure of human subjectivity as the site of its essential provenance." See "Kant's Thesis about Being," 359.

23. Kant, *Critique of Pure Reason*, B xvi–xvii. By changing our language concerning objects from "beings in themselves" to a consideration of things as objects of our conceptual construction, Kant has shifted the fundamental standpoint of knowledge, as he is very much aware, in his selection of the Copernicus metaphor.

24. Again, reference is made to the work of Dreyfus and Taylor, and the need to recover a "contact epistemology." Cf. footnote 15 *supra*.

25. Thatcher, *The Ontology of Paul Tillich*, 2.

26. See Thomas Kuhn, *The Structure of Scientific Revolutions* (Chicago: University of Chicago Press, 1996). It would not be too much off point to posit that Kuhn's conception of "paradigm" shift is only possible on the basis of his recognition of the scientific consequences of the move from classical metaphysics to ontology.

27. Thatcher, *The Ontology of Paul Tillich*, 3; Martin Heidegger, *Being and Time*, trans. John Macquarrie and Edward Robinson (Oxford: Blackwell, 2001), 31.

28. In point of fact, it no longer makes sense to call the modern subject a "subject" at all, which is why A. N. Whitehead was more accurate in speaking of it alternatively as a "superject" (*Science and the Modern World* [New York: Pelican Mentor Books, 1948], 166).

29. Martin Heidegger, "What Is Metaphysics?" in *Basic Writings*, ed. David Farrell Krell (New York: Harper and Row, 1977), 97.

30. It is crucial to understanding Heidegger's position to see that he maintains a strict distinction between "to be" and "to exist." For him, "[t]he being that exists is the human being. The human being alone exists. Rocks are, but they do not exist. Trees are, but they do not exist. Horses are, but they do not exist. Angels are, but they do not exist. God is, but he does not exist. The proposition 'the human being alone exists' does not at all mean that the human being alone is a real being while all other beings are unreal and mere appearances or human representations. The proposition 'the human being exists' means: the human being is that being whose Being is distinguished by an open standing that stands in the unconcealedness of Being, proceeding from Being, in Being" (Heidegger, "Introduction to 'What Is Metaphysics?'" in *Pathmarks*, ed. William McNeill [Cambridge: Cambridge University Press, 1998], 284). It is

important to notice that Heidegger adds this remark in a subsequent introduction to his "What Is Metaphysics?" perhaps because he intuited that his initial answer to the question failed to avoid the very subjectivism he was seeking to critique.

31. Heidegger, "Letter on Humanism," in *Pathmarks*, ed. William McNeill (Cambridge: Cambridge University Press, 1998), 243.

32. See Heidegger's use of "tradition" and the way in which he believes that Immaneul Kant's "interpretation of being . . . name[s] the fundamental trait that forms the process of the entire history of philosophy" in Martin Heidegger, "Kant's Thesis about Being," in *Pathmarks*, ed. William McNeill (Cambridge: Cambridge University Press, 1998), 337–38, 359. If what I have claimed about Kant is correct, then this shows us the fundamental ambiguity of Heidegger's enterprise, a critique of Kant while remaining faithful to him.

33. Heidegger, "Phenomenology and Theology," in *Pathmarks*, ed. William McNeill (Cambridge: Cambridge University Press, 1998), 41.

34. Ibid., 43.

35. Heidegger is not rigidly consistent throughout his work in his usage of the distinction between ontology and metaphysics. For example, he has said of metaphysics that it "is inquiry beyond and over beings which aims to recover them as such and as a whole *for our grasp*." Given that Being is the only thing Heidegger posits beyond beings, metaphysics must be "ontological" in nature here. Nevertheless, the ontic-al aspect of metaphysical science remains present in the definition, in as much as it is a science concerned with "recovery . . . for our grasp" (Heidegger, "What Is Metaphysics?" 109).

36. One example of how this occurs is illustrative of the general spirit I think hovers over his work. As the Christian metaphysical tradition has amply shown, speaking of an absolute "necessity" with respect to human being creates an ontological reduction which is problematic, not only for Christian theology but for its own internal coherence. If humanity is "needed" by the divine, then God's being becomes dependent on the act of creation, and indeed identical with it, in violence to the traditional understanding of divine transcendence vis-à-vis creation. The transcendent is immanentized in this failure to retain the "independence" of divine being with respect to human being. It is by this immanentization of the conception of God as creator-in-need-of-his-creation that subjectivism arises on the back end in Heidegger's thought.

37. Heidegger takes up this question directly in his letter to Ernst Jünger, published as "On the Question of Being," in *Pathmarks*, 291–322. However, I find his answers evasive and question-begging, thus inadequate to the problematic relation between metaphysics and ontology as he conceives them.

38. Heidegger, "Letter on Humanism," 243.

39. Ibid.

40. Ibid., 240.

41. See Heidegger's attempt to put forward a positive thinking of nihilism, "On the Question of Being," 309ff.

42. Heidegger, "Letter on Humanism," 240.

43. Ibid.

44. Those interested in Thatcher's criticism of Tillich will find a pertinent list of the errors Tillich's ontological eclecticism produces here: *The Ontology of Paul Tillich*, 160–61.

45. Ibid., 163.

46. Ibid., 158.

47. Thatcher simply mentions this as an aside, but a genealogical account of Western antimetaphysical discourse, at least as it relates to theology, can be found in James Richmond, *Theology and Metaphysics*, 1–48. For a fuller elaboration of its philosophical sources, see Brad Gregory, *The Unintended Reformation* (Cambridge: Harvard University Press, 2012), 25–73.

48. See Etienne Gilson, *Christian Philosophy*, trans. Armand Maurer (Winnipeg: Hignell Printing, 1993).

49. Thatcher, *The Ontology of Paul Tillich*, 164.

50. Ibid., 166.

51. Ibid., 165.

52. Ibid.

53. See Etienne Gilson, *The Unity of Philosophical Experience* (New York: Scribner's Sons, 1950), 34–37. In terms of how "theologism" acts philosophically, Gilson defines it as "using reason against reason in behalf of religion," and convincingly argues that its necessary conclusion is philosophical skepticism, proved by repeated "experiments" in the history of philosophy.

54. Erik Peterson has articulated this need for a realist metaphysics as a requirement for any theology whose authorization derives from the fact of the Incarnation of Son—that is, for any *Christian* theology. See Erik Peterson, "What Is Theology?" in *Theological Tractates*, trans. Michael J. Hollerich (Standford: Standford University Press, 2011), 1–14.

55. John 18:36.

56. Some of these ideologies are Marxist or socialist in nature, as was the case for a generation of radical liberation theologians, but some are philosophically liberal and seek to support democratic and liberal forms of government, such as the authors of so-called *Radical Political Theology* or Francis Fukuyama. In my understanding these latter also count as "totalitarian ideologies" to the extent that their political mechanisms are taken as most fully realizing the possibilities of human nature—that is, they are teleologically "final" political forms, indifferent to any ultimate relationship to "the Kingdom of God"; or, as the case may be, claiming for themselves the right to establish such a relation apart from the Church. See Francis Fukuyama, *The End of History and the Last Man* (New York: Penguin, 1992); and Clayton Crockett, *Radical Political Theology* (New York: Columbia University Press, 2011).

57. Thatcher, *The Ontology of Paul Tillich*, 163. Emphasis in the original.

58. As cited in Richmond, *Theology and Metaphysics*, 17.

59. Ludwig Feuerbach, *The Essence of Christianity*, trans. George Eliot (Mineola: Dover Publications, 2008). Sigmund Freud, *The Future of an Illusion*, trans. James Strachey (New York: W.W. Norton, 1989).

60. This has tended to be the claim from the side of theologism—that is, that rational testimony concerning divine reality is an act of epistemological hubris. However,

as Brad Gregory has shown, the inverse is in fact the case, as it purports to pronounce limits upon human knowledge, on the basis of a univocal conception of human reason, in a way that is at odds with the Incarnation of the Son and the sacramental life of the Church. See Gregory, *The Unintended Reformation*, 44–73.

61. This noncompetitive and complementary relationship is formally articulated within magisterial Catholic social teaching in *Fides et Ratio* (Second Vatican Council, *Fides et ration*, accessed December 18, 2018 http://w2.vatican.va/content/john-paul-ii/en/encyclicals/documents/hf_jp-ii_enc_14091998_fides-et-ratio.html).

62. *Gaudium et Spes*, §36 (Second Vatican Council, *Gaudium et spes*, accessed December 18, 2018 http://www.vatican.va/archive/hist_councils/ii_vatican_council/documents/vat-ii_const_19651207_gaudium-et-spes_en.html).

63. Those interested in this aspect of the argument will find Etienne Gilson's *The Unity of Philosophical Experience* a valuable guide to the discussion.

64. Romano Guardini, *The End of the Modern World*, trans. Joseph Theman and Herbert Burke (New York: Sheed and Ward, 1956), 55.

65. Modernity's essential revolutionary-reactionarianism produces many a supple irony. Karl Barth is just such an ironic figure, being implicated in appropriating a Kantian anthropology, even though for ostensibly theological purposes. Matthew Rose has persuasively argued that Barth's acceptance of the Kantian subject, as evinced in his reaction against any "natural theology," undoes his otherwise important theological work. Matthew Rose, "Karl Barth's Failure," *First Things* 244 (June/July 2014): 39–44.

Other current voices likewise relying on Kantian subjectivity, but with a decidedly antitheological agenda can be found in Radical and death-of-God theology circles. Cf. Clayton Crockett, *A Theology of the Sublime* (New York: Routledge, 2001).

66. See Charles Taylor, *A Secular Age* (Cambridge: Harvard University Press, 2007), esp. 159–211.

67. Alasdair MacIntyre, *Three Rival Versions of Moral Enquiry* (Notre Dame: University of Notre Dame Press, 1990).

68. Most notably, Richmond, Gregory, and Blanchette. See Oliva Blanchette, "Are There Two Questions of Being?" *Review of Metaphysics* 45 (1991): 259–87.

69. Louis Dupré, *The Passage to Modernity* (New Haven: Yale University Press, 1993), 249ff.

70. Ibid. While in general I agree with Dupré, both that modernity as a cultural "event" did happen and was premised on a changed metaphysical view of the state of things (including the concept of "the State"), I do not agree with his judgment that modernity succeeded "in rendering all rival views of the real obsolete" (249), nor with his judgment that humans have within their mental power, the ability to "change the nature of the real" (252). I view these slippages in his otherwise careful articulation of the need to recover theological "transcendence" as damaging to that end precisely in so far as they are concessions to an "unreal" modern ontology that would seem to have been successful in putting God to death.

71. Such as the so-called "myth of religious violence." See William T. Cavanaugh, *The Myth of Religious Violence* (Oxford: Oxford University Press, 2009).

Chapter Fourteen

The Eucharist Makes the Church Repent

Eucharistic Ecclesiology and Political Theology

Daniel Wright

Two of the most significant theological trends to emerge in the last century are eucharistic ecclesiology and political theology, yet the relationship between the Church's sacramental existence *ad intra* and its ethicopolitical identity *ad extra* remains unclear. Eucharistic ecclesiology prioritizes the eschatological dimension of the Church made manifest in the "sacrament of sacraments" while political theology prioritizes the historical dimension. Thus, the two fields face unique temptations. Eucharistic ecclesiology can foster an otherworldly disinterestedness toward the concerns and problems of this world, as if the Church remains above and beyond inconsequential, quotidian existence. Political theology, on the other hand, tends to reduce the Church to a community of individuals with shared social and political goals, as if there is no hope beyond what can be achieved in history. The challenge—and value—of correlating eucharistic ecclesiology and political theology is in reconciling a robust anticipation of the eschaton with an equally robust commitment to address the social evils in the world. In other words, the challenge is to explain how the Eucharist which "makes the Church" is both eschatological and historical.

In this chapter, I discuss the different ways in which Metropolitan John Zizioulas and William Cavanaugh attempt to reconcile the eschatological and historical dimensions of the Eucharist and why neither is ultimately successful. Despite their differences, Zizioulas and Cavanaugh agree that the best human efforts to imitate Christ involve struggling against sin rather than overcoming it. On this basis, I argue that Zizioulas and Cavanaugh lead us to understand political theology as descriptive of the Church's penitential action in the world, which is both from and for the Eucharistic event. In short, eucharistic ecclesiology demands a political theology in the same way that the Eucharist demands repentance.

ZIZIOULAS AND EUCHARISTIC ECCLESIOLOGY

The Church's foremost apologist for eucharistic ecclesiology, Zizioulas claims that the Eucharist is somehow "both a historical *and* an eschatological event."[1] To describe the Eucharist in relation to history and the eschaton, Zizioulas often refers to a scholia attributed to Maximus the Confessor on Dionysius the Areopagite's work which says, "[The Areopagite] calls 'images (eikones) of what is true' the rites that are now performed in the synaxis.... For these things are symbols, not the truth.... For the things of the Old Testament are the shadow; those of the New Testament are the image. The truth is the state of things to come."[2] From this passage, Zizioulas gathers that the Eucharistic liturgy is sourced in the eschatological future rather than the historical past. "In other words," says Zizioulas, "the cause of 'what is accomplished in the synaxis,' lies in the future.... The Kingdom which is to come, a future event, being the *cause* of the Eucharist, gives it its true *being*."[3] So the Eucharist is distinct from other historical events because it is caused by the future. That is, "the Eucharist is not a repetition or continuation of the past, or just one event amongst others, but it is the penetration of the future into time."[4]

For Zizioulas, then, the Eucharist is discontinuous with the historical flow of events; it does not belong to any causal chain that can be traced backward in time but enters time from the eschatological future beyond time. Put this way, the historical character of the Church seems questionable, and the Eucharist seems more like an eschatological parenthesis within history rather than part of history. For this reason, Zizioulas is accused of employing an "overrealized eschatology."[5] Miroslav Volf argues that Zizioulas "has no place systematically in the experience of salvific grace for the theologically necessary presence of unredemption."[6] If the Church is defined by eschatological union with God, then "the historical character of the church, if the latter genuinely is to be a church, [is] transcended."[7] The Church is constituted by an eschatological event that transcends the historical consequences of the Fall. Therefore, the Church exists beyond sinfulness and death even though members of the Church continue to sin and die. Volf thus explains "that the eschaton is realized exclusively in the Eucharist means not only that only eucharistic communities constitute the church in the full sense of the word, but that they are indeed the church *only during the actual Eucharistic synaxis*."[8] The Church seems to come into existence with each Eucharistic event only to vanish again as the people re-enter the world of sin and death. With good reason, Volf questions "why the dispersed church is then to be called 'church' at all in the proper sense of the term."[9]

Zizioulas attempts to answer the question of the historical Church by spelling out the ethical implications of the Eucharist for the Church outside the liturgy. He argues that "the moral life follows from the *transformation* and *renewal* of humanity in Christ, so that every moral commandment appears and is understood only as a consequence of this *sacramental* transformation. In such a vision of ethics," he continues, ". . . moral conduct is understood as a continuation of the liturgical experience."[10] For Zizioulas the Church is "transfigured in order to transfigure" the world.[11] However, after making this claim concerning the extension of the liturgy into the world, Zizioulas immediately takes it back. He explains that he "does not mean to say that a eucharistic vision will provide a solution to the moral problems of our society."[12] He specifically rejects any version of the social gospel:

> Therefore the Eucharist will always open the way not to the dream of gradual perfection of the world, but to the demand for heroic ascesis, an experience of kenosis and of the cross, the only way in which it is possible to live the Eucharist in the world until the victory of the Resurrection at the end of time. At the same time, the Eucharist offers the world the experience of this eschatological dimension that penetrates history in the eucharistic communion and makes possible our deification in space and time. Without this dimension, no missionary method, no intelligent diplomacy, no system of morality will transfigure the contemporary world into Christ.[13]

Here we see what Zizioulas means when he speaks of "the eucharistic vision of the world" as "a continuation of the liturgical experience." He does not mean that the iconic manifestation of the eschaton is carried out into the world in order that the world be transformed into the Kingdom of God. Nor does he mean that the eschatological communion of the Eucharist persists in the time between liturgies such that the Church never fully re-enters the world of sin and death. For Zizioulas, the liturgical experience continues beyond the liturgy itself as an ascetic imperative—a call to imitate the crucified Christ.

Zizioulas asserts that "as an image of the Kingdom, the Eucharist makes us appreciate more deeply the contrast between the world as it is, and the world as it will be in the last times."[14] For this reason, "the eschatological character of the Eucharist does not attenuate but rather intensifies the struggle against the evil which surrounds us."[15] But again, this struggle against evil is not for the sake of perfecting the world, nor for the sake of bringing about the Kingdom of God. Outside of the liturgy, the Eucharist can only be lived in the mode of ascesis, which Zizioulas defines in terms of imitating the kenosis of Christ on the Cross. Zizioulas is clear that the fullness of eucharistic communion is not possible outside of the liturgy because the Eucharistic event is a foretaste of the ontological transformation that will only be fulfilled in the eschaton. Outside of the liturgy, under the conditions of the fallen world, we can only anticipate the eschaton by struggling against sin in obedience to God:

> The Eucharist is witness to a morality that is not an historical evolution but an ontological grace, acquired only to be lost again, until on the last day it will be acquired definitively.... The Liturgy [is] a solemn celebration from which the faithful return to the world full of joy and charism. But in crossing the threshold of the church, they find an unabated struggle.... The Eucharist has given them the strongest assurance of the victory of Christ over the devil, but upon this earth, this victory will ever be a victory of 'kenosis,' the victory of the cross, the victory of heroic ascesis—as it has been understood and lived in Eastern monasticism.[16]

For Zizioulas, the Eucharistic event is a matter of ontological participation in the resurrected Christ while asceticism is a matter of moral imitation of the crucified Christ. The Church does not cease to exist outside of the Eucharistic liturgy but perdures in a different mode. In the event of the Eucharist, the Church is iconic, but in its ascesis, the Church is mimetic.[17] This brings us back to our initial question regarding the relationship between the Church *ad intra* and the Church *ad extra*. Except now, we must ask whether eucharistic participation in the resurrected Christ renders the ascetic imitation of the crucified Christ ultimately inconsequential and unnecessary—that is, whether ethicopolitical actions are inconsequential and unnecessary.

Zizioulas claims that love is the tie that binds the Eucharist and ascesis, for love transcends the boundary between history and eschaton. Citing 1 Corinthians 13, which contrasts the temporary nature of the gifts of prophecy, tongues, and knowledge to the unending nature of love, Zizioulas comments:

> The eschatological character of the Eucharist is essentially linked to the eschatological character of love, which is the experiential quintessence of the Kingdom. All asceticism and all cleansing from the passions is in essence a precondition for the Eucharist, because the Eucharist cannot be understood apart from love. Love is not simply a virtue; it is an ontological category, not simply an ethical one. Love is that which will survive into the 'age which does not end or grow old' when all the gifts which impress us today, such as knowledge, prophecy, etc., will pass away.[18]

Love has two dimensions corresponding to the two dimensions of the Church. Moral love is a virtue achieved by ascesis and belongs to the realm of history, while ontological love belongs to the eschatological Kingdom and is manifested in the Eucharist. Thus, if love will survive into the eschaton, it will do so in its ontological mode and not its ethical mode. This is why Zizioulas says that asceticism is a *precondition* for the Eucharist. Just as

Christ could not experience the resurrection without first dying on the Cross, neither can we approach the Eucharist without first taking up our own crosses and imitating Him (Matt 16:24; Luke 9:23). In this light, we see that asceticism plays a necessary role in the life of the Church, but it is a means and not an end. "The ascetic life culminates in the Eucharist."[19]

For Zizioulas, whatever is achieved by ascesis is achieved in the realm of morality, not in the realm of ontology. When Zizioulas claims that ascesis is a *precondition* for the Eucharist, he does not mean that attaining moral love by ascesis in any way merits the ontological love granted in the Eucharist. In fact, ascesis has nothing to do with achieving spiritual or ethical fulfillment. "Ascetic life aims not at the 'spiritual development' of the subject but at the giving up of the Self to the Other . . . that is, at love."[20] Ascetic love is kenotic self-discipline and self-denial. Zizioulas's point is that focusing on one's own spiritual development is all too often, even necessarily, a selfish endeavor. To overcome self-love, which is the root of all evil, one must acquire an "understanding of the Other as having primacy over the Self," even to the point of self-sacrifice and self-condemnation.[21] It is exactly this kenotic notion of ascesis that Christ exemplifies on the Cross and that we are called to imitate. Asceticism is therefore a response to the Fall; it is not a matter of imitating Christ's sinless life but his sacrificial death wherein he took on the sins of others. Ascetic love is perfected not in sinlessness but in kenotic selflessness, even self-condemnation.

In defining asceticism in terms of self-condemnation, Zizioulas follows the ascetical theology of Saphrony Sakharov whose spiritual master St Silouan the Athonite passed on the famous saying: "Keep thy mind in hell and despair not." This axiom highlights the dialectic of self-condemnation and hope of the ascetic. It harkens back to the ancient saying attributed to Nilus of Ancyra: "The beginning of salvation for everyone is to condemn himself." At the same time it refers to the eschatological hope that results from Christ's conquering of hell.[22] But there is a missing link here between self-condemnation and the hope of salvation. Though Christ has made salvation possible, hope in the eschatological Kingdom is dependent upon repentance. Thus, we see that Silouan's axiom is, at root, a reformulation of the gospel message: "Repent, for the Kingdom of God is at hand!" Or, in the context of eucharistic ecclesiology, we might paraphrase the axiom rather clumsily as: "Practice ascesis, that you may enter the Kingdom of God foretasted in the Eucharist!"

Ascesis is repentance. But this is deceptively simplistic if we do not take into account the capacious nature of repentance in the patristic tradition.[23] When Nilus and Silouan speak of self-condemnation, they prescribe not only individual repentance but radically communal repentance—that is, taking responsibility for the sins of others. Zizioulas explains that the desert Fathers, in particular, emphasized this way of imitating Christ:

> They insisted that the Other should be kept free from moral judgement and categorization. This they achieved not by disregarding evil but by transferring it from the Other to the Self. . . . The theological justification is Christological: Christ himself made his own the sins of others on the Cross, thus paving the way to self-condemnation so that the others might be justified. 'Christ became a curse for us' (Gal. 3:13). 'For our sake he [God] made him to be sin who knew no sin, so that in him we might become the righteousness of God' (2 Cor. 5:21).[24]

Ascetic love requires the sacrifice of the self for the other. Zizioulas relates that a certain monk confessed and did penance for the sin of another as if it were his own; and another monk prayed that the devil which possessed his brother might pass into himself.[25] Zizioulas is particularly interested in the sixth-century Desert Father Zosimas, who not only forgives the offense committed against him but regards "the Other as a benefactor for having helped him to blame himself for this evil act."[26] Zizioulas argues that such acts of self-condemning love are not only for monks and extremists but for all Christians. "The essence of Christian existence in the Church is *metanoia* (repentance). . . . For we all share in the fall of Adam, and we all must feel the sorrow of failing to bring creation to communion with God and the overcoming of death."[27]

But Zizioulas stops short of setting up "heroic ascesis" as a principle of social ethics, and he does so for two reasons. First, he says that "it would be inconceivable to regulate social life on such a basis, for there would be no room for *law and order*." Since justice is the fundamental principle of morally organized societies "any transference of moral responsibility for an evil act from the person who committed it to someone else would be totally unethical." This leads Zizioulas to claim that heroic ascesis is "inapplicable to social life." The logic of penitential love which comes from the Kingdom is at odds with the logic of justice rooted in history. Zizioulas rejects political theology because heroic ascesis is not sustainable as a rational or practical ethic, just as the social gospel is not sustainable as a faithful theology.[28]

Second, Zizioulas argues that adopting heroic ascesis as the foundational principle for social ethics would be self-defeating. He explains: "Love cannot be turned into an institution. This is not to say that the Church could ever be inactive in the world: when someone is hungry, you share food with him. . . . [The Church's] action is personal, rather than institutional. . . . If charity becomes managed and administered, the Church will be driven by secular imperatives and cease to love, for love must always be free."[29] Zizioulas worries that if heroic ascesis, which imitates the crucifixion and awaits the eschatological Kingdom, is institutionalized, it will devolve into a secularized social gospel which passes over the crucifixion and attempts to achieve the eschatological Kingdom by its own efforts. In other words, political theology shifts the task of taking responsibility for the other away from the individual and toward an impersonal institution, which cannot help but treat its ethicopolitical goals as ends in themselves rather than penitential prerequisites of Eucharistic participation; political theology is all politics and no theology.

Zizioulas presents a reasonable case for the incompatibility of eucharistic ecclesiology and political theology. However, his rejection of political theology seems to confirm the charge that his eucharistic ecclesiology entails that the Church is purely eschatological and thus ceases to exist in the historical world between liturgies. Outside the liturgy, the Church disperses into individuals with common beliefs and a selfless, penitential commitment to others. The irony of this position is that if these individual Christians come together and form an organized structure by which they may more effectively and comprehensively accept responsibility for others, then, according to Zizioulas's logic, these individuals thereby cease to love rather than increase their love. But Zizioulas does not have the last word on the topic. There are other ways to construe the relationship between eucharistic ecclesiology and political theology that aim to uncover their compatibility.

CAVANAUGH AND POLITICAL THEOLOGY

Like Zizioulas, William Cavanaugh also claims that the Eucharistic event constitutes the Church as both eschatological and historical. But in contrast to Zizioulas, Cavanaugh seeks to show that the Eucharist is directly involved in ethics and politics. For Cavanaugh, "the Eucharist is the ongoing action of Christ in the Spirit to go out from the altar into the streets and reconcile the world to the Father."[30] The result is that while Zizioulas struggles to explain how the eschatological Eucharist can enter into history, Cavanaugh struggles to explain how the historical Eucharist can transcend history.

Cavanaugh sets up his eucharistic political theology by appealing to the liturgical theology of Alexander Schmemann. In contrast to theologians like Louis-Marie Chauvet, for whom the liturgy can be defined as a Christian ritual which occupies a liminal position between the sacred and the profane, Cavanaugh claims that for Schmemann the Christian liturgy calls the sacred/profane distinction into question.[31] Cavanaugh explains that "the liturgy of the Church enacts a foretaste of the Kingdom on earth, which signifies precisely the blessing and transformation of everyday life. The cordoning off of a separate 'sacred' realm is precisely the denial of the eschatological import of the Church's liturgy, because it reinforces the status quo of worldly order."[32] Thus Cavanaugh argues that "the Eucharist spills well beyond the confines of the altar and out into the world. . . . Members of the Body of Christ who participate in the Eucharist take the social action performed and envisioned in the action of the altar out into the streets and invite others to participate."[33] Cavanaugh calls his eucharistic political theology a "counter-politics" because it is "deeply involved in the sufferings of this world" and is therefore neither otherworldly and sectarian nor amenable to the "politics of the world which killed its savior."[34] For Cavanaugh, "the point is not to politicize the Eucharist, but to 'eucharistize' the world."[35]

For examples of "eucharistizing" the world, Cavanaugh turns to the work of the Vicariate of Solidarity and the Sebastian Acevedo Movement in Chile under the Pinochet regime. Both of these were Christian activist groups whose activities neither directly depended on the celebration of the Eucharistic liturgy nor excluded non-Christians from participation. Still Cavanaugh makes the strong claim that their actions were eucharistic in the proper sense and not the weaker claim that their activities simply share certain ritualistic commonalities with the Eucharist. "The point," says Cavanaugh, "is rather that the same Spirit of Christ who makes the Church in the Eucharist, who calls together bodies into the Kingdom of God, is also at work in these movements producing new types of social bodies . . . that participate in the Body of Christ."[36]

Yet despite his rejection of the sacred/secular distinction, Cavanaugh employs a similar distinction between the liturgical Eucharist and the historical or political Eucharist when he admits that the Church's "politics will always be infected with finitude and sin,"[37] and that the Eucharist judges and calls into question not only the world's politics but the Church's politics as well.[38] So if the Eucharist really does spill beyond the confines of the altar and into the world, it is ineluctably tainted and diluted with finitude and sin in the process. The problem is that Cavanaugh needs the liturgical Eucharist to manifest the perfection of the eschaton in order for it to stand in authoritative judgment over the imperfect politics of both the world and the Church. Therefore, if certain social and political actions can be called Eucharistic, it is only insofar as they are attempting to imitate the eschatological Kingdom within history and not because God is at work in them in the same way that God is at work in the liturgy. To suggest otherwise entails that either (a) these social and political actions manifest the perfection of the eschaton just as the liturgical Eucharist does or (b) the liturgical Eucharist is infected with finitude and sin just as our social and political actions are. But, as we have just seen, Cavanaugh explicitly rejects the former and implicitly rejects the latter. Thus, Cavanaugh's contention that political actions can be Eucharistic seems ultimately untenable.

Cavanaugh covers over the difference between the perfection of the liturgical Eucharist and the imperfection of political activities that imitate the Eucharist by arguing that "the holiness of the church is visible in its very repentance for its sin."[39] He reasons that

> Sin is not just something that obscures the true nature of the church, any more than the cross was just an unfortunate thing that happened to Jesus in the course of his salvation of the world. Sin is an inescapable part of the church *in via,* just as the cross is an essential part of the drama of salvation. The existence of sinful humanity in the church does not simply impede the redemption that Christ works in human history, but is itself part of the story of that redemption. . . . However, the story can only be told in a penitential key.[40]

For Cavanaugh, political actions are eucharistic when they visibly express the holiness of the Church through repentance. "The church's proper response to being taken up into the life of God is not smug assurance of its own purity, but humble repentance for its sin and a constant impulse to reform."[41] Cavanaugh even cites Zizioulas's use of the desert Fathers—that is, Nilus of Ancyra and Zosimas—but he reads these Fathers somewhat differently than Zizioulas. Referring to self-condemnation and taking on the sins of others, Cavanaugh writes:

> The distinction between my sin and your sin is relativized. Christ himself has obliterated this distinction, choosing to take on the sins of others in his suffering on the cross. Those who would follow this act of kenosis must do likewise, and recognize the solidarity of all sinners. To do so is simultaneously to recognize the social nature of holiness, which is visible precisely in the penitence of the church.[42]

In contrast to Zizioulas, who stresses the personal nature of repentance as a precondition for communion in the Eucharist, Cavanaugh focuses on the social dimension of both the Eucharist and repentance. For Cavanaugh, social sin is overcome by social communion—which takes place both within and beyond the liturgy. But here again Cavanaugh relies on something similar to the sacred/secular distinction; this time elaborated as the difference between the sinless perfection of the liturgical Eucharist, which takes us up into the life of God, and the sinful imperfection of the historical Eucharist, which, like the Cross, is an inescapable part of the penitential story of redemption.

The Eucharistic event does not spill out into the streets and take on an ethicopolitical character, as Cavanaugh claims, without undergoing a fundamental change. By Cavanaugh's own logic, inside the liturgy the Eucharist is an eschatological gift of communion, but outside the liturgy it is a finite and sinful response to finite and sinful historical realities. Therefore, we cannot speak of the Eucharist in the streets without equivocation. Still, even if Cavanaugh's contention that the Eucharist overflows the confines of the liturgy is problematic, his avowal of the social nature of repentance is a helpful corrective to Zizioulas's pessimism regarding political theology.

THE EUCHARIST AND POLITICAL THEOLOGY

Both Zizioulas and Cavanaugh distinguish the perfection of the eschatological Eucharist from the sinfulness of the historical world and argue that living the Eucharist in the world is defined by repentance. However, they define the relationship between the Eucharist and repentance in different ways. For Zizioulas, ascetical repentance is a precondition of eucharistic participation and therefore culminates in the Eucharist. But for Cavanaugh, repentance is somehow identified with the Eucharist as its extraliturgical manifestation or fulfillment. Or more to the point, repentance is a consequence of the eucharistic event, the overflowing of eucharistic communion out into the streets in the form of political activism. In short (and perhaps to oversimplify the difference), Zizioulas claims that ascetic repentance precedes the eucharistic event, while Cavanaugh holds that the eucharistic event precedes ascetic repentance.[43]

Now, there are a number of good reasons for siding with Zizioulas over Cavanaugh regarding the relationship between the Eucharist and repentance. Just as the eschaton is the end of history, surely the eschatological Eucharist is the end of historical ascesis and repentance. This is why the sacrament of penitence precedes, and is a precondition of, participation in the Eucharist, and why communicants confess themselves to be "chief among sinners" in the liturgy immediately before the Eucharist. Moreover, this is why ascetic fasting during the week is not a continuation of the previous Eucharist but a preparation for the next Eucharist—penitentially remembering Christ's betrayal and crucifixion in expectation of the Resurrection which is celebrated on Sunday as the eschatological Eighth Day.

Yet Cavanaugh's emphasis on the continuity of the liturgical Church with the historical Church can help provide a solution to Zizioulas's inability to justify the existence of the Church outside of the liturgy. Sunday is not only the Eighth Day but also the first; it is both eschatological and historical. The liturgy proclaims the Eucharist as "for the forgiveness of sins, and for life everlasting"—a twofold blessing that signals the two dimensions of the event. On the one hand, the Eucharist is part of a historical cycle wherein it both requires and begets repentance for the sake of forgiveness and spiritual progress toward greater depths of ascetic repentance; and on the other hand, it is a proleptic culmination and eschatological end of this historical cycle. There is both continuity and discontinuity between the community that repents and the community that celebrates the Eucharist. The Eucharist is simultaneously a spur to repentance and also the end of repentance.

But even if we acknowledge the two dimensions of the relationship between the Eucharist and ascetic repentance, it does not necessarily follow that eucharistic ecclesiology can be reconciled with political theology. Recall that Zizioulas poses two potent objections to turning ascetic repentance into an organized social struggle. In sum, he claims that ascetic repentance is at odds with justice and that institutionalized ascetic repentance becomes involuntary and leads to secularization. To respond, we must first question the opposition between repentance and justice. Zizioulas declares,

> It would be inconceivable to regulate social life [according to heroic ascesis], for there would be no room for *law and order* if this attitude to the Other were to become a principle of ethics. Given that justice is a fundamental principle of ethics and law, any transference of moral responsibility for an evil act from the person who committed it to someone else would be totally unethical.[44]

The claim is that a society regulated by a principle of ascetic repentance would necessarily reject law and order in favor of unjustly transferring responsibility from the guilty to the innocent. But such a society would not, in fact, be regulated by ascetic repentance. For if the transference of moral responsibility to an innocent person is imposed rather than freely accepted, then it is no longer repentance. Such a society would not have abandoned law and order but simply chosen to order itself according to unjust laws. Thus, Zizioulas is correct to say that "it would be inconceivable to regulate social life on such a basis," but this is not because ascetic repentance would leave no room for law and order. In fact, repentance presupposes law and order. Without some form of law and a sense of justice, we cannot judge good and evil; and we cannot repent for sin if we cannot recognize it.[45] Heroic ascesis begins with an understanding of justice but views it as a means rather than an end in itself. The two are not antithetical; rather, heroic ascesis exceeds the limits of justice.

Zizioulas's second objection to political theology concerns its tendency to reduce the Church to an institution with a social agenda in competition with other secular institutions. He argues:

> The Church is transcendent of secular institutions, so it does not compete with them. As a sign of the limits and transience of all institutions, the Church prevents every worldly claim from becoming totalitarian. . . . The Church can live

in the world without becoming absorbed into organized social outreach or into politics, just as it can without retreating into quietism.[46]

Because the Church exists from the eschatological future, it is not transient but transcendent. Zizioulas warns that if the Church commits to "worldly claims," then it loses its transcendent identity; it ceases to be the Church. Instead, the Church is meant to proclaim the eschatological Kingdom and prophetically expose the limitations of "worldly claims" and politics. To avoid secularization, Zizioulas reasons that the Church's ascetic love and mission in the world must be practiced on a personal, rather than institutional, basis: "When someone is hungry, you share food with him. The more of your eschatological identity you carry with you, the more you will love and come to the aid of whoever needs your help, whatever it costs you."[47] Outside of the liturgy, the Church disbands into isolated individuals, which, as noted above, seems to preclude the community of the faithful from historical existence. For Zizioulas, if the Church exists in the world, it does so as a secular institution.

As we have already seen in our discussion of Cavanaugh, Zizioulas is right to point out the difficulty of reconciling the historical and eschatological dimensions of the Church. By rejecting the sacred/secular distinction and claiming that "the Eucharist is the ongoing action of Christ in the Spirit to go out from the altar into the streets and reconcile the world to the Father," Cavanaugh implies that either the historical world is sinless as part of the eschatological communion of the Eucharist, or that the eschatological communion of the Eucharist is sinful as part of the historical world—neither of which is theologically acceptable. While it would be a mistake to conclude that Cavanaugh's political theology is therefore purely secular, Zizioulas's objection to political theology helps explain why Cavanaugh has trouble allying the transcendent Eucharist with transient concerns. But perhaps Zizioulas goes too far in suggesting that a eucharistic political theology is impossible. Indeed, there are other ways to articulate a political theology grounded in eucharistic ecclesiology.

Aristotle Papanikolaou has Cavanaugh in mind when he laments that "what the eucharistic and communion ecclesiologies do not fully nuance is how Christians do not live up to being Christians."[48] His point is that if eschatological communion is foretasted in the Eucharist and then taken out into the streets, then we should expect churches to be virtually sinless communities of selfless love working to transform the world around them. The fact that eucharistic communities fail to live up to this expectation, "does not negate the validity of [eucharistic ecclesiology], but it does mitigate the claim of identification of the Eucharist with the kingdom of God."[49] Papanikolaou argues that eucharistic ecclesiology expects too much from the Eucharist and not enough from the faithful.

Papanikolaou's solution is to incorporate the Christian ascetical tradition into eucharistic political theology. Even though "the Church is most Church in the Eucharistic assembly," the Church images the eschatological Kingdom in ascesis as much as in the Eucharist. Thus, "some eucharistic assemblies image the *eschaton* to a greater degree than other communities, and this difference in degree depends on how each of the individual members of the community are integrating into their lives the ascetical spirituality of the tradition."[50]

Papanikolaou is particularly interested in "the political space" as "an arena of ascetical struggle" in which Christians find "an opportunity to move toward deeper love of God and neighbor."[51] But in the sphere of secular politics, the goal of imaging the Kingdom of God must be reimagined as pursuing the "common good" for all people, regardless of religious commitments. For Papanikolaou, the common good is not identical to the eschatological good, just as the Eucharist is not identical with the eschatological Kingdom; the Eucharist "is the realization of a proleptic communion . . . analogically related to the eschatological good."[52] But in this case, the Eucharistic event seems entirely inconsequential, both for political theology and for the Church. Though Papanikolaou recognizes that "the very point of asceticism is . . . a movement toward a communal Eucharistic act," his notion of ascesis as proleptic and analogical communion leaves nothing for the Eucharist to offer that is not already achieved by ascesis. By "mitigating" the identification of the Eucharist with the Kingdom and making ascesis proleptic and analogical, Papanikolaou reduces the Eucharist to a ritualized expression of an already realized communion; the Eucharist is made redundant. Papanikolaou's political theology expects too much from ascesis and not enough from the Eucharist. Thus, in different ways, the political theologies of Papanikolaou and Cavanaugh seem to confirm Zizioulas's objection to political theology. Both theologians struggle to reconcile the transience of "worldly claims" with the transcendence of the Eucharistic event because they make the communion offered in the Eucharist available outside of the liturgy.

The only way to preserve the centrality of the Eucharist is to acknowledge it as a unique possibility of proleptic, eschatological communion. Thus, Zizioulas is right to point out that the "ontological grace" offered by the Eucharist is "acquired only to be lost again, until on the last day it will be acquired definitively." But Zizioulas portrays this experience as an individual loss and therefore as a call to individual repentance rather than a communal loss and a call to communal repentance.

Cavanaugh is helpful here. His reading of the desert Fathers points out the "deeply social nature" of sin and repentance. In fact, ascetic repentance cannot be an individual endeavor because it entails a recognition of the solidarity of all humans as sinners, complicit in the fallen nature of the world. There are evils in the world for which the repentance of individuals is inadequate. Individuals cannot take responsibility for large-scale or systemic evils. Social evil requires social repentance.

Even though the faithful lose the ontological grace of communion upon leaving the liturgical space, this momentary grace remains present with them in the form of a moral imperative for penitential communion. Political theology risks secularizing the Church only to the extent that it confuses the moral imperative for secular communion with the sacred foretaste of ontological communion. But when political theology is identified with penitence, the Church is able to maintain the priority of sacred communion without trivializing secular forms of communion.

CONCLUSION: EUCHARISTIC ECCLESIOLOGY AND POLITICS AS PENITENCE

If the goal of political theology is to articulate a way in which the Church may be actively involved *in* the world without being *of* the world, then it seems perfectly reasonable to identify the Eucharistic event as the paradigmatic political act of the Church because the Eucharist is the nexus of history and the eschaton. This can be fleshed out in one of two ways: either the Eucharist is politicized or politics is eucharistized. In the former case, the Church becomes insular and segregated from the world because it makes political decisions and actions as exclusive as the sacraments. In the latter, the Church all but loses its identity by sacrificing the uniqueness and exclusivity of its sacraments for the sake of finding common cause with the world. If these are the only options, then the Church must choose between preserving its faith commitments and participating in the public sphere.

But there is a third option. In order to reconcile eucharistic ecclesiology with political theology, we must recognize that even though the Eucharist cannot be political and politics cannot be eucharistic, the two are inseparable insofar as the Eucharist demands repentance and repentance is political. Eucharistic ecclesiology teaches the Church to engage the world penitentially, to see politics as penitence, and vice versa. As Alexander Solzhenitsyn writes: "The gift of repentance, which perhaps more than anything else distinguishes man from the animal world, is particularly difficult for modern man to recover. . . . Repentance is the first bit of firm ground underfoot, the only one from which we can go forward not to fresh hatreds but to concord."[53]

The Church's political mission is to repent and thereby call the world to repentance by example. The political Church does not condemn sinners but stands in solidarity with them in recognition of a common affliction. Likewise, the Eucharist does not teach us how to live in the Kingdom but how far we are from the Kingdom. It demands that we live our lives in the manner of Abba Bessarion who upon seeing a sinner turned out of the church arose and joined him saying, "I, too, am a sinner."[54] The Eucharist not only makes the Church, it makes the Church repent.

NOTES

1. John D. Zizioulas, *Lectures in Christian Dogmatics*, ed. Douglas H. Knight (New York: T&T Clark, 2008), 153.
2. Maximus the Confessor, *Commentary on the Ecclesiastical Hierarchy*, PG 4: 137; John Zizioulas, *The Eucharistic Communion and the World*, ed. Luke Ben Tallon (New York: T&T Clark, 2011), 44.
3. Zizioulas, *Eucharistic Communion*, 45.
4. Zizioulas, *Christian Dogmatics*, 155.
5. Miroslav Volf, *After Our Likeness: The Church as the Image of the Trinity* (Grand Rapids, MI: Eerdmans, 1998), 101.
6. Ibid., 101.
7. Ibid., 102.
8. Ibid.
9. Ibid.
10. Zizioulas, *Eucharistic Communion*, 129.
11. Ibid., 130.
12. Ibid.
13. Ibid., 131.
14. Ibid., 80.
15. Ibid.
16. Zizioulas, *Eucharistic Communion*, 130.
17. In contrast, Nicholas Loudovikos draws from Maximus the Confessor to argue that "icon" and "mimesis" mutually imply one another such that the Eucharist not only participates in the Kingdom but also imitates it. Furthermore, participation and imitation are available outside the Eucharistic event as well through the divine energies. Thus, Palamite theology leads Loudovikos ultimately to reject eucharistic ecclesiology in favor of an "apophatic ecclesiology." Nicholas Loudovikos, "*Eikon* and *mimesis*: Eucharistic ecclesiology and the ecclesial ontology of dialogical reciprocity," *International Journal for the Study of the Christian Church* 11, nos. 2–3 (2011): 123–26; *Church in the Making: An Apophatic Ecclesiology of Consubstantiality* (Yonkers, NY: St. Vladimir's Seminary Press, 2016).
18. Zizioulas, *Eucharistic Communion*, 76.

19. John D. Zizioulas, *Communion and Otherness: Further Studies in Personhood and the Church*, ed. Paul McPartlan (New York: T&T Clark, 2006), 85.

20. Ibid., 84.

21. Ibid.

22. Nilus, PG 79: 1249; Zizioulas, *Communion and Otherness*, 82.

23. In a study of early Eastern asceticism, Alexis Torrance establishes a hermeneutical framework for interpreting references to repentance in the New Testament and Church Fathers: "Three forms of repentance make up the proposed interpretative framework: 1) an initial repentance, applied to the beginning or new beginning of Christian life, wherein the person takes stock of his or her life, and turns it Godward; 2) an existential repentance, applied to the Christian life more generally, wherein the way of the Christian is, at root, one of μετάνοια; 3) Christ-like repentance, in which the Christian effectively repents for other people, bearing their sin and healing their estrangement, by virtue of the gift of Christ" (*Repentance in Late Antiquity: Eastern Asceticism and the Framing of the Christian Life c. 400–650 CE* [Oxford: Oxford University Press, 2012], 47).

24. Zizioulas, *Communion and Otherness*, 82–83.

25. Ibid., 82–83, n. 183.

26. Ibid., 83.

27. Ibid., 4.

28. Ibid., 87.

29. Zizioulas, *Christian Dogmatics*, 127.

30. William T. Cavanaugh, "The Church in the Streets: Eucharist and Politics," *Modern Theology* 30, no. 2 (2014): 392.

31. Ibid., 388.

32. Ibid.

33. Ibid., 391.

34. William T. Cavanaugh, *Torture and Eucharist: Theology, Politics, and the Body of Christ* (Oxford: Blackwell, 1998), 14.

35. Ibid., 14.

36. Cavanaugh, "The Church in the Streets," 391.

37. Ibid., 392.

38. Ibid., 389.

39. William T. Cavanaugh, *Migrations of the Holy: God, State, and the Political Meaning of the Church* (Grand Rapids, MI: Eerdmans, 2011), 165.

40. Ibid., 163.

41. Ibid., 165.

42. Ibid., 166.

43. To be clear, Cavanaugh rejects the use of the Eucharistic event as a model to be imitated subsequently in the world. Instead he includes the Church's action in the world within the very definition of the Eucharist. Still, the liturgical dimension of the Eucharist precedes the historical/political dimension.

44. Zizioulas, *Communion and Otherness*, 87.

45. Cf. Romans 7:7.

46. Zizioulas, *Christian Dogmatics*, 127.
47. Ibid.
48. Aristotle Papanikolaou, *The Mystical as Political: Democracy and Non-Radical Orthodoxy* (Notre Dame, IN: University of Notre Dame Press, 2012), 85.
49. Aristotle Papanikolaou, "Integrating the Ascetical and the Eucharistic: Current Challenges in Orthodox Ecclesiology," *International Journal for the Study of the Christian Church* 11, nos. 2–3 (2011): 184.
50. Papanikolaou, "Integrating the Ascetical and the Eucharistic," 186.
51. Papanikolaou, *The Mystical as Political*, 154.
52. Ibid., 157.
53. Alexander Solzhenitsyn, "Repentance and Self-Limitation in the Life of Nations," in *The Solzhenitsyn Reader: New and Essential Writings 1947–2005*, eds. Edward E. Ericson Jr. and Daniel F. Mahoney (Wilmington, DE: ISI Books, 2006), 529–30.
54. Benedicta Ward, ed., *The Sayings of the Desert Fathers, The Alphabetical Collection* (Kalamazoo, MI: Cistercian Publications, 1975), 42.

Chapter Fifteen

How Realistic Are Christian Politics?
A Case for Eschatological Realism
Logan M. Isaac

Long before Oxford moral philosopher and Christian Realist Nigel Biggar reacted against the "wishful thinking" of pacifism in his 2013 monograph, *In Defence of War*, Mennonite theologian John Howard Yoder lampooned realists as "pie in the sky" for their failure to articulate a biblically realistic account of secular political claims upon Christians. Christian realism, associated with Reinhold Niebuhr, was a reaction against the Social Gospel movement of the late nineteenth century, which sought to change the world for the better through good Christian deeds. Niebuhr sensed a hint of Pelagianism and was concerned that the theology behind the movement had a dangerously naïve theology of sin; he focused his work on reminding the Church that our place within a fallen world sometimes called for necessary but limited evil to restrain humanity's inclination toward atrocity. Yoder's trepidation about realism, on the other hand, was that even well-intentioned means without an end can rationalize any evil by attaching means to poorly defined and inadequately shared goods, such as justice. Indeed, a central criticism by pacifists is the realist impulse to control history through political violence.[1] Can we have both realism and pacifism, or does being one necessarily exclude us from being the other?

REALISM VERSUS PACIFISM

Following WWII, the question of war and peace was dominated by Niebuhr's realist school of thought. Niebuhr's political realism contributed to America's reluctant entrance into WWII and continued to hold sway well into the conflict in Korea and America's entry into Vietnam. Politics, for Niebuhr, rotate around a mixture of power and desire. In his essay "Augustine's Political Realism,"[2] Niebuhr explains political and moral realism as "the disposition to take all factors in a social and political situation which offer resistance to established norms into account, particularly the factors of self-interest and power."[3]

He critiqued pacifism for its sectarian attitude toward the world in which it lived and was dependent upon. Namely, pacifism failed to be considerate of the reality of a pluralistic world in which conflicting interests, while ideally mediated by mutuality and political compromise, were (in "reality") settled by recourse to violence. According to Niebuhr, a world without violence was a utopian ideal, an "illusion,"[4] which he combatted via appeals to realism. Walter Rauschenbusch's Social Gospel movement of the late nineteenth century was the primary target for Niebuhr's theology, which he insisted held a too optimistic (and heretical) view of human nature. As the political unfolding of Social Gospel theology, pacifism held too optimistic a view of international relations and represented an unrealistic "idealism." Pacifism was irresponsible, failing to acknowledge what he saw as the reality human sinfulness, "the power and persistence of self-love,"[5] and the clear necessity of intervening violence to keep evil in check.

Following the disastrous results of the war in Vietnam, however, Yoder gained prominence as a proponent of pacifism by directly countering the realist school of thought. In his magnum opus, *The Politics of Jesus*, Yoder satirically referred to his own methodology as "Biblical realism" in a direct shot across the bow of Niebuhr's use of the qualifier "Christian."[6] As a member of the Anabaptist branch of Christian denominations, he knew he entered the fray as an underdog both numerically and theologically. He cites Niebuhr's 1935 *Interpretation of Christian Ethics* specifically as representative of a "mainstream" way of doing political theology.[7]

Yoder coined the term "Biblical realism" primarily (if not exclusively) as a dig against realism, since he saw Niebuhr as playing down the role of the Bible in shaping Christian convictions in the political sphere. It is no coincidence, for example, that the classical tenets of the just war criteria are not modeled after Biblical precepts; though, thanks in part to Niebuhr's popular appeal, they enjoyed massive revival leading up to the two world wars.[8] In fact, a key tenet of disagreement between pacifism and realism is the nature of Christology and the incarnation. Realists emphasize the sacramental nature of Jesus in his role as priest in the *munus triplex*. As priest, his primary function is sacerdotal, not exemplary. The emphasis is on Christ's, rather than human, agency.

Pacifists like Yoder, meanwhile, will often insist that fundamental to the incarnation, and indeed to the entirety of God's self-disclosure in "the Word" as both Christ and scripture, is an ethic of imitation. Yoder specifically cites

Niebuhr's 1935 *Interpretation* as opposing the "ethic of imitation" by which pacifism is known. Pacifism argues that central to Jesus's role as priest is to be an example to follow by *all believers* as "a royal priesthood, a holy nation."[9] Rather than focusing on Jesus as priest, however, their main arguments usually focus on Jesus as king, as sovereign over the whole world, ruling as he is from "the right hand of the throne of God."[10]

Crucial to this debate is therefore the nature of the kingdom that is often described as being both "now and not yet." Realists emphasize the *not yet*, seeing a world at war to which the Church is responsible as neighbor and which Christ will finally redeem at his second coming or *parousia*.[11] For them, the kingdom will be consummated and cannot be ushered forward by any human effort. Pacifists, on the other hand, emphasize the *now*, insisting that the kingdom comes "on earth as it is in heaven" precisely by the community called to discipleship by embodying Christian principles; the kingdom has been inaugurated and is now breaking forth into the world through the witness of the saints.

However, Yoder's claims about the Bible are only coherent within a community for which scripture is existentially foundational. If the Kingdom is really "real," then which camp can or should be using the term "realism" and what does it have to do with ontology, the attempts by fallible, finite humans to define actual, infinite reality itself? If scripture is to be ontologically determinative, then it means that Christians must derive our definition of "reality" by starting with the Word of God, not with what we perceive. As creatures corrupted from birth, our very ability to sense or reason is touched by sin; we cannot do so clearly, but "in a mirror, dimly."[12] If the Church precedes the world in every way, then we do not owe the world justice, or even peace, but honesty. As Yoder's disciple Stanley Hauerwas phrases it, "the first task of the Church is to make the world the world, not to make the world more just."[13] No matter what we think or see when we hear of war and rumors of war, the world is in fact "very good."[14]

Therefore, if we look at the world and believe it is bad because it is filled with violence, then we believe a type of lie, perhaps even our own. Creatures *doing* bad does not mean they *are* bad, and if they are in fact very good, then eschatological realism will serve as an ontological anchor, pulling us into the creatures God made us to be by insisting that to be realistic is to live into who and what we truly are.

I agree with Yoder that holding to the doctrine of *prima scriptura* is profoundly realistic and, with him, I object to realist claims that biblical pacifism is reducible to "prophetic irrelevance."[15] But more than simply filling out the wrinkles of his discarded verbiage, I want to explore a particular kind of Biblical realism in light of claims Yoder makes about the centrality of pacifism for Christian ethics, one which includes a robust eschatology.[16] Before we can do that, we must look at the parallels between what we have been calling realism and the study of reality itself, of ontology.

REALISM AND ONTOLOGY

Besides Augustine, Niebuhr also derives his realism from Machiavelli, for whom "the purpose of the realist is 'to follow *the truth* of the matter rather than the imagination of it.'"[17] It follows that politics is necessary in order for nations to interact with minimal violence; diplomacy, negotiation, and conflict being tangible manifestations of politics for the realist. In Niebuhr's essay on Augustine's political realism, he is careful to differentiate between "political and metaphysical theory," the former being the subject of his inquiry and the latter falling outside his purview. However, the distinction between politics and metaphysics is not clear, for precisely what he can mean by truth is open to debate. An account of truth implies a metaphysics, must derive from an account of ultimate reality, but Niebuhr reduces "truth" in his essay to the same "social realities" which criticizes idealists for failing to appreciate. This double-speak undermines his argument by relativizing the "truth" which both realists and idealists supposedly follow.[18]

The reality is that politics has a story. For Aristotle, politics signified the organization of human relationships in order to create and preserve goods, material and immaterial alike. Natural resources and manufactured goods were as worthy of being held in common as were virtues like courage or wisdom. Goods served the purpose of preserving the *polis*, or city-state, and of promoting the highest good as justly as possible. The modern world, however, produced a distinction between public and private spheres of life, thereby reducing "politics" to a derogatory term connoting the public exercise of *power over* goods. What is meant by "polis" went from city-state to the whole world, a cosmo-polis. Historian Roland Bainton insists this cannot fit with the Greek usage, as the city-states, "sovereign states of approximately equal strength" were one of many; a peer among regional entities exercising "relative equality of power."[19] No such balance exists in the modern world, nor could it possibly exist if polis means the entire earth, for where would we find its peer?

Modern notions of politics instead focus on conflicting self-interests and the power dynamics necessary to maintain their tenuous balance. Nowhere is this more apparent than in international relations, defined as it is by recurring violence. Goods have lost their meaning in the same way politics has been reinvented to imply power and self-interest. Divorced from telos, from purpose and function, one can rationalize any evil by attaching method to poorly defined and inadequately shared goods. For whom is a war just? The victors. It should come as no surprise that a central criticism by pacifists is the realist impulse to control the world through political violence. But the permissibility of violence for realists only makes sense if reality is primarily defined by the material realm, what Niebuhr would call "political realism."

Ingolf Dalferth's essay on Karl Barth's eschatological realism outlines three major realms in which realist claims engage, namely ontology, semantics, and epistemology.[20] In the interest of time, we will only touch on the first two. According to Dalferth, "Ontologically, the realist holds that there is a reality independent of the human mind and our social constructions of reality."[21] Which is to say that reality exists apart from our means of representing it. A second element of realism, one we will return to later, is that semantically, realism maintains that "truth [cannot] be reduced to verifiability."[22] In other words, just because one cannot verify that something is real, that does not mean it fails to be real.[23]

What Niebuhr called "metaphysical realism," based rather on an *immaterial* meaning, may be a stand in for ontology and is a very close parallel to eschatology. A Christian "metaphysical reality" is determined not by reason, but by revelation. For Niebuhr, the intelligibility of reality was critical, for to journey beyond reason was to enter the realm of illusion. Unfortunately he crafts few constructive claims about realism, with a vast majority of his essay spent critiquing "idealism."[24] Reality, however, is not the absence of illusion any more than peace is the absence of war. Yoder's criticism zeroed in on this, insisting that a politics without eschatology was a politics without Christ, and a Christian account of the world without Christ at its head is not only heretical, but also ontologically inconceivable.

Niebuhr resisted what he saw as the idealist impulse to imagine that a better world exists or is possible by human hands, insisting instead on what he (or Machiavelli) called "the truth of the matter." A Yoderian account, on the other hand, insists that reality is a product of divine creative intent, not dependent upon finite human intellect, begun for and oriented toward a nonviolent "end." Scripture makes it clear that God ordained a body, not a program or institutions, to bear witness to the nature and totality of creation's subordination to its Creator. Applying eschatology to political realism gives Christians a glimpse at their distance from God precisely so that they make apparent the world's inability to discover its own being apart from the Word of God.

If Christ is indeed Lord and present as the Word when the world was created *ex nihilo*, then the God to whom Jesus and his body bear witness determines reality, the Word is ontologically determinative. An essentially human institution, religious or secular, is inherently finite and highly suspect as an interpreter of reality insofar as reality is radically independent of humanity. Niebuhrian realism, therefore, is problematic as long as it ascribes "reality" to a location other than the world revealed by Scripture. What realists might be calling "reality," Yoder turned the tables by insisting realism was in fact a creaturely construct and therefore ultimately illusory.

This begs to the ultimate question Christ poses, "Who do you say that I am?"[25] If Christ is really Lord, the very Word present at and for Creation, then the world is ontologically determined by a particular person, namely the incarnate Son of God, who by Christ truly affirmed the (real) world we see when we look out our windows. Furthermore, God's self-disclosure through scripture makes the Bible a carrier of ontological determination. If this is all true, then no "realism" is truly Christian without a firm scriptural foundation.

John Zizioulas is helpful for constructing an eschatological realism as he shows that ontology must be about particularities like the life, death, and resurrection of a Jewish rabbi in first-century Palestine. Rather than deriving ontology from universals, what he calls "the closed ontology of the Greeks,"[26] the Christian tradition insists "being is caused in a radical way by *someone*— a particular being."[27] Sensible reality, which is to say the only reality to which human knowing has access, does not move from universal forms to particular substances, but from a particular person, one whose very name denies derivability and rejects human coherency, who calls themself "I am that I am." In other words, within a particularly scriptural ontology, a Biblical realism (to use the Yoderian phrase) "particularity is to be understood as causative and not derivative."[28] The same linguistic fluidity is reflected in the use of the name Israel to mean both the individual person who "wrestled with God" as well as the twelve tribes who carried on that pugilistic tradition. For finite creatures, being is derived via a uniquely Biblical phenomenon Zizioulas calls "corporate personality"[29] from "the person of Adam."

However, this might need to be teased out a bit. Zizioulas must mean something more like "first family" since Adam fails to be the "reality of communion"[30] that his account of personhood describes. Even with all the animals created in the search for a partner, Adam is alone in his creatureliness without another person, which God calls "not good."[31] The "corporate personality" of which Zizioulas writes is coherent only in *human* relationship. "Adam" has no such corporate-ness apart from the persons who made him "humanity" (namely, Eve). Likewise, "Israel" had no corporeality apart from the hypostasis of the twelve tribes that the name implied. The emphasis on corporate personality for the purposes of eschatological realism is intended to show that the ontology of humanity ought to derive from particular Biblical precepts, that scripture is ontologically determinative. This helps us see the way in which reality is coherent for Christians only insofar as it aligns with the central authoritative force common to our many diverse communities.

ESCHATOLOGICAL REALISM

As a distinctively eschatological task, realism reminds us that humanity both comes from and will return to God. As for the in between, the now-not-yet of the kingdom to which we are called, language is crucial. When translated as "end," the Greek *eskhatos* is pregnant with meaning. "End," after all, can mean both the chronological conclusion of time but also the purpose or function of a thing, in this case its *telos*. Therefore, human being is what Alan Torrance calls an "eschatological process of becoming."[32]

Insisting on a thick meaning of eschatology as "end" not only recovers the Aristotelian nuance of *polis* by insisting that politics has a *telos*, but it also unites the chronological inevitability to which humans are bound as creatures on the one hand, with the teleological trajectory of all creation as intended by its Creator on the other. A fundamental premise of a particularly scriptural account of reality insists that the Church, being Christ's body on earth, precedes the world ontologically and semantically. This is true both in a thin, chronological sense, in that the body of Christ existed at a time that precedes all creation, but also in a thick eschatological sense as well. It is not simply that God will bring *about* the end of the world, but that God *is* the end of the world.

Eschatological realists insist against the false assumption that sin is essential to human nature. Torrance may be one such realist, insisting "Properly functional human nature, therefore, requires to be conceived first and foremost eschatologically."[33] God being "the beginning and the end," the "alpha and omega," places teleology and eschatology in very close relationship. This helps us contextualize the canonical Biblical witness because it gives us a picture of what we truly are as creatures before sin attached itself to the world (Genesis 1 & 2) and what we are to become once more when sin has been finally been driven from our midst (Revelation 21 & 22).

Centering theological anthropologies in Genesis 3, as Niebuhr does, makes it impossible to adequately appraise sin and, in the process, it keeps us from fully understanding God. To speak of a "Fall" is already to speak of an elevated position as our normative, ontological state of moral or political being. To say that we are corrupted assumes the nature essential to our being precedes corruption. Though the world may appear to be ruled by the prince of darkness, looks can be deceiving. We are given a glimpse of who and whose we are in the apocalypses of our forebears, the poetry of Milton, in the fantasy of Tolkien, and the imagination of Bill Watterson. This is where Dalferth's second tenet about realism comes critically into play. In terms of semantics and meaning, "truth [cannot] be reduced to verifiability."[34] Although reality being independent of the human mind means we cannot conceive of it fully in truth, it also means realness radically surpasses the empirical method and the scope of human senses as a whole. Rather than trying to rationalize it, we might consider imagining it instead. In fact, imagining the totality of God's reign on earth is precisely what we get in apocalyptic literature of the prophets and peppered throughout the Gospels and the book of Acts. A biblical, eschatological imagination gives voice to the finitude of sensible human reason and perception, and it may be the best way to comprehend human being.

As for politics, an eschatologically determined definition of reality suggests Niebuhr had a low view of the real sovereignty Christ has over actual worldly affairs. If we privilege human perception, we will declare, with Niebuhr, that "the truth of the matter" is quite grim and requires the intervention of supposedly just violence. But Christ is with us, whether it looks like it or not, because we are in Christ. We do not derive politics from what we see and hear, but from who and whose we are, in whose image we are made.

Yoder's politic theology is ontologically sound insofar as it locates both sovereignty and functional anthropology outside this world we think we see. The nexus of reality, in Biblical terms, is not in this world dominated by corrupted humanity. It is somewhere else, somewhere synonymous with the heavens, where Christ rules from the right hand of the Father. What Paul calls "authorities" are not ultimate, only provisional. As Christ makes abundantly clear, they "would have no authority . . . at all unless it had been given you *from above*."[35] When Christ "comes again," it would be more accurate to call it a re-entry into the limits of creaturely sensible perception and chronological captivity. As for our genesis, sin does not alter our ontological substance, only attaches to it. Christ restores us to who we really are, which will be "new" only to us, not to God and therefore not "in reality" or in truth.

As for everyday life, an eschatological realism is political in as far as it is to be instructive to our daily lives, as far as it gives us an ethic for how to act in relationship with one another. With Yoder, we must affirm that Christ indeed provides an ethic to live by. This is not to reduce him to mere sage, as the historical Jesus quest has tried to do, but to elevate the *exemplary* function to equal status with the *sacramental*. Preeminent moral philosopher Alasdair MacIntyre insists, "The whole point of ethics . . . is to enable man to pass from his present state to his true end."[36] True end evokes both human telos as well as humanity's end as revealed by scripture. The fundamental claim made by an eschatological realism is that the church precedes the world in every way. Our creator determines who and what we are, and our being is derived from something that predates sin. Eschatological realism is neither unrealistic nor irresponsible, it is in keeping with the beings we were created to be and which our narrative trajectory clearly encompasses. The distinct political calling of the Church is to live "now" into the "not yet" eschatological vision, to theological performances that reveal the realness of the kingdom.

Let's pretend I have a friend, a friend who stretches the boundaries of what it means to be a friend, especially in the Aristotelian sense. This "friend" is kind of a jerk or at least he seems to be by all rational accounts. Being Biblically realistic might suggest we are to turn the other cheek if they strike us, or to go the extra mile if they burden us with their own heavy load. But being particularly eschatological in our dealings with them requires us rather to see and to believe that this person is in fact "very good," that his being a jerk is merely a ruse, a fleeting result of being temporarily captive to time and materiality as a finite being. Being realistic in this sense forces us not only to love our enemies, but to cease having them altogether. This is a realism that begins and ends with Jesus, a politics based not on what we see around us, but on the One who sees us and loves us despite our being jerks to him and to one another.

CONCLUSION

Though Niebuhr has reigned supreme as the major proponent of Christian realism, we have seen that in fact there are competing claims as to what a distinctively Christian realism must be. Against Niebuhr's account, pacifist Yoder referred to his Anabaptist exegetical methodology as Biblical realism, however cursory his titling may be. We recounted the overall trajectory of realism and discussed the implications of Yoder's emphasis, namely that any Biblical account of reality and being must focus especially upon the Bible and encompass a thick view of eschatology as not merely a chronological end but as humanity's teleological end as well. With the help of Barth and Zizioulas, we gestured toward such an eschatological realism that assumes ontological primacy in the Word of God, which is the body of Christ, before the world. This primacy assumes not just a political sovereignty but also ethical necessity. In all, we have sided with Yoder's realism but called attention to a need for greater focus on the particularities of the Bible, and the special relevance of apocalyptic literature for deriving a fuller perspective on human nature, its origins, and its end.

The political differences between the pacifist and realist claims, as I have described them, part most clearly on the question of the extent to which the eschaton is realized in the world we inhabit. In terms of scripture, the Cross must define reality, though pacifists and realists will disagree as to the material implications. Pacifists like Yoder emphasize an inaugurated eschatology, that Jesus's life was not merely sacramental but exemplary; he showed us how to live and gave little attention to the "political" machinations the world might concoct because their "reality" was fleeting and illusory (which only makes Niebuhr's modern rhetorical moves somewhat ironic). "The kingdom is here" might be the pacifist refrain. On the other hand, realists are hesitant to endorse such a theology because of the Pelagian influence the Social Gospel movement left, of God's kingdom being subject to human influence. Realists would emphasize that "the kingdom is coming." To hold these two in sharp contrast to one another is to hold a thin view of *eskhatos*, as though it can only be one or the other, only past or future. A thicker view of reality, one we have been calling eschatological realism, grounds itself not only in chronology, but teleology as well; the end is both anticipated as a future moment and yet mysteriously within each of us right now.

More work must be done to address the implications of an eschatological realism such as I have described. Perhaps most critically, moral philosophers and theological ethicists must continue to ask if and how human creatures realize the "end" for and toward which we have been created, if reality is truly determined by scripture. Further, to what extent is human captivity to (and observations of and through) time ontologically credible? If it is true that in our present state we see and think "dimly," then we would be wise to take our own observations with a grain of salt, especially if our conclusions tend toward descriptions that privilege our corrupted senses and intellect. An eschatological realism forces us to trust the authority of scripture for our definition of reality. We are to live as though the way it *will be* is the way it *is*, regardless of our finite human capacity to comprehend the world in all its richness, because "reality" is determined by God. Humans are called "very good," but we fell from our created state; we fell out of right relationship with God. As fallen creatures on the journey of redemption, or return to our true state, our telos is at an incline, it is not a flat path for the faint of heart.

NOTES

1. This claim is the sixth of ten in Stanley Hauerwas, "Reforming Christian Ethics: Ten Theses," in *The Hauerwas Reader* (Durham, NC: Duke University Press, 2001), 113.

2. Reinhold Niebuhr, *Christian Realism and Political Problems* (Fairfield, NJ: Augustus Kelley, 1966), chapter 9.

3. Niebuhr, *Problems*, 114.

4. According to Niebuhr, idealism is particularly marked by its pursuit of such illusions. Niebuhr favors this word in describing what he calls "idealism" throughout the essay.

5. Niebuhr, *Problems*, 138.

6. John Howard Yoder, *The Politics of Jesus: Vicit Agnus Noster* (Grand Rapids, MI: Ethics & Public Policy Center, 1972), viii, x, 4, 136.

7. Ibid., 4.

8. Phillip Wynn's book, *Augustine on War and Military Service* (Minneapolis, MN: Fortress Press, 2013) as well as Roland Bainton's *Christian Attitudes on War and Peace* (cited below) both describe the rise in interest in just war, and its misled attribution to Augustine, as having begun no earlier than the escalation of force that led to WWI.

9. 1 Peter 2:9, New Revised Standard Version. All citations of scripture, unless otherwise noted, are NRSV.

10. Hebrews 12:2.

11. The Latin word most commonly translated from Greek *parousia* is "advent." The ascension therefore was not a departure of Jesus, but an arrival, a *parousia* at the right hand of the Father, from which he *currently* rules over all of creation, all of reality. Karl Barth agrees, claiming that Easter and Pentecost are also "parousia" (*Church Dogmatics*, IV/3 [Peabody, MA: Hendrickson Publishers, 2010], 293 ff).

12. 1 Corinthians 13:12.

13. Stanley Hauerwas, *Hannah's Child: A Theologian's Memoir* (Grand Rapids, MI: Eerdmans, 2010), 158.

14. Genesis 1:31.

15. John Howard Yoder, *Christian Witness to the State* (Harrisonburg, VA: Herald Press, 2002), 7.

16. Yoder makes the connection between eschatology and pacifism abundantly clear in his essay, "Peace without Eschatology?" It originally appeared in 1961 but was published posthumously in *The Royal Priesthood*, ed. Michael Cartwright (Harrisonburg, VA: Herald Press, 1998), 143–67.

17. Niebuhr, *Problems*, 114. Emphasis added is my own. Niebuhr's reference to Machiavelli's fifteenth chapter of *The Prince* is not cited, but Marriott's 2006 translation is nearly word for word; "to follow up the real truth of the matter than the imagination of it."

18. Niebuhr, *Problems*, 114.

19. Roland Bainton, *Christian Attitudes to War and Peace* (Eugene, OR: Wipf & Stock, 2008), 33. Bainton insists this balance was what made these "Hellenic feuds" just and legal in the eyes of the Greeks.

20. Ingolf Dalferth, "Barth's Eschatological Realism," in *Karl Barth: Centenary Essays*, ed. S. W. Sykes (Cambridge: Cambridge University Press, 2009), 16–17.

21. Ibid., 16.

22. Ibid.

23. According to Robin Lovin in *Reinhold Niebuhr and Christian Realism* (New York: Cambridge University Press, 1995), three different "realisms" are considered

by Niebuhr: political, moral, and theological. More detail is also given in her *Christian Realism and the New Realities* (New York: Cambridge, 2008), 6–11.

24. Even Lovin identifies this as a problem with Niebuhr's work, saying "the meaning of 'realism' emerges primarily in a negative assessment of 'idealism'" (*Reinhold Niebuhr*, 4).

25. Matthew 16:15, Mark 8:29, Luke 9:20.

26. John Zizioulas, *Being as Communion* (Yonkers, NY: Saint Vladimir's Seminary Press, 1985), 39.

27. John Zizioulas, *Communion and Otherness* (New York: T&T Clark, 2006), 104.

28. Ibid., 104.

29. Ibid., 105.

30. Ibid., 107.

31. Genesis 2:18.

32. Alan Torrance, "Is There a Distinctive Human Nature? Approaching the Question from a Christian Epistemic Base," *Zygon* 47, no. 4 (2012): 907.

33. Torrance, "Distinctive," 912.

34. Dalferth, "Barth," 16.

35. John 19:10.

36. Alasdair MacIntyre, *After Virtue* (South Bend, IN: University of Notre Dame Press, 2010), 54.

Bibliography

Andreopoulos, Andreas. "Eschatology in Maximus the Confessor." In *The Oxford Handbook of Maximus the Confessor,* edited by Pauline Allen and Bronwen Neil, 32–40. New York: Oxford University Press, 2015.

Aquinas, Thomas. *The Summa Theologica of Thomas Aquinas*, vol. 1, Part 1. Translated by Fathers of the English Dominican Province. New York: Cosimo, 2007.

Aristotle. "Metaphysics." In *The Complete Works of Aristotle: The Revised Oxford Translation, vol. 2*, edited by Jonathan Barnes, translated by W. D. Ross, 1552–1728. Princeton: Princeton University Press, 1984.

Augustine. *Confessions*. Translated by Henry Chadwick. Oxford: Oxford University Press, 2008.

Bainton, Roland. *Christian Attitudes to War and Peace*. Eugene, OR: Wipf & Stock, 2008.

Baker, Matthew. "'Alles Verständnis ist Interpretation': Neo-Patristic Synthesis and Philosophical Hermeneutics—Georges Florovsky and Hans-Georg Gadamer in Conversation." Unpublished paper, 2012.

———. Unfinished PhD Diss., Fordham University, 2015.

Balthasar, Hans Urs von. *Cosmic Liturgy: The Universe according to Maximus the Confessor*. Translated by Brian E. Daley. A Communio Book. San Francisco: Ignatius Press, 2003.

———. *Kleiner Diskurs über die Hölle* (Einsiedelen: Johannes Verlag, 2007).

———. *Présence et pensée: essai sur la philosophie religieuse de Grégoire de Nysse*. Paris: Beauchesne, 1988.

Barth, Karl. *Church Dogmatics*. Peabody, MA: Hendrickson Publishers, 2010.

———. *Church Dogmatics 1.1.* Edited by G. W. Bromiley and T. F. Torrance. London: T&T Clark, 1975.

———. *Church Dogmatics 1.2.* Edited by G. W. Bromiley and T. F. Torrance. London: T&T Clark, 1956), 793.

Basil the Great. *Basil the Great: On the Holy Spirit*. Translated by David Anderson. Crestwood, NY: St Vladimir's Seminary Press, 1997.

Bathrellos, Demetrios. *The Byzantine Christ: Person, Nature, and Will in the Christology of Saint Maximus the Confessor*. The Oxford Early Christian Studies. Oxford: Oxford University Press, 2004.

Batllo, Xavier. *Ontologie scalaire et polémique trinitaire*. Münster: Aschendorff, 2013.

Berdyaev, Nikolai. *The Origin of Russian Communism*. Ann Arbor: University of Michigan Press, 1960.

———. *The Russian Revolution*. Ann Arbor: University of Michigan Press, 1961.

———. *Slavery and Freedom*. Translated by R. M. French. San Rafael: Semantron Press, 2009.

Betsakos, Vasilios. Στάσις ἀεικίνητος. Ἡ ἀνακαίνιση τῆς Ἀριστοτελικῆς κινήσεως στὴ θεολογία Μαξίμου τοῦ Ὁμολογητοῦ [Ever-Moving Repose: The Renewal of Aristotelian Movement in the Theology of Maximus the Confessor]. Athens: Armos, 2006.

Blanchette, Oliva. "Are There Two Questions of Being?" *Review of Metaphysics* 45 (1991): 259–87.

Blanco, Pablo. *Joseph Ratzinger. Razón y Cristianismo. La victoria de la inteligencia en el mundo de las religiones* (Madrid: Rialp, 2005).

Blowers, Paul. *Exegesis and Spiritual Pedagogy in St. Maximus the Confessor*. Notre Dame: University of Notre Dame Press, 1991.

———. "Realized Eschatology in Maximus the Confessor, *Ad Thalassium* 22." In *Studia Patristica,* vol. XXXII, edited by Elizabeth Livingston, 258–63. Leuven: Peeters, 1997.

Bonner, Gerald. *Freedom and Necessity: St Augustine's Teaching on Divine Power and Human Freedom*. Washington DC: The Catholic University of America Press, 2007.

Bradshaw, David Houston. *Aristotle East and West: Metaphysics and the Division of Christendom*. Cambridge: Cambridge University Press, 2004.

Bulgakov, Sergius. *The Orthodox Church*. Crestwood, NY: St Vladimir's Seminary Press, 1985.

Bussanich, John. "Plotinus's Metaphysics of the One." In *The Cambridge Companion to Plotinus*, edited by Lloyd P. Gerson, 38–65. Cambridge: Cambridge University Press, 1996.

Capps, Walter H. *Religious Studies: The Making of a Discipline*. Minneapolis: Fortress Press, 1995.

Cavanaugh, William T. "The Church in the Streets: Eucharist and Politics." *Modern Theology* 30, no. 2 (2014): 384–99.

———. *Migrations of the Holy*. Grand Rapids, MI: Eerdmans, 2011.

———. *The Myth of Religious Violence*. Oxford: Oxford University Press, 2009.

———. *Torture and Eucharist*. Malden, MA: Blackwell, 1998.

Collingwood, R. G. *The Idea of History*. Oxford: Clarendon Press, 1946.

Conrad-Martius, Hedwig. *Das Sein*. Munich: Kösel, 1957.

Constas, Maximos. *The Art of Seeing: Paradox and Perception in Orthodox Iconography*. Los Angeles: Sebastian Press, 2014.

Crockett, Clayton. *Radical Political Theology*. New York: Columbia University Press, 2011.

———. *A Theology of the Sublime*. New York: Routledge, 2001.

Crouzel, Henry. *Origen: The Life and Thought of the First Great Theologian*. Translated by A. S. Worrall. Edinburgh: T&T Clark, 1989.

Cunningham, Lawrence S. "Reflections on *Introduction to Christianity*." In *Exploration in the Theology of Benedict XVI*, edited by John C. Cavadini, 142–54. Notre Dame: University of Notre Dame, 2012.

Dalferth, Ingolf. "Barth's Eschatological Realism." *Karl Barth: Centenary Essays*, edited by S. W. Sykes, 14–45. Cambridge, UK: Cambridge University Press, 2009.

Daniélou, Jean. *From Glory to Glory: Texts from Gregory of Nyssa's Mystical Writings*. Crestwood, NY: St Vladimir's Seminary Press, 1961.

———. "La Colombe et la ténèbre dans la mystique byzantine ancienne." *Eranos Jahrbuch* 23 (1954): 400–405.

———. *L'être et le temps chez Grégoire de Nisse*. Leiden: Brill, 1970.

———. *The Lord of History: Reflections on the Inner Meaning of History*. Translated by Nigel Abercrombie. London: H. Regnery, 1958.

Delumeau, Jean. *Sin and Fear: The Emergence of a Western Guilt Culture*. New York: St Martin's Press, 1990.

Denzinger, Heinrich, and Adolf Schönmetzer, eds. *Enchiridion Symbolorum*. Fribourg: Herder, 1976.

Doucet, Marcel. "Dispute de Maxime le Confesseur avec Pyrrhus. Introduction, texte critique, traduction et notes." PhD thesis, Université de Montréal, Institut d'Études Mediévales, 1972.

———. "Vues récentes sur les métamorphoses de la pensée de saint Maxime le Confesseur." *Science et Esprit* 31, no. 3 (1979): 269–302.

Dreyfus, Hubert, and Charles Taylor. *Retrieving Realism*. Cambridge: Harvard University Press, 2015.

Dupré, Louis. *The Passage to Modernity*. New Haven: Yale University Press, 1993.

Evdokimov, Paul. *Orthodoxie*. Neuchatel: Delachaux Niestlé, 1959.

Fagerberg, David. *On Liturgical Asceticism*. Washington, DC: The Catholic University of America Press, 2013.

Feuerbach, Ludwig. *The Essence of Christianity*. Translated by George Eliot. Mineola: Dover Publications, 2008.

Florensky, Pavel. *At the Crossroads of Science and Mysticism*. New York: Semantron Press, 2014.

———. *Iconostasis*. Crestwood, NY: Saint Vladimir's Seminary Press, 1996.

———. *The Pillar and Ground of the Truth*. Princeton: Princeton University Press, 1997.

———. *Salt of the Earth, an Encounter with a Holy Russian Elder: Isidore of Gethsemane Hermitage*. Platina, CA: Saint Herman of Alaska Brotherhood, 1999.

Florovsky, Georges. *Collected Works of Georges Florovsky*. Vol. 2, *Christianity and Culture*. Belmont, MA: Nordland Publishing, 1974.

———. *Collected Works of Georges Florovksy*. Vol. 13, *Ecumenism I: A Doctrinal Approach*. Translated by Roberta Reeder. Vaduz, Europa: Büchervertriebsanstalt, 1987.

———. *Ways of Russian Theology*, vol. 2. Belmont, MA: Buchervertriebsanstalt, 1987.
Florovsky, Georges, and Andrew Blane. *Georges Florovsky: Russian Intellectual and Orthodox Churchman*. Crestwood, NY: St. Vladimir's Seminary Press, 1993.
Flynn, Gabriel, and P. D. Murray. *Ressourcement: A Movement for Renewal in Twentieth-Century Catholic Theology*. Oxford: Oxford University Press, 2012.
Franchetti, Cody. "Nominalism and History." *Open Journal of Philosophy* 3, no. 3 (2013): 401–12.
Freud, Sigmund. *The Future of an Illusion*. Translated by James Strachey. New York: W.W. Norton, 1989.
Friedman, Michael. *Kant and the Exact Sciences*. Cambridge, MA: Harvard University Press, 1992.
Frings, Manfred S. *The Mind of Max Scheler: The First Comprehensive Guide Based on the Complete Works*. Milwaukee, WI: Marquette University Press, 1997.
Fukuyama, Francis. *The End of History and the Last Man*. New York: Penguin, 1992.
Gadamer, Hans-Georg. *Truth and Method*. London: Bloomsbury, 2004.
Garrigues, Jean-Miguel. *Maxime le Confesseur. La charité, avenir divin de l'homme*. Théologie historique 38. Paris: Beauchesne, 1976.
Gilson, Etienne. *Christian Philosophy*. Translated by Armand Maurer. Winnipeg: Hignell Printing, 1993.
———. *The Unity of Philosophical Experience*. New York: Scribner's Sons, 1950.
Gregory, Brad. *The Unintended Reformation*. Cambridge: Harvard University Press, 2012.
Gregory of Nyssa. *Commentary on Songs of Songs*. Edited Richard A. Norris Jr. Atlanta, GA: Society of Biblical Literature, 2012.
Guardini, Romano. *Das Ende der Neuzeit*. Basel: Hess Verlag, 1950.
———. *The End of the Modern World*. Translated by Joseph Theman and Herbert Burke. New York: Sheed and Ward, 1956.
Guyer, Paul. *Kant's System of Nature and Freedom*. New York: Oxford University Press, 2005.
Guyer, Paul, and Allen Wood. "Introduction to the *Critique of Pure Reason*." In Immanuel Kant, *Critique of Pure Reason*. Translated by Paul Guyer and Allen Wood. Cambridge: Cambridge University Press, 2000.
Hanna, Robert. *Kant, Science, and Human Nature*. New York: Oxford University Press, 2006.
Hauerwas, Stanley. *Hannah's Child: A Theologian's Memoir*. Grand Rapids, MI: Eerdmans, 2010.
———. *The Hauerwas Reader*. Edited by John Berkman and Michael Cartwright. Durham, NC: Duke University Press, 2001.
Heidegger, Martin. *Being and Time*. Translated by John Macquarrie and Edward Robinson. Oxford: Blackwell, 2001.
———. *Ontology: The Hermeneutics of Facticity*. Translated by John van Buren. Bloomington: Indiana University Press, 1999.
———. *Pathmarks*. Edited by William McNeill. Cambridge: Cambridge University Press, 1998.

———. "What is Metaphysics?" In *Basic Writings*, edited by David Farrell Krell, 89–110. New York: Harper and Row, 1977.
Hengel, Martin. *The Son of God: The Origin of Christology and the History of Jewish-Hellenistic Religion.* Eugene, OR: Wipf and Stock, 2007.
Hong, Howard V., and Edna H. Hong, ed. and trans. *Søren Kierkegaard's Journals and Papers*, vol. 1–6. Princeton: Princeton University Press, 1967–1978.
Hunt, Anne. "The Trinity through Paschal Eyes." In *Rethinking Trinitarian Theology: Disputed Questions and Contemporary Issues in Trinitarian Theology*, edited by Giulio Maspero and Robert J. Wozniak, 472–90. New York: T&T Clark, 2012.
Jenson, Robert. *Systematic Theology*, vol. 2. Oxford: Oxford University Press, 1999.
John of Damascus. *An Exact Exposition of the Orthodox Faith.* Edited by B. Kotter. Berlin: Walter de Gruyter, 1973.
Kant, Immanuel. *The Critique of Judgment.* Translated by James Meredith. Oxford: Clarendon Press, 1952.
———. *Critique of Pure Reason.* Translated by Norman Kemp Smith. London: Macmillan, 1929.
———. *Critique of Pure Reason.* Translated by Paul Guyer and Allen Wood. Cambridge: Cambridge University Press, 2000.
———. *Groundwork of the Metaphysic of Morals.* Translated by H. J. Paton. New York: Harper Perennial, 1964.
———. "Idea for a Universal History with a Cosmopolitan Aim." In *Idea for a Universal History with a Cosmopolitan Aim: A Critical Guide,* edited by Amélie Oksenberg Rorty and James Schmidt. New York: Cambridge University Press, 2009.
———. *Religion within the Boundaries of Mere Reason.* Edited and translated by Allen Wood and George Di Giovanni. Cambridge: Cambridge University Press, 1998.
Karayiannis, Vasilios. *Maxime le Confesseur. Essence et énergies de Dieu.* Théologie historique 93. Paris: Beauchesne, 1993.
Kierkegaard, Søren. *Concluding Unscientific Postscript to the Philosophical Crumbs.* Edited and translated by Howard V. Hong and Edna H. Hong. Cambridge: Cambridge University Press, 2009.
———. *The Prayers of Kierkegaard.* Edited and translated by Perry D. Le Fevre. Chicago and London: University of Chicago Press, 1956.
———. *Sickness unto Death.* Edited and translated by Howard V. Hong and Edna H. Hong. Princeton: Princeton University Press, 1980.
———. *Søren Kierkegaard's Journal and Papers.* Vol. 1, *A–E*. Edited and translated by Howard V. Hong and Edna H. Hong. Princeton: Princeton University Press, 1967.
———. *Søren Kierkegaard's Journal and Papers.* Vol. 3, *L–R*. Edited and translated by Howard V. Hong and Edna H. Hong. Princeton: Princeton University Press, 1975.
———. *Søren Kierkegaard's Journal and Papers.* Vol. 4, *S–Z*. Edited and translated by Howard V. Hong and Edna H. Hong. Princeton: Princeton University Press, 1975.

———. *Stages on Life's Way*. Edited and translated by Howard V. Hong and Edna H. Hong. Princeton: Princeton University Press, 1991.

Kisiel, Theodore. *The Genesis of Heidegger's Being and Time*. Berkley: University of California Press, 1993.

———. "On the Genesis of Heidegger's Formally Indicative Hermeneutics of Facticity." In *Re-thinking Facticity*, edited by François Raffoul and Eric Sean Nelson, 41–69. Albany: State University of New York Press, 2008.

Kraft, Victor. *The Vienna Circle: The Origin of Neo-Positivism, a Chapter in the History of Recent Philosophy*. New York: Greenwood Press, 1953.

Krieg, Robert A. "Kardinal Ratzinger, Max Scheler und eine Grundfrage der Christologie." *Theologische Quartalschrift* 160 (1980): 106–22.

Kuhn, Thomas. *The Structure of Scientific Revolutions*. Chicago: University of Chicago Press, 1996.

Lacan, Jacques. "Problèmes cruciaux pour la psychanalyse. Séminaire [XII,] 1964–1965." Edited by Michel Roussan. Paris: Editions de l'Association Freudienne Internationnal, 2000. Unofficial edition, commercially not available.

Laird, Martin. "Apophasis and Logophasis in Gregory of Nyssa's Commentarius in Canticum Canticorum." *Studia Patristica* 37 (2001): 126–32.

Lasch, Christopher. *The Culture of Narcissism*. New York: Norton, 1978.

———. *The Minimal Self*. New York: Norton, 1984.

Léthel, François-Marie. *Théologie de l'agonie du Christ. La liberté humaine du Fils de Dieu et son importance sotériologique mises en lumière par saint Maxime le Confesseur*. Théologie historique 52. Paris: Beauchesne, 1979.

Levinas, Emmanuel. *Totality and Infinity: An Essay on Exteriority*. Translated by Alphonso Lingis. London: Kluwer Academic Publishers, 1991.

Lindbeck, George. *The Nature of Doctrine: Religion and Theology in a Postliberal Age*. London: Westminster John Knox Press, 1984.

Loudovikos, Nikolaos. "Being and Essence Revisited: Reciprocal Logoi and Energies in Maximus the Confessor and Thomas Aquinas, and the Genesis of the Self-referring Subject." *Portuguesa de Filosofia* 72, 1 (2016): 117–46.

———. *Church in the Making: An Apophatic Ecclesiology of Consubstantiality*. Translated by Norman Russell. Yonkers, NY: St. Vladimir's Seminary Press, 2015.

———. "Consubstantial Selves: A Discussion between Orthodox Theology, Existential Psychology, Heinz Kohut, and Jean-Luc Marion." In *Personhood in the Byzantine Christian Tradition: Early, Medieval, and Modern Perspectives*, eds. Alexis Torrance and Symeon Paschalidis (New York: Routledge, 2018), 182–96.

———. "*Eikon* and *Mimesis*: Eucharistic Ecclesiology and the Ecclesial Ontology of Dialogical Reciprocity." *International Journal for the Study of the Christian Church* 11, no. 2–3 (2011): 123–36.

———. *A Eucharistic Ontology: Maximus the Confessor's Eschatological Ontology as Dialogical Reciprocity*. Translated by Elizabeth Theokritoff. Brookline, MA: Holy Cross Orthodox Press, 2010.

———. "Possession or Wholeness? St. Maximus the Confessor and John Zizioulas on Person, Nature, and Will." *Participatio: Journal of the Thomas F. Torrance Theological Fellowship*, no. 4 (2013): 258–86.

———. "Striving for Participation: Palamite Analogy as Dialogical Syn-energy and Thomist Analogy as Emanational Similitude." In *Divine Essence and Divine Energies: Ecumenical Reflections on the Presence of God in Eastern Orthodoxy*, edited by Constantine Athanasopoulos and Christian Schneider, 122–48. Cambridge: James Clarke and Co., 2013.

———. "Δι-εννοημάτωσις or Inter-meaningfullness: Reading Wittgenstein through Gregory Palamas' and Thomas Aquinas' readings of Aristotle." In *Ludwig Wittgenstein between Analytic Philosophy and Apophaticism*, edited by Sotiris Mitralexis, 151–65. Newcastle Upon Tyne: Cambridge Scholars, 2015.

———. Ἡ κλειστὴ πνευματικότητα καὶ τὸ νόημα τοῦ ἑαυτοῦ. Ὁ μυστικισμὸς τῆς ἰσχύος καὶ ἡ ἀλήθεια φύσεως καὶ προσώπου [Closed Spirituality and the Meaning of the Self: Christian Mysticism of Power and the Truth of Personhood and Nature]. Athens: Ellinika Grammata, 1999.

———. Οἱ τρόμοι τοῦ προσώπου καὶ τὰ βάσανα τοῦ ἔρωτα [Terrors of the Person and the Torments of Love]. Athens: Armos, 2009).

———. Ὀρθοδοξία καὶ ἐκσυγχρονισμός. Βυζαντινὴ ἐξατομίκευση, κράτος καὶ ἱστορία, στὴν προοπτικὴ τοῦ εὐρωπαϊκοῦ μέλλοντος [Orthodoxy and Modernization: Byzantine Individualization, State and History, in the perspective of the European Future]. Athens: Armos, 2006.

———. Ψυχανάλυση καὶ ὀρθόδοξη θεολογία. Περὶ ἐπιθυμίας, καθολικότητας καὶ ἐσχατολογίας [Psychoanalysis and Orthodox Theology: On Desire, Catholicity and Eschatology]. Athens: Armos, 2006.

Louth, Andrew. "French Ressourcement Theology and Orthodoxy: A Living Mutual Relationship?" In *Ressourcement: A Movement for Renewal in Twentieth-Century Catholic Theology*, edited by Gabriel Flynn and Paul D. Murray, 495–507. Oxford: Oxford University Press, 2012.

Lovin, Robin. *Christian Realism and the New Realities*. New York: Cambridge University Press, 2008.

———. *Reinhold Niebuhr and Christian Realism*. New York: Cambridge University Press, 1995.

Ludlow, Morwenna. *Gregory of Nyssa, Ancient and (Post)modern*. Oxford: Oxford University Press, 2007.

MacIntyre, Alasdair. *After Virtue*. South Bend, IN: University of Notre Dame Press, 2010.

———. *Three Rival Versions of Moral Enquiry*. Notre Dame: University of Notre Dame Press, 1990.

Machiavelli, Niccolò. *The Prince*. Translated by W. K. Marriott, 1958. Accessed December 1, 2015. http://www.gutenberg.org/files/1232/1232-h/1232-h.htm

Mahn, Jason A. *Fortunate Fallibility: Kierkegaard and the Power of Sin*. Oxford: Oxford University Press, 2011.

Manoussakis, John Panteleimon. *God after Metaphysics: A Theological Aesthetic*. Indiana Series in the Philosophy of Religion. Bloomington: Indiana University Press, 2007.

Mantzaridis, Georgios. *The Deification of Man: St Gregory Palamas and the Orthodox Tradition*. Crestwood, NY: St Vladimir's Seminary Press, 1984.

Maspero, Giulio. "L'ontologia trinitaria nei Padri Cappadoci: prospettiva cristologica." In *Trinità in relazione: Percorsi di ontologia trinitaria dai Padri della Chiesa all'Idealismo tedesco*, edited by C. Moreschini. Panzano in Chianti, FI: Edizioni Feeria, 2015, 69–91.

———. "Patristic Trinitarian Ontology." In *Rethinking Trinitarian Theology: Disputed Questions and Contemporary Issues in Trinitarian Theology*, edited by Robert J. Wozniak and Giulio Maspero (London: T&T Clark, 2012), 211–29.

Mateo-Seco, Lucas Francisco. *Estudios sobre la cristología de San Gregorio de Nisa.* Pamplona: Eunsa, 1978.

Mateo-Seco, Lucas Francisco, and Giulio Maspero. *The Brill Dictionary of Gregory of Nyssa*. Translated by Seth Cherney. Leiden: Brill, 2009.

Maximus the Confessor. *Ad Catholicos per Siciliam constitutos (Theologica et polemica ix)*. Edited by François Combefis. PG 91: 112C–32D.

———. *Ad Marinum presbyterum (Theologica et polemica i)*. Edited by François Combefis. PG 91: 9A–37D.

———. *Ambigua ad Iohannem*. Edited and translated by Nicholas P. Constas. In *Difficulties*, 1:62–450; 2:2–330.

———. *Ambigua ad Thomam*. Edited and translated by Nicholas P. Constas. In *Difficulties*, 1:2–58.

———. *Capita de caritate*. In *Capitoli sulla carità*, edited by Aldo Ceresa-Gastaldo: 48–238. Rome: Editrice Studium, 1963.

———. *Capita theologica et oeconomica*. Edited by François Combefis. PG 90: 1084A–1173A.

———. *Capita x de duplici uoluntate Domini (Theologica et polemica xxv)*. Edited by François Combefis. PG 91: 269D–73D.

———. *De eo quod scriptum est, « Pater, si fieri potest, transeat a me calix » (Theologica et polemica vi)*. Edited by François Combefis. PG 91: 65A–69A.

———. *Disputatio cum Pyrrho*. Edited by François Combefis. PG 91: 288A–353B.

———. *Distinctionum quibus res dirimuntur definitiones (Theologica et polemica xvii)*. Edited by François Combefis. PG 91: 212C–13A.

———. *Exemplum epistulae ad episcopum Nicandrum de duabus in Christo operationibus (Theologica et polemica viii)*. Edited by François Combefis. PG 91: 89C–112C.

———. *Liber asceticus*. In *Maximi Confessoris Liber asceticus*, edited by Peter Van Deun and Steven Gysens: 4–123. CCSG 40. Turnhout: Brepols; Leuven: Leuven University Press, 2000.

———. *Maximi Confessoris Opera Omnia, Tomus primus*. Edited by François Combefis. Patrologiae Cursus Completus. Series Graeca 90, edited by Jacques-Paul Migne. Paris: Migne, 1865.

———. *Maximi Confessoris Opuscula exegetica duo*. Edited by Peter Van Deun. Corpus Christianorum. Series Graeca 23. Turnhout: Brepols/Leuven: Leuven University Press, 1991.

———. *Mystagogia*. In *Maximi Confessoris Mystagogia: una cum latina interpretatione Anastasii bibliothecarii*, edited by Christian Boudignon: 3–74. Corpus Christianorum. Series Graeca 69. Turnhout: Brepols, 2011.

———. *On Difficulties in the Church Fathers*. Edited and translated by Nicholas P. Constas. Vol. 1, *Ambigua to Thomas*; *Ambigua to John* 1–22, vol. 2, *Ambigua to John*, 23–71. Dumbarton Oaks Medieval Library 28–29. Cambridge, MA; London: Harvard University Press, 2014.

———. *Orationis dominicae expositio*. Edited by Peter Van Deun. CCSG 23: 27–73.

———. *Quaestiones ad Thalassium*. In *Maximi Confessoris Quaestiones ad Thalassium una cum Latina interpretatione Joannis Scotti Eriugenae iuxta posita*, edited by Carl Laga and Carlos Steel: 7:3–539; 22:3–325. Corpus Christianorum. Series Graeca 7, 22. Turnhout: Brepols; Leuven: Leuven University Press, 1980–1990.

———. *Quaestiones et dubia*. In *Maximi Confessoris Quaestiones et dubia*, edited by José H. Declerck: 3–170. Corpus Christianorum. Series Graeca 10. Turnhout: Brepols; Leuven: Leuven University Press, 1982.

———. *Spiritualis tomus ac dogmaticus . . . ad sanctissimum Dorensem episcopum Stephanum (Theologica et polemica xv)*. Edited by François Combefis. PG 91: 153B–84C.

———. *Tomus dogmaticus ad Marinum presbyterum (Theologica et polemica xx)*. Edited by François Combefis. PG 91: 228A–45D.

———. *Variae definitiones (Theologica et polemica xiv)*. Edited by François Combefis. PG 91: 149B–53B.

Maximus the Confessor, Thalassius, and Theodore Raïthu. *Maximi Confessoris Opera Omnia, Tomus secundus, Thalassi Abatis, Theodori Raithuensis Opera*. Edited by François Combefis, Franz Oehler, and André Galland. Patrologiae Cursus Completus. Series Graeca 91, edited by Jacques-Paul Migne. Paris: Migne, 1863.

McPartlan, Paul. *The Eucharist Makes the Church: Henri de Lubac and John Zizioulas in Dialogue*. Edinburgh: T&T Clark, 1993.

Michel, Virgil. *The Liturgy of the Church*. New York: The MacMillan Company, 1937.

Migne, Jacques-Paul, ed. *Patrologiae Cursus Completus, Series Graeca*. 162 vols. Paris, 1857–1866.

Misler, Nicoletta. *Beyond Vision: Essays on the Perception of Art*. London: Reaktion Books, 2002.

Mitralexis, Sotiris. *Ever-Moving Repose: A Contemporary Reading of Maximus the Confessor's Theory of Time*. Eugene, OR: Cascade/Wipf and Stock, 2017.

Moutsoulas, Elias. Γρηγόριος Νύσσης, Βίος, Συγγράμματα, Διδασκαλία [Gregory of Nyssa. Life, Writings, Teachings]. Athens: Eptalophos A.B.E.E., 1997.

Mühlenberg, Ekkehard. *Die Unendlichkeit Gottes bei Gregor von Nyssa. Gregors Kritik am Gottesbegriff der klassischen Metaphysik*. Göttingen: Vandenhoeck und Ruprecht, 1966.

Murphy, Murray. *Philosophical Foundations of Historical Knowledge*. Albany: State University of New York Press, 1994.

Murphy, Nancey. *Theology without Foundations: Religious Practice and the Future of Theological Truth*. Edited by Stanley Hauerwas, Nancey Murphy, and Mark Nation. Nashville, TN: Abingdon Press, 1994.

Nichols, Aidan. *The Theology of Benedict XVI*. London: Burns and Oats, 2007.

Niebuhr, Reinhold. *Christian Realism and Political Problems.* Fairfield, NJ: Augustus Kelley Pubs, 1966.

———. *The Nature and Destiny of Man: A Christian Interpretation.* New York: Charles Scribner's Sons, 1980.

Nielsen, Kai. *An Introduction to the Philosophy of Religion.* New York: St. Martin's Press, 1983.

Norris, Richard A. *Gregory of Nyssa: Homilies on the Song of Songs.* Atlanta: Society of Biblical Literature, 2012.

Øhrstrøm, Peter, Henrik Schärfe, and Sara L. Uckelman. "Jacob Lorhard's Ontology: A 17th Century Hypertext on the Reality and Temporality of the World of Intelligibles." In *Conceptual Structures: Knowledge Visualization and Reasoning,* edited by Peter Eklund and Ollivier Haemmerlé, 74–87. Berlin: Springer, 2008.

O'Meara, Dominic J. *Plotinus: An Introduction to the Enneads.* Oxford: Clarendon Press, 1993.

Pannenberg, Wolfhart. *Basic Questions in Theology.* Translated by George H. Kehm. Philadelphia, PA: Westminster Press, 1969.

———. *Jesus—God and Man.* Translated by Lewis L. Wilkins and Duane A. Priebe. Philadelphia, PA: The Westminster Press, 1977.

———. *Systematic Theology,* vol. 3. Translated by Geoffrey W. Bromiley. Grand Rapids, MI: William B. Eerdmans Publishing Company, 1998.

Papanikolaou, Aristotle. "Integrating the Ascetical and the Eucharistic: Current Challenges in Orthodox Ecclesiology." *International Journal for the Study of the Christian Church* 11, no. 2–3 (2011): 173–87.

———. *The Mystical as Political: Democracy and Non-Radical Orthodoxy.* Notre Dame, IN: University of Notre Dame Press, 2012.

Perišić, Vladan. *Theological Disambiguations: An Unconventional Handbook of Orthodox Theology.* Los Angeles: Sebastian Press, 2012.

Phillips, D. Z. *Faith after Foundationalism.* London and New York: Routledge, 1988.

———. *Wittgenstein and Religion.* New York: St. Martin's Press, 1994.

Pippin, Robert. *The Persistence of Subjectivity.* New York: Cambridge University Press, 2005.

Plantinga, Alvin. *Warranted Christian Belief.* Oxford: Oxford University Press, 2000.

Pseudo-Maximus the Confessor. *Diuersa capita ad theologiam et oeconomiam spectantia deque virtute et uitio (xxvi-d).* Edited by François Combefis. PG90:1188A9-392A.

Pyman, Avril. *Pavel Florensky: A Quiet Genius.* New York: Continuum Publishing, 2010.

Quine, Willard Van Orman. *Theories and Things.* Cambridge, MA: Harvard University Press, 1981.

———. "Two Dogmas of Empiricism." In *Problems in the Philosophy of Language.* Edited by Thomas M. Olshensky. New York: Holt, Rinehart and Winston, 1969.

Ratzinger, Joseph. *Church, Ecumenism and Politics: New Endeavors in Ecclesiology.* San Francisco: Ignatius Press, 2008.

———. "Das Ende der Zeit." In *Joseph Ratzinger Gesammelte Schriften,* edited by Gerhard Ludwig Müller. Vol. 10, *Auferstehung und ewiges Leben,* 602–19. Freiburg-Basel-Wien: Herder, 2012.

———. "Das Offenbarungsverständnis und die Geschichtstheologie Bonaventuras." In *Joseph Ratzinger Gesammelte Schriften*, edited by Gerhard Ludwig Müller. Vol. 2, *Offenbarungsverständnis und die Geschichtstheologie Bonaventuras*, 53–661. Freiburg im Breisgau: Herder, 2009.

———. "Die Bedeutung der Väter für die gegenwärtige Theologie." *Theologische Quartalschrift* 148 (1968): 257–82.

———. *Dogma and Preaching: Applying Christian Doctrine to Daily Life*. Edited by Michael J. Miller. Translated by Michael J. Miller and Matthew J. O'Connell. San Francisco: Ignatius Press, 2011.

———. *Dogma und Verkündigung*. München-Freiburg: Erich Wewel Verlag, 1973.

———. "Einführung in das Christentum. Vorlesungen über das Apostolische Glaubensbekenntnis." In *Joseph Ratzinger Gesammelte Schriften*, edited by Gerhard Ludwig Müller. Vol. 4, *Einführung in das Christentum*, 31–322. Freiburg im Breisgau: Herder, 2009.

———. *The End of Time? The Provocation of Talking about God*. Edited and translated by Matthew Ashley. New York: Paulist Press, 2004.

———. "*Eschatologie. Tod und ewiges Lebe*." In *Joseph Ratzinger Gesammelte Schriften*, edited by Gerhard Ludwig Müller. Vol. 10, *Auferstehung und ewiges Leben*, 602–19. Freiburg-Basel-Wien: Herder, 2012.

———. *Eschatology: Death and Eternal Life*. Translated by Michael Waldstein. Washington, DC: The Catholic University of America Press, 1988.

——— *Glaube–Wahrheit–Toleranz. Das Christentum und die Weltreligionen*. Freiburg im Breisgau: Herder, 2005.

———. *Im Anfang schuf Gott. Vier Münchener Fastenpredigten über Schöpfung und Fall*. München: Erich Wewel Verlag, 1986.

———. *In the Beginning. A Catholic Understanding of the Story of Creation and Fall*. Translated by Boniface Ramsey. London: T&T Clark, 1995.

———. *Introduction to Christianity*. San Francisco, CA: Ignatius Press, 1990.

———. *Introduction to Christianity*. Translated by J. R. Foster. San Francisco: Ignatius Press, 2004.

———. *Jesus of Nazareth: From the Baptism in the Jordan to the Transfiguration*. Translated by Adrian J. Walker. New York: Doubleday, 2007.

———. *Jesus of Nazareth: Holy Week. From the Entrance into Jerusalem to the Resurrection*. Translated by the Vatican Secretariat of State. San Francisco: Ignatius Press, 2011.

———. "Jesus von Nazareth. Vom Einzug in Jerusalem bis zur Auferstehung." In *Joseph Ratzinger Gesammelte Schriften*, edited by Gerhard Ludwig Müller. Vol. 6.1, *Jesus von Nazareth*, 415–635. Freiburg-Basel-Wien: Herder, 2013.

———. "Jesus von Nazareth. Von der Taufe im Jordan bis zur Verklärung." In *Joseph Ratzinger Gesammelte Schriften*, edited by Gerhard Ludwig Müller. Vol. 6.1, *Jesus von Nazareth*, 127–413. Freiburg-Basel-Wien: Herder, 2013.

———. "L'interpretazione biblica in conflitto: problemi del foundamento ed orientamento dell'esegesi contemporanea." In *L'esegesi cristiana oggi*, edited by Luciano Pacomio and Ignace de La Potterie, 93–125. Casale Monferrato: Piemme, 1991.

———. *On the Way to Jesus Christ*. Translated by Michael J. Miller. San Francisco: Ignatius Press, 2005.

———. *Pilgrim Fellowship of Faith: The Church as Communion*. Edited by Stephan Otto Horn and Vinzenz Pfnur. Translated by Henry Taylor. San Francisco: Ignatius Press, 2005.

———. *Principles of Catholic Theology. Building Stones for a Fundamental Theology*. Translated by Mary Frances McCarthy. San Francisco: Ignatius Press, 1987.

———. *Theologische Prinzipienlehre. Bausteine zur Fundamentaltheologie*. Erich Wewel Verlag: München, 1982.

———. *Truth and Tolerance: Christian Belief and World Religions*. Translated by Henry Taylor. San Francisco: Ignatius Press, 2004.

Renczes, Philipp Gabriel. *Agir de Dieu et liberté de l'homme. Recherches sur l'anthropologie théologique de saint Maxime le Confesseur*. Cogitatio fidei 229. Paris: Cerf, 2003.

Richmond, James. *Theology and Metaphysics*. London: SCM Press, 1970.

Ricoeur, Paul. *Lectures 2. La contrée des philosophes*. Paris: Seuil, 1999.

Rose, Matthew. "Karl Barth's Failure." *First Things* 244 (June/July 2014): 39–44.

Rousseau, Jean-Jacques. *The Social Contract*. Edited by Tom Griffith. Hertfordshire: Wordsworth Editions, 1998.

Rowland, Tracey. *Ratzinger's Faith. The Theology of Pope Benedict XVI*. New York: Oxford University Press, 2008.

Russell, Norman. *The Doctrine of Deification in the Greek Patristic Tradition*. Oxford: Oxford University Press, 2004.

Santayana, George. *The Letters of George Santayana*, vol. 5, Book I. Edited by William G. Holzberger. Cambridge: MIT Press, 2001.

Second Vatican Council. *Gaudium et Spes*. Accessed August 1, 2017.

Schmemann, Alexander. *Celebration of Faith*. Vol. 3, *The Virgin Mary*. Crestwood: St. Vladimir's Seminary Press, 1995.

———. *The Eucharist*. Crestwood, NY: St. Vladimir's Seminary Press, 1990.

———. *Introduction to Liturgical Theology*. Crestwood, NY: St. Vladimir's Seminary Press, 1966.

———. *The Journals of Father Alexander Schmemann 1973–1983*. Crestwood, NY: St. Vladimir's Seminary Press, 1990.

———. "Liturgy and Eschatology." In *Liturgy and Tradition: Theological Reflections of Alexander Schmemann*, edited by Thomas Fisch. Crestwood, NY: St. Vladimir's Seminary Press, 1990.

———. *Liturgy and Tradition*. Edited by Thomas Fisch. Crestwood, NY: St. Vladimir's Seminary Press, 1990.

———. *Of Water and the Spirit*. Crestwood, NY: St. Vladimir Seminary Press, 1974.

Schmemann, Alexander. "Problems of Orthodoxy in America: The Canonical Problem, " in *St. Vladimir's Seminary Quarterly*, no 2, 1964, 71.

Schneewind, J. B. *The Invention of Autonomy*. New York: Cambridge University Press, 1998.

Sheehan, Thomas. "A Paradigm Shift in Heidegger Research," *Continental Philosophy Review* 32, no. 2 (2001): 1–20.

Simeon the New Theologian. *The Discourses*. Translated by C. J. De Catanzaro. New Jersey: Paulist Press, 1980.

Skliris, Stamatis. *In the Mirror: A Collection of Iconographic Essays and Illustrations*. Los Angeles: Sebastian Press, 2007.

Slesinki. Robert. *Pavel Florensky: A Metaphysics of Love*. Crestwood, NY: Saint Vladimir's Seminary Press, 1984.

Solzhenitsyn, Alexander. "Repentance and Self-Limitation in the Life of Nations." In *The Solzhenitsyn Reader: New and Essential Writings 1947–2005*, edited by Edward E. Ericson Jr. and Daniel F. Mahoney. Wilmington, DE: ISI Books, 2006. Originally published in Alexander Solzhenitsyn, ed., *From under the Rubble*. Translated by A. M. Brock, Milada Haigh, Marita Sapiets, Hilary Sternberg, Harry Willetts, and Michael Scammell. Boston: Little, Brown, and Company, 1974.

Spira, Andreas. "Le temps d'un homme selon Aristote et Grégoire de Nyssa." *Colloques internationaux du CNRS* (Paris 1984): 283–94.

Strawson, P. F. *Skepticism and Naturalism: Some Varieties*. New York: Columbia University Press, 1985.

Sudduth, Michael. *The Reformed Objection to Natural Theology*. London and New York: Routledge, 2009.

Taylor, Charles. *Hegel*. Cambridge; New York: Cambridge University Press, 1975.

———. *A Secular Age*. Cambridge: Harvard University Press, 2007.

Thatcher, Adrian. *The Ontology of Paul Tillich*. Oxford: Oxford University Press, 1978.

Thistleton, Anthony. *New Horizons in Hermeneutics: The Theory and Practice of Transforming Biblical Reading* (Grand Rapids, MI: Zondervan, 1992).

Tilley, Terrence W. "In Favor of a 'Practical Theory of Religion': Montaigne and Pascal." In *Theology without Foundations: Religious Practice and the Future of Theological Truth*, edited by Stanley Hauerwas, Nancey Murphy, and Mark Nation. Nashville, TN: Abingdon Press, 1994.

Tillich, Paul. *Theology of Culture*. New York: Oxford University Press, 1964.

Tollefsen, Torstein T. *Activity and Participation in Late Antique and Early Christian Thought*. Oxford: Oxford University Press, 2012.

———. *The Christocentric Cosmology of St. Maximus the Confessor*. Oxford Early Christian Studies. Oxford: Oxford University Press, 2008.

Torrance, Alan. "Is There a Distinctive Human Nature? Approaching the Question from a Christian Epistemic Base." *Zygon* 47, no. 4 (2012): 903–17.

Torrance, Alexis. *Repentance in Late Antiquity: Eastern Asceticism and the Framing of the Christian Life c.400–650 CE*. Oxford: Oxford University Press, 2012.

Tzamalikos, Panayiotis. *Origen: Philosophy of History and Eschatology*. Leiden: Brill, 2007.

Van Huyssteen, J. Wentzel. *Essays in Postfoundationalist Theology*. Grand Rapids, MI: William B. Eerdman's Publishing Co., 1997.

Veyne, Paul. *Writing History: Essay on Epistemology*. Translated by Mina Moore Rinvolucri. Manchester: University Press, 1984.

Volf, Miroslav. *After Our Likeness: The Church as the Image of the Trinity*. Grand Rapids, MI: Eerdmans, 1998.

Ward, Benedicta, ed. *The Sayings of the Desert Fathers: The Alphabetical Collection*. Kalamazoo, MI: Cistercian Publications, 1975.
Whitehead, A. N. *Science and the Modern World*. New York: Pelican Mentor Books, 1948.
Wojciech, Jacek. "Katholische Theologie." In *Die Religion in Geschichte und Gegenwart VI*, edited by Kurt von Galling. Tubingen: J.C.B. Mohr, 1962.
———. *La foi comme dialogue. Une introduction à la théologie de J. Ratzinger*. Paris: Institute Catholique, 1991.
Wolfe, Judith. *Heidegger's Eschatology: Theological Horizons in Martin Heidegger's Early Work*. Oxford: Oxford University Press, 2013.
Yannaras, Christos. *De l'absence et de l'inconnaissance de Dieu, d'après les écrits aréopagitiques et Martin Heidegger*. Translated by Jacques Touraille. Théologie sans frontières 21. Paris: Cerf, 1971.
———. *The Enigma of Evil*. Translated by Norman Russell. Brookline: Holy Cross Orthodox Press, 2012.
———. *On the Absence and Unknowability of God*. Translated by Haralambos Ventis. London: T&T Clark, 2005.
———. *Orthodoxy and the West*. Brookline, MA: Holy Cross Orthodox Press, 2006.
———. *Person and Eros*. Translated by Norman Russell. Brookline, MA: Holy Cross Orthodox Press, 2007.
———. *Philosophie sans rupture*. Translated by André Borrély. Perspective orthodoxe 7. Genève: Labor et fides, 1981.
———. *Six Philosophical Sketches*. Athens: Ikaros, 2011.
———. Έξι φιλοσοφικές ζωγραφιές [Six Philosophical Sketches]. Athens: Ikaros, 2011.
———. Προτάσεις Κριτικής Οντολογίας [Prototypes of Critical Ontology]. Athens: Icaros Publications, 1985, 2010.
———. Το ρητό και το άρρητο [The Effable and the Ineffable]. Athens: Ikaros, 1999.
Yoder, John Howard. *Christian Witness to the State*. Harrisonburg, VA: Herald Press, 2002.
———. *The Politics of Jesus: Vicit Agnus Noster*. Grand Rapids, MI: Ethics and Public Policy Center, 1972.
———. *The Royal Priesthood*. Edited by Michael Cartwright. Harrisonburg, VA: Herald Press, 1998.
Žižek, Slavoj. *On Belief*. Thinking in Action. London: Routledge, 2001.
———. *The Fragile Absolute; or, Why Is the Christian Legacy Worth Fighting For?* Wo Es war. London: Verso, 2000.
———. *The Puppet and the Dwarf: The Perverse Core of Christianity*. Short Circuits. Cambridge, MA: MIT Press, 2003.
Zizioulas, John. *Being as Communion: Studies in Personhood and the Church*. Crestwood, NY: St. Vladimir's Seminary Press, 1985.
———. *Communion and Otherness: Further Studies in Personhood and the Church*. London: T&T Clark, 2007.
———. *Eucharist, Bishop, Church: The Unity of the Church in the Divine Eucharist and the Bishop during the First Three Centuries*. Translated by Elizabeth Theokritoff. Brookline, MA: Holy Cross Orthodox Press, 2001.

———. *The Eucharistic Communion and the World*. London: T&T Clark, 2011.
———. *Lectures in Christian Dogmatics*. London: T&T Clark, 2009.
———. *The One and the Many: Studies on God, Man, the Church, and the World Today*. Alhambra, CA: Sebastian Press, 2010.
———. "Person and Nature in the Theology of St Maximus the Confessor." In *Knowing the Purpose of Creation through the Resurrection: Proceedings of the Symposium on St Maximus the Confessor, Belgrade, October 18–21, 2012*, edited by Maksim Vasiljević, 85–113. Alhambra, CA: Sebastian Press and Faculty of Orthodox Theology, University of Belgrade, 2013.
Zoumboulakis, Stavros. Το περιοδικό 'Σύνορο' και ο Χρήστος Γιανναράς. Η θεολογική πρόταση της αποηθικοποίησης του Χριστιανισμού ["The 'Synoro' Journal and Christos Yannaras: The Theological Proposal for a Demoralization of Christianity"]. In Αναταράξεις στη μεταπολεμική θεολογία—Η "θεολογία του '60" [*Turbulence in Post-War Theology: The Theology of the '60s*], edited by Pantelis Kalaitzidis, Thanasis N. Papathanasiou, and Theofilos Abatzidis, 315–26. Athens: Indiktos Publications, 2009.

Index

Andreopoulos, Andreas, 90, 93, 95
apologetics, 7, 8, 19
apophaticism, 26, 32, 33
a posteriori, 5, 46, 56, 128
Aquinas, Thomas, 45, 145, 150, 159, 160, 224–25, 241, 242
Aristotle, 24, 28, 35, 37, 42, 50, 93, 100, 106, 111, 160, 167, 183, 211, 217, 222, 223, 228, 241, 258, 263, 268
  Aristotelian, 4, 24, 41, 42–43, 50, 52, 53, 62, 63, 271, 273
ascesis, 249–53, 256, 257, 259
Augustine, 102, 145, 158, 195, 202, 203, 266, 268, 275
autonomous, 14, 83, 84–88, 93, 164
Avatar (movie), 143, 144

Bacon, Francis, 4
Barth, Karl, 7, 8, 121, 190, 246, 269, 273, 275, 276
Basil of Caesarea, 32, 36, 44
beauty, 6, 28, 42, 78
being *qua* being, 37, 38
Berdyaev, Nikolai, 173–88
Bulgakov, Sergei, 99, 145, 158, 174

Cappadocian, 25, 27, 32, 44, 51, 59, 132

Catholic, 65, 69, 79, 144, 158, 173, 184, 190, 192, 246
Cavanaugh, William, 246, 247, 253–56, 258, 259, 262
Christianity, 3, 8, 12, 14, 16, 21, 38, 58, 75, 88, 111, 123, 133, 159, 175, 176, 177–179, 182, 183, 185, 189, 191–92, 199, 200, 209, 221, 237, 245
Christendom, 15, 62, 191
cogito, 6
communion, 32, 33, 39, 53, 69–70, 78, 90, 92, 109, 112, 113, 114, 115, 117, 122, 141, 153, 156, 157, 198, 249, 252, 255, 256, 258, 259–60, 270
corruption, 114, 126, 154, 157, 231, 271
Crucifixion, 52–53, 56, 111, 182, 253, 256

Daniélou, Jean, 26, 29–30, 34, 35, 198
Dasein, 40, 101–5, 110, 112, 118, 119, 165, 229, 231
desire, 14, 28–29, 30, 31, 48, 85, 86, 87, 101, 102, 128, 129, 145, 147, 150, 157, 169, 177, 193–94, 209, 210, 211, 231, 266
despair, 110, 126, 206–9, 212, 213–16, 238, 239, 251
dogmatics, 5, 73

293

ecclesiology, 68–70, 72, 109–10, 113, 120, 136, 155, 247, 248, 251, 253, 257, 258–59, 260, 261, 263
empiricism, 4, 5, 17, 19, 39, 164
epektasis, 26, 27, 28–29, 31, 32, 33–34
eros, 48, 169, 171
eschatology, 15, 41, 43, 47, 49, 50, 55, 89–91, 100, 102, 108, 109, 110, 113, 114–16, 119, 122, 126, 129, 137, 143, 144, 147, 148, 149, 151, 152–55, 248, 268, 269, 271, 273–74, 275
   eschaton, 47, 49, 51, 52, 53, 57, 102, 108, 111, 113, 126, 128, 130, 137, 247, 248–50, 254, 256, 259, 260, 274
Eucharist, 57, 58, 65, 70, 71, 92, 93, 106–8, 109–14, 115, 120, 122, 123, 127, 129, 131, 134, 135, 136, 137–38, 139, 141, 150, 153–54, 157–58, 159, 247–63

faith, 3, 6, 8, 11, 14, 16, 20, 21, 30, 31, 39, 41, 58, 93, 114, 127, 131–32, 135, 139, 141, 179, 185, 186, 189, 191–92, 196, 206–10, 212, 213–214, 215, 235, 236, 237, 260
falsifiable, 3, 14, 15, 16
Florensky, Pavel, 66–67, 68, 72, 73, 74, 77–78, 79, 80, 81
Florovsky, Georges, 15, 99–100, 106, 107, 108, 109, 114–17, 118, 120, 121, 122, 123, 126, 130, 131, 134, 135, 139, 153, 154, 174, 185

Gadamer, Hans Georg, 99–100, 104, 107, 113, 114, 120, 121, 126, 128, 132, 137, 140
German idealism, 39
Gethsemane, 52
Gregory of Nyssa, 24, 25, 29, 32, 34, 36, 138, 160

Hegel, Georg Wilhelm Friedrich, 39, 40, 46, 47, 83, 87, 94, 106, 111, 207

Heidegger, Martin, 17, 40, 58, 99–123, 137, 151, 153, 164, 170, 185, 199, 227, 228–32, 236, 239, 243–44
Hellenism, 134, 136, 164
Heraclitus, 4, 51, 143, 170
heteronomous, 86, 87, 93
history, 3, 4–5, 13, 14, 15–16, 21, 23, 27, 33, 34, 37, 38–41, 46–47, 48, 49, 50, 51–52, 53, 54, 55, 57, 65, 66, 71, 75, 77, 78, 83–84, 87, 88–93, 94, 101, 104–6, 108, 110–11, 112–13, 114–17, 119, 121, 122, 123, 125, 126, 128, 129, 130, 133, 134, 135, 136, 137, 139, 140, 141, 149–50, 151, 153–54, 156, 173, 174–75, 179, 180, 181, 183–84, 185, 188, 189, 190–92, 200, 201, 207, 214, 227, 228, 235, 236, 238, 242, 244, 245, 247, 248, 249, 250, 252, 253, 254, 255, 256, 260, 265
Holy Spirit, 24, 39, 114, 130, 132, 136, 139, 140, 197
Hume, David, 5, 6–7, 11
hypostasis, 42, 44, 49, 51, 57, 155, 160, 169, 170, 270
hypostatic otherness, 12

imitatio Christi, 92
immortality, 42, 56, 125, 135, 196
Incarnation, 15, 27, 38, 39, 46, 48, 88, 90, 91, 130, 136, 140, 152, 157, 182–83, 192, 237, 240, 245, 246

Jesus Christ, 13, 15, 26, 27, 29, 33, 41, 44, 46, 47, 48, 50, 51–53, 54, 55–56, 57, 69, 70, 71, 72, 74, 80, 86, 88–93, 109, 110, 111, 112, 113, 114, 116, 117, 123, 125–26, 127, 128, 129, 130, 131, 132, 133–34, 135, 136, 137, 139, 140, 141, 149, 153, 155, 156, 157, 178, 182, 183–84, 186, 187, 192, 194, 199, 201, 203, 206–7, 212, 216, 235, 247, 249–55, 256, 258, 262, 266–67, 269–70, 271–73
jurisdiction, 74

Kant, Immanuel, 4–7, 11, 17–18, 21, 39, 83–93, 94, 103, 118, 137, 151, 156, 211, 226–28, 230, 238–39, 242, 243, 244, 246
kenosis, 249–50, 255
Kierkegaard, Søren, 7, 9, 101, 102, 119, 205–16, 217

Leibniz, Gottfried, 84, 211, 225–26, 227, 242
Levinas, Emmanuel, 13, 21
lex credendi, 3
lex orandi, 3, 75–76
Lindbeck, George, 8, 9, 20
liturgy, 60, 65–80, 81, 108, 109, 114, 117, 120, 141, 199, 248, 249–50, 253–56, 258, 259
Locke, John, 4, 5
Logos, 27, 35, 45–49, 51, 53, 60, 61, 89–93, 131, 143, 207
Lossky, Vladimir, 153, 174
Louth, Andrew, 159, 184
Luther, Martin, 7, 100, 101, 102, 118, 191, 242

MacIntyre, Alasdair, 239, 246, 272, 276
Marx, Karl, 39, 40, 176–78, 180, 245
Maximus the Confessor, 15, 37, 40–48, 50–54, 56–57, 58, 59, 60, 61, 62, 63, 84, 89, 90–93, 95, 110, 115, 117, 122, 128, 131, 132, 133, 137, 138, 139, 140, 141, 145, 146, 147, 148–49, 152, 153, 155, 156–57, 159, 248, 261
McPartlan, Paul, 61, 154, 160, 262
metaphysics, 4, 5, 7, 13–14, 17–18, 21–24, 25, 37, 40–41, 50, 86, 111–12, 152, 175, 186, 221–39, 241, 242, 243, 244, 245, 268
Middle Ages, 66
Modernity, 4, 7, 11, 13, 23, 246
Moses, 28, 29

narcissism, 143, 152, 158
nihilism, 40, 177, 211, 244

Orthodox, 5, 11–13, 59, 66, 70, 77, 95, 99, 108, 109, 116–17, 120, 126, 129, 132, 143, 145–46, 153, 156, 173–74, 184, 185, 263

Paley, William, 7
Pannenberg, Wolfhart, 107, 115–16, 117, 120, 123, 126, 130, 133, 135, 139, 141, 147
Papanikolaou, Aristotle, 258–59, 263
Plantinga, Alvin, 9, 11, 20
Platonic, 4, 24, 56, 137, 150, 164
postmodernity, 23
prolepsis, 129, 130, 214, 215

Quine, Willard van Orman, 5, 17, 19, 84

Ratzinger, Joseph (Pope Benedict XVI), 34, 66, 68, 69, 70, 71, 72, 73, 79, 80, 189–98, 199, 200, 201, 202, 203
Renaissance, 4, 12, 66–68, 83
Resurrection, 41, 49, 51, 53, 56, 59, 77, 91, 121, 125, 127, 128, 130–37, 139, 140, 157, 160, 201, 249, 256
Romanides, John, 12, 153, 155, 156
Rorty, Richard, 18, 19, 94

salvation, 70, 102, 113, 117, 128, 134, 139, 140, 144, 147, 189–92, 193, 198, 200, 205, 251, 255
Schmemann, Alexander, 66, 74–77, 80, 253
subjectivity, 83–88, 93, 207, 216, 230, 243, 246

telos, 48–49, 56, 61, 88, 109, 116, 117, 148, 223, 268, 271, 272, 274
Tillich, Paul, 88, 95, 108, 109, 121, 228, 229, 232–33, 245
transcendence, 5, 26, 29, 32, 41, 59, 75, 91, 112, 130, 144, 148, 189, 192, 194, 198, 199, 210, 223–24, 225, 235, 237, 240, 241, 244, 246

Trinitarian, 12, 14, 16, 32, 34, 38, 39, 58, 120, 122, 140, 195, 198
tropos, 48, 49, 51, 55, 56, 61, 110

Universals, 4

Vatican II, 69, 73

Western, 43, 73, 99, 107, 111, 140, 143, 144–45, 147, 151, 153, 158, 173, 230
Wittgenstein, Ludwig, 5, 6, 8, 9–11, 15, 17, 19, 20, 151–52, 156, 160, 163

Yannaras, Christos, 12–15, 58–59, 86, 100, 122, 153–56, 160

Zizioulas, Metropolitan John of Pergamon, 12, 13, 56, 61, 99–117, 118, 120, 121, 122, 126, 130–31, 135–36, 137, 139, 140–41, 153–54, 156, 247–53, 255–59, 270, 273
Zoumboulakis, Stavros, 11, 12–13, 21

About the Contributors

On May 16, 2015, **Matthew Baker** was posthumously awarded a doctorate in theology from Fordham University. Baker published and presented various scholarly works on such thinkers as St Irenaeus, Origen, St Ephrem the Syrian, St Athanasius, Clement of Alexandria, Karl Barth, T. F. Torrance, Martin Heidegger, John Zizioulas, and, most notably, Georges Florovsky. Zizioulas and Aristotle Papanikolaou (Baker's PhD dissertation adviser), along with other contemporary scholars, recognized Baker as a brilliant and devout theologian, a rising star in the world of theology. Tragically, on March 1, 2015, at the age of thirty-seven, Baker was killed in a car accident.

David W. Fagerberg is professor in the department of theology at the University of Notre Dame. He holds master's degrees from Luther Northwestern Seminary; St. John's University, Collegeville; and Yale Divinity School; and the PhD from Yale University. His work first explored how lex orandi is the foundation for lex credendi (*Theologia Prima: What Is Liturgical Theology?* [Chicago: Hillenbrandbooks, 2003]). Into this he integrated the Eastern Orthodox understanding of asceticism as preparing the liturgical person (*On Liturgical Asceticism* [Washington, DC: The Catholic University of America Press, 2013]) to live that liturgical life in the world (*Consecrating the World: On Mundane Liturgical Theology* [Kettering, OH: Angelico Press, 2016]). He returned to Schmemann in *Liturgy outside Liturgy* (Hong Kong: Chorabooks, 2018).

Demetrios Harper is a Byzantine studies postdoctoral fellow at the Medieval Institute, University of Notre Dame, and a visiting research fellow at the University of Winchester, UK. He also serves as the assistant editor of

Analogia: The Pemptousia Journal for Theological Studies. His research interests are varied but focus especially on philosophical theology, ethics, and patristics, and he has authored several articles and book chapters on topics related to both philosophical and theological ethics. Most notable among his recent publications are his monograph *The Analogy of Love: St Maximus the Confessor and the Foundations of Ethics* (Crestwood, NY: SVS Press, 2018) and the anthology *Christos Yannaras: Philosophy, Theology, Culture* (New York: Routledge, 2018), which he coedited with Andreas Andreopoulos.

Isabel C. Troconis Iribarren has a PhD in systematic theology from the Pontifical University of the Holy Cross (Rome) and is assistant of Trinitarian theology and eschatology at the theology faculty of the Pontifical University of the Holy Cross (Rome). Her publications include "L'antropologia ratzingeriana dell'*imago Dei* come risposta al dilemma dello storicismo teologico," in *Storia e Mistero. Una chiave di acceso alla teologia di Joseph Ratzinger e Jean Daniélou* (Roma: Edizioni Santa Croce, 2016), and "Teleología en libertad. La verdad de la historia según Joseph Ratzinger," in *Annales Theologici* 32 no. 2 (2018): forthcoming.

Logan M. Isaac is an independent scholar who spent over six years in the United States Army, including a deployment to Iraq in 2004. Following a 2006 discharge, he earned a master of theological studies from Duke University in 2013 and a master of letters in systematic and historical theology from the University of St Andrews in 2015. Although he has been published in academic outlets such as *The Sage Encyclopedia of War: Social Science Perspectives*, ed. Paul Joseph (Thousand Oaks, CA: SAGE Publications, 2016), he directs most of his energies toward cultivating healthier public discourse at the intersection of Christian doctrinal traditions and the experience of armed service. Noted for his intellectual dexterity as a theologian-practitioner, his first book received a *Publishers Weekly* starred review and he has been featured on the cover of *Christianity Today Magazine*. He maintains an online presence at www.iamloganmi.com.

Andrew T. J. Kaethler is academic dean and assistant professor at Catholic Pacific College in Langley, BC, Canada. He received his doctorate in systematic theology from the University of St Andrews. His research interests and publications have primarily centered on theological anthropology and eschatology, particularly concerning the theology of Joseph Ratzinger and Alexander Schmemann. He has published in *Modern Theology*; *Logos: A Journal of Catholic Thought and Culture*; *New Blackfriars*; *Forum Philosophicum*; and *Mitteilungen Institut Papst Benedikt XVI*. In a somewhat different direction, in 2017 he wrote the introduction and notes to a republication of Georges Bernanos's novel *Joy* (Tacoma, WA: Cluny Media, 2017).

The Very Reverend **Nikolaos Loudovikos** is professor of dogmatics and philosophy at the University Ecclesiastical Academy of Thessaloniki, Greece; honorary research fellow at the University of Winchester; and visiting professor at the Institute for Orthodox Christian Studies, Cambridge. His recent monographs in English include *A Eucharistic Ontology: Maximus the Confessor's Eschatological Ontology of Being as Dialogical Reciprocity*, trans. Elizabeth Theocritoff (Brookline, MA: HC Press, 2010) and the forthcoming *Church in the Making: An Apophatic Ecclesiology of Consubstantiality* (New York: St Vladimir's Press).

Giulio Maspero is professor at the faculty of theology of the Pontifical University of the Holy Cross (Rome). He is member of the Association Internationale des Etudes Patristiques (AIEP) and a full member of the Pontifical Academy of Theology (PATH). He has published mainly on Gregory of Nyssa, Trinitarian theology, and the relationship between philosophy and theology. In particular, he has published *Trinity and Man* (Leuven: Brill, 2007) and has directed, together with L. F. Mateo-Seco, *The Brill Dictionary of Gregory of Nyssa* (Leuven: Brill, 2009) and, together with R. Wozniak, *Rethinking Trinitarian Theology* (London: T&T Clark, 2012). His most recent monographs are *Uno perché trino* (Siena: Cantagalli, 2011), *Essere e relazione* (Rome: Città Nuova, 2013), and *Dio trino perché vivo* (Brescia: Morcelliana, 2018), the latter devoted to the pneumatology of the Greek Fathers.

Sotiris Mitralexis is assistant professor of philosophy at the City University of Istanbul (İstanbul Şehir Üniversitesi) and visiting research fellow at the University of Winchester. He has been Seeger Fellow at Princeton University, visiting fellow at the University of Cambridge's Faculty of Divinity and visiting senior research associate at Peterhouse, Cambridge. He received a doctorate in philosophy from the Freie Universität Berlin, a doctorate in theology from the Aristotle University of Thessaloniki, and a degree in classics from the University of Athens. His publications include *Ever-Moving Repose: A Contemporary Reading of Maximus the Confessor's Theory of Time* (Eugene, OR: Cascade Books, 2017).

Daniel S. Robinson's research follows the trajectory of Greek intellectual history from the Hellenistic period into the Christian era. After completing an MA in Orthodox studies at the Patriarch Athenagoras Orthodox Institute, he studied ancient philosophy at the University of California Berkeley and earned his doctorate in history at the Graduate Theological Union. His particular interest lies in the Greek Fathers' use of philosophy toward the systemization of a Christocentric ethics. Dr. Robinson currently teaches in philosophy and history departments in the San Francisco Bay Area. He is the author of *Fate, Freedom, and Happiness: Clement and Alexander on the Dignity of Human Responsibility* (Piscataway, NJ: Gorgias Press, 2018) and "Epistemological Agreement in Eastern and Western Christian Personalisms," *Arc—The Journal of the Faculty of Religious Studies* 40 (2012): 13–54.

Jared Schumacher is assistant professor of theology and Catholic studies at the University of Mary in Bismarck, North Dakota. His research interests include moral theology, Catholic social teaching, and political theology. His dissertation investigates the historical relationship between Church and State in philosophy and theology and develops an interpretation of Catholic social teaching as (im)political theology. Recently he published "The Unbearable Present: Reflections on the Homelessness of Secular Modernity," in *Narrating Secularisms: Being between Identities in a Secularized World*, eds. William Desmond and Dennis Vanden Auweele (Washington DC: The Council for Research in Values and Philosophy, 2017), 45–78.

Dionysios Skliris received a doctorate from the Faculté des Lettres et Sciences Humaines of the University of Paris (Sorbonne—Paris IV). He studied classics and theology at the University of Athens and completed a master's degree in late antique philosophy at the University of London (King's College) as well as a master's degree in Byzantine literature at the University of Paris (Sorbonne—Paris IV). He is currently a teaching fellow at the University of Athens's faculty of theology.

Chris Doude van Troostwijk is a Dutch philosopher and theologian. He is professor of philosophy and philosophical ethics at the Luxembourg School of Religion and Society and affiliated as researcher and lecturer at the Protestant Theological Faculty of the University of Strasbourg. He holds the Mennonite Chair for Liberal Theology at the Free University in Amsterdam. His current research project "Philosophies, Theologies and Ethics of Finance" is concerned with providing an alternative ontology and ethics of money. His last published work, with Matthew Clemente, is *Richard Kearney's Anatheistic Wager* (Bloomington: Indiana University Press, 2018).

Maxim Vasiljević, Bishop of Western America (Serbian Patriarchate), is professor of Patristics at the University of Belgrade. In 1999 he defended his doctorate in the field of dogmatics and patristics at the University of Athens.

He continued postdoctoral studies at the Sorbonne in the field of Byzantine history, while also delving into the theory and practice of art at the French Academy of Fine Arts in Paris. His scholarly books, studies, and articles include essays on the Fathers and Saints of the Church, including *History, Truth, Holiness* (Los Angeles: Sebastian Press 2011) and *Against the Self-Evident: Theology as a Surprise* (Crestwood, NY: Saint Vladimir's Seminary Press, forthcoming).

Haralambos Ventis is assistant professor of the philosophy of religion at the faculty of theology, University of Athens. He has studied philosophy and theology, and holds doctorates from Boston University School of Theology and the Katholieke Universiteit Leuven, Institute of Philosophy. He has published papers in various theological journals and is the author of two books, *Eschatology and Otherness* (Athens: Gregoris, 2005) and *The Reductive Veil: Post-Kantian Non-representationalism versus Apophatic Realism* (Katerini: Epektasis, 2005).

Daniel Wright received a PhD from the University of Virginia in 2018 with a dissertation entitled *Communion and Being: Re-Thinking Ontology and Morality with John Zizioulas.* He currently lives in Brookline, Massachusetts, with his wife and three children while obtaining an M.Div. from Holy Cross School of Theology.

Christos Yannaras is professor emeritus of philosophy at the Panteion University of Social and Political Sciences, Athens. He studied theology at the University of Athens and philosophy at the Universities of Bonn and Paris. He received a doctorate from the Faculté des Lettres et Sciences Humaines of the University of Sorbonne and a doctorate from the faculty of theology of the Aristotle University of Thessaloniki. He has been nominated doctor of philosophy *honoris causa* at the University of Belgrade, at St. Vladimir's Seminary, New York, and at the Holy Cross School, Boston. He served as visiting professor at the Universities of Paris (the Catholic faculty), Geneva, Lausanne, and Crete.

www.ingramcontent.com/pod-product-compliance
Lightning Source LLC
Chambersburg PA
CBHW021819300426
44114CB00009BA/241